SAPPHO'S LEGACY

SUNY series, Praxis: Theory in Action

Nancy A. Naples, editor

SAPPHO'S LEGACY

Convivial Economics on a Greek Isle

Marina Karides

SUNY
PRESS

Published by State University of New York Press, Albany

For information, contact State University of New York Press, Albany, NY
www.sunypress.edu

Library of Congress Cataloging-in-Publication Data

Name: Karides, Marina, author.
Title: Sappho's legacy : convivial economics on a Greek isle / Marina Karides.
Description: Albany : State University of New York Press, [2021] | Series: SUNY series, praxis: theory in action | Includes bibliographical references and index.
Identifiers: LCCN 2020048647 (print) | LCCN 2020048648 (ebook) | ISBN 9781438483054 (hardcover : alk. paper) | ISBN 9781438483047 (pbk. : alk. paper) | ISBN 9781438483061 (ebook)
Subjects: LCSH: Women in cooperative societies—Greece—Lesbos (Municipality) | Food cooperatives—Greece—Lesbos (Municipality) | Lesbos (Greece : Municipality)—Social conditions.
Classification: LCC HD3424.G82 L4753 2021 (print) | LCC HD3424.G82 (ebook) | DDC 334/.68479500820949582—dc23
LC record available at https://lccn.loc.gov/2020048647
LC ebook record available at https://lccn.loc.gov/2020048648

10 9 8 7 6 5 4 3 2 1

SAPPHO'S LEGACY

Convivial Economics on a Greek Isle

Marina Karides

SUNY
PRESS

Published by State University of New York Press, Albany

For information, contact State University of New York Press, Albany, NY
www.sunypress.edu

Library of Congress Cataloging-in-Publication Data

Name: Karides, Marina, author.
Title: Sappho's legacy : convivial economics on a Greek isle / Marina Karides.
Description: Albany : State University of New York Press, [2021] | Series:
    SUNY series, praxis: theory in action | Includes bibliographical references and
    index.
Identifiers: LCCN 2020048647 (print) | LCCN 2020048648 (ebook) | ISBN
    9781438483054 (hardcover : alk. paper) | ISBN 9781438483047 (pbk. : alk.
    paper) | ISBN 9781438483061 (ebook)
Subjects: LCSH: Women in cooperative societies—Greece—Lesbos
    (Municipality) | Food cooperatives—Greece—Lesbos (Municipality) |
    Lesbos (Greece : Municipality)—Social conditions.
Classification: LCC HD3424.G82 L4753 2021 (print) | LCC HD3424.G82
    (ebook) | DDC 334/.68479500820949582—dc23
LC record available at https://lccn.loc.gov/2020048647
LC ebook record available at https://lccn.loc.gov/2020048648

10 9 8 7 6 5 4 3 2 1

For Pano and Ambrose, of course

And in loving memory of my grandparents,
Πάνος καί Γιωργία Ρούβαλη,
their return to Greece left us a trail to follow

About the rhythms now: the kalamatiano, as you mention, is played at music nightclubs and it is used to colour particular points, but one cannot dancing like this [sic], because each rhythm is written for the dancer's step especially in row dances. Moreover, the description you give of the Zeymbekiko is rather "touristic" and it reminds us of the Zorba the Greek. The Zeymbekiko existed before the period between the wars and the rembetika songs. It is a traditional male dance performed since the 17th century on the east islands of the Aegean Sea (Samos, Chios, Mytilini etc.) and on the coasts of Minor Asia. The rhythm and especially the variation you mention, is played somehow slowly and "widely" (9/4). There is a great difference in the style, which is not the same with the maqsum. In rembetika songs it is played faster. I remind you that, since the Zeymbekiko is strictly a male dance, its execution must be as plain as possible, although nowadays it is danced by little girls, too.

—Manthos Garlofis
http://www.khafif.com/rhy/garlofis/garlofis.htm

It will also become apparent that anarchist principles are active in the aspirations and political action of people who have never heard of anarchism or anarchist philosophy. One thing that heaves into view . . . is mutuality, or *cooperation without hierarchy or state rule*. Another is the anarchist tolerance for confusion and improvisation that accompanies social learning, and confidence in spontaneous cooperation and reciprocity.

—James C. Scott *Two Cheers for Anarchism* (2012, xii)

Contents

Illustrations

Figures

Table

Preface

τάδε νῦν ἐταίραις   these things now for my companions
ταῖς ἐμαῖς τέρπνα κάλως ἀείσω   I shall sing beautifully

—Sappho, fragment 160, Carson's (2003) translation

This volume was composed amid numerous travels and many hurri-
canes, multiple earthquakes, and two magnificent eruptions of the
Kīlauea Volcano, all forcing regular evacuations. It concludes, ironically,
during a pandemic and under a stay-at-home order in Hawai'i. Greece is
gaining a bit of recognition for limiting the spread of the coronavirus.
Yet, so often with public commentary on Greece, any triumph is framed
with disbelief and puzzlement, often in condescending language (e.g.,
Giugliano 2020). This book stands against such evaluations, positing
Greece's "spontaneous alternative culture" (Leontinidou 1990) as an
explanation for its societal success. The hosting and endurance required
of independent dining and drinking venues—no matter how tiny, how
rural, or how small a menu—are the heart of this book and where a good
chunk of it was written. With the increased cognizance of the extent to
which they provision public conviviality and cope economically, *Sappho's
Legacy* is an opportunity to cherish them.

An incredible amount of appreciation goes to Mary Kazazi, resident
intellectual of Skala Eresos. To advance my Greek language skills, I was
directed to Mary's traditional stone home and entered into a patio so
lush with trees and native plants, it is conceals the house from view. I
left seven years later, with a dear friend, one who I have been able to
share in many drinks and meals along Skala Eresos's balconies. Mary has
been influential in my understanding of Greek politics, economics, and

social life. She encouraged me to challenge the demarcation between ancient and modern Greece as an act of cultural appropriation. Her expressed love for her nation, its intellectual and artistic histories and acute memory for historical detail, whether it involves happenings in Athens or Eresos a few days, years, decades, centuries, or millennia ago, made her my ideal tutor.

There are many others throughout Lesvos whom I am indebted to for all forms of assistance with this research, access to government offices and officials, tipping me off on high-stake political forums to attend, and the good times and good food, as was shared with Delia Curro, that comes with a study of convivial economics. Debby from Heliotopos deserves special appreciation for indulging my children, providing transport, and feeding us. She and her partner, Patrick, permitted us to extend our stay at Heliotopos and introduced me to a wide range of travelers to Eresos. The willingness of people to share their stories is what my work depends upon. Each of the women's cooperatives hosted me for visits, and I am eternally grateful to members for sharing their time, memories and critical thoughts, as well as their recipes. I am especially appreciative of the members of the Agra, Molyvos, Mesotopos, and Parakila cooperatives to which I lived nearest while in Lesvos and visited most. The unpacking of the lesbian enclave of Eresos was informed by the research of University of Aegean anthropologist Venetia Kantsa, and I thank her for a brief but important meeting in Mytilini. Without the time granted to me by lesbian entrepreneurs and their employees, and by visitors to Skala Eresos, my work could not expand upon the social history of the lesbian enclave, including interviews with many women who have been returning to Skala Eresos since the mid-'70s. Their stories create a deep imagining and a nostalgia for gathering in a place where gender and sexual freedom for women has some scope. The ethnic Greek proprietors of enterprises in Skala Eresos also were extremely hospitable in meeting with me time after time and providing instruction in how they conduct business that were essential for building an understanding of alternative economics as practiced on Greek islands.

My mother, Lina Karides, is the person who I thank most for the tremendous amount of good I am fortunate enough to have in my life and for safeguarding my Greek identity. Learning how to drive to take me and my brother to Greek school, to Greek Orthodox Church, to learn Greek dances, poems, and march in Greek parades, she secured for me the Greek language skills and cultural orientation that enabled the completion of this research. Her emphasis on academics and love of politics and economics have served me and my sibling incredibly well.

Denise Bauman, my treasured German American friend, who together from toddlers we navigated our child of immigrant experiences, aided me in recent years through the sometimes challenging environment women in academia face, urging me to complete this volume. Kerri Gayatri Fulford also has been there every step of the way, grounding me from when my journey to become an academic began in Athens, Georgia. My darling brother, Constantine Karides, also applied his remarkable capacities to keep me moving forward in my career as did Joya Misra, with her friendship and advice. Like Sappho, I have been lucky enough to be surrounded by creative groups of women and this includes Margaret Darr, Miss Susie K., Cassandra Snyder, Francine Stock, and Katrina Zech. My very first thoughts about economics practiced convivially are grounded in their home of New Orleans. I also celebrate the many musicians in the Crescent City for performative lessons in listening to rhythms.

A special appreciation goes to Eva Silot Bravo and her son, Joao, with whom we lived life in Miami. Her fierce intellectual capacity, as she completed her dissertation, pushed my thinking on alternatives with her expertise on Cuba and its transnational alternative music scene. Also in Miami, David R. and Lola Brown and Heidi and Spiro Giannopoulos are thanked for vetting many of the stories in this book. Gabriella Zamora and Aubrey Russell, Mary Harris and her family, Nadége Altidor, and Nina and Paul Martin provided very big ears and incredible insights on everyday economics as microentrepreneurs in the Miami scene who lived lives globally—Mexico, Haiti, Austria, England, and France—offering me much comparative fuel as I developed my analysis of convivial economics in Greece.

The external reviewers provided exceptional guidance and insight. I am indebted to them for their careful evaluation, willingness to read between the lines, and well-crafted commentary though any errors are mine. The kind and serene editorial management of Rebecca Colesworthy and Ryan Morris has been reassuring as has been the resolute staff of SUNY Press. Colleagues in my life who I owe gratitude include Ivy Ken (who provided crucial feedback on this volume at a critical time), Katia Perea, Cynthia Hewitt, Linda Grant, Melissa W. Wright, Laura Chason Love, Patricia Widener, and Noralis Rodriguez-Coss (for our work in island feminisms). I also thank Christopher Chase Dunn, Jackie Smith, Marilyn Grell-Brisk, and Manisha Desai who, unbeknown to them, kept me roped into scholarship as a profession and as a social justice project.

My dear colleagues in Hawai'i, Yolisa Duley and Jennifer L. Stotter, and former students and new friends Jennifer Chai, Audrey Kamai, Trixie Croad, Kanoe Case, and Kaylee DeCambra, provided wonderful insights listening to my thoughts on the subtleties of islandness, race, ethnicity, and sexuality in Europe by offering comparative discussions on the complicated racial, ethnic, and indigenous context in the settler state of Hawai'i.

For the last six years I have lived in the green forest richness of Puna by the dynamic ocean that surrounds the island of Hawai'i. Thinking through occupation, colonization, and the autochthonous concerns of islanders from this space and Kanaka Ōiwi scholarship on it has enhanced this manuscript. I thank Gail Makuakāne-Lundin for her sponsorship to attend indigenous conferences and events. I am especially appreciative of Kumu Pele Kaio, his halau, Unulau, and his instruction through hula that have enhanced my consideration of islands and their diaspora and the keeping of cultural practices.

The warmth and welcome of Jennifer Chai's and Jennifer L. Stotter's families and the intuition of their daughters, respectively, Makana Kushi and Chloe Stotter-Ruley, as well as Gayle Chavez, Kau'i Kalili, Kekaikane-Olaho' Lindsey, Connie Cappos, Cherie Kauahi, Laurie Mengel, Huihui Kanahele-Mossman, and Kanoe Casem-Ka'awaloa, also helped in my progress toward completing this volume in Hawai'i. I appreciate Karen L. Harper, Loke Aloua, Sunny Arishiro, Julianna Davis, Kristin Bacon, Kaylee DeCambra, Noreen Kohl, Mary Jo Riehm, and Penn Pantum-sinchai for their various forms of research support and Amiti Maloy for her assistance with indexing. Nathalie Rita, especially, has been essential in supporting my research; I deeply appreciate her editorial work and friendship. I am also thankful for the warm welcome by the College of Social Sciences and the Department of Geography and Environment at the University of Hawai'i at Mānoa, my new academic home that made it possible for me to complete the last stages of this volume.

This book gains from the love of my father, Antonis Karides, and his enthusiasm and labor in food and conviviality; my niece, Luciana, and nephews, Cassius and Brunello, who ask about the book; my κουνιάδα or sister-in-law, Angela; and my father-in-law, Arthur M. Kastler. My children, Pano and Ambrose, have lived with this book more than half their lives, traveling to Greece regularly, attending school in Eresos, being drafted from one home to another, witnessing me write, revise, repeat, keeping their charm and being gentle guests in the homes of others. I am forever beholden to my adored and adoring spouse, Arthur O. Kastler, for providing the space and time for me to work on this volume for days on end. He is a fine musician learning to play island sounds on string instruments and a home chef preparing delightful meals with local ingredients from where my work takes us. Reliably entertaining and nourishing us, he also dedicated his time refining the references in this book.

The research conducted for this volume began with my being granted a Fulbright Research Scholar (Greece) award in 2008, which facilitated the research and assisted me in bringing my family along. It is worth noting that the Fulbright Program in Greece was the first in Europe and is the second longest running Fulbright Program in the world. I also acknowledge the several small grants I received from the College of Arts and Letters and the Division of Research at Florida Atlantic University, my academic home during some of this research.

The exchange offered in the epigraph of chapter 7 is from *A Bit of Fry and Laurie*, "Gordon and Stuart Eat Greek," series 1, episode 3, British Broadcasting Corporation, which aired January 27, 1989. Appreciatively, permission was granted via Hamilton Hodell, Career Management for Extraordinary Talent, 20 Golden Square, W1F 9JL London, United Kingdom.

An earlier version of chapter 8 was published as "An Island Feminism: Convivial Economics and the Women's Cooperatives in Lesvos" in *Island Geographies: Essays and Conversations*, edited by Elaine Stratford, 78–96 (New York: Routledge, 2017).

Tzeli Hadjidimitriou, photographer and cinematographer, generously granted permission for the use of her photographs. Tzeli's photos lends a pictorial credence to the physical beauty of Lesvos and its gendered spaces. All pictures were taken within the last decade, about the time it took to complete the research and writing of this book. I also owe Tzeli many thanks for her willingness to think through analyses about her island. Tzeli identifies as a researcher of authenticity, an independent filmmaker, fine art photographer, and writer from Lesbos, Greece. She studied Direction of Photography for the Cinema in Rome and in Greece she received a certificate in video montage. She has produced five documentaries about life in Greece, screened at film festivals globally and her photography is shown in museums and galleries in Greece and abroad.

Figure 1.1. Taverna paper tablecloth with map of Lesvos/Ambrose and Pano Kastlides. Across Greece, tables at tavernas or restaurants are customarily covered with paper tablecloths. The paper tablecloths, often decorated with a map of the locale, are clipped to the sides of tables by the waiter as one sits down for a meal. This tablecloth was gifted to me by a taverna owner in Skala Eresos after our interview to bring home as a memento.

PART I

ΚΑΛΩΣΟΡΙΣΕΣ

So when the guest comes to you as a host, you as a host get to tell them you're quite happy to be at their service: *"well may you be commanding me."*

—Nick Nicholas, Modern Greek linguist (2016)

I do not know how it is, but I always feel at home with these people [the Turks] and can get out of them just what I like; but it is a very different thing with the Greeks, who shuffle and shuffle, and you never can depend upon them for a moment.

—Lady Hester Stanhope (1846, 109) in a letter from Rhodes

CHAPTER ONE

Prolegomenon

If we confine our historical scrutiny to revolutionary success, we discount that vast proportion of human social action which is played out on a humbler scale. We also evade, by teleological reasoning, the real questions that remain as to what *are* the transformative motors of history.

—Jean Comaroff (1985, 261)

It was late September, the summer season was ending, and the school year about to begin. The narrow streets of Skala Eresos were all but empty—just a few cafés and tavernas that line the Aegean shore were open for business. In this seaside village on the Greek isle of Lesvos, tourists, travelers, and local Greeks sat in relaxed conversations over drinks on wooden balconies perched by the sea. Cobbled and concrete streets separate diners from kitchens and storefronts that waiters walk across to serve true oceanside meals—a scene typical of Greece's coastlines.

I felt like I missed the better part of a great party. Many of the local residents were leaving their seaside summer homes and returning with children and potted plants in hand back to the upper village of Eresos, a few miles uphill, or to homes in Athens, Greece's capital, or Mytilini, the island's largest town. The unseasonably warm Mediterranean weather in 2008 held open more than the handful of dining venues that usually remain after summer's end. These businesses, along with a few bakeries and grocery shops, serve the small community of Skala's several hundred yearlong residents and straggling visitors who appear on occasion during the island's cold, wet winter.

Having come to Lesvos for research, I considered who I might interview in this evaporating beach town. My plan had been to study the women's food cooperatives that operate in villages throughout the island as a form of gendered models of alternative economics. Yet I could not relinquish an interest in the lesbian microenterprises and tourist enclave in Skala Eresos, which had piqued my interest during a visit to the island almost two decades prior.* Skala Eresos is an archetypal Greek island village steeped in Greek Orthodoxy, agriculture, fishing, and tourism and also the proclaimed birthplace of Sappho, the famed ancient Greek lyrical poet, who wrote about her love of women.** The lesbian hotels, cafés, and bars—such as Sappho's Garden—owned and visited by both ethnic Greek and transnational lesbians seemed to easily coexist with traditional Greek *kafeneions* or coffee shops, which are recognized as bastions of Greek masculinity (Papataxiarchis 1991). I decided also to explore the mingling that occurs at Skala Eresos' diverse drinking and dining venues based in lesbian and traditional Greek sociality and enterprise, as a way to further study the local, alternative economics practiced on Greek isles.

In its analysis of alternative economic practices, *Sappho's Legacy* weds the women's village cooperatives that operate throughout Lesvos with the lesbian-owned microenterprises in the village of Skala Eresos, presenting both of them as spatiotemporal alternatives to neoliberal economics and gendered, heterosexist normativities. The start of my fieldwork in late September 2008, which continued intermittently through May 2016, coincides with the global financial crisis. News of the high wire act

---

*Throughout I use the term "lesbian" or "lesbian identified" with the awareness that the term is both historically specific (Faderman 1992) and that "place is central to the form identities take" (Browne and Ferreira 2015, 4). Furthermore, I follow Browne and Ferreira's (2015, 5–6) argument that while the term may be "fluid and constructed in spatial and temporal ways," "lesbian" highlights the heterosexism and patriarchy in the politics of sexualities, and it remains a way that people, including the women in Lesvos I interviewed, chose to identify. I refrain from using LGBTQ+ because this conception was not relevant to the time period I am most focused on and would conflate, for example, the experiences of lesbian and gay travelers with that of trans travelers. I apply the term "queer" when discussing theoretical perspectives post-1991 but generally not in reference to groups or earlier writings on lesbian, gay, bisexual, and trans communities. I distinguish between Lesbian, a native resident of Lesvos, and lesbian, a sexual orientation, but mostly apply the phrase "residents of Lesvos" to the former for greater clarity.

**I sometimes qualify Greek with "ethnic" to indicate the autochthonous people of Greece. When referring to Greek culture or other social aspects, I refrain from this to recognize the many other races and ethnic groups that live in Greece and participate in or create Greek culture.

of traditional investment firms and hedge funds and their surreptitious management of the US housing market had broken just a few days after arriving in Lesvos. Tied to the US financial scandal was the unscrupulous lending practices of banks within the European Union (EU), which would eventually bang Greece and other peripheral EU nations (Ireland, Spain, Portugal) up against the bulwark of global capital.

To a certain extent, *Sappho's Legacy* became an account of Greek islanders' interpretations and responses to this crisis. The multiple years in which I returned to the field were a propitious moment to study small-scale local, collective, and community-minded economic practices in Greece. My timing lent insight into how these island enterprises survived, and even succeeded, during unfavorable economic circumstances. I explore the ways in which they conduct business—pricing, lending, gifting, wages, purchasing, trading, rent agreements, work schedules—to support the survival of the wider community. *Sappho's Legacy* illustrates how groups that have been marginalized or discriminated against socially, are less privileged economically, or are geographically distant from centers of capitalism seek or create economic alternatives for the purpose of autonomy, community, and convivial work (Simone 2004; Hau'ofa 1994; Illich 1973).

This volume documents how the local, subaltern economic logic of Greeks and the everyday economic practices of autonomous cooperatives and microenterprises on Greek islands remain stubbornly resistant to neoliberalism.* Though outlying and small, understanding how these

---

*There exist wide debates on the meanings of globalization, neoliberalism, and economic development in the social sciences (i.e., Harvey 2005; Kellner 2002; Guillen 2001; MacLean 2000). My use of the terms here distinguishes neoliberalism as the Washington Consensus–promoted ideological shift from state-led or Keynesianism development strategies to an increased capital bias that limits state regulatory capacities and supports privatization but relies on governments' facilitating capital expansion. Neoliberal tenets have shaped development strategies in most of the globe, encouraging an uneven, interdependent system of production and consumption (McMichael 2008; Klak and Conway 1998). Some use globalization and neoliberalism interchangeably (see Harvey 2005), but the social movement literature in particular demonstrates that the term "globalization" denotes not only the concentrated networks of capitalism but also those of the global justice movement (Smith et al. 2008; Brecher, Costello, and Smith 2000) to create a "globalization from below" (Smith et al. 2008; Starr 2000). Or, in the case of the migration literature, globalization reflects the increase in transnational livelihoods that blur national borders and the large portion of the world's population that maintain diasporic rather than national identities (Kraidy 2005; Braiziel, and Mannur 2003; Hall 2003).

local island enterprises persist in defying norms of global capitalism draws attention to less studied transformative motors of history (Comaroff 1985). Even as the European Union, International Monetary Fund, and European Central Bank, popularly referred to as "the troika," demanded economic and cultural capitulation, many Greek islanders and those attracted to them seemed to reject the fundamental ethos by which global capital stands. *Sappho's Legacy* is about how *convivial economics* are generated by subaltern groups in peripheries, and how gender and sexualities inform the creation of food and drink venues—bars, cafés, cooperatives, and restaurants—that offer both opportunities for leisure and employment. In naming convivial economics, I draw inspiration from *The Tools of Conviviality* (1973, 18) by Ivan Illich, an anarchist and academic outsider (Hoinacki 2002), whose book emphasized "personal energy under personal control" for the advancement of a just economy. Contributing to the recent fields of island studies, food studies, and alternative economics, my research of economic alterity on Lesvos considers how island societies may be inclined to meet the needs of the environment and the community first, offering a counter to the failure of continental-centered neoliberal approaches.

The Organic and Attritional Alterity of Cooperatives and Microenterprises

Both the women's cooperatives and the local and lesbian enterprises in Skala Eresos speak to economic alternatives in island societies and the ways gender, sexuality, ethnicity, nation, and tourism shape those alternatives. While mainstream economic development discourses now address gender differences, most often by co-opting feminist analyses to promote neoliberal agendas (Bedford 2009), an appreciation of intersectionality (Ken 2011; Choo and Ferree 2010; Hill-Collins 1990), or that gender, sexuality, race, ethnicity, or nation intersect to inform economic choice is limited in both the academic and popular alternative economic literature (for examples, see Mason 2016; Burlingham 2005; Botsman and Rogers 2011; Wright 2010; Hess 2009; Laville, Leveseque, and Mendell 2006). Given their marginalization in the formal labor market, women and groups snubbed in the formal economy due to social identities or island geographies seek and make alternatives to conventional economics. This volume brings an intersectional approach and geographical awareness to alternative economics including an appreciation that sexualities are constitutive of economic practice.

Based in Greek cooperative traditions and located in island village communities, the women's cooperatives on Lesvos represent an *organic* resistance to neoliberalism. The women's cooperatives have evolved from a long tradition of cooperatives production in Greece where there is evidence of over a century of sailors, shepherds, fishers, artisans, and farmers working collectively, in formal or loosely organized cooperatives, distributing income equally or by the type of work, and collaborating on financial decisions (Petropoulo 1993). The women's cooperatives in Greece were also prompted by development strategies in the 1980s and later with the formation of the European Union to advance agrotourism and increase women's employment in rural and island regions.

Arriving from their nearby homes, often by foot to their production and retail facilities in the village square, during mornings and after the traditional Greek midday break, women's cooperative members across Lesvos keep a similar routines of work. Preparing pastries, savory treats, and fruit preserves, the women are working in constant engagement with each other and rely on one another to make production plans and coordinate kitchen duties, while they discuss current events and politics with demitasses of Greek coffee. They ply and fold thin layers of dough, sometimes rolled over ten feet on a table between them, which they turn into artistic patterns and shapes flavored and embellished with a variety of local nuts, fruits, and honey.

Table 1.1. Women's Cooperatives on Lesvos in 2012

Village	Year Initiated	Membership
Agra	1998	15
Anemotia	1998	10
Asomotos	1998	4
Ayia Paraskevi	1999	11
Ayiassos	1998	12
Filia	2004	11
Mesotopos	1998	34
Molyvos	2004	13
Parakila	2001	16
Polichnitos	1997	9
Petra	1982	unknown
Skalachori	2000	17

The data in this table represents a snapshot of the membership of the island's women's cooperatives. Between 2008 and 2019 only one cooperative had closed on Lesvos. Women's cooperatives such as those I study in Lesvos are found throughout rural villages in Greece. Although there is a central organization that hosts awards and annual meetings, the cooperatives operate independently.

The table provides the names of the cooperative villages, the years the cooperatives were established, spanning from 1982 to 2004, and membership, ranging from four to 34 members, in 2012. The organizational forms of cooperatives vary depending on their scale and the product or services provided; however, cooperatives are generally owned by employees and democratically governed by members (Wright 2010; Hacker 1989). The International Labor Organization (2002) defines a cooperative as "an autonomous association of persons united voluntarily to meet their common economic, social and cultural needs and aspirations through a jointly owned and democratically controlled enterprise." Cooperatives are also characterized by transparency where production and managerial information is distributed equally among leadership and workers, there is an equal share in profits, and decisions are made collectively (Bernstein 1982).

In the push toward alternative economics, cooperatives are being revisited as a form of economic governance that depend neither on the logic of accumulation nor on state control (Restakis 2010). Beyond the commitment to ensure fair and safe labor, cooperatives rely on solidarity and a mutually constructed vision of the enterprise, countering hierarchical models of business management. Motived by the camaraderie they held with each other, each of the women's cooperatives I met had developed such models, engaging and articulating their own planning process and vision of the cooperative.

Like the women's cooperatives, the locally run and family owned microbusinesses that dominate Lesvos and many Greek islands are also examples of what I classify as *organic economic alterity*, which display grassroots subaltern economic sensibilities. Contributing to the organic economic alterity in Greece are the numerous enterprising efforts of mostly Northern Europeans who relocate to Lesvos and to other Greek isles. Many of the lesbians who initiated enterprises in Skala Eresos left urban and suburban regions and material pursuits to set up a small enterprise in a far-flung island village. I refer to this desertion of the dominant economy and entry into the Greek island microeconomy as *attritional economic alterity*.

Lesbian-centered microenterprises constitute approximately one-third of the enterprises in summertime Skala Eresos. While some of the current lesbian entrepreneurs originally arrived in Skala in the late 1980s, there was also a newer generation of lesbians, those that first came to Skala a decade or more later, who established enterprises shortly after their arrival. Several of the first set of lesbian entrepreneurs to open businesses in Skala Eresos in the 1990s continue to operate the same or different businesses from those they started. These women often mentor, advise, and encourage new prospective lesbian business owners. All of the lesbian businesses in Skala that have operated for at least a decade involve ethnic Greek lesbians in ownership or management. Many of these enterprises consist of partnerships between ethnic Greek and Northern European women.

Microenterprises, defined as businesses with fewer than nine employees, make up the vast majority of enterprises in Greece (ILO 2019). Over the last several decades, microenterprises became a topic of interest for international development agencies. Initially, microenterprises, or subsistence and self-employment strategies, in much of the Global South as well as Greece were widely criticized by modernization proponents and theorists and considered to thwart economic development. By the early 1990s development approaches toward microenterprises transformed with a neoliberal policy agenda. Small informal urban and rural enterprises of the Global South were now viewed as opportunities for development by the policymakers and international institutions that once dismissed them (Karides 2005; Otero and Rhyne 1994). Whereas microenterprises had been most closely associated with the informal sector that involves legal economic activity conducted off the books and entities not in compliance with government regulations or not reporting earnings in an official capacity (Rakowski 1994; Portes 1983), the shunning of them seemed to have simply vanished in development policy circles. Supporting poor entrepreneurs was envisioned as a viable *neoliberal* path for development (Jurik 2005; Karides 2005).

Neoliberal support of microenterprises in the Global South grew out of the failures of modernization to create the industrialization and employment expected by its advocates (Karides 2005). With nowhere to turn, the "development set" (Coggins 1976) shaped by and shaping neoliberalism claimed the survival efforts in the Global South as their own novel strategy for economic development, relieving the state as well as capital from employment creation and placing it in the hands of the jobless (Karides 2010; Jurik 2005; Servon 1999).

Notwithstanding the association of microenterprises with the informal sector, as an international development strategy, or a last resort for earnings, I reframe microenterprises within the alternative economic literature. Often created and depended upon by marginalized groups and by those in marginal locations for the purpose of supporting subsistence and one's community, they have been an important source of economic survival (Osirim 2009; Karides 2005; Creevey 1996). Furthermore, women, indigenous groups, persons of color, and other subalterns prefer the autonomous conditions of work that operating a microenterprise offers, including options to care for and respond to the needs of one's locality. Microenterprises are also established to avoid the discriminatory and biased overseers found in formal employment, even if the earnings are less and the labor more encompassing (Karides 2010; Campbell 1987). In Greece, microenterprises epitomize Greek life, suiting Greeks' "anti-authoritarianism and independent streaks" (Hartocollis 2015).

Sappho's Legacy addresses the subalternity of the women's cooperatives and Greek and lesbian microenterprises to consider how they may offer alternative pathways for development that are not formally institutionalized or state-centric, but local, immediate, and convivial. Throughout time and in various locations, concentrations of locally embedded small-scale enterprises have with little recognition changed the world. We have a lot to learn from Greek islanders and their resilience and preservation of an economic culture that generously hosts visitors and migrants, who sometimes are able to establish their own alternative economic enterprises on Greek islands.

The next few sections review literature and conceptual influences that help me to frame what I have experienced throughout Greece and studied in Lesvos. I use *convivial economics* to refer most directly to the alternative economic forms and practices engaged in by subaltern groups and those living in subaltern locations, that are oriented toward the collective success of enterprises, sociable, and in support of local community, rather than emphasizing individual economic achievement.

Enterprising Resistance

The women's cooperatives across Lesvos and enterprises in Skala Eresos, which are inspired by conviviality and reliant on shared labor, resist co-optation and are less acquiescent to dominant economic ideologies and norms. James C. Scott (1985, 229), an academic force in subaltern and anarchist theory, explains the advantage of everyday forms of resistance: "Unlike hierarchical formal organizations, there is no center, no leadership, no identifiable structure that can be co-opted or neutralized. These forms of resistance will win no set-piece battle but are admirably adopted to long run campaigns of attrition."

Scott's oft-cited (1985) study of Malaysian peasants, *Weapons of the Weak*, was a tribute to the potency of a subordinate class's ability to deconstruct, dismiss, and resist hegemonic ideologies. Through detailed ethnography, Scott (1985, 1979) shows how peasants reject and challenge the philosophies of the dominant class. His work confronted mainstream scholarship (Moore 1978; Bourdieu 1977; Piven and Cloward 1977) that identified ideological hegemony or the mass acceptance of what is deemed "inevitable" by the dominant class. Scott (1985) added to perspectives on resistance of dominant political economic systems, suggesting that it is not necessarily measurable by intention and organized collective action. Scott identified a whole realm of activities that Malaysian peasants engaged in, which were separate from formal or collective protest, that countered the dominant discourse of efficiency. This enabled Scott (1985, 287) to address the distinction between "real" versus "token" forms of resistance that characterized early social change and social movement literature and to suggest: "The privileged status accorded organized movements, I suspect, flows from either of two political orientations: the one, essentially Leninist, which regards the only viable class action as one led by a vanguard party serving as a 'general staff,' the other more straightforwardly derived from a familiarity and preference for open, institutionalized politics as conducted in capitalist democracies."

Real resistance had been limited to organized and systematic efforts motivated by a revolutionary consciousness. Even though unorganized or individual acts may negate the logic of the dominant system, they were considered opportunistic or self-indulgent accommodations within the system. Scott (1985) confronts this interpretation by stressing that academic literature had misunderstood the political and social struggles of those marginally located. Defying dominant understandings at the time, he argued that repeated and independent acts of self-preservation that do not adhere to the dominant ideology signified a form of resistance. The cornerstone of Scott's argumentation is that, while not systematic or driven by revolutionary thought, independent acts of resistance may synergize to challenge the prevailing system. The collective impact of daily, local forms of resistance is echoed in Scott's most recent works (2012, 2017) in which he continues to explore anarchic, daily, or small-scale forms of resistance as a challenge to global capitalist expansion.

More recently, Marxist sociologist Erik O. Wright (2010) outlined a variety of alternative strategies for dismantling capitalism, but he seems to have reconstituted a hierarchy of resistance similar to the one that Scott (1985) reproached. Wright (2010, 288) describes small, local independent efforts as *interstitial strategies* that "operate outside the state and try as much as possible to avoid confrontations with state power," sharing the core tenet of building counterhegemonic institutions in society. Wright (2010) shelves interstitial strategies for their perceived associations with anarchist traditions. Like many social scientists (Piven and Cloward 1977; Moore 1978; Bourdieu 1977), he deemed the small, local, and mundane as being less able to counter hegemony.

Revisiting conceptualizations of resistance is essential for envisioning how small convivial enterprises may offer a counterpoint to global capitalism. The current flurry of enterprises in the Global North that identify as "local," "communal," "community," "subsistence," "diverse," "social," "solidarity," "human," or "sharing" has activated academic research on the potential of alternative economics. Though previous scholarship has disregarded local, small, and collective alternatives as motors of social change, recent inquiries, including this one, are reviving assessments of these initiatives as forms of resistance.

Markedly, three literatures focused on autonomous small-scale, artisanal, micro-scaled enterprises blossomed between the late 1950s and early 1970s: European protocapitalism (Frank 1996; Butlin 1986; Chirot 1985; Black 1984; Berg, Hudson, and Sonenscher 1983; Wolf 1982; Wallerstein 1974), hippie or counterculture economics (Cotterill 1983; Illich 1973; Schumacher 1973; Bookchin 1969; Belasco 1989), and "third world" development (McClelland 1967; Geertz 1963; Tax 1956; Redfield 1962). These frames of analysis, which developed contemporaneously but separately, are all equally relevant for assembling a conceptual location of the nonexpansionary small-scale, autonomous enterprises I study in Lesvos. The protocapitalism or the creation of cottage industries and guilds in the medieval era, the cooperative and commune movement of the 1960s, and the informal sector in cities of the Global South influenced patterns of economic development in their own time and place by pursuing economic forms that countered the prevailing economic system.

In numerous historical moments, subaltern groups, and those in subaltern locations, have sought to construct small independent and autonomous economic solutions when the dominant economic system was failing. By doing so they created a path for an alternative economics. Although too early to evaluate, the current burst of alternative economic activities—such as bartering, community gardens, fair trade, collective ownership, alternative lending schemes, sharing, housing or consumer cooperatives, community currency, and convivial microenterprises and self-employment—may also be shifting economies away from the domination of neoliberalism (Mason 2016; Gibson-Graham 2006).

As a whole, though, the alternative economy literature makes little sense of how social inequalities and groups marginalized by race, ethnicity, indigeneity, gender, and sexuality shape the growth and development of alternative economic projects and practices. There is limited consideration of the Global South and the informal character of alternative economic practices in peripheral locations or how the rhythms of a place—its history, culture, or geography—may shape the possibilities of economic alterity. Adding a subaltern perspective to the study of resistance and economic alterity may help elucidate the ways in which convivial economics is a habit of the marginalized or the subaltern. Subaltern studies evolved from a critique of colonial and elite perspectives in South Asian history that "failed to account for the dynamic and improvisational modes of peasant political agency" (Chaturvedi 2000, viii). Grappling with Marxist thought, subaltern studies expanded resistance beyond class consciousness, an approach particularly embraced by South Asian and Latin American scholars (see Rodríguez 2001).

A significant momentum in subaltern literature, and one that provides insight for convivial economics, has been its focus on everyday acts of resistance. Scholars within the subaltern tradition consider daily challenges to the dominant system as enduring and in the long run possibly more effective in their slow and almost imperceptible transformation of subordinating conditions. A subaltern approach is cognizant of the nonhegemonic or counterhegemonic values carried by marginalized groups that resist, restrict, or qualify hegemony. E. P. Thompson (1978, 163) states: "Whatever this hegemony may have been, it did not envelop the lives of the poor and it did not prevent them from defending their own modes of work and leisure, and forming their own rituals, their own satisfactions and view of life." In taking stock of contemporary economic alterity there is much in the Greek case to suggest that what is being defended contemporarily by the Greek population is "their own modes of work, leisure, rituals, satisfactions, and view of life" (Thompson 1978). According to Lila Leontidou (1990), a scholar of Greek urban development, Greece diverges from Northern Europe by the ways in which Greeks resist capitalism. She explains that the traditional left is uneasy with Greece's "spontaneous alternative culture" and does not accept "informality, communal life and socializing, song and football attendance, or mutual aid and illegal building" as oppositional (Leontidou 1990, 2). Leontidou (1990, 2) writes, "Cities of the North, mostly cold and disciplined, contrast with the light, heat and spontaneity of Southern cities and the corresponding popular attitudes. Mediterranean labouring people have their own ways of opposing capitalism and confronting poverty and exploitation." The convivial economics found in Lesvos may very well capture the Mediterranean's unique ways of opposing capitalism.

Naming who or what exactly is subaltern is a task that has hounded the field and includes a range of traits, characteristics, and experiences that might qualify. Antonio Gramsci's own position on the subaltern also has been variously described. Gramsci (2003, 191), who grew up on the island of Sardinia where his experiences of marginality as an islander appear to have been influential, recognized that even in medieval Europe "the subaltern groups had a life of their own . . . institutions of their own." In effect, by identifying the subjectivity of subordination, Gramsci substantiates a subaltern consciousness, extending the possibility of rejecting hegemonic discourse beyond the proletariat (Mignolo 2005, 381).

Other well-regarded subalternists have characterized the subaltern. O'Hanlon (2000, 105) suggests that "when we are talking about the subaltern, we are referring to a presence which is in some sense resistant: which eludes and refuses assimilation into the hegemonic." Arnold (2000, 32–33) claims that at a minimum the subaltern can be "regarded as little more than a convenient shorthand for the variety of subordinate classes—industrial workers, peasants, laborers, artisans, shepherds and so forth." Or as Gayatri Spivak (1993, 2194) most notably put forth: "The 'subaltern' always stands in an ambiguous relation to power—subordinate to it but never fully consenting to its rule, never adopting the dominant point of view or vocabulary as expressive of its own identity." Feminists, queer theorists, and postcolonial analyses have expanded the scope of subaltern identities to include those constructed as the "Other" by dominant frames. These studies have highlighted the ways in which gender, race, ethnicity, sexuality, and nation work as categories of privilege and subordination that attempt to legitimize economic and social disparities. Subaltern analyses keep in view dynamics—both structural and discursive—that sustain systems of power and modes of resistance (Gandhi 1998), lending powerful insight for exploring alternative economics as a tool of the marginalized.

Islandness

If alternative economics, broadly conceived, offer a pathway to more just economies, it is critical to understand where they do and can occur. Unless anywhere is possible, the spatial dimension of economic alterity requires more consideration (Leyshon and Lee 2003; Lobao, Hooks, and Tycamyer 2007). Islandness—or the perspective that living and working on an island comes with a distinct set of social and economic features and orientations (Baldacchino 2006; Hau'ofa 1994; McCall 1994)—significantly shapes the economics practiced on Lesvos.

As finite locations that have incurred the wrath of colonial projects and as robust sites of local forms and thought, islands provide subaltern space (Clayton 2010). Islands remain at the fringe of mainstream development that conceives of disparate places as interchangeable, absent of particularisms, and without requirement of diversified approaches. Moreover, the perceived or real remoteness of islands, as imagined paradise and exceptions to mainland lifestyles, suspend islands as places that attract subalterns and others seeking to delink from the dominant system.

Although the term "subaltern" had been rarely used to describe space, Daniel Clayton (2010) opened it to human geography and others in the field have followed suit (see Jazeel and Legg 2019). Clayton (2010) applies subaltern to describe locations where antisystemic or counterhegemonic projects develop. Clayton (2010, 249) distinguishes subaltern space "first, as a space of domination, the abject and disquieting space in which people are placed and kept in situations of subordination, a closed and contained space of difference; and second, as a resistant and anticipatory space within the past and the present, from which, it is hoped, domination will or can be subverted or overturned. [And] . . . an alternative and counter-hegemonic space in which the desire and ability to fracture and challenge power is imagined and enacted." Because the production of space is geographically and historically contingent (Lefebvre 1991), it is in local sites, with discourses and structures that have not been grasped by apparatuses of power or which refuse to acknowledge them, where subalternity can exist.

By conceiving attachment to place as parochial or a form of separatism, more than one alternative economics perspective slights the notion that location matters (Wright 2010; Hess 2009; Gibson-Graham 2006). Yet downgrading spatial attachments or geographic identities seems to stem from more privileged outposts. David Harvey (2000, 556) explains: "The depiction of others' geographical loyalties as banal or irrational . . . helps foster ignorance and disinterest in the lives of those others; meanwhile space after space is opportunistically demonized or sanctified by some dominant power as a justification for political action. Such biased geographical knowledges, deliberately maintained, provide a license to pursue narrow interests in the name of universal good and reason." Appreciating subaltern space as a platform from which actions and perspectives counter dominant frames, *Sappho's Legacy* addresses alternative economics as strategies of place. Some places, like islands, may lend themselves to organic or attritional economic alterity, or both, more than others. The replication of these qualities in other geographies is a potential avenue by which alternative economies can expand.

Islands and archipelagos have been places not only of colonial domination. They are also liminal spaces existing between societies that bridge cultural and social forms of exchange, including Pacific, Caribbean, and Mediterranean island groups. The Aegean Islands are especially suitable for thinking about islands as *borderlands* and places of interchange and opportunities for novel exchange (Anzaldúa 1999). Located in the still contested waters between Greece and Turkey—a geographical, economic, and ideological partition that constructs "east" and "west"—places Lesvos and other Aegean Islands as borderlands (Mignolo and Tlostanova 2006; Anzaldúa 1999). Islands present possibilities for both geographic and epistemic distance from modern dominant ideologies. According to Mignolo (2011, 1), border thinking occurs "wherever the conditions are appropriate and the awareness of coloniality (even if you do not use the word) comes into being." The subalternity of the economic practices found in Lesvos, and across much of Greece and its islands, implies a type of border thinking that collides with the EU's neoliberal agenda attesting to Greece's geo-historic peripherality in Europe.

The study of islands originally emphasized their isolation, cultural distinctions, and perpetual dependency (see Hau'ofa 1994). However, analyses focusing on the vulnerability and remoteness of islands, and islanders, have faded among those who study islands. Instead, the rather recent island studies framework, or nissology, seeks to understand "islands on their own terms" (Hau'ofa 1994; McCall 1994; Baldacchino 2006; Brinklow 2011). Early nissological literature was devoted to unpacking "islandness," or the distinct experience, quality, and phenomena of islands. Despite the diversity across islands, the study of islandness seeks to provide a basis for introducing a conceptually cohesive island studies perspective. Grant McCall (1994, 1), a geographer who helped found the field of island studies, proposed nissology "as a rhetorical, subaltern discourse for islanders as well as for understanding islands in their stewardship of two-thirds of the resources of the planet." Yet island studies is only beginning to consider the inequities and structures of bias and discrimination that are shaped by islandness and contained by islands (Karides 2017).

The resilience, reciprocity, and self-reliance of island populations, and locally informed cultures around food, sociality, and environment, are traits that may prove useful as we seek a better balance between economy, ecology, and society. Given that current mass-scale production systems, or the current world-system, have likely reached their ecological limits, exacerbated poverty, and deepened social divides, insights into how to proceed to build better futures are imperative (Calhoun and Derlugian 2011; Restakis 2010). Because of their unique geographies

Figure 1.2. Contemporary Sappho statue at Skala Eresos's port/courtesy of Tzeli Hadjidimitriou. The seaside village of Skala Eresos is bordered by its port on one side and a small mountain on the other. This sculpture by Ross Macaulay is set next to a wood bench that overlooks Skala Eresos's tiny marina where local fishers keep their boats.

and histories, island spaces are fertile ground for convivial economics to flourish. Islands reflect distinct patterns of both human movement and settlement, which provide unique insights into the basis for alternative economic development. Islands include large populations of people who have resided on them for generations that sustain organic economic alterity. Many mainlanders migrate, permanently or semipermanently, to build lives around the subaltern logic of island spaces, the roots of attritional economic alterity.

Sappho's Lesvos

Because it is Sappho's informal community of women who engaged in creative, convivial, and collective work on Lesvos that inspires the direction and title of the volume, I devote some attention to her story as backdrop. The sexual orientation and poetry of Sappho, and the multiple interpretations of them, have inspired countless scholars to ruminate on their implications. The intimacy and the bonds among the women in the cooperatives and the lesbian enterprises in Eresos, and the positive evaluation they have of themselves in their production, seems to at least echo the enchantment that appears in the writings of Sappho. It is Sappho's poetry that inspired my first journey to Lesvos (Barnard 1958). Eventually my attention was drawn to tracing the rhythms of the subaltern economics that capture the daily life and exchange in the Aegean and the gendered spatiality of Greek islands.

Most Mediterranean islands are referenced in Greek mythology and hold at least a bit of ancient history. Lesvos's story, for whatever reasons, seems to be gynocentric and shapes the arguments developed in this book. The island of Lesvos is recognized for having a culture in which women had greater freedoms than in other places of ancient Greece (Slatkin 2000). Many of its ancient cities were named after the granddaughters of the Greek Titan Helios and continue to retain these names. The Byzantines presented the island as a dowry to a Genoese prince in 1335, a practice of marriage proposals that some ethnic Greek residents informally continue on the island to this day. And it is on Lesvos where Orpheus's head washed ashore and was collected and buried by the sometime resident Muses (Watson 2013).

The cultural richness of Greece's third largest island reveals a timeline of some of the world's masterful artists, poets, and philosophers, who were either born and raised in Lesvos or traversed through the island. Theophrastus, for instance, a student of Plato who successfully replaced Aristotle as the head of the Peripatetic school, was originally from Eresos. The well-known novelist Stratis Myrivillis and the poet Odysseus Elytis—whose poetry was recognized in 1979 with a Nobel Prize for Literature—are acclaimed artists with ties to Lesvos. Despite her spectacularity, Sappho, the lyrical poet who lived on the island more than 2,500 years ago, is sometimes given little or no adulation as a master of arts and letters in many histories of Lesvos that one might find on the internet, in travelogues and guidebooks, or in national tourism paraphernalia.*

Yet Sappho and her works have been heralded among others by Greeks, Victorians, and lesbians. Sappho is best known for her poetry and is one of the lyric canonical poets who were required study for the educated aristocracy in Classical Greece. Many academic accounts address the magnificent artistic and cultural influence of Sappho, past and present (Reynolds 2000; Snyder 1997; Wilson 1996; Harris 1996; Williamson 1995; Snyder 1994). Sappho's poetry is highly regarded during her lifetime and in centuries after. That she was named "the Tenth Muse" by Plato is repeated in vast writings on her life and work, particularly in Victorian literary circles, and was also the name of a central lesbian café-bar in Skala Eresos.

---

*See, for example, the 2007 Road Editions map of Lesvos, published in Athens, that remains the most thorough and widely used map of the island by locals and visitors. It does not include even a mention of Sappho in its historical summaries of major persons and events. See also the *Lesvos Guide 2007: Life In Style*, published by Empros, a local newspaper. One of the only locally produced Lesvos guides in English, it mentions Sappho along with Alcaeus, another lyric poet, and suggests that "according to some rumors they were much more than simple friends" (2007, 3). In its review of Eresos, the guide does not mention it as Sappho's birthplace nor is the lesbian tourist scene discussed. However, the page does include an advertisement for Antiope, a women-only hotel in the village. Finally, in the *Tourist Guide Holidays in Lesvos*, 2008, the title page on the section previewing Eresos refers to the village as having "the scent of Sappho," it seems in an attempt to not completely slight the historical figure and offer a nod to the lesbian tourism to the village. On the other hand, Tzeli Hadjidimitriou's (2012) *Girls Guide to Lesvos*, whose photos grace this volume, provides historical information on Sappho and her ties to Skala Eresos, a discussion of the village as a lesbian tourist destination, as well as offering general tourist information for the island.

Sappho's repertoire included love poems and erotic verses demonstrating a deep sensitivity to human emotions and connectivity (Rayor 1991). She was aware of the novelty of her topics in writing such as is evident in her well-cited fragment 16, Carson's (2003) translation:

Ο]ἰ μὲν ἰππήων στρότον οἰ δὲ   Some men say an army of horse and
    πέςδων,   some men say an army on foot
οἰ δὲ νάων φαῖς᾽ ἐπ[ἰ] γᾶν   and some men say an army of ships
μέλαι[ν]αν ἔ]μμεναι κάλλιστον,   is the most beautiful thing on the
ἔγω δὲ κῆν᾽ ὄτ—   black earth. But I say it is
    τω τὶσ ἔπαται   what you love.

Remarkably, Sappho's lyrics were concerned with an appreciation for everyday life and social relationships, raising these topics to the level of poetics during the grand era of Classical Greece—a time in which war and gods were all anyone wrote about (Rayor 1991). Her poetry carries sociological insights, as she gave empirical fodder—stories of women, her daughter, or details of interactions—for her philosophical musings about love, sexuality, and personal interactions.

Many writers and scholars highlight Sappho's poetic professions of love for the women in her life as a demonstration of her same gender attraction. As evidence they point to the fragments (approximately 650, with two new poems found in 2004 and 2014) of her poetry that were not lost in translation, decayed, or destroyed by the Byzantines (Mendelsohn 2015). In many of these fragments, Sappho vividly describes her adoration for women (Way 1920, 14). Consider fragment 31, Carson's (2003) translation:

και γελαίςας ἰμεροεν, το μ᾽ ἡ μάν   And lovely laughing—oh it
καρδίαν ἐν ςτήθεςιν ἐπτόαιςεν   puts the heart in my chest on wings
ὡς γὰρ <ἐς> ς᾽ ἴδω βρόχε᾽ ὡς   for when I look at you, even a
    με φώνη-   moment, no speaking
        ς᾽ οὐδέν ἐτ᾽εἴκει   is left in me

Debates on whether or not the group of women who Sappho wrote about engaged in sexual exchanges is as lively in the streets of Lesvos's villages as in the academy. The Victorian literati, for example, were enamored with Sappho. They forced her sexual leanings into heteronormativity, as they envisioned her community of women as a finishing school for girls. Others, however, argue that Sappho led a *thiasos* or religious cult for Aphrodite with related ritual sex work. It is critical to underscore that the veracity of both claims is limited, and a more modified view is that Sappho's circle consisted of women who arrived from other regions for the purpose of learning and sociality; it seems a foreshadow of the current pattern of visitors to the Aegean island and Skala Eresos, Sappho's presumed birthplace. However, the opening of gay and queer scholarship has lent academic credibility to the readings of Sappho's homoeroticism, with scholars sticking close to Sappho's original poetry in their interpretations and contextualizing these with discoveries regarding sexuality and ancient Greek social life.

In Sappho's Lesvos, sexual relations and contact between same gendered persons were not aberrant. Yet, as Calame (1996), Greene (1996), Snyder (1997), and others document, Sappho's love for women was denied by authoritative ancient texts of later eras, when it was considered to mar a woman's character. Books by Greene (1996), Williamson (1995), and Snyder (1997) describe the altered pronouns in translations from Greek-to-Roman and Greek-to-English to heterosexualize Sappho's life and writings. These changes mark attempts to mask Sappho's sexual involvement with women and the arts and sociality carried out by a community of women who surrounded her (Calame 1996). The scrutiny and denial of Sappho's love life was unique to her; the homoeroticism practiced by the men of her era has not received the same criticism and denial by scholarly communities nor by the Greek public (Greene 1996; Harris 1996).

Although debates abound, the first use of the term "lesbian" to demarcate women's sexual expression seems to have occurred in a Greek comedic play in the fifth century BC. The term was used to refer to the sexual prowess of Lesbian women but not necessarily as homoerotic. At the turn of the twentieth century, German and English sexologists, such as Havelock Ellis, began using "lesbian" to refer to "female same sex relationships," which they defined as socio-pathological, grounding a homophobic medicalization of sexuality. German and English psychologists' choice to use Lesvos as the referential base for same-sex relations between women, at a time when peer writers and literary critics devoted so much attention to denying Sappho's same gender attraction, is ironic. Both cases reflect the larger legacy of Northern Europeans appropriating Greece and Greek culture, with little awareness of doing so, to serve their own purposes.

As the term "lesbian" became the common reference to women attracted to women, it seems those who are from Lesvos have stopped referring to themselves as Lesbians. Unlike other Greek islands, Lesvos is commonly denoted as Mytilini, the island's capital, including on airline and ferry schedules, and in travel books, implying a distancing from the term that likely reflects homophobia.* There is still ongoing contestation of the term "lesbian," which is exemplified in a recent lawsuit over the term. In 2008, a resident of Lesvos sued the Homosexual and Lesbian Community of Greece—the only registered organization in Greece using the term "lesbian" to refer to same-sex relationships between women—over whether this term can be used to refer to women who love women. The plaintiff in this suit attempted to reappropriate the term to refer only to the people from Lesvos. The plaintiff stated that the suit "was not an aggressive act against gay women" and that the usage of "lesbian" as a referent to same-sex sexuality began only recently (Brabant 2008; Flynn 2008; Wright 2008). Much was made by critics of the lawsuit, since the term "lesbian" is sanctioned by the United Nations, leading many blogs to decidedly describe the legal case as ignorant and vengeful.

I happened to be in Lesvos during the summer of the trial and listened to discussions about the lawsuit. There was little doubt for most I spoke with in the villages of Lesvos that the decision to sue by the plaintiff derived from personal grudges rather than a real interest in saving the term "lesbian" for those from Lesvos. The case ruled against the plaintiff and in favor of the organization permitting the use of the term "lesbian" by the Homosexual and Lesbian Community of Greece to refer to same-sex relations between women. Whether it is Lesvos's historical fate of gynocentrism, an outcome of European appropriation, or contemporary lesbian tourism, lesbianism remains a distinctive rhythm in the island's past and recent social history.

Methodology: Rhythmanalysis

I utilize rhythmanalysis, an intuitively attractive method to grapple with interacting temporalities of social forces and the island geography of the Aegean. A novel approach, rhythmanalysis is just beginning to be

---

*There are multiple spellings of Mytilini, the capital of Lesvos. I follow Kantsa's (2002) usage.

applied empirically (Lyon 2018; Reid-Musson 2017; Nash 2016). Bridging history, especially the long historical perspective of world-systems (Chase-Dunn and Hall 1997), with ethnography, scholars have sought to situate everyday experiences in a historical frame that accounts for varying multiscalar political-social-cultural influences (Gille and Ó Riain 2002; Naples and Desai 2002; Burawoy 2000). This section offers a summary of rhythmanalysis, its evolution, and why I select it as a methodological framework.

Lucio Alberto Pinheiros dos Santos, a Brazilian philosopher writing in 1931, first introduced the concept of rhythmanalysis as the phenomenology of rhythms. He defined it as a method for knitting together the material, biological, and psychological to make sense of human experience (dos Santos 1931). It was not until the late fifties, when Gaston Bachelard (1991) picked up dos Santos's exploration of rhythmanalysis to codify his arguments on the discontinuity of the human experience, that rhythmanalysis was brought to the European intelligentsia. Bachelard was attracted to dos Santos's formulation of the phenomenology of rhythms because he saw it supporting his arguments that the experience of reality and time is a series of events and occurrences or rhythms. In his *The Dialectic of Duration* (1991), Bachelard challenges philosopher Henri Bergson (and Auguste Comte), who argued that the accumulation of knowledge is unbroken and the experience of time or memory is continuous, a single duration rather than a system of instances.

Henri Lefebvre, a founding theoretician of human geography, brought rhythmanalysis to fruition as a method of analysis, bridging his work on everyday life with his study of the production of space. Lefebvre (1984, 74–76) explores how rhythms show movement, "they gauge time (and are measured by it) and are of specific quality and always in relation to each other." The repetition of rhythms can be either cyclical (like a clock) or linear (like a series of blows by a hammer) and account for everything: the routines of everyday life, traffic lights, urban systems, the cycles of an economy, a heartbeat, a neighborhood, and waves (Lefebvre 1984). According to Lefebvre, rhythms are never singular, but they exist as a plurality and are only understood in relation to one another.

To study or explain society, especially modern society, a rhythmanalyst must observe, listen to, and identify the particular rhythms of a context and how they interplay with one another (Lefebvre 2004). Thinking about social phenomena as a multitude of rhythms moving in relation to one another and influenced by place is what attracts me to rhythmanalysis.

It allows for making sense of the range of influences on Lesvos and their timing, from ancient to contemporary, that come together to provide conditions for an island microeconomy in which a lesbian enclave and women's cooperatives can flourish.

Lefebvre (2004, 20) considered rhythmanalysis as a "new science of society" and insists that "a rhythmanalysist can listen to a house, a street, a town as one listens to a symphony." This, then, is how I listened to the cooperatives and microenterprises in Lesvos, the local patterns in the village context in which they thrive, and the transnational array of forces that have come to shape the social politics and economics of Greek islands. A rhythmanalytical approach helps make visible the traditions of ancient Greece in the everyday practices of contemporary Greek islanders, and how this intertwines with currents of gender and sexuality, tourism, and the social politics of the EU. The flowering of a contemporary lesbian community and village women's cooperatives on Lesvos, two millennia after Sappho's collective, appeals to rhythmanalytical consideration.

Understood as rhythms, inequalities may be examined as deep patterns with stronger or weaker influence on a particular place at various moments (Reid-Musson 2017). Rhythms retain fluidity—continually interacting with other rhythms and circumstances and shifting as they are impacted by social change—opening the possibility of a new or renewed and unforeseen "rhythm" that introduces itself into the existing amalgam of rhythms. For contemporary social sciences in which we are simultaneously becoming more aware of the socioeconomic-cultural-ecological interconnections around the world and of the personal, psychological, and biological depths of humanity—all of which can be envisioned as interacting rhythms—rhythmanalysis may provide a more comprehensive study of these interactions and mobilities.

Musical rhythms often are noted by general listeners only when there is a good deal of discord or heightened interactions among them. It is often only a musician or a music aficionado who is truly able to describe the various rhythms at play in a successful piece of music. The work of social scientists is to distinguish social processes so that others—readers, students, colleagues—can *hear* them. Embracing rhythmanalysis as a method can help increase attention to the numerous, overlapping, and shifting strands in the formation of societies and places, and identify spaces of social change. Unlike other methodologies, the examination of social institutions, inequalities, cultural identities, or political legacies as a rhythm advances a grasp of the fluidity of social life. The constant shifting of influences, and the temporal strengthening or weakening of rhythms, echoes a queer theoretical understanding of how social norms and practices are shaped (Butler 1990).

A Rhythmanalyst in Lesvos

The natural and social rhythms of island life in the Mediterranean were marked as providing therapeutic value in many of my conversations with locals, visitors, and migrants. Indeed, the sociality of the Mediterranean lifestyle and diet have long been thought to provide better health and longer life, a position that has recently gained scientific merit (Buettner 2015; Trichopoulo et al. 2003). Living in Skala Eresos, I succumbed to the local rhythms, developing a daily schedule that just may have organized Greek life since ancient times. Rather than living by the "work continuously—no time for lunch—burn the midnight oil" routine of many US academics, I changed my work habits, more so than I ever did. While I maintained the intensity of a field researcher, I learned quickly that making phone calls and arranging interviews in the midafternoon was not acceptable.

For data collection, I used ethnographic methods of observation and participation, conducting in-depth interviews and several short surveys. I attempted to operationalize rhythmanalysis by paying attention to the timing of larger political economic influences of Greek social history and the impact on the specific social worlds I studied and interacted with in Lesvos. I focused on how these rhythms intersect with long-held cultural practices and alterations ushered in by Northern Europe at various stages of Greek island development. The majority of my data was collected in the summer and autumn of 2008, July 2009, and between April and August 2012. I also returned to Greece and met with key informants and contacts in March 2014 and August 2016.

Visits with Women's Cooperatives

I scheduled regular meetings with the women's cooperatives interspersed throughout the island, allowing me to eventually master driving around winding gravel mountain roads at night, in deep fog and soft rain. I conducted informal semistructured focus group interviews with twelve cooperatives at least two times; a thirteenth, that I had met with once in 2008, closed by the time of my second return. Depending on what day or time I arrived the number of participants in focus groups varied due to the scheduling of work shifts. Along with formal interviews, I visited each of these cooperatives multiple times during each research trip. Even when I did not have a meeting scheduled, I often stopped by to have a coffee and a chat, quite customary in Greece, after being welcomed to do so, when I drove across the island. In several of the cooperatives, I was a regular, making weekly visits that kept me informed of the latest happenings given the volatile period during which I chanced to be conducting this research. All in all, I conducted approximately eighteen focus group interviews with an average of four cooperative members participating per meeting as well as approximately thirty informal meetings, visits, or observations.

Each of the women's cooperatives I interviewed provided me with pastries to sample as I sat down to talk with them. Their offers were generous and captured the giving emblematic of Greek enterprises. As a gracious Greek guest, I ate them, no matter how many I encountered in a day. Each time, I also offered to pay, even though I knew that my money would not be accepted. I managed, however, to purchase boxes of Greek cookies (*koulouria*), liqueurs made with local fruits, weighty baklava, and preserves that I was able to share and gift to acquaintances in Eresos.

My interviews with the cooperatives focused on their origin stories, the daily rhythm of work, membership, customer base, wages, governance structures, and relationships with other cooperatives or the larger network of cooperatives throughout Greece. Along with gathering information on the practicalities of cooperative life, such as how work schedules are organized, how items are priced, inventory is managed, and the domain of ingredients, I learned about the political situation of cooperatives vis-à-vis the Greek economic crisis and changes in state government policies. I also learned about members' families, how long they have worked in the cooperative and the reasons why, the care and concern they had for one another and their village, and a good bit about local agriculture, wild harvesting, and Greek food preparations and their regional varieties.

My meetings with the women's cooperatives opened the opportunity for in-depth discussions with local village women, which I could not carry out with most of the ethnic Greek women in Eresos who, despite my Greek ethnicity, may have just as well identified me as another Northern émigré in the village. The conversations and meeting held with the women's cooperative members grounded me in the realities of daily life and the concerns of island women in Lesvos. Among the cooperatives I visited and conducted interviews with, the high value placed on collectivity, sociality, and autonomy was almost universal. At a few of the cooperatives, I often had to reexplain that I was not connected to the state or a representative of the EU, but that I had a genuine independent interest in how and why women create flexible, convivial, and communal work on islands. In addition to interviews with cooperative members I also conducted informal semistructured interviews with a few government officials, such as those in the Ministry of Agriculture, who had overseen programs for the development of women's cooperatives. These interviews provided insight into the economic development of women's cooperatives as well as on the contemporary issues and policies facing them.

With the exception of the cooperatives in Molyvos and Ayiassos— the former a highly touristic and architecturally superb village with somewhat upscale visitors and the latter a village that bustles with religious tourism to its monastery in a mountainous region rich with wild herbs and chestnut trees—the cooperatives were located in much smaller and quieter villages. Most of the cooperatives were found in the agora or the marketplace, where most shops in Greek island villages are located. The agora is a holdover from ancient times that continues to be identified by official street signs for even the tiniest of villages.

In summer, most Greek island villages receive tourists, who vary by the length of stay and connection to the village. Some tourists are village kin returning from Athens for the summer, while others, arriving from abroad, stop by for the afternoon to visit the cooperatives for a taste of a deeply local interpretation of Greek pastries and pies. But in the late fall and winter months only Mytilini, the island's economic center, hosts a sprightly social life. Even the most popular villages of Eresos and Molyvos are generally devoid of visitors in winter and the colder autumn months. Year-round islanders retreat into the autumn harvesting of olives and acquiesce to winter's rhythm of tranquility dotted with religious holidays, which are celebrated with pastries and savories from the cooperatives.

COLLECTING STORIES IN SKALA ERESOS

In Skala Eresos, I became embedded in the local communities by participating in numerous events and actively joining various social scenes. In

2008, almost every weekday morning, with the exception of strikes and holidays, I dropped my elementary school–aged children off at school, a neoclassical building built with funds provided by a well-off Eressian living in Australia. I picked them up at 12:30 p.m., the end of the school day for kindergarteners and early elementary students, waiting with other parents and relatives. While I had spent significant time as a single person traveling Greece and visiting relatives, in working and sending children to school I learned a great deal more about the daily rhythm of Greek village life.

Along with sending my children to the local public school, I joined the Parent Teacher Association (PTA), which gave me access to community affairs. I spent most evenings in the lesbian bars, hippie/alternative hangouts, or distinctly Greek tavernas and coffee shops. I realized that as well as local Greek residents, Skala Eresos held a yearlong lesbian and alternative community, indicating that there were plenty of people left to interview when I first arrived in the fall of 2008. With the dwindling tourist season came less work and social obligations both for the business owners and workers in Skala Eresos. There was more time for extended conversations, and several events to witness and join, as winter's quiet befell the Aegean on my first research trip.

I conducted audio recorded interviews with approximately seventy persons from a range of backgrounds and relationship to Skala Eresos. Among them about a third included generational residents of Skala from elite and peasant backgrounds, owners of enterprises, ranchers, and farmers. I also interviewed European lesbians including English, German, French, Dutch, Belgian, Spanish, Italian, and ethnic Greek lesbians, most of whom were in their forties and fifties, and many who held businesses or worked in them. I also met with members of Skala's community that identify as British ex-pats, and at least ten Northern European women who were married to or divorced from ethnic Greek men. The youngest person I interviewed was a twenty-one-year-old college student who works in Skala during summers, the eldest, a Greek Communist Party war hero at eighty-eight. Of this broad population of interviewees, I asked participants about their perceptions of life in Skala Eresos, how they experienced the seasonal rhythms and different communities, the kinds of changes or development they might like to see, or what they prefer remain the same. Many spoke about the volatile political climate, telling me about the politicians they favored or the ones they did not, and concerns with the EU and its attempts to infringe on Greek political and economic autonomy. Most of my interviews lasted a little more than an hour, while others carried on late into the evening, eventually merging into discussions as part of a larger social gathering at one of the many dining venues in Skala. Along with these formal interviews, I spent hundreds of hours in conversation with individuals or groups about the social diversity in Skala Eresos.

At last count in 2016, there were approximately sixty-three micro-enterprises in Skala Eresos. More than half of these enterprises serve food and drinks, and are the emphasis of this research. In Greece food and drink enterprises hold specific designations that limit or permit the types of items they can sell. For example, restaurants and tavernas can serve the broadest array of food items and drinks, but kafenions, the quintessentially Greek coffee shops that evolved from the Ottoman Empire (Quaraert 2005), can offer limited fare such as pressed sandwich items and alcohol offerings are generally limited to ouzo. Bars are the businesses that can serve a range of liquor but also hold a limited food menu, for example no prepared seafood or cooked meats. Usually served along with drinks ordered at Greek bars are small mezzes, such as olives, nuts, or chips, that arrive without request. Cantinas, often food trucks found near the seaside during summer, are even more limited, able to serve only premade food items, such as sandwiches, soft drinks, and beer but not wine or liquor. Souvlaki places were their own category of enterprise, and, what may or may not be obvious, the only locale where one could purchase souvlaki.

Other enterprises that make up the microeconomy of Skala Eresos include a few small markets, all of which have a constant flow of customers, a couple of bakeries where daily bread is purchased for afternoon meals, about four tourist shops that sell beach items such as floaties, towels, and plastic toys as well as the usual tourist "tchotchkes," a travel agency, a car rental service, and a fine jewelry store and gift shops with artisanal items. There is only one hotel upon the shoreline in the village of Skala Eresos, while most of the others, not more than five, are found in the back of the village, in the valley. Many tourists find accommodations through the traditional rooms-to-let that characterizes Greek island travel. And, as required by state law, there is a pharmacy available in all Greek villages.

About a third of the enterprises were operated by one or two women. A good number were run collectively by families or couples, and referred to as a family business. Approximately 30 percent of the business owners in Skala Eresos identified as lesbians, with the vast majority of these enterprises in food and beverage, and I interviewed the majority of these owners. Many of the lesbian enterprises and those initiated by Skala's bohemian set could be considered examples of attritional economic alterity, enterprises started by foreigners or urban ethnic Greeks leaving their homes and seeking to secure livelihoods consistent with the rhythm of Greek island life. A large group of enterprises in Skala are organic, developed within the local Eressian community, sometimes passed down from a previous generation. Over the eight-year period of my research, I witnessed younger persons comanage businesses with parents or grandparents and leadership transitioning from one generation to the other.

I attempted to visit each of these businesses as I made my rounds in the village. During my late autumn stay, I was a regular visitor to the few shops in Skala that remained open including two locally owned Greek tavernas, a bar owned and frequented by lesbian identified women, and a lesbian owned restaurant where people from all groups ate. I also was a regular at the bakeries and small markets. In the summer months, with an increased array of businesses, my regular locations expanded. Although I managed to visit and have at least a drink or meal in all of Skala's enterprises, I maintained a few regular spots. This included three locally owned Greek tavernas, a bar and a restaurant each operated by Greek alternatives or self-identified bohemians from urban regions, a traditionally Greek locally owned coffee shop, three lesbian bars that were owned and frequented by lesbians who relocated to Skala Eresos permanently or semipermanently, and two lesbian restaurants. The time I was able to sit at these venues afforded me opportunities to deepen my ties and conversations with owners and workers in them, giving me keen insight into the daily workings of the convivial economics at play. In 2012 I conducted a basic survey of food and beverage enterprises in Skala Eresos. Through these surveys I accumulated a range of information on when enterprises were established. The earliest continuing enterprise was a kafenion established in the 1960s and the most recent was a kebob house opened by a Turkish and Greek lesbian couple in 2016. The majority of enterprises were established in the 1990s when Northern European tourism to Greece was on the rise.

The majority of Skala Eresos's microenterprises hired less than five employees, in many cases family members, friends, spouses, or partners, even during the busy season of August. Similar to inquiries I made of the cooperatives, I was especially interested in identifying from where the ingredients arrived to help determine the extent of a local food system. I also surveyed Skala's business owners on whether and what kind of support they received from the government to which the typical response was "τίποτα" (tipota) or nothing. Their position on government was mostly critical. A preference for autonomy from the state, to be further articulated, is not only a response to the political maneuvers in regard to Greece's contemporary debt crisis, but also reflective of long historical rhythms of the political and economic independence of Greek islanders.

In July 2009 and 2012 I conducted a brief survey by approaching persons I perceived to be tourists. I completed thirty of these, which consisted mostly of questions requiring short answers such as "Are you on vacation? What brings you to Skala Eresos? Have you been here before? And do you return often? What do you enjoy most? Do you dine out? Has this changed? How long is your stay?" as well as identifiers of ethnicity or race, gender, income level, and residence. In some cases, the surveys were filled by respondents while I sat with them, with others I attempted to capture their brief answers verbatim. With at least two-thirds of the surveys I conducted, conversations extended for some time after the completed survey and I attribute this to the natural sociability of Greek venues and congeniality of persons on holiday.

The informality and immediacy of island life in the Aegean took me by surprise. I came with the assumption of scheduling interviews with at least a week's notice, a ridiculously long time in the context of Lesvos, and rural islands, where everything from a medical appointment to a haircut or a meeting with the school principal is addressed almost as soon as needed. As long as I stuck to the daily rhythms of village life, my meetings and the events I attended moved as if choreographed.

I could be waiting at the porch of Adonis's Café gazing across the sea to the enormous rock that sits unnaturally in its perfection at the center of Skala Eresos's bay, meet with a German lesbian homeopath who has lived on and off in Eresos for almost twenty years, and arrange another interview with a passerby all in one afternoon. Or, if in a casual conversation someone was identified to be informative for my research, I could schedule a visit with her shortly after or be brought to her directly. While every meeting has its utility and all conversations in the field can provide some unexpected perspective, several times I found myself in the awkward position of talking with persons simply to follow patterns of respectability and in obligation to an informant. Without exception, though, interviews and meetings generously were granted, and from each I took something of the richness of Lesvos and its opportunity for economic conviviality.

The decidedly seasonal life of Lesvos, including the ebb and flow of tourism, weather patterns, and holidays, makes rhythmanalysis a useful prism for articulating convivial economics as they occur on the island. Thinking rhythmically we can discern the flux in social and economic life, historically and contemporarily, and how, despite oscillating rhythms, we find solidly identifiable places.

A Road Map for *Sappho's Legacy*

Sappho's Legacy is divided into three parts. Part 1: Καλωσόρισες, named after the Greek greeting of welcome to those just arrived, consists of three chapters. This first chapter is a welcome to the social cultural landscape of Lesvos. I have presented perspectives on subalternity and resistance and islands to locate the women's cooperatives and microenterprises in the alternative economy literature. After I addressed Sappho's legacy, I concluded by making a case for rhythmanalysis as a methodological orientation. Chapter 2 grounds the volume in a set of theoretical perspectives on alternative economy. Four central frameworks of contemporary alternative economics are reviewed—social economy, solidarity economy, localism, and diverse or community economics. This is followed by a fuller articulation of convivial economics that roots economic alterity in the strategies of subaltern groups and those living in subaltern locations that sustain community. The third chapter is focused on Greece's political-economic development, the onset of the global economic crisis, and the substantial role cooperatives and microenterprises play in the nation's economy. It highlights the ways in which alternative economics is a matter of course in Greece, as are active public protests and agitation—both of which represent counters to contemporary capitalism. The chapter historicizes the nation's current economic circumstances as a legacy of its economic and social peripheralization in Europe. I develop this rhythm of analysis by drawing attention to particular historical moments that showcase Europe's condescension toward Greece through biased representations of its populations and policies that burdened Greece economically. Europe's patronizing attitude toward Greece was evident in EU forums addressing its economy over the last decade. I consider both the political volleying around Greece's economic crises and the negative stereotyping of Greek enterprises and economic practice in popular media. My goal is to distinguish Greece's convivial economics vis-à-vis EU's march toward neoliberalism.

The Rhythm Section, the second part of the volume, includes three chapters each dedicated to a major rhythm of Greek island life and enterprise. These include host-guest relations in chapter 4, which explores φιλοξενία (filoxenia), a Greek style of hospitality, from its ancient foundations to its perpetuation in island tourism, as a dominant cultural rhythm.* Relying on historical, mythological, and anthropological accounts of Greece, I try to make φιλοξενία palpable, first by tracing contemporary aspects of Greek tourism to ancient Greek forms of receiving foreigners and noting the public space of the village square in Greek islands as grounds for convivial economics. I also explore Northern Europeans' attitude of entitlement toward Greece and their simultaneous disdain and attraction to Greek alterity as a historical rhythm. Chapter 5 presents a

---

*Φιλοξενία (filoxenia), hospitality. Throughout the volume I use the Greek alphabet and spelling of words and sometimes phrases that relay concepts or expressions that I perceive as not offering the same richness in meaning when translated or transliterated. In the first uses of such a term I follow with a transliteration of the word or phrase in a parenthesis and provide a footnote with a definition drawn from *Mandesson's Modern English-Greek Dictionary* (1995) as there are too few of these to substantiate a glossary. However, these definitions often don't carry the depth of cultural meaning that I may elaborate more fully in the text to express the concept I hope to convey. As ku'ualoha ho'omanuwanui (2014) writes of translations of her own Hawaiian language: "No language thoroughly translates the gradations of meanings of the original language into the 'target' language." In most instances, I also follow Kanaka Ōiwi scholars; I present first in Greek phrases that were originally written in the language. For this volume this includes fragments of Sappho's poems and an exchange from Aristophanes's comedic play, *Lysistrata*. For each of these I selected recent translations that present both the original Greek along with the English translation. I also arrived at Carson's (2003) translation of Sappho, Johnston's (2017) translation of *Lysistrata*, and the first woman's translation of *The Odyssey* by Wilson (2017) because they do not adorn or reinvent the original Greek as with Victorian English translators and offer a contemporary voice. For Greek terms, such as taverna, that are regularly used by non-Greeks, most of which are in reference to places that are likely to be visited by tourists or Greek foods they might eat, and place names, such as villages, islands, or cities in Greece, I transliterate into English using common phonetic spellings. In a few cases, such as in text from interviews, I provide the Greek in parenthesis usually to call attention to a Greek idiom. The translation into English of my interviews conducted in Greek are my own.

sociohistorical analysis that draws attention to the gendered-sexualized spatiality of Greek islands. I review scholarship that reflects on ancient Greek patterns of gendered spatiality and anthropological research that shows how women in the past and present transgress the rhetoric of spatial boundaries to meet practical needs. A spin around most Greek islands, especially in late morning and afternoon, will find a mass of local Greek men publicly gathering in cafés and eateries, arguably a display of Greek masculinity (Papataxiarchis 1993). It is this tradition of homosocial gathering that the rise of contemporary tourism, especially independent women tourists, along with the women's cooperatives and lesbian enclaves have refashioned. Chapter 6 articulates island food systems as a third central rhythm. This chapter responds to the growing food studies literature, and considers its proliferation in relation to food tourism and islands. I contribute to the vibrant conversation currently in food studies by offering a contemplation of how island geographies contour local food systems. I also consider how alternatives such as organic, local, and small-scale farming have been characteristic of islands, hippies, and peasants predating the current flurry of these activities now being celebrated. Together the three rhythms presented in part 2 have sustained both a convivial and gendered pattern of economy on Greek islands that new groups have amended and engineered to sustain their own convivial enterprises on them.

Part 3: Hospitable Shores is largely empirical, blending ethnography and historical analysis to elucidate the above rhythms in Lesvos. Chapter 7 depicts Skala Eresos, providing a history of the seaside village's modern development that initiated in the early 1900s when families, who had escaped the piracy of previous centuries by settling in nearby mountains, returned to reestablish a coastal community. I articulate the fine sociality of island societies as it occurs in Skala Eresos, and how it interacts with island migration and tourism to shape a convivial local economy. The chapter showcases the relationships among Skala Eresos's microenterprises across Greek businesses and bohemian microenterprises, which all cater to the local population and Greek and foreign tourists. Chapter 8 centers on Skala Eresos becoming a premier site for lesbian travel and tourism. Based on in-depth semistructured interviews, I explore the relationships between Greek islanders and their Northern visitors as well as the impact of homophobia on lesbian tourism. Chapter 9 details the workings of the women's cooperatives and the political and economic climate under which they have come to create and manage a feminist economic alterity. These cooperatives have a positive impact on their village communities economically and by virtue of the space they provide women to socialize. I review their histories of development, the success of the cooperative model, and their engagement with the state. The chapter also considers their relationship with island place and gendered work in food production. I explore how the cooperatives have evolved including trading their goods across Greece and further abroad.

The coda provides a conclusion reflecting on convivial economics as a matter of contemporary resistance to neoliberalism and Greece's past, challenging the bifurcation of Greek cultural and socioeconomic history into the modern and the ancient. I review perspectives of alternative economics and the prospects they hold for the future. Reaffirming the rhythms of Lesvos convivial economics: hospitality and mobilities, gendered and sexualized spatiality, and island food practices, that combine on Greek islands as a buttress for convivial economic culture to sustain itself, I consider the current circumstance of Greece.

What this book describes as Greek convivial economics became a notable aspect of Greece's contentious negotiations with the EU, the International Monetary Fund, and the European Central Bank throughout the economic crisis. Greeks' methods of conducting business and their work ethic was essentialized and used to legitimize the severe austerity measures that impoverished Greece. The broad protests of the Greek population, such as the march of over 25,000 Greek citizens on November 12, 2015, projected Greek opposition to parliamentary legislations set to deconstruct livelihoods into forms that contradict Greek economic culture. What *Sappho's Legacy* seeks to showcase is how the day-to-day organic economic alterity of small, local, Greek island enterprises achieves material needs and local sociality, accommodates strangers and newcomers with hospitality, and resists neoliberalism. Island dynamics of reciprocity are evident in the communities of women in Lesvos who participate in cooperatives throughout the island or form the lesbian enclave in Eresos. Acting as "insurgent architects," these women attempt "to shape their own beingness," not condemning themselves to work paths set out by external structures and values (Harvey 2000, 235). They are part of a long tradition of islanders meeting material needs while maintaining an everyday life based in flexibility, generosity, and sustainability.

CHAPTER TWO

The Master's Tools Will Never Dismantle the Master's House

For the master's tools will never dismantle the master's house. They may allow us temporarily to beat him at his own game, but they will never enable us to bring about genuine change.*

—Audre Lorde (1984, 2)

The other level is that of ordinary people, peasants and proletarians, who, because of the poor flow of benefits from the top, skepticism about stated policies and the like, tend to plan and make decisions about their lives independently, sometimes with surprising and dramatic results that go unnoticed or ignored at the top. Moreover, academic and consultancy experts tend to overlook or misinterpret grassroots activities because these do not fit in with prevailing views about the nature of society and its development.

—Epeli Hau'ofa (1994, 2)

Global capitalism has made achieving economic security or survival an increasingly challenging feat, especially for the most marginalized among us. Despite the difficulty, some people have succeeded in establishing enterprises that aim to reach beyond the neoliberal goal of profit maximization. They have chosen to provide socially necessary goods and services, support ecological interests, and provide spaces of

---

*The chapter's title is borrowed from the title and passage of an essay in Audre Lorde's (1984) volume, *Sister Outsider*. This sentiment and Lorde's essay capture the alterity in convivial economics.

37

sociality. These goals often involve the prioritization of autonomy over expansion and the balancing of personal life and work—traits of a convivial economy. For some who engage in such enterprises, the refutation of neoliberal methods represents an active choice that involves departing from mainstream income earning practices, as was reflected in many of the lesbian enterprises and hippie or alternative enterprises found in Skala Eresos. For others, a noncapitalist ethos is more indicative of economic geographies as found in the women's cooperatives and Greek microenterprises in island spaces (Peck 2013).

Conceptions of what counts as work have changed through time, shaped by culture and location (Weeks 2011; Applebaum 1992). Whether people are born in remote villages on Greek islands or relocate to them from elsewhere, the reasons people establish businesses and create livelihoods speak to sociological interests around how, why, and where people work. What people do to earn an income is delimited by a host of factors: poverty, familial expectations, immobility, job opportunities, race and ethnic bias, discrimination and social expectations around gender and sexuality, or the demands of the contemporary capitalist economy. The enterprises I studied in Lesvos suggest that for many, concern over the well-being of society and environment also drives entrepreneurial, employment, and residential choices.

This chapter explores four theoretical framings of what is generally referred to as alternative economics, including social economy, solidarity economics, localism, and community or diverse economies. My research in Lesvos contributes convivial economics as a perspective that highlights economic alternatives as creative and communal economic strategies of marginalized peoples and places. Convivial economics emphasizes the "unnoticed" activities that, as Hau'ofa (1994) and others assert, are often misunderstood and mislabeled by mainstream models of development (Escobar 1995). The women's cooperatives studied in Lesvos are based on collective labor and ownership, as they draw from Greek traditions of cooperative and communally driven economics. They fit neatly into articulations of alternative economics including "the social economy" (Wright 2010; Laville, Levesque, and Mendell 2006; Moulaert and Ailenei 2005), "the solidarity economy" (Allard, Davidson, and Matthaei 2008), and "community or diverse economies" (Gibson-Graham 2006). However, microenterprises and small businesses, such the enterprises in Skala Eresos, are a more contested terrain in the alternative economic literature. Even though microenterprises may empower local economies socially and politically (Hess 2009), maintain fair labor practices, and support autonomy, many traditional Marxists and advocates of cooperative movements suggest that they are particularly susceptible to the profit motive of capitalism. Yet the small scale and intentions of these enterprises often lead them to operate outside capitalist (and socialist) principles of mass production and consumption (Hess 2009) and to resist centralized bureaucratic control, which often support a local economy. These smaller and micro entities may be better able to control the principles of enterprise and prioritize environmental viability, autonomy, or creative expression in one's work, over capital expansion and profits (Schumacher 1973).

Alternative Economics

Academic debates and discussions around the possibilities of alternative economies are relatively recent. These conversations have emerged as more and more individuals and communities across the globe are developing ingenious solutions to the problems wrought by the last several decades of neoliberalism. While there is limited consensus on what economic practices may or may not be reasonably included in the term "alternative economics," it generally refers to the broad set of income earning practices that challenge capitalism by not adhering to neoliberal ideals to seek profit maximization at all costs but rather assume social responsibility and are ecologically benign (Hart, Laville, and Cattani 2010; Kelly 2010, Zsolanai 1993).

Recently there has been an expansion in the nomenclature used to describe alternative economic practices including subsistence, sharing, participatory, human, generative, dissident, as well as other terms with regional relevance that may capture some nuance. Here, however, I focus on four established perspectives within the alternative economics literature to contrast and locate *convivial economics*, which theoretically frames the type of enterprises studied in Lesvos. Each of these four paradigms—social economy, solidarity economy, localism, and community or diverse economies—offer a distinct conceptualization for how to best resist and shift economic practices away from neoliberalism.

SOCIAL ECONOMY

Rooted in Northern Europe (Laville, Levesque, and Mendell 2006; Moulaert and Ailenei 2005, 238), the social economy refers to the injection of social justice into production and allocation systems (Moulaert and Ailenei 2005). Laville, Levesque, and Mendell (2006, 7) explain that "the social economy originated in Europe, by the nineteenth century it emerged in North America as well, particularly in Canada and Quebec with its ties to the United Kingdom and France as well as other European countries, especially Germany and Belgium." The phrase "social economy" can be traced back to French economist Charles Dunoyer, who coined the term in 1830 to advocate for a moral approach to the economy. A set of French researchers, such as Frederic Le Play (1864), Charles Gide (1912), and Leon Walras (1896), later expanded the concept into its own field of study (Moulaert and Ailenei 2005). Social economy became known as the "science of social justice" or "the study of all efforts made to improve the condition of the people" (Gide 1912, 10, quoted in Moulaert and Ailenei 2005, 2049). These scholars—who witnessed the rise of exploitive working and poor living conditions during the Industrial Revolution—identified the cooperative, associative, and mutual aid practices people used to counter capital's excess as a "social economy."

Laville and colleagues (2006), Wright (2010), and others rejuvenated these original conceptions of the social economy to understand contemporary economic entities, such as nonprofit organizations, that have developed to address the negative effects of neoliberalism. More than other perspectives on alternative economics, the social economy is tied to traditional sociological thought and frameworks that privilege the ability of the state and government agencies to institutionalize progressive practices. However, it differs from the study of welfare states, as it assesses the means by which nongovernmental organizations can direct the provision of social goods leading to state centralization, rather than assuming the a priori redistributive force of the state.

The social economy perspective, especially as articulated in the US, generally excludes entities such as microenterprises and small independent cooperatives as significant movers of social change. The progress of the social economy is often measured by the extent to which agencies that provide social goods, such as childcare or healthcare, are scaled up and linked to the state, thereby creating a pathway to socialism (Wright 2010; Laville, Levesque, and Mendell 2006). Yet this approach often neglects more informal and negotiated relationships around the distribution of social goods that can also challenge neoliberalism. The social economy orientation also fails to address environments in which weak or hostile

governments are unable to support or rebuff the expansion and centralization of nonprofit organizations and other related entities.

SOLIDARITY ECONOMY

The solidarity economy is rooted in the Global South, particularly Latin
America. Unlike other alternative economic perspectives, it is tied to
grassroots global justice movements. The first use of "solidarity economy"
is attributed to Chilean philosopher Luis Razeto, who in the 1980s designated solidarity economic enterprises to be inclusive of Factor C—the
principles of cooperation, co-responsibility, communication, and community (Allard, Davidson, and Matthaei 2008). Some networks, such as the
European Social-Solidarity Network and the Intercontinental Network
for the Promotion of the Social Solidarity Economy, have been able to
bridge the social economy and the solidarity economy. However, advocates of the solidarity economy offer a distinct perspective on alternative
economics. Ethan Miller (2006), for instance, an author and activist
in the US cooperative movement, explains in an online essay that the
objective of the solidarity economy is to connect "islands of alternatives
in a capitalist sea." Solidarity economic activists seek to network these
largely independent low-capital entities to build them as a significant
counter to capitalism. Working from this perspective, proponents imply
it is bottom-up or grassroots alternatives to production, consumption,
and exchange that are creating new economic cultures.

Unlike the social economic alternative, the solidarity economy
grew from the everyday strategies of the poor and marginalized in Latin
America who were contending with the negative impact of structural
adjustment policies. These policies were imposed by the World Bank, the
International Monetary Fund, and the US on indebted nations around
the globe through the 1980s, forcing governments to cut social services
and state employment, increase taxes on basic goods, and deregulate
economic and environmental laws. Other requirements for IMF loans
included privatizing state industries and natural resources, devaluing
currency, and reserving most of a nation's GNP for servicing debt. The
consolidation of "Third World debt" saved private lenders, such as large
banks, from losing on their investments, while simultaneously opening
up Global South nations to exploitation by global capital. Transnational
corporations were enabled to cheaply purchase the assets of nations forced
to devalue currencies, spread exploitive labor conditions, and make gains

through deregulated financial systems. The structural adjustment policies asserted a US hegemony dominated by corporations, thereby driving a neocolonial and neoliberal world order that offered almost no benefit to nonelite populations in the Global South.

Lila Leontidou (1990, 1) suggests that Mediterranean Europe holds aspects of society and cultural forms associated with Latin America, as well as Africa, due to similar histories of economic interference, unstable and dictatorial governance, and coloniality: "Greece has been in many ways close to peripheries: a long period of its modern history was spent under Ottoman rule, and then under British and US neocolonial domination. In the postwar period, as it passed from peripheral to semi peripheral status in the world economy, however, it became more like the rest of the Mediterranean societies, and developed certain important differences from Northern Europe." The structural adjustment policies Greece endured in recent years are strikingly reminiscent of the debt restructuring experiences of Latin America. For example, when they first began to address Greece's debt in 2010, the troika enforced the same type of austerity measures that had failed across the globe decades earlier. By 2015, the failure of these measures was clear, as all aspects of the Greek economy had worsened since the implementation of these policies. However, the troika's response was to accelerate the program of austerity, ignoring the will and desperation of the Greek people who had voted for an alternative. Writing from an African standpoint on the failed experiences with structural adjustment policies, Gueye (2015) explains that "concerning Greece, the EU has not heeded the structural-adjustment lessons. . . . Like structural adjustment in the past, Greek bailouts have saved foreign financial institutions, not the people."

Neoliberal austerity measures have forced poor and middle class persons across the globe—especially women—to advance independent economic strategies to meet basic needs (Acosta-Belen and Bose 1995; Pyle and Ward 2003). In Latin America and the Caribbean, for example, communities have organically created solidarity economic forms, such as neighborhood kitchens, collective lending, subsistence agriculture, and informal small and microenterprises, preceding current conceptualizations of alternative economics (de Soto 1989). In China as well, informal relationships, such as social solidarities within communities, facilitate the provisioning of public goods to villages (Tsai 2007). These efforts are often the result of people hatching creative solutions to survive in the face of governmental absence and a lack of public or private employment opportunities.

The contemporary movement of the solidarity economy is centered on the idea that cooperatives are vehicles for overcoming neoliberalism. In summer 2019, the UN held its first conference devoted to assessing the role of social and solidarity economies for sustainability and development as both hold social and environmental objectives (Yi et al. 2019). Proponents of cooperatives are unconvinced that principles of solidarity could be sufficiently incorporated by privately owned enterprises that do not adhere to collective ownership because of the possibility of exploitation (including self-exploitation). Yet the local and independent initiatives of poor, marginalized, and low-income groups, which inform the foundation of the solidarity economy perspective, are not necessarily collectively owned (Allard, Davidson, and Matthaei 2008; Miller 2006). The survival strategies and informal economics pursued by women, families, and extended kin networks arose out of community needs, operating around the provision of social goods and services or the extension of informal credit. In some social, cultural, and geographic contexts, where the collective good or community survival is an orienting principle, collective ownership in the form of cooperatives may not be necessary for principles of solidarity to operate.

Localism

Localism, with its growing momentum as an alternative economic strategy, is founded on the belief that small and locally owned businesses are the centerpiece for an alternative political economy. David Hess (2009, 51), who studied localist movements in the urban US, defines it as a "political project of building an alternative economy that is distinct from the world of the large publicly traded corporation." He (2009) argues that at our historical juncture, localism may be capable of challenging corporate domination. He compares the growth of "buy local" campaigns and contemporary consumerist movements to the anti-chain-store movement of the Progressive Era, suggesting that once again small businesses and social justice issues are linked, forming the grounds for a localist social movement.

Unlike left critiques that have been focused on the reformation or regulation of corporations, localists seriously consider the ways in which locally owned small shops, microenterprises, and nonprofits can challenge neoliberalism by creating alternative economic structures in a locality. Support for small and local business development once existed in the sociology of development. In their analysis of the role of small businesses in the success of the ethnic enclaves of Miami, Portes and Stepick (1993, 5) state: "In a 1946 report to the US Senate, C. Wright Mills raised a related issue, namely whether cities suffered when their economies became dominated by outside interests. Mills denounced footloose corporate capitalism. . . . Mills proposed to the Congress a program to revitalize local business on the theory that community-based enterprises were more egalitarian and more responsive to local welfare. Critics called Mill's position retrograde." The public intellectualism of Mills likely guided his appreciation of the value of locally embedded enterprises that are not beholden to stockholders. Urban sociologists have also analyzed the differences between the operation of local capital and national or transnational capital, finding that the latter has a detrimental effect on local communities (see Logan and Molotch 1987). Jane Jacobs's renowned classic, *The Death and Life of Great American Cities* (1961), also broadly argues that small, local enterprises sustain community connections and economic investments in a neighborhood. Yet these articulations have been largely neglected by the corporate trajectory of urban development, prior to the recent and rising calls for local economies.

Several popular volumes backing small businesses and local economies written by authors such as Michael Shuman (2000, 2007, 2012) and Bo Burlingham (2007) have promoted small, local enterprises, economic networks, and stock exchanges as the ultimate model for local control and economic success. While these authors and others aspire for localism, their orientation seems geared toward smart and efficient business practices based in a market economy. They give limited recognition to the impacts of social inequalities and the uneven opportunities of a gendered and racialized capitalist economy. They may reflect a distinct movement away from corporate expansion and centralized ownership, and in some cases promote sustainability, but these strategies are largely tied to the mechanics of capitalism with interest in expanding profits although within local networks.*

---

*For example, in his study, Hess (2009) distinguishes between two organizational networks of localist movements in the US: the American Independent Business Alliance (AMIBA), which seeks local economic empowerment, self-sufficiency, and political autonomy, and the Business Alliance for Local Living Economies (BALLE), which includes principles of ecological sustainability and community benefits as part of its mission. Although BALLE stands for just and environmentally safe communities, both organizations are interested in the benefits of local capitalist growth although not corporate expansion.

For Hess (2009), the advantage of a local economy is tied to the ability of local and privately held businesses to respond and reinvest in their communities. Earnings of local businesses are often invested locally rather than distributing profits among distant shareholders and workers (Shuman 2012; Hess 2009; Logan and Molotch 1987). As private entities, small businesses are free to respond to local environmental concerns rather than the profit margins that drive publicly traded corporations. Advocates also suggest that locally potent economies can better determine the pricing of products rather than corporate-dominated ones in which residents must contend with price increases set at faraway headquarters. Rather, members of a community can negotiate with local retailers (Hess 2009).

The opportunity to consolidate political power through local ownership as a way to counter corporate interference and competition is arguably another strength of localism. A network of local business owners can not only offer an economic advantage for local communities but also advocate for government policies that are supportive of small businesses. Aligned with progressive and left movements, the reorientation of small business owners toward a local polity strengthens the basis for resisting neoliberalism that for Hess (2009, 57) "represents a political development of potential historical consequence." The rescaling of the market becomes a vehicle by which to challenge centralized control of the global economy. Ideally, through "independent and local ownership" the neoliberal paradigm is replaced with motives for quality, equity, environment, and community, as is "the goal of extending that project to locations throughout the world in the form of a global economy based on locally owned independent enterprises" (Hess 2009, 52).

Detractors of localism argue that rather than supporting political and economic empowerment, local business development is a ploy for further entangling communities in neoliberal economics. For example, "buy local" campaigns may ultimately represent a consumerist movement driven by neoliberal subjectivities or "middle class retreatism" when they fail to operate in the spirit of economic alterity (Szasz 2007). In chapter 6, where I consider the possibilities of alternative and local food systems, I address more fully the contradictions of consumer activism.

Localist and alternative movements rooted in the Global North, typically developing in privileged communities, seem less fixed on poverty reduction and marginal communities (see Kelly 2010; Hess 2009). Hess (2009) discusses how black men and women in the US are 50 percent more likely to start small business than their white counterparts, but they are more likely to fail. Beyond this, though, his volume takes little account of marginal populations and marginal locations nor does it acknowledge how localist strategies have been enacted from these identities and locations. Hess (2009) also characterizes the informal sector in Latin America as a failure of neoliberal development, rejecting microenterprises as localist initiatives. Contemporary studies of US or Global North localism can be somewhat myopic, as they can be negligent of how localism operates as a varied and an organic phenomenon and a strategy of survival in economically disadvantaged regions.

Community and Diverse Economies

Julie Gibson and Katherine Graham (2006), a pair of feminist human geographers, who have gone by the pen name J. K. Gibson-Graham, sought to discursively undermine the hegemony of "capitalocentrism" or the tendency to perceive capitalism, rather than alternatives, everywhere. According to Gibson-Graham (2006), not only the academy but also the general public have been subject to capitalocentric logic that limits a sense of self and possibility. Gibson-Graham (2006) reflect on how subjects are constituted and how they can shift and create new identities for themselves despite the hegemony of capitalocentric discourse. They describe both psychoanalysis and Buddhism as the two methods for self-transformation that can be applied to building a dis-identification with individuality and the economic subjection that centuries of capitalistic thought has imposed. In essence, Gibson-Graham's (2006) community economics, steeped in Foucauldian discourse analysis, is about changing "subjects" to endow them with economic identities independent of capitalism.

Gibson-Graham (2006, 86) also seek to replace traditional conceptions of community development that tie location to identities with a "vision of an ethical space of decision-making." Gibson-Graham (2009) resist community identities as a source of social and economic transformation based on the position that they are essentially exclusionary in nature. Yet this leaves little consideration for how collective identities have provided for economic and social survival for marginalized groups and regions. This includes ethnic communities, lesbian and gay enclaves, and indigenous communities that have been able to survive and maintain geographic and social space precisely because of what might be considered a strategic essentialism (Spivak 1993).

Gibson-Graham (2006) made their own attempts to shift subjectivities in a set of action research projects in which they engaged directly with community members in Australia. They (2006, 133) explain that "from the outset, we saw our projects as aimed at mobilizing desire for noncapitalist becomings." Gibson-Graham (2006, 134) identified themselves as holding a higher status position in the communities they worked within. They explained that community participants "invested power in our status and formal knowledge." Rather than refuse it, they accepted it as a method by which to make their knowledge desirable, comparing their efforts to that of a psychoanalyst.

Gibson-Graham's discursive approach to alternative economics seems riddled with privilege. Gibson-Graham's (2006) decision to not diffuse their power seems to confer a hierarchy between the experiential knowledge of their participants and their academic expertise. Also concerning is that Gibson-Graham had no long-term trajectory planned for their engagement. They explain that they were forced to end their involvement with the Australian group and that of their community field workers due to funding and resources. They (2006, 162) conclude, "It is possible to cultivate subjects for a community economy, but that disclosing and sustaining new worlds requires nourishment over more than a few years."

Gibson-Graham's (2006, 170) efforts at resubjectivation sought to encourage and inspire the public to stop waiting for "capitalism to give them a place in the economy" or believing "that outside assistance is necessary if needs are to be met." Instead, they encouraged people to actively construct "their economic lives on a daily basis, in a range of noncapitalist practices and institutions." Despite their energies and recognition that alternatives to capitalism exist, Gibson-Graham (2006) seem to overstate the extent to which people identify themselves in capitalocentric ways, particularly in application to regions that are geographically removed from capitalist centers or corporate entities. Their recent work, with coauthors Jenny Cameron and Stephen Healy, *Take Back the Economy* (2013), applies the term "reframing" with a presentation of their iceberg model of the global economy, in which "wage labor producing for a market in a capitalist firm" is just the tip of the iceberg. In it they implore readers to act like others who have selected to opt out of the "machine economy."

The strength of alternative or nonmainstream economic projects, such as cooperatives, microenterprises, alternative food networks, and sustainable communities, are founded in their own self-generation as they have persisted and reappeared through history. These entities have not required academic leadership for their development, though collaborations can be effective. Many marginalized communities that have engaged with academics have been critical of how researchers use communities for their own professional benefit, leave or abandon them with little to no benefit, or misrepresent them.

To a great extent Gibson-Graham's (2006) approach assumes that capitalist or neoliberal rhetoric has ensnared most of us, neglecting how those on the margins (hooks 1984) construct work-lives that are independent of capitalocentrism. In my own fieldwork on the informal sector, microenterprises, and cooperatives across island regions, interview participants have rarely expressed that they expect or hope that capital or the state will give them a place in the economy. This type of assumption might hold true in highly regulated economies dependent on macrolevel infrastructure, but in my research in an array of locales—including the informal sector in New Orleans, street vendors in Port of Spain, Trinidad, local food systems in Florida and Hawai'i, and microeconomies in Greece and the Republic of Cyprus—interview participants independently initiated enterprises for autonomy and subsistence. In many instances these practices allowed them to escape the racism or gender bias entrenched in formal work structures, while also helping their communities by providing informal and uncalculated assistance to those in need and with similar endeavors.

Economic alternatives may be driven, to various degrees, by locally and culturally defined economic practices that organically reject the ideals of neoliberal governance, formal job structures, and rigid employment regimes. Although Gibson-Graham's (2006) discursive approach is rightfully critical of academia for limiting theorization of economic alternatives, I am skeptical of a vanguard pose often invoked by academics involved in community action projects. It seems unaware of the economic wisdom and solidarity I have heard on city streets, in rural communities, in villages, on islands, and in the Global South, demonstrating a counterhegemonic logic from which much can be learned for building an alternative economy and the literature on it.

To various degrees the social and solidarity economy, localism, and community and diverse economics incorporate the kind of convivial economics I seek to elaborate in my analysis of the lesbian enterprises, the village women's cooperatives, and in the microeconomies of Lesvos, Greece. Yet as a whole the alternative economy literature makes little sense of how inequalities based in race, ethnicity, gender, sexuality, nation, and place shape the growth and development of alternative economic projects and practices.

Convivial Economics:
Organic and Attritional Economic Alterity

Drawing from Ivan Illich's (1973) book, *The Tools of Conviviality*, in addition to subaltern, queer, and feminist economic perspectives, I develop the concept of convivial economics as a way to interpret the economic entities created by marginalized groups and in marginal locations. Convivial economics refer to practices that neither adhere to nor adopt the dominant principles of neoliberal economics. Instead, they advance and sustain a sociable, caring, and local orientation to economy. Mainstream analyses rarely consider the social and cultural importance of economic enterprises that are situated within distinct spaces and shaped by regional interests and community ties. Convivial economics, and its organic and attritional forms, emphasizes the everydayness of social and economic resistance.

This section develops the concept of convivial economics. I also explore the influence of context on economic relationships, arguing that islands are conducive for the development of convivial economics due to the effect of "islandness" on economic exchanges. Lastly, I attend to the scale of enterprises as it relates to convivial economics, adapting E. F. Schumacher's (1973) "small is beautiful" thesis to further consider Lesvos's economic landscape and its cooperatives and microenterprises.

Neoliberal capitalism has created a set of global conditions in which most people struggle to achieve material well-being, find work/family/leisure balance, and live in a healthful environment. Illich's (1973) advocacy for "tools that guarantee the right to work with independent efficiency" was in advance of recent formulations, but it is consistent with the current thrust of alternative economic practices that attempt to redress the limitations of neoliberalism. According to Illich (1973), the tools for conviviality are framed by three values—survival, justice, and self-defined work.

Illich (1973) describes industrialization or large-scale production in which workers are no longer directly in control of their labor as a failure in development. His critique of capitalist production, but also of socialism, is that workers are not in direct control of "tools," which would include systems of production and decision-making or administration. For conviviality to occur there must be "autonomous and creative intercourse among persons, and the intercourse among persons with their environment; and this in contrast with the conditioned responses of persons to the demands made upon them by others" (Illich 1973, 11). Illich's emphasis on "personal energy under personal control" characterizes many of the alternative economic efforts occurring around the globe (Amin 2009; Hess 2009; Gibson-Graham 2006; Leyshon and Lee 2003; Grimes and Milgram 2000).

Alfons Garrigós (2002), an adherent of Illich's, adds that Illich's focus on personal and community relations and distrust of technological solutions for development were tied to his appreciation of limits. Garrigós (2002, 122) argues that, for Illich, limit "is the condition of the possibility of hospitality." The organization of our economic and political structures should not be shaped by the arrogance of unlimited technicians and politicians, but approached with the humility of a guest and with the hospitable treatment of all groups rather than relegating them to cold institutions. The alternative enterprises on Greek islands, and the overall condition of Greek society and economy, seem limited by the possibility of hospitality.

In Lesvos, both the women's cooperatives and microenterprises reflect the autonomous and creative conditions of labor described by Illich (1973). The women's cooperatives grew from an island history of agricultural cooperatives, political autonomy, and gendered spatial customs that gave way to collective self-reliance. Northern European and Athenian lesbians left urban careers to relocate to Skala Eresos and develop microenterprises to create livelihoods that they could shape to live more freely and independently.

Feminist and queer scholars (Cantú, Naples, and Vidal-Ortiz 2009; Jacobsen and Zeller 2008; Valocchi 2005; Matthaei 1998; Gibson-Graham 1996) have written about how economic choices, opportunities, and practices are shaped by heteronormativity and patriarchy. These perspectives challenge political economy perspectives that continue to neglect the ways in which the organization of work, development, and ownership are gendered and sexually uneven (Badgett and Williams 2008). Bridging feminist and queer insights with alternative economics perspectives, I try to showcase how those who are socially or geographically marginalized, or both, deftly create economies or forms of exchange that daily challenge neoliberalism, provide conviviality, and sustain communities.

THE EVERYDAYNESS OF THE ECONOMY

Henri Lefebvre (1984) and Michel de Certeau (1984), both eclectic French scholars, were captivated by the impact of modernity on daily human practice. They found that everyday activities, including economics, represented a rich arena from which one could assess social transformation. Both food studies and gender studies have also considered that "the daily life of ordinary people is not only worthy of study but necessary to any understanding of past and present worlds" (Avakian and Haber 2005, 16). Given its continued engagement with conceptions of resistance (Chandra 2015) and everyday forms of it (Vinthagen and Johansson 2013), subaltern analysis is an effective frame for alternative economy. As a body of scholarship, "the critique of everyday life" showcased the significance of our daily activities for understanding macro-level processes often eclipsed by sociology's emphasis on institutional structure, quantifiable patterns, or government policy.

In his inquiry into everyday life, de Certeau (1984) became particularly critical of academic assumptions that people lived their lives "passively . . . guided by established rules." He strived to draw attention to everyday practices or the "way of doing things" rather than leaving them as the "obscure background of social activity." He believed that everyday acts revealed, not individualized behaviors, but "modes of operations" or "schemata of action." De Certeau (1984, xiv) highlighted the regular subversions of the dominant social order in modern society, opposing the grid of discipline Michel Foucault articulated as modernity. De Certeau (1984, xiv) beckons: "It is all the more urgent to discover how an entire society resists being reduced to it [dominant order], what popular procedures (also "miniscule" and quotidian) manipulate the mechanisms of discipline and conform to them only in order to evade them, and finally, what ways of operating form the counterpart." The ways in which groups or individuals perceive structural constraints—and how they choose to challenge, negotiate, undermine, or adapt them—can be made visible when we focus on the everyday exchanges, most particularly economic ones. Focused on the daily economic practices of post-Soviet populations to discern change in economic practice, Stenning et al. (2010, 242) argue that the informal and reciprocal exchanges that operated during the communist regime were retained in ways that now "domesticate" neoliberalism and "subvert the market agendas of powerful actors."

Daily economic practices, such as nonmonetary exchanges, no-interest loans, gratis or gift items or assistance, sharing goods or tools, and a preference for local development over increasing profits are traits of alternative economies (Gibson-Graham 2006). Organic economic forms, such as the women's cooperatives, that are shaped by regional geographies and conscripted by culture and social mores or attritional economic enterprises, created by those who chose to leave the mainstream economy, can be conceived as "the clandestine forms taken by the dispersed, tactical, and makeshift creativity of groups or individuals" (de Certeau 1984, xiv) to resist or alter the dominant system.

In the Aegean, the growth of contemporary local economies, especially in agriculture and tourism, is shaped by a cultural logic that also tames neoliberalism, or shuns it outright. For instance, in many of the negotiations among women's cooperatives members I witnessed, production was not shaped by a cost-benefit analysis, but was dictated by preparing food items that reflect a local identity, such as chestnut inspired deserts by the Ayiassos cooperative, even if it meant both more cost and effort and less profit.

Convivial economic exchange characterizes Greece at large, which might be conceived as an island-informed society. In Athens, which holds the largest number of theaters and active theater-goers in Europe (Billington 2020), ticket prices were reduced during the economic crisis so everyday working people might attend. Another example of a convivial, rather than a neoliberal, approach to mundane economics is the expansion of bartering and solidarity structures during Greece's crisis ridden period (Malamidis 2020). Widely covered by the mainstream English press was the trade system established in Volos (Alderman 2015; Donadio 2011). Located in northern Greece, the city established a local currency that temporarily replaced the euro as a way to assist families' ability to purchase local and much-needed goods.

Collective mechanisms of survival and grassroots economics grounded in the Global South and semiperipheries, such as Greece, are not given the credit they deserve in the new literature on the social, solidarity, or diverse and community economies and localism. The economic spontaneity, informal associations, and localized solutions in poorer or geographically marginalized regions are not sufficiently appreciated as precedents and examples of alternative economics. Economic alterity may be more readily available in particular social historical contexts and geographies. Lefebvre and Régulier (2000, 233), in comparing Northern and Southern Europe, defines the differences between the two regions as such: "Mediterranean cities appear to have always lived and still live within regimes of compromise. . . . Such a metastable state results from the fact of the polyrhythmical. *One could not over-emphasize this form of alliance, the compromise, which historically differs from that of the Sworn*

Community. In Nordic and oceanic cities one can expect more regulated time, linked to contractual rather than ritual forms of association" (italics added). Despite all the negative attention Greece received internationally regarding its economic practices, a "regime of compromise" enabled the survival of smaller economic entities in Greece's urban centers and its remote island regions, because it is counteractive to the contractual logic of neoliberalism. The means by which locals, lesbians, and others who have relocated to Lesvos are able to create convivial spatial-temporalities also exemplify the grassroots or spontaneous and convivial development that Leontidou (1990) describes as Mediterranean. With a sizeable number of microenterprises and a network of large and small cooperatives, Greece's sociopolitical forms, cultural practices, and its geography of islands seem to provide a context for organic and attritional economic alterities to prosper.

The economic practices I recorded primarily occur within Greek island villages and are shaped indelibly by local cultural forms that have been practiced on Greek islands for an enormous length of time. Yet they also depend on successful transnational and cross-cultural economic exchanges. Some of the women's cooperatives send their products as far away as Australia and the Democratic Republic of Congo, where Greek-Lesbian enclaves exist. The microentrepreneurs in Skala Eresos, including those owned by Greeks and alternative foreigners and lesbians, must negotiate the demands and expectations of primarily Northern European and ethnic Greek tourists and vacationers who arrive each summer. To maintain their convivial enterprises, women's cooperative members and island microentrepreneurs moved deftly around patronizing attitudes and negative stereotypes of lesbianism or Greekness, or both, in doing business and maintaining conviviality in the context of transnational island tourism.

The Importance of Being an Island

I locate convivial economics as a practice of islanders and in recognition of islands as subaltern spaces and geographies of cosmopolitanism and colonialism. Early writing assumed the idleness and dependency of island populations. As I briefly referred to in the introduction, with the emergence of island studies in the mid-1990s a reconception of islands, islanders, and the potentiality of island-thinking for global concerns has advanced. Island scholarship proposes that island living provides a distinct set of opportunities for localized creative action (Shofield and

George 1997) and that the particular conditions historically faced by
islanders may engender resourcefulness and resilience and "the generation
of imaginative developmental alternatives" (Baldacchino 2006). Though
convivial economics transpires in other locations, my conception of it
is tethered to expanding island studies.

Writing from a position of Oceanic centrality, Epeli Hau'ofa
(1994) influentially argued for the social and ideological strength of
Pacific islanders and their mobility, challenging the early frames in
island development that defined islands as "too small, too poor, and too
isolated to be able to rise above the condition of dependence." Rather,
Hau'ofa (1994) explains that the ocean is a medium that links islands
to other places rather than isolates them. Epeli Hau'ofa (1994) was first
to articulate an "island studies perspective" that challenged the fairly
downbeat approach toward island societies that was fixed in anthropology
and geography. He (1994, 5) explains that his own initial views adopted
coloniality, saying he "was so bound to the notion of 'smallness,' that
even if we improved our approaches to production . . . the absolute size
of our islands would still impose such severe limitations that we would
be defeated in the end." By revisiting the cosmologies and knowledges
of Pacific islanders, Hau'ofa (1994) shifted the discourse from islands as
perpetually dependent and small to that of "a sea of islands" in which
the breadth and width of space and resources is defined not just by "dry
surfaces," as in mainland frameworks, but by the reach of the seas and
the stars that guided islanders to traverse them.

Hay (2006) and McCall (1994) critique using islands metaphor-
ically because they have often served as an image for "backwardness,
irrelevance, and anti-social self-indulgence" (McCall 1994, 3). Although
they are often conceived of as remote and insulated, islands have been
deeply embedded in global processes, which has contributed to their
distinction (Terrell 2004). For example, Klak and Conway (1998) argue
that the Caribbean islands represent the first true cosmopolitan place in
the world. Unlike noncoastal mainland regions, "connectedness describes
the island condition better than isolation" and "island boundaries
invite transgression" (Hay 2006, 23). Others have broadened the scope
of island studies by "envisioning the archipelago" to recognize "island
spaces as inter-related, mutually constituted and co-constructed," which
has encouraged the further theorization of connections among islands
and between islands and mainlands, thereby challenging the tropes of
island isolation and singularity (Stratford et al. 2011, 113).

Furthermore, islanders are mobile, historically leaving for new opportunities and "enlarging their worlds" beyond the shorelines (Hau'ofa 1994). For many island societies the diaspora communities retain close ties, economically and socially, and these reciprocal relations are integral to the survival and success of island communities (Hau'ofa 1994). The transnationalism of islands also is shaped by legacies of colonization and islands being exploited militarily by colonial states to legitimize occupation. Finally, island tourism, through an influx of visitors and tourists, very often an exploitive dynamic, contours island development as transnational space. Island tourism is attractive not only because of warm weather and the tropical island motif, or the natural beauty of warm and cold-weathered islands, but also the geographic diversion it offers for mainland residents. For persons, likely with economic privilege, who seek reprieve from the large scale of mainland societies or urban centers, many islands are appealing due to their scope, nature, and sparse populations (Shofield and George 1997).

Despite the mobility that characterizes islands and islanders, including the to and fro of native island populations and the seasonal sojourners attracted to them, islands' cultural and social identities remain tenacious (Suwa 2007; Baldacchino 2006; McCall 1994). In Greece, the continuous parade of tourists and conquerors over millennia did not halt Greek islanders from retaining cultural practices. The Greek archipelagos—Ionian, Aegean, Cyclades, Dodecanese, and Sporades— are recognized for having unique qualities, as does the island of Crete. Many of the traditions across Greek islands are still deeply influenced by Byzantium or the Greek Orthodox Church. In the case of the Aegean, there are also strong influences from the Ottoman Empire. Greek islands also retain facets of their ancient societies, such as rituals of host-guest relations, evident throughout the Greek islands, that will be further explored in chapter 4.

Shima, a Japanese concept of islandness, helps to explicate the social distinctiveness of islands. Shima takes the island landscape and its social dimensions as a single totality, envisioning the ways in which one's livelihood molds and is molded by an acute sense of context or the experience of "being possessed and possessing" (Suwa 2007). It differs from mainland sensibilities where endless space or urban intensity offers a continuously shifting milieu. The women's cooperatives sprouted from a distinct local, regional, and geographical context shaped by particular economic and political histories—a shima. On the other hand, the lesbian

enterprises in Skala Eresos, and by extension the lesbian tourism that
arose in the early 1980s, laid claims to village space, capturing one-third
of summertime enterprises. In so doing, these women created a lesbian
shima. A tight relationship with the local and natural environments, or
an intimate familiarity with one's place and space, is a feature conducive
to convivial economics.

That islands warrant special concerns for economic development
was first put forth globally during United Nations meetings in 1972,
which were largely driven by a dependency perspective (Briguglio 2000;
Josling 1998). Initial steps toward official recognition of the unique
qualities of island economies provided island states a vehicle for modi-
fying and even resisting patterns of liberalization and deregulation. An
island-centered approach logically challenges the neoliberal cornerstone
of a single policy solution for national economies of any scope—large,
small, poor, rich, indebted, post-disaster, industrial, service—incognizant
of the need for diversified or alternative approaches based in geographic
and environmental considerations for economic development (Briguglio
2000; Escobar 1995).

Placing islands at the center of the world-system recognizes that
"islands are the frontline zones where problems of environment and development unfold" (Baldacchino 2006, citing Kofi Annan, Secretary-General
of the United Nations). Early theoretical attention to islands was drawn
by McCall (1994), who exposed the weakness of mainstream paradigms
through the proposition that islands offer unique insights for critiquing
mainstream capitalist development. McCall (see Baldacchino 2006, 10)
suggests that "if the twentieth century had been the century of mainland,
industrial, large-scale, continental progress . . . perhaps the twenty-first
century could prove that of island, small-scale, service-driven." The threat
to cultural and economic autonomy and ecological instability that islands
have been facing for some time is being understood and more directly
felt by continental populations, even those living beyond the coastline.
"Thinking like an island" (Chirico and Farley 2015) is gaining currency
in academic settings by those concerned with economic development
that is ecologically unsustainable.

Convivial enterprises are found throughout history and in various
locations. Islands that have been marginalized by mainland and mainstream
demands, yet are decidedly integral to global development, present a distinct opportunity for considering convivial economics and how marginal

groups have come to develop them. Because islands are suited for growing small local enterprises and microeconomies, even alongside large-scale developments, and quite often retain a cosmopolitan population, we can harness from them lessons for supporting convivial microeconomies and a sense of shima that may be fruitfully applied elsewhere.

While economic alterities are made by daily practice and informed by geographies, the scale or size of enterprises is also a condition of economic conviviality. As mass production, consumption, and media expanded by leaps and bounds throughout the US and Europe in the 1960s, concerns about it were first raised by the "cultural turn" in Marxism. How would the proletariat develop consciousness with the expansion of capital's new ideological machinery? These critics (Debord 1967; Adorno 1966) attributed the loss of human connection and creativity to the scale of industrial production. Other opponents to mass society were concerned with the ecological damage that large-scale production caused (Shiva 1988; Pepper 1984; Lovelock 1979; Schumacher 1973; Carson 1962). In essence, it was the size of capitalist organizations and their destructive capacities that provoked a worldwide call for small-scale businesses, markets, communes, collectives, and conviviality as an alternative to ever-expanding capitalism in the 1970s. "Small is beautiful"—an idiom made famous by E. F. Schumacher's book, *Small Is Beautiful: Economics as if People Mattered* (1973)—offered a unique challenge to capitalist expansion at a time when socialism, large and bureaucratic, was highlighted as the progressive alternative among activists and academics in the Global North. In the Global South, where small-scale, self-created, income-earning activities still dominated and supported large swaths of the urban and rural populations, modernization proponents readily critiqued them as detrimental to economic development as they defined it.

Like Illich (1973), Schumacher (1973) emphasized that technology and processes should be affordable, accessible, and suitable for smaller entities. Schumacher (1973) argued that small-scale operations, no matter their numbers, are less likely to be harmful to the natural environment than large-scale ones. Socially and ecologically a place could more easily recoup from the impact of multiple small encroachments than from singular larger entities simply due to the size of the enterprise. *Small Is Beautiful* (1973) articulates a basic logic of the benefits of small-scale production (regardless if they are collectively owned) for ecological sustainability and that it is better suited for humane working conditions.

Summary

To various degrees the social and solidarity economy, localism, and community and diverse economies all incorporate the kind of convivial economics I identify in the lesbian enterprises, the village women's cooperatives, and the microeconomies of Lesvos, Greece. Yet, as a whole, the alternative economy literature makes little sense of how social inequalities and marginalized identities around ethnicity, gender, sexuality, and geography shape the growth and development of alternative economic projects and practices.

With the exception of solidarity economy perspectives, the literature largely fails to consider the Global South and the character and parameters of alternative economic practices in peripheral locations more generally. Importantly, these perspectives do not examine how the rhythms of place, historically, culturally, and geographically configured, may facilitate or thwart alterity. A focus on subaltern groups and subaltern locations, grounded in the views of those who create and work in alternative economic enterprises, is essential for broadening conceptualizations of alternative economics.

The social economy perspective is largely wedded to an active state and the advancement of institutional structures. Although social economy theorists (Wright 2010; Laville, Leveseque, and Mendell 2006) recognize small cooperatives and microenterprise and local economies as interstitial strategies, they generally discount independent economic efforts that are privately based or microenterprises as fundamental to building a social economy. The perspective is positioned in wealthier Global North contexts in which both government and foundations can be rallied for funding, which are considered central to developing the social economy. The social economy approach gives little space for more informal and negotiated relationships that are valued by small and microenterprises and in peripheralized economies.

The solidarity economy is movement oriented, based in the Global South, and links collectively owned enterprises or similar efforts locally as well as cross-nationally. It resists the inclusion of self-employed, small, and microenterprises because of the possibility of exploitation. More than other perspectives, it recognized the ingenuity and grassroots efforts of the most marginalized groups for building a foundation of economic alterity. The solidarity economy is also grounded in attachment to place and identities and envisions itself as a global social movement.

Also focused on mobilization, localism addresses the effectiveness of place attachment for building local economies that eschew or resist corporate intervention economically and politically. Among alternative economic perspectives, it is most committed to showcasing the effectiveness of locally based enterprises as a model for development. Yet it also favors the Global North by overlooking the extent that informal relationships, especially in less privileged locations, facilitate the survival of small and microenterprises that often operate within community networks. The growing alternative food systems movement and research describes the many opportunities available for local economies, but remains inattentive to the lengthy history and persistence of local food systems in the Global South.

Gibson-Graham's (2006) diverse economies approach is committed to shifting academic and public discourse to reduce the centrality of capitalism. Yet this approach is resistant to including locally based initiatives that are inscribed in community identities. Gibson-Graham (2006) has helped to lift academic thought, particularly in human geography, to see beyond "the end of history" (Fukuyama 1992), the permanence of capitalism, and the doldrums of a waning socialism. They have also facilitated scholarly recognition that alternatives do exist, and that these alternatives take up a large portion of the economic landscape. Yet, contrary to Scott (1985) and subaltern analysis that recognize that counterhegemonic understandings of economy and society are rooted in the marginalized, Gibson-Graham (2009, 170) argue that an intentionally managed discursive shift is necessary for "most people in both developed and developing nations" to advance and acknowledge economic alternatives. Gibson-Graham (2006) presume people to be hoodwinked by capital's discourses, even as they identify the prevalence of non-capital-centric activities.

Distinct from these central perspectives on alternative economics and others, convivial economics contends that economic alternatives historically have been driven by those less privileged in the dominant economic system and that the geographic or spatial context informs grassroots possibilities of congenial and hospitable forms of economic exchange. Greece, a nation that has been both marginalized and colonized and serves as a cultural and physical border of a divided global landscape, is defined by its islands as much as it is by Athens. Greece's conundrum—its uneasy fit in the European Union and the derisive evaluation its economy receives by many EU leaders—may be as much an outcome of the convivial economics currently practiced by its population as it is of a global reckoning with the limits of neoliberalism.

CHAPTER THREE

Of Greek Islands and Microentrepreneurs

Neoliberal Battles and the Marginalization of a Nation

Like a shifting layer of sand these loosely composed tribes of many different peoples lie across Greece; calling themselves Greek indeed. . . . you must look upon the modern Greeks as a nation of mongrel element & a rustic. . . .

—Virginia Woolf ([1906] 1992, 340)

The story is about me and people I know. It's about Greece and its politics, about the repeated frustrations of my people to obtain independence from foreign domination and the lousy Greek politicians who served those powers.

—Melina Mercouri (1971, 1)

This past Monday I was asked to sign a public letter. Brief but heartfelt, it reminded the British of all that we owe the Greeks and urged that we lend them our support. It was to be published in a London paper just hours before the Greeks began to renege on what they owe us—or at least the International Monetary Fund.

—Armand Marie Leroi, *New York Times*, July 3, 2015

By late 2009, when the debt crisis struck Europe, the Greek government and wealthy elites began to draw Europe's ire for the scale of Greece's debt. Greece's small and family enterprises—pigeonholed as unprincipled even before the onset of the Greek economic crisis—were also blamed for the nation's financial position. Northern European politicians and media stereotyped Greeks as lazy, working less than their Northern Europeans counterparts, overspending, waiting for handouts, and deceitful (Inman 2015; Miller 2015; Tzogopoulos 2013; Kulish and Ewing 2012; Zarkadakis 2011; Besancenot and Grond 2010; Margaras 2010). These are well-worn ethnic stereotypes of modern Greeks, applied as much by past British authors, such as Virginia Woolf in 1906, as they are by present ones. Greek journalists, academics, and allies publicly challenged what they identified as unfair typecasting of Greek workers across the European press, arguing that it was "bordering on racism" and reliant on "quasi-Orientalism" (see Leontidou 2014 and Malkoutzis 2011).

The attention drawn to Greek microbusinesses focused on factors such as a perception that workdays and hours of operations were too short and that financial management was too informal. The Greek economy was critically characterized as an "Ottoman Bazaar" (see Hartocolis 2015) in one *New York Times* article, which is based on the assumption that bartering and bargaining with small independent vendors is a less preferable form of transaction than corporate or formalized modes of trade—a starkly Global North perspective.

The Greek microenterprise sector captures a greater portion of the economy than is typical in most of Europe (European Commission 2010). One cannot claim that the modern Greek economy ever thrived in a capitalistic sense. Yet a centerpiece of this book is the argument that local, small, and collective enterprises have supported the integration of home and work life across Greece with an economic conviviality that promotes sociality and fairness, delineating an alternate measure of success.

A broad range of Northern European observers have assumed authority to pontificate on ethnic Greeks' daily economic practices. One illustration is the BBC 5 live radio interview recorded in July 2015 with English novelist Louis de Bernières. Having written a popular novel set on a Greek island, he was asked to comment on Greeks and their crisis:

> You know it's their own fault but, all the same, the methods that have been used to get them out of it is just systematically making things worse and worse. . . . They've got to get in the habit of self-sufficiency in a way that isn't ducking and diving. . . . That, for example, you've got to be able to go to a restaurant and pay with plastic. The reason they always

ask for cash is, of course, because you don't have to pay any tax on it. If you're just after survival of your own family or your own business, you are not going to be doing the country much good. . . . They are what they are.

Negative commentary on Greek work ethics and business strategies like this one are informed by long-standing assumptions about small-scale entrepreneurs and businesses in peripheral and semiperipheral regions. Critical of what he described as the "bazaar economy," anthropologist Clifford Geertz (1963, 28–29, 35) dismissed the economic viability of the small, local economies that he observed during his fieldwork in Indonesian villages: "It has the disadvantage that it turns even the established businessman away from an interest in reducing costs and developing markets and toward petty speculation and short-run opportunism. . . . The trader is perpetually looking for a chance to make a smaller or larger killing, not attempting to build up a clientele or a steadily growing business." Geertz's (1963) opposition to microbusinesses and local economies reflects his embrace of modernization. Contemporary critiques of Greece's economic organization also assume the superiority of liberalized markets, large-scale export-oriented enterprises, and the entry of transnational capital. Summarily discounted in EU commentary on Greece is the dynamism and conviviality that exists among Greek microenterprises and the wide range of cooperatives that have managed to survive the economic crisis and the onslaught of austerity measures.

Greece's economic and social subordination in Europe is a rhythm that has been sustained since the founding of modern Greece in the early 1800s and dissolution of the Ottoman Empire (Kitidi and Chatzistefanou 2011). This chapter orients readers to the contemporary Greek context by first addressing the recent difficulties between Greece and the EU and IMF in the handling of the debt crisis since 2010. It then contextualizes the contemporary era by reviewing three historical moments that highlight Greece's marginalization in Europe. The neoliberal cadence of the EU, and the Greek population's resistance to it, embodies an enduring clash between Greece and its wealthier and more powerful European nations. For the objective of this volume, it is crucial to underscore that islands and microenterprises, which distinguish Greece's socioeconomic landscape from most of its neighbors, were especially disfavored by austerity measures applied by the IMF and EU bodies.

Neoliberal Rhythms

The EU was supposed to form a political alliance across Europe, but it resulted in a strategy of regional development grounded in a neoliberal ideology. The EU was formalized in 1993 after building on decades of unification efforts by European nations. Despite regular disparagement by Northern European counterparts, Greece was included as one of the twelve original signatories of the Maastricht Treaty, the founding document of the EU that outlined its political framework, as well as the financial obligations of nations in the union.

In 1997, the EU's Stability and Growth Pact solidified the EU's fiscal rules, which made the neoliberal commitments of the EU particularly evident. Widely critiqued for centralizing fiscal authority and reducing financial maneuverability, the Stability and Growth Pact obliged EU nations to stay within 3.0 percent of their GDP in deficit spending, which entailed aggressive fiscal oversight and limited structural expenditures. The European Fiscal Compact amped up the Pact in 2012, as it increased restrictions and fined nations for exceeding the debt ratio limitation, thereby "burying Keynsianism" (Jones 2011). Not addressed in the establishment of EU financial agreements and examined in this chapter were the large debts Greece has incurred throughout its history. Though Greece's battle with the Ottomans and struggle against Nazi Germany secured Europe's political and economic interests, it landed Greece in a financially precarious position from its initial formation into a modern state. Further lending in recent years by European nations to Greece, occurred so that it could meet the requirements for EU entry, again saddling the nation with debt and enriching Northern European nations. Not only were some Northern European nations made wealthier by interest on borrowed money but also because EU lenders obliged Greece to make purchases, for example of expensive infrastructure, from them. The history of Greek debt formation contests the view that Greece owes any amount to the EU, UK, or IMF.

Greece's incessant confrontations with neoliberal policies in the last decade suggest how incongruent the unforgiving principles of economic austerity are with Greek culture. For example, the prospect of foreclosures on primary homes—a condition imposed by the troika—had not been practiced in Greece, and it continues to be considered immoral regardless of debt. The population's alternative logic to that of neoliberalism was made even more evident during the January 2015 elections, when the openly left, antiausterity SYRIZA (Radical Left-Social Front Coalition) party came into power.

Tensions over Greece's large national debt, which first appeared in late 2008, and its status within the EU reached their highest pitch in the summer of 2015. Front-page news worldwide ran taunting headlines implying that Greece's economy was on a precipice. For example, the *New York Times* ran a cover story asking, "Is Greece Lehman Brothers, or Is It Radio Shack?" Meanwhile, the BBC and MoneyCNN, respectively, ran stories titled "Greek Debt Crisis: The Final Showdown" and "No! Votes Shocks Europe." One *New York Times* article (Higgins and Kanter 2015) starts with "frustrated European leaders gave Greece until Sunday to reach an agreement to save its collapsing economy from catastrophe." For much of the mainstream press, Greece's only option for survival depended on SYRIZA capitulating to the International Monetary Fund, the European Union, and the European Central Bank. The overwhelming coverage of Greece by mainstream international news sources and the invariable chorus of political and economic commentators insisted that there was no alternative for Greece to survive outside the EU, despite its own population's willingness to make that attempt.

The global attention to Greece's economy and vituperative language regarding ethnic Greek economic habits and political resistance to neoliberalism may have been an early hint that the global economic status quo was indeed unraveling. What had the "Mediterranean race" unleashed? The Greek public was demanding solutions beyond the narrow economic policies drawn from the Washington Consensus or rather the "rigidity or inflexibility of the rules and principles of the Berlin Consensus" (Pantazi 2015). The heightened attention to Greece's crisis included those personally and politically impacted by the fate of the nation, those reliant on the neoliberal order, and social justice activists, researchers, practitioners, and everyday people who were seeking alternatives to neoliberalism.

In Greek lore, the island of Lesvos is particularly noted for its resistance to capitalism. Lesvos continues to be referred to as the "red island" due to its identification with the Greek Communist Party (KKE), the strength of the leftist National Liberation Front and the Greek People's Liberation Army (ELAS) during and after World War II, and the continuation of left-leaning politics, generally. Greece's national elections in May and June of 2012 were especially volatile as the population was responding to the austerity measures being implemented by the Panhellenic Socialist Movement (PASOK), the governing socialist party. Among a slate of almost ten parties, Lesvos's population largely voted for two prominent left parties, the KKE and SYRIZA. In the May 2012 elections, 31.50 percent of the population voted for either the KKE or SYRIZA with the KKE leading by about 2 percent. Then, in the June revote, this combination increased to 33.80 percent with a shift toward SYRIZA.

SYRIZA and the KKE campaigned against "the Memorandum"—the agreement in 2010 between the Greek government and the troika (the European Commission, European Central Bank, and IMF)—that imposed the first set of harsh and widely criticized austerity measures. At the beginning of 2015, a constitutional requirement declared the necessity of a snap election due to the failure to elect a president. During this January 2015 election, 10.8 percent of the Lesvos vote went to the KKE. Another 32.9 percent supported SYRIZA, reaffirming its status as the red island, as it helped oust the two political parties, PASOK and New Democracy, that had governed Greece for decades.

With the onset of the economic crisis, a nationally staked alternative to neoliberalism was tangible. The global public was taken aback by the fierce resistance of the Greek population, as they overwhelmingly rejected further austerity measures, even though it was a decision that risked Greece's EU membership. The now infamous Oxi (no) vote—in which 61 percent of Greek voters rejected the "bailout" conditions offered by the troika at the risk of a "Grexit"—was clearly unexpected by the IMF and members of the European Commission and European Central Bank. Initially stammering in shock at the outcome, EU politicians soon turned against Greece and the SYRIZA party with a vengeance.

A *Financial Times* (July 13, 2015) report described Europe's finance ministers as "lashing out," as they "lectured" and "crucified" Greek prime minister Alexis Tsipras and Greek finance minister Euclid Tsakalotos. In the final meetings held by the European Council that paved the way for Greece's third loan agreement with the troika, Tsipras capitulated to the demands of the EU Council to the great disappointment of many, not least of all Greek residents. Having held firmly against austerity measures for its first six months in office, SYRIZA's leadership agreed to additional measures, as they secured a third loan that allowed Greece to service what even the IMF regards as an unsustainable amount of debt. The measures gave Greece an even worse deal than what the troika had offered in its first set of negotiations, as they involved heavy taxation and vast privatization. Greece's political leaders were accused of bluffing and holding no real plan for exiting, even though Yanis Varoufakis, the provocative former finance minister of SYRIZA, adamantly stated that there was a plan for Greece's departure from the EU, advancing the prospect of a parallel currency (Varoufakis 2017).

In a final European parliamentary meeting, Guy Verhofstadt, who represented a free market group from Belgium with participatory access to the meetings, heartily chastised Tsipras. A video of the six-minute confrontation went viral, and Verhofstadt has since claimed to have given Greece "a lesson." In effect, the series of meetings by EU governing bodies on Greek debt and EU status in July 2015 showcased an assumed authority and righteousness of EU technocrats who accept neoliberalism as prima facie economic logic, refusing the consideration of alternatives.

In scolding Tsipras, Verhofstadt concludes, "Finally, let's end, propose to end, the privileges in your country." Among a list of Greece's privileged entities including Greek ship owners, the Greek Orthodox Church, political parties, and the military was "the privilege of the Greek islands." The erasure of this "privilege" amounted to a 30 percent reduction in the value added tax (VAT) rate for Greek islands, which was used to assist many tiny remote island village populations with living costs that are inherently higher by virtue of their location. The European Commission also increased the tax rate for hotels and restaurants—primarily small and locally owned microenterprises—which are the bread and butter of Greek island tourism and the core of Greece's convivial economics. Although the EU and the United Nations have supportive measures for island-centered policies, they were ignobly ignored in the European Commission's arrangements for addressing Greece's debt and strategies for growth. Instead, both islands and microenterprises seemed to have been harshly reprimanded in the austerity measures that were supposedly intended to revamp Greece's economy.

Interestingly, the EU parliamentary discussions in 2015 did not include an analysis of the centrality of Northern European tourism to the Greek economy, which accounts for approximately 18 percent of its GDP. Tourism also was rarely considered in the media coverage on the Greek economic crisis. Yet, Greece's relatively depressed economy, delightful climate, and glorious shores, as well as its distinct pace of life, makes the Greek islands an ideal and affordable vacation spot for many Northern European travelers of all classes.

Over 90 percent of Greek tourists arrive mostly from Northern European nations. Visitors from the United Kingdom, followed by Germany, account for the largest portion of Greece's visitors. Other regions, including Asia and the Americas, trail behind the tourism of Northern Europeans. Since 2015, Greece has received more than 20 million visitors annually. Though tourism declined with the pandemic in 2020, Greece continues to be a revered tourist destination. Among the consequences of being a vacation zone are the false assumptions that get promoted regarding the practices, needs, and work lives of island hosts.

A few days after Tsipras's submission to the loan conditions of the European Council, the Greek parliament was mandated to vote on these measures. Zoe Konstatopoulou (2015), president of the Greek parliament at the time, utterly rejected the timeline, as the legislator argued that these

> conditions are blatant blackmail by foreign governments of European Union member states on this government and on the members of parliament. . . . implementation would result in a major intervention in the functioning of justice and the exercise of the fundamental rights of the citizens, tearing down . . . the functioning of Greek democracy. . . . the message which is being sent by the creditors is that democratic processes are futile, that direct democracy as expressed by citizens . . . is irrelevant. . . . Coercion is not an agreement, blackmail is not an agreement.

Many of Greece's political leaders and the majority of its population openly opposed the continued suppression of Greece's anti-neoliberal position. Yet, the Marxist-identified prime minister succumbed to the immense power of global capital, as he hoped that Greece might overcome the destructive logic of neoliberalism if it could swallow one more round of the troika's austerity measures. The forceful imposition of neoliberalist stratagem seems to indicate a forced logic, inconsistent with the sensibilities of many populations and regions. It was clear that Greeks directly and openly resisted neoliberal programs with large public protests and with their votes. But, it is also Greeks' *everyday* economic practices that privilege community, personal ties, and sociality, revealing a daily defiance of neoliberalism.

The Northern Europeans I interviewed in 2008, 2009, and 2012— both before and after the public's realization of the weight of Europe's financial crisis—complained that Greeks were "inefficient," "lacking industry," "slow," "inconsistent," "lawless," "loud," and "lazy." Their views mirrored the stereotypes offered by Northern European politicians, press, and commentators, as they debated the imposition of austerity measures on Greece.

For many Northern Europeans in Lesvos, however, there is also an emphatic attraction to the rhythms of Greek island life. Northern Europeans who had both permanently and semipermanently relocated to the island had grumbled about the restricted, materialist, and isolated lives that they lived in their nations of origin. They often described their work lives as competitive and demanding, claiming that Greece and its islands are a haven, a place of freedom.

Greece's Peripherality

The belittlement of Greeks by Europeans did not begin with the economic crisis of the 2010s. Instead, there is a historical precedent shaping the relationship between Greece and Europe. Edward S. Forster (1958, 20), a British historian of modern Greece, in a somewhat florid telling of its history, explains in a footnote: "The fact that Greeks leaving their native lands for France or England still talk of going to Europe is an excellent illustration of their feelings of isolation . . . from the civilized world." Implicit in Forster's (1958) claims are not only the separate spheres by which Greece and Europe were conceived during the 1950s, but also the culturally biased sentiments long held about modern Greece. The erasure of Greeks' history begins with the appropriation of the "birthplace of civilization" from Greece by Europe, veiling the relative backwardness of Northern European regions when ancient Greece (800 BC to 500 BC) was thriving politically and culturally, especially during its Classical era (fifth and fourth centuries BC). Forster (1958), like many others, identifies "civilization" as belonging to Northern Europe. In their introduction to *Women Writing Greece*, Kolocotroni and Mitsi (2008, 11) explain the ancestral confiscation of ancient Greece: "In the era of high imperialism, the response to Greece has to be examined in the context of the imperial project, which connected the British, rather than the lowly modern Greeks, to the ancient Athenians."

British women writers in particular readily separated ancient Greece from its modern inheritors. An English scholar of women and queer travel writings in colonial context, Churnjeet Mahn (2016) dissects texts of British women's writing on Greece at the time of its independence from the Ottoman Empire. Referring to British women travelers, Mahn (2016, 5) asserts: "They either ignored the native Greek populations as an irrelevant element to their experience of travel or as children in terms of a civilization whose progression was hampered by an inherently Oriental nature." By making claims in their writings that, although lamentable, Greeks had been tainted by "the Orient," Mahn (2016, 5) argues, "British women sought to position themselves closer to antiquity by temporally distancing modern Greece from a contemporary frame of reference." Furthermore, Victorians had cast Greece as enslaved by the Orient and waiting to be freed by England, to which English women writers fastened their own efforts of liberation (Mahn 2016). With ample textual analysis, Mahn (2016, 8) asserts that English women's anthropological accounts of the late 1800s "placed Greek women above Turks, but behind British women," problematizing the liminality or loss of purity of modern Greek women, so that "British women could be the authentic Greek" and "more legitimate heirs of the Ancients" (Mahn 2016, 8).

Beyond discursively laying claims to ancient Greece, further solidifying British ties to ancient Greece were the many artifacts that were taken or "looted" by Britain, as stated by Greece's minister of culture Antonis Samaras, in 2009, when the new Acropolis Museum was opened (Itano 2009). Like colonized nations, Greece awaits the return of material artifacts of its treasured past. Displaying empty showcases, the new Acropolis Museum highlights the absence of pieces like the Parthenon Marbles that are still maintained by the British Museum. The request for the return of the Parthenon Marbles was a central project of Melina Mercouri in her role as the minister of culture in the 1980s. The evaluation of ancient Greece as the heritage of Europe, and not Greece, is quite comprehensive. Consider that the publication of *Black Athena* (Bernal 1987), which attests to the Afro-Asiatic roots of ancient Greece, provoked a great deal of academic controversy. It stemmed not only from the substance of Bernal's analysis but also because his claim dismantles the "white" foundation of Western civilization.

Herzfeld (2002) describes Greece as a "crypto-colony," which captures and complicates the ambiguity of its cultural and economic location in Europe. Although part of Europe, modern Greece has served the sociopolitical interests of its wealthier neighbors from its inception. Rather than being integral to the European project, Greece is better understood as a borderland manipulated to secure the political and economic interests of its Northern neighbors. As stated earlier, the Aegean islands, in particular, sit conspicuously in the midst of the constructed boundary of "east" and "west," blurring the distinctions between the two worlds that so many scholars and pundits, including those in postcolonialism, rely upon.

The next sections briefly consider three occasions—the founding of modern Greece (1821–1932), the aftermath of World War II (1946), and the Fascist regime (1967–74)—each an example of European suppression of Greece. The purpose of highlighting these three moments in a book on alternative economic practices on Lesvos is to track rhythmical patterns in Greece's sociopolitical development that lay the grounds for an alternative economic framework.

Modern Greece was born in part from the interests of England, France, and Russia that sought to overcome the Ottoman Empire. The liberation of Greece in the 1800s was surely wanted by Greeks who desired to free themselves from the Ottomans, who had ruled the region since 1453. Yet the relationship between Greeks and their Ottoman occupiers was tangled, as many wealthy and educated Greeks held positions of power during Ottoman rule, in roles such as political advisors and educators. Some Greeks also maintained control over their wealth, land, and trade during the Ottoman period (Milton 2008). Because Ottoman governance took a hands-off approach, it allowed for the political and economic autonomy of isolated villages, such as those in Lesvos. For instance, judicial cases were handled by village priests and communally controlled agriculture dominated the Aegean islands under Ottoman reign. Centuries under Ottoman rule also had significant cultural and economic effects, especially on the eastern side of Greece. Commentary on the social and economic ties between Lesvos and Turkey's eastern shores was part of public discourse on the island and regularly percolated as a topic in my interviews. Europe's refugee crisis in 2015–16, which resulted in rafts full of families fleeing economic and political violence arriving on the shores of the village of Eftalou in Lesvos from Turkey, also alerted much of the globe to the slim separation of the "east" from the "west."

The subordination of Greece was abundantly apparent when England, France, and Russia appointed a young Bavarian prince as the first king of "independent" Greece as war against the Ottoman's carried on. These "Great Powers" were seeking to hinder what they considered to be anarchic forms of governance that existed in Greece under the loose rule of the Ottomans. King Otho arrived to Greece in 1833, at the age of seventeen, with an all-German council serving in positions of governance. A new form of centralized government was imposed on Greek communities that had been able to govern themselves under the Ottomans. Forster (1958, 13) describes the impact of Europe's imposed authority: "The administration was entirely centralized, and no advantage was taken of the communal system which already existed and might well have been used for local self-government in a country of which the physical features necessitate numerous isolated communities. The financial state of the country, with the load of debt incurred during the war, was hopeless from the beginning, and oppressive taxation drove many of the peasants to take to the hills." By 1843, the German monarch had been limited by the formation of a constitutional government. It was only in the early 1900s, with pressure from Greeks who desired an independent state, that the Republic of Greece was founded with the signing of the Treaty of Lausanne.

Buoyed by the goal of independence and Europe's encouragement, the modern Greek nation sought geographical expansion to incorporate regions that had once been part of ancient Greece. This included the eastern coast of Anatolia (or Micro Asia), which contains the city of Smyrna, once a vibrant urban and cosmopolitan center just an hour and a half ferry ride from Lesvos. Several of the families I came to know in Skala Eresos had parents and grandparents that had held businesses and resided in Smyrna, as they had maintained trade between the island and the now Turkish mainland.

Yet Greece's attempt in the early 1920s to take Smyrna and the surrounding regions caused a fierce response by Turkey, which was developing its own nationalist sentiment under the Turkish National Front and the defeat of the Ottomans in World War I. In 1922, Turkish nationalist forces violently entered Smyrna, setting the city afire with disastrous results. The British, Italian, and American navies, which were anchored in the city's port, have been reprimanded for letting Smyrna burn (Milton 2008). Many of the thousands of mostly Greeks and Armenians who stood waiting on the quay just beyond the conflagration were never rescued. Historian Giles Milton (2008), in his book *Paradise Lost*, describes the rich culture, ethnic diversity, and trade that evolved in the city and its demise in the Catastrophe of Smyrna. The British and US military warships purposefully selected not to "arrange any kind of humanitarian endeavors" to rescue Greek and Armenian citizens. Despite pleas from anguished officers, due to official orders from above to maintain neutrality, thousands were left to their deaths (Koktzoglou and Shenk 2020).

The disaster at Smyrna mitigated the project of Greek expansion. In the 1920s, Greece and Turkey formally agreed to a population exchange in which 1.2 million Turkish-speaking Greek Orthodox citizens were expelled from Turkey and 400,000 Greek-speaking Muslims were forced from Greece into Turkey. Approximately 60 percent of Lesvos's population is considered to be descendants of the Greek refugees from Turkey. Many of those I interviewed cite this as contributing to the compassion the islanders offered to the swell of refugees who landed on Lesvos in 2015.

Another illustration of Greece's expendability in Europe is reflected in its economic and political outcomes after World War II, which was in contrast to the postwar experiences of other nations that struggled against the Nazis. The unusual strength of Greek leftists, who coordinated and fought Greece's campaign against the Nazis, has been well documented and applauded in histories of the resistance (Mazower 2000). Yet, after the victory over Nazi Germany was achieved, the Greek population was sacrificed once again (Mazower 2000). British forces under Winston Churchill, fearing the strength of Greece's National Liberation Front and its leftist orientation, shot into Greek crowds who were welcoming Britain's arrival (Vulliamy and Smith; 2014 Mazower 2000).

Instead of hailing the National Liberation Front and their welcome of British troops, Britain provided weaponry to right-wing Greeks, including politicians that had fled Greece or allied with the Nazi regime (Vulliamy and Smith 2014). In its interest to quash the Greek left, Britain perpetrated violence against the very people who had assisted in the defeat of Nazi Germany, plunging Greece into a violent civil war (1946–49). The British, US, and European actions or inactions, as the case may be, demonstrated a willingness to exploit Greece in order to secure their own political and military interests. The political stability of Greece, the integrity of its national government, and the everyday lives of Greeks were of no significance to a European-US world order that was defining itself in opposition to communism. The backdoor agreement between Russia and Britain, which divvied up Southern Europe, meant that members of the Greek Communist Party and the National Liberation Front would not receive assistance from the Soviet Union.

Unlike the celebration of war heroes in Allied nations, in Greece a white or conservative terror, backed by the English and US government, was unleashed. The Greeks who had fought the Nazis were imprisoned,

persecuted, and subject to mass killings. When Britain decided it could
no longer afford to support royalist Greece, President Harry Truman
picked up the battle against leftists. Concerned with keeping Greece
from communism, Truman initiated the use of proxy wars in Greece and
established the Truman Doctrine, which together were violently applied
decades later to Central America.

As a final insult, World War II reparations to Greece were never
properly handled, and in this regard Greece is the exception among
nations that joined the Allies to overcome Germany (Mazower 2000).
Some financial settlements between Greece and Germany, to address
the costs of the Nazi occupation to Greece, were paid in 1960 and
1990. In April 2015, in the context of Greek debt negotiations, leaders
of the SYRIZA party made a formal request for Germany to complete
repayment of the debt Germany still owes Greece from World War II,
provocatively suggesting it would confiscate German property if the debt
was not paid. A few left-leaning political parties in Germany agreed
to the financial obligation, but the matter never moved forward and
was considered a political ploy by SYRIZA. Yet by drawing on history,
SYRIZA was locating Greece's dire economic circumstances as part of
long trend of its peripheralization within Europe.

A final example of the quasi-European status of Greece is evident
in the neglect and disregard within the European Community (EC) of
neofascism and the military junta, the Regime of Colonels, that ruled
Greece between 1967 and 1974. Melina Mercouri's statement in the
epigraph at the start of this chapter is in relation to this period, but
its applicability to Greece's past and present geopolitical location and
socioeconomic circumstances is salient. Internationally, even though the
Swedish government urged the EC to take a stance against Greece's
fascist regime, the EC took no formal action. Rather than Europe or
the US intervening to stem fascism in Europe, Northern Europeans
began vacationing on Greek islands. Greeks living abroad rallied for
Europe's attention to the loss of civil rights, political imprisonments,
and the torture deployed by the Regime of Colonels. A young Greek
university student from the Ionian island of Corfu immolated himself in
1970 in the central plaza in Genoa, Italy—a striking example of how
ethnic Greeks attempted to gain Europe and the world's attention to
the tyranny clutching their nation.

The ultimate downfall of the Regime of Colonels was due to the
uprising of Greek students that amassed at the Polytechnic University
where they developed a radio station to relay a message of resistance, at

a time when fascists controlled all Greek media outlets. On November 17, 1973, after three days of the student occupation, the regime aggressively sent tanks to the university, leading to twenty-four deaths, mostly of bystanders. November 17 is still commemorated as a public holiday in Greece, as it marks the loss of life and the risks students took to liberate Greece from fascism. It is also the name of a present-day Greek radical leftist group. While Europe neglected Greece's plight under fascism, the US backed the Regime of Colonels. As the US has done in countless nations, the infringement of rights and democracy was justified by its struggle against communism with the primary purpose being to expand capitalism. The demise of the junta and the drafting of a postfascist democratic modern Greece was a nationally autonomous effort.

These historical cases illustrate that the political and economic integrity of Europe excludes Greece from its boundaries. This was most recently substantiated by the secret "Plan Z," a premediated strategy for Europe's success in the event of "Grexit" should Greek banks collapse. The plan was furtively developed in 2012 by German economist Jörg Asmussen; Thomas Wieser, an Austrian Finance Ministry official; Poul Thomsen, a Danish IMF official; and Mark Buti from the European Commission. They intentionally excluded all Greek officials, did not keep a paper trail or compose any digital communications of their design to shutter all ATMs, isolate Greek banks, and impose currency controls if Greece had refused the terms of the financial package being proposed by the troika. For EU officials, including German prime minister Angela Merkel—who was firmly aware that a plan was under way—the strategy was to preserve Northern Europe while Greek officials were kept in the dark and the wider Greek population was to be thrown to the wolves for disobeying neoliberalism (Spiegel 2014).

These historical moments reveal the many ways in which Europe has repeatedly infringed on Greek values, needs, and lives when its own political interests or power and wealth could be furthered. In effect, autonomy, grassroots action, local development, and self-reliance as a means of survival are in part an inheritance from Greece's recent past and its peripheral location in Europe.

The Hellenism of Cooperatives and Microenterprises

Cooperatives and microenterprises—small, often family owned and operated businesses employing nine or fewer persons—have been dominant economic units in Greece for some time. Microenterprises constitute 96.5 percent of the businesses in the Greek private sector, and they employ just over half of the population. As stated, Greece's microenterprise sector stands out even among EU nations, in which small and medium-size enterprises make up a large portion of economies (GSEVEE et al. 2014). The size and scale of Greek enterprises secures an intimacy between customers and proprietors, which was evident and easy to document in Lesvos, with this familiarity playing a significant role in the conviviality of island economics. Smaller enterprises are an embedded part of the Greek landscape with state policies disallowing large-scale developments and enterprise on most islands. Only on some islands, such as Crete, Santorini, and Mykonos, Greece's most expansively touristed island, do large-scale high-end hotels and resorts exist. Most of the accommodations on Lesvos are microenterprises or modest, locally owned hotels. Upscale accommodations are found in Molyvos and Skala Eresos has a resort style facility, owned locally, but managed by an English company catering to upscale British tourism.

Cooperatives, as described in the introduction, are also endemic to Greece. Their history has been detailed by University of Aegean sociologist Ioannis Nasioulas (2012) who chronicles their development, suggesting that Greece, not England, hosted them first and documents formal cooperatives appearing in Greece as early as the 1770s. The legacy of Greek cooperatives, particularly in relation to larger agricultural cooperatives includes, at times, heavy-handed state control. Agricultural cooperatives were often utilized to create political patronage and to secure a food supply to the growing urban industrial sector. During Greece's military dictatorship (1968–74), cooperatives were forced to abide by the demands of the regime, producing directly for the state. And in the 1980s, under the newly elected government of PASOK (Greece's Socialist Party), the cooperative movement expanded with state funds and support.

Nassioulas (2012, 145) also recognizes Greece as a nation with historical conditions to support a social economy including an "age-old community system that held up through the Ottoman Empire" that was foundational to Greece's nation building at the start of the twentieth century. Some of the original Greek cooperatives, such as those tied to olive oil or dairy production, continue through the present. I was able to visit some of these old dairy and olive cooperatives in Lesvos and witness their working. During an interview in the upper village of Eresos, I was brought into office of the Lesvos cooperatives where I was invited to review bookkeeping records in aged binders catalogued by decade starting with the 1920s.

Theorizing the role of cooperatives is tied to broader concerns of successfully embedding the economic in the social fabric of society (Polanyi 1944). Marxian criticisms of cooperatives as an avenue forward from capitalist exploitation abound. For example, like the solidarity economy concern that microenterprises will succumb to capitalist principles, Marxists were worried that cooperatives would eventually do the same. In Greece, cooperatives appear as a persistent method of organic economic alterity, despite economic challenges to liberalize the economy. Globally, cooperatives continue to build momentum as one of the new (or renewed) forms of economic governance that depend neither on the logic of accumulation nor on state control (Fonte and Cucco 2017; Ken and Elizalde 2016; Jessop 2001).

Across Europe cooperatives are expanding, as nearly one in four new enterprises are said to be part of the social economy and are holding substantial market shares in various industries (European Commission 2020, 2011). As in Greece, state laws in Italy, France, Belgium, Spain, and Portugal have been passed to better define cooperatives, particularly social cooperatives, recognizing them as an expanding movement that can benefit the economy. For Greece, the cooperative movement is a local strategy and needs to be recognized as such, rather than as an imported strategy. Despite the origin stories of cooperatives lying in England, Greek island communities deserve a closer look for the early foundations of cooperatives.

A Recap

Greece's long tumble in financial crisis and the austerity measures imposed did not result in Greeks succumbing to neoliberal logic. Instead, the nation's strong basis in community-centered and collective economics held rhythms that Greeks drew upon to retain their social and economic forms and contribute to their population's survival. Greek sensibilities of a moral economy contrasts with the Berlin Consensus and the severe austerity measures that SYRIZA initially boldly resisted. Greece seems to be Northern Europe's counterrhythm.

Greece's historical marginality in Europe, showcased in the few examples depicted in this chapter, sculpts its practice of convivial

economics. The Northern European media, politicians, and public deride
Greeks for their own forms of economy, often misperceiving them as
outcomes of disorganization or underhandedness, rather than a strong
foundation in ethics of provisioning for others, as well for the *oikos* or
the family, home, and well-being. Even the adoring public commentaries
by Northern European literary figures and their petitions for keeping
Greece in the EU still foisted blame for Greek debt on the "charming"
traits of Greeks, rather than on the neoliberal practices of the global
economy and the tightfisted economic policies of the EU.

PART II

THE RHYTHM SECTION

In order to grasp and analyze rhythms, it is necessary to get outside them, but not completely: be it through illness or technique. A certain exteriority enables analytic intellect to function. However, to grasp a rhythm it is necessary to have been grasped by it; one must let oneself go, give oneself to its duration.

—Henri Lefebvre, "Seen from a Window" (2003, 27)

CHAPTER FOUR

For the Love of Strangers and Enterprise

Νυν δ'επεί ημετέρην τε πόλιν καί γαιαν ικάνεις, ούν έσθήτος δεθήσεαι
ούτε τε' άλλου, ων επέοιχ' ικέτην ταλαπείριον 'αωτιάσαντα.

But since you have arrived here in our land, you will not lack for
clothes or anything a person needs in times of desperation.

—Homer, *The Odyssey*, 6:191–193, Wilson's (2017) translation

Greece has made me think about everything statistics don't tell
you. No European country has been as battered in recent years. No
European country has responded with as much consistent humanity
to the refugee crisis. . . . There have been clashes, including on
Lesbos, but almost none of the miserable bigotry, petty calculation,
schoolyard petulance, and amnesiac small-mindedness emanating
from European Union countries further north.

—Roger Cohen, *New York Times*, July 2015

Various historical and mythological accounts convey distinct forms of
receiving and greeting visitors during Greece's ancient period from
Odysseus forward. Anthropologists of modern Greece suggest that, for
Greeks, moral worth is marked by the extent of one's hospitality (Cowan
1991; Papataxiarchis 1991; Herzfeld 1987). Presently, family and friends
who emigrate from Greek islands and return annually—likely for summer holidays—are welcomed with a feast similar to those practiced in
the past. A generous welcome, which is often given to contemporary
visitors and tourists arriving to Greek islands, has been widely described
by travelers and documented in Greek travel literature, and may help

explain why many of Greece's tourists are returning visitors (estimated at 80 percent in Lesvos by hotel proprietors) even during Greece's recent difficult political and economic climate.

Tourism is an interaction between hosts and guests, one that often provokes social change (MacCannell 2013; Smith 1989). The ritual of host-guest relations as a defining feature of Greek islands is likely shaped by the geographical boundaries of residents who historically could identify visitors arriving on its shores. Yet island populations also are noted for being exclusive and resisting the influence of outsiders. McCall (1994, 4) sets forth eight island characteristics. Among them: "A fifth, and most obvious trait, is that islands are bounded entities in a way that continental cultures are not. There is a clear ideological, if not practical division between an in-group and an out-group: us and them, for islanders." McCall's (1994) broad assessment has been supported by research on island identities in *Shima* and *Island Studies Journal*, the two central academic journals in island studies. Insular networks often preclude social or political access to visitors and newly arrived residents. It is also captured by the concept of shima—the Japanese concept of islandness that was described in chapter 2—as it addresses the intimate, mutual relationship between the social and ecological on islands, which may *eventually* be realized by new residents.

Gayatri Spivak (1993) articulates "strategic essentialism" as a method by which nonelite groups organize themselves collectively, despite differences, into categories to resist and challenge oppressive forces. Islanders with histories of visitations—including colonizers, voyagers, tourists, and intruders—make use of strategic essentialism to retain their cultural integrity. They are a global group struggling with various life-threatening conditions, such as sea level rise, cultural survival, and depopulation, and are collectively strategizing to resist the onslaught of continental tourists, experts, and interlopers.

This chapter addresses both the hospitality and exclusiveness of islanders from a Greek island standpoint. Φιλοξενία (filoxenia), or "love of foreigners or strangers," is an explicit orientation toward visitors that characterized ancient Greece and applies presently, profoundly shaping the generous character of contemporary Greek enterprises. I conceptualize Greek constructs of "foreigners" and how this is negotiated in Lesvos by tracing the rhythm of hospitality from Greece's ancient rituals to their contemporary expressions, as described by both hosts and visitors. This nuanced and delicately balanced relationship of hospitality and degrees of foreignness help sustain the *convivial economics* on Greek islands, as it enables local and nonlocal populations to retain cultures of community and enterprise. The chapter frames the discussion of hospitality, exclusivity, and enterprise in Lesvos within an island studies framework, emphasizing islands as subaltern space. As a marginal locales, I argue that islands are opportune for the emergence and perpetuation of convivial economics.

Esoteric Island Hospitality

In cases of aggressive interlopers, the generous welcome of islanders has proven detrimental. For instance, rather than acting as proper guests, Christopher Columbus and Captain James Cook, and their compatriots, accosted their hosts. Had they not, the bridges of altruism offered by island societies might have provided a much better model for trade and exchange, rather than the grief and pain caused by occupation, colonialism, and genocide.

Colonialists and new imperialists demeaned and attacked their indigenous island hosts, characterizing them as naïve, ignorant, or undeveloped (Sheller 2003; Césaire 2001; Hau'ofa 1994). The generosity offered by indigenous island groups to the first European arrivals in the Caribbean and Pacific is well documented, as is the violence towards these populations. The hospitality of the indigenous population of Hawai'i, who maintain a deeply articulated practice of *aloha* that includes a welcoming spirit of community and mutual regard, is a profound case in point. In *Aloha Betrayed*, political scientist and Hawaiian studies scholar Noenoe Silva (2004) explores how the "aloha" Kanaka Maoli offered to Europeans, and later Americans, was mistook and manipulated by foreigners seeking access and gain in the islands, leading to the continued illegal occupation of the Hawaiian Kingdom by the US.

For Greek society, φιλοξενία or the generosity of spirit to foreigners remains a fundamental rhythm that continues to play an important role in establishing the mores for interactions between islanders and visitors. Stephen Mitchell (2011), the highly regarded translator of poetry and myth, explains the centrality of host-guest customs in the introduction to his translation of *The Iliad*. Hospitality was a rule of conduct in ancient Greece that was understood as sacred. To assist readers in making sense of Homer's epic tale on the events that sparked the Trojan War, Mitchell (2011, xxiii) elucidates:

> A host is obligated to entertain his guest with the utmost
> generosity, to provide for his comfort and safety . . . while
> the guest is bound to honor his host and treat him with equal
> respect. The mutual bond between host and guest is more
> than a matter of courtesy. It is, in the moral world, what the
> law of gravity is in the physical world: the force that holds
> things together and prevents society from flying apart into
> lawlessness and savagery.

For ancient Greeks hospitality was upheld by religious beliefs—gods awarded those who provided hospitality to strangers and punished those with unwelcoming behaviors. The Odyssey, considered Homer's follow-up to The Iliad, is thematically driven by the prominence Greeks make of host-guest relations. At the end of The Odyssey, the underside of the virtue of hospitality is explored. Upon finally returning to his beloved Ithaca after his long seafaring journey, Odysseus finds his wife, Penelope, and his son, Telemachus, hosting zealous suitors who are jockeying for Penelope's hand in marriage in anticipation of the pronouncement of Odysseus's death. Much is made of the wine and delicacies that Penelope provides to the men in waiting. Only by appreciating the code of hospitality as a matter of family honor can the oddness of hosting prurient suitors awaiting the death of one's spouse be understood.

Narratives from Greek mythology are replete with articulations of the hospitality visitors receive when arriving to islands. In one story Zeus, the ruler of the gods of Mount Olympus, transforms into a peasant traveler to assess whether his most ardent law, hospitality, is sufficiently exercised by mortals. These mythological or religious stories are literary artifacts of the ways in which hospitality is a central moral code of Greeks. Historian M. I. Finlay's The World of Odysseus (2002), a landmark study in the sociology of ancient worlds, directly attends to the concept of "xenia" or φιλοξενία, which refers to the custom of offering protection and hospitality to strangers. Finlay argues that in early Greece the appropriate greeting of foreigners was fundamental to the advancement of civil life.

Anthropologists of modern Greek village life also identify distinct cultural forms of host-guest relations in their research (Papataxiarchis 1991). The term φιλοξενία continues to be actively used by Greeks to refer to the hospitality and friendship granted to foreigners in Greek communities. Evthymios Papataxiarchis (1991, 165), a foremost anthropologist in Hellenic studies, explains that "in principle, the outsider is subjected to filoxenia (hospitality), which etymologically refers to a feeling of amity and friendship towards the xenos."

THE CASE OF KERASMA

As a rhythm of visitation, φιλοξενία was established long before the arrival of foreign tourists to Greek shores, yet it continues to pattern the Greek travel industry. One expression of φιλοξενία is found through κέρασμα (kerasma), which simply translates to "treat," and can refer to the giving of drinks, coffee, pastries, or small gifts to new and return-ing visitors, customers, friends, or family members.* Many travelers to Greece confirm that they were greeted with such treats upon arrival by acquaintances, hotel owners, or wait staff. Under capitalist principles, a gift offered by an enterprise is often used to seek an increase in profits. In Greece, however, almost all dining venues provide some type of κέρασμα, making it a useless vehicle for attracting customers. Instead, gifts are offered as a means of providing welcome and an opportunity for exchange and communication, a delight in hosting, rather than for the purpose of increasing revenue.

Researchers in Greece also are categorically received as guests (see Papataxiarchis 1991). In my own experience of dining in various Greek venues in urban and rural settings with differing company that has included children, grandparents, tourists from the US, Germany, and the Netherlands, old wealth and new wealth Greeks, lesbians and gay men, the gifting of deserts and drinks by food enterprises was extended regardless of my company. In bakeries, an extra pastry is sometimes added to purchases free of charge. Or, after expressing curiosity about an item, patrons may be offered not a taste, but a serving. And as stated earlier, in almost every interview or meeting I completed with a cooperative or the owners of eateries, I was offered a beverage or something delicious to eat gratis. Even as Greek enterprises endured austerity measures, resulting in the loss of income and access to cash, they continued to offer κέρασμα.

I spoke with business owners in Greece about κέρασμα to explore why this was so habitual. In a small city in the Peloponnese, where I was visiting family members, I went to dine at a recommended restaurant.

*κέρασμα (kérazma), treat, treating, offering a drink.

The charming proprietor offered my companion and I a glass of a delicious cherry liqueur at the end of the meal. It was May 2016, and EU
bodies were demanding yet another round of austerity measures. I asked
the owner why she continues to offer κέρασμα and does not consider
charging. Her response was curt, "They are not going to make barbarians
of us yet." She then softened, and asked, "What is the sense of having
a business if one is unable serve and cater to customers, share gifts, and
make good company?" My questioning of κέρασμα, regardless of how I
framed it, continued to come across as nonsensical in interviews with
proprietors in Skala Eresos. Answers from participants included, "You
give fruit to thank the guests," "What else would you do?," or "This is
how we make friends." The contemporary embodiment of κέρασμα is
emblematic of the moral code described of ancient Greece and is part of
the national habitus (Bourdieu 1967) of Greek entrepreneurial activity.

This spirit of gifting was reflected in a conversation I had with a
younger owner, Katarina, a Greek lesbian in her early thirties who had
opened a bar café in Skala Eresos a year into the economic crisis.* When
I asked about the extra drinks and desserts one seems to receive when
dining in Greece, she offered a comparison with her own experience as
a customer in the UK: "If you are English, you don't offer an extra shot.
In England they don't do that. But for me, if someone has a few drinks,
is it OK not to give them a shot? We [Greeks] have to do it, we have
less excuses in some things. I never expect it in England, to get a free
shot. It's a Greek thing, the κέρασμα." Katarina's insights distinguish a
cultural difference in food and drink establishments between Greece and
Britain. Her claim does not diminish the sensibility of British establish-

---

*Although I have applied names that reflect ethnic Greek backgrounds where
applicable, with the exception of well-known public government officials the names
used throughout the volume are entirely pseudonyms. Since many of the women
or lesbian travelers to Europe arrive at different periods, there are multiple stories
told that unfold at different time periods. Following other ethnographers in rural
communities (see Lynch 2007, 247), in some cases to further assure privacy I have
conflated stories of participants or "changed certain cosmetic details of their stories"
or altered dates when it would not misdirect the ethnographic content. Because this
volume traces the influence of island place, the rise of the women's cooperatives,
and the distinction of Skala Eresos as a well-known and first lesbian tourist enclave
in Europe, all of which are essential to the telling of convivial economics, I have
maintained the names of villages and the island Lesvos.

ments, nor does she suggest that the Greek habit of κέρασμα is unsound. Instead, the characterization of κέρασμα as not being a choice enables an appreciation for the ways in which economic conviviality is bound to the Greek identity and an organic aspect to Greek business activity.

The pricing of items at tavernas, cafes, and cooperative is another example of the φιλοξενία embedded in the culture of Greek business practices. Goods are typically sold with an interest in covering the cost of the primary ingredients, overhead, and making a profit. Yet each of the several modes of alternative economics described earlier—social and solidarity economy, localism, and community or diverse economics—argue for different principles to guide economic decisions, such as meeting the needs of the local community, ecological concerns, or resisting corporate capitalism. In Lesvos, pricing also was shaped by a concern for protecting customers' dignity, and in the interest of supporting public sociality.

I asked members of the various cooperatives how they decided to price their food items. Joanna, a member of one of the cooperatives in the northern part of the island, explained that they price "by the pocket," meaning the price is determined by what they think the customer can afford to pay. I wondered how they determined who could afford to pay more or less, but this was a matter of island social conditions, in which there was a shared understanding of neighbors' economic standing. Cooperatives' pricing was not determined by how much they could squeeze from better off customers, but by how to serve less prosperous ones. In Parakila, cooperative members collectively debated the subject of pricing. They concluded that if a patron could "help" the cooperative they should, and if the cooperative could "help" a customer they would.

Two cooperative members from Skalachori, whom I met in 2012, explained that all their pricing was driven by the strain of the economic crisis. Pricing was a matter of coordinating the survival of the cooperative, the village, and the island. In their strategies of price setting, the businesses and cooperatives in Greece sought to balance the pride of their customers with the goal of keeping their enterprises open. Cooperative members' prices were shaped by a caretaking spirit, which ensured that even local villagers who were financially struggling would be able to purchase some basic food items. This type of transaction was often hidden or conducted slyly, so that the customer in receipt would not feel despondent about their financial circumstances.

In Skala Eresos, I found a similar pattern in regard to pricing during the economic crisis. Pavlo, the proud owner of a long-standing taverna in Skala Eresos, explains: "I haven't changed the prices for two years and the quality is the same. The Greeks and the Europeans have less. It's a psychological violation to people to not be able to eat [out]. He'll eat out, but eat less." Pavlo's business practices holds insight for appreciating how φιλοξενία is entrenched as a trait of Greek dining venues. First, Pavlo's business absorbs the increase in the cost of living that began to affect Greeks in 2010 due to ramped up taxation. Instead of increasing his prices or seeking a wealthier clientele, Pavlo wanted to continue offering his customers the opportunity to gather socially. Greek dining entrepreneurs, such as Pavlo, recognize public dining as a social necessity and he considers himself a host to its fulfillment, which is not just a matter of gain, but a virtue in itself.

After completing a delightful afternoon meal of tsipoura (sea bream), beet greens, and island-made ouzo with a friend, I had the opportunity to discuss the routine of business ownership with another taverna owner, Georgios. Both my dining companion and the owner come from well-established families in Skala Eresos. I was asking Georgios how he managed between the high-volume tourist season and the absence of tourists in winter months. The story he decided to share captures the φιλοξενία inherent in the Greek perspective of enterprise:

> We aren't open in the usual way [in winter]. But we are here and we cook something for lunch and so if anyone stops by we have something to offer them—it could be lentils, or scordalia and bacalao. Once, a Japanese woman came here, she was here to visit the birthplace of Sappho [he chuckles]. She came to eat and we invited her to have a meal with us. We joked that my wife was the descendent of Sappho. At the end of the meal she asked to pay, and we were surprised, we said, "No, you came to eat with us." The next summer we saw her, again, she came back to see us.

For Weber (1978), a defining feature of capitalism is the separation of home and work, which helped solidify the formal and instrumental character of capitalist production (Collins 1986). In Greece, however, this separation has not articulated, as microenterprises that are small and local are a mainstay of the economy and regularly tied to family dwellings. Even in larger scale enterprises or government bureaucracies, it seems that daily life in Greece continues to be patterned around cultural values of hospitality, familiarity, and care, rather that the "rationality" of capitalism.

When Georgios states that his taverna does not stay open in the usual way, he explained that his business is not open as a charging enterprise. Instead, it remains open in case a traveler needs a meal. In many Greek island households, women act as household managers, and they typically prepare large afternoon meals. For many families who run food enterprises, the household is adjacent to or part of the business property, which may also be used as the family kitchen. The household-enterprise nexus also supports a convivial economics, where food service becomes an extension of one's household. Georgios's story of the visitor from Japan exhibits this attribute.

The rhythm of φιλοξενία also is apparent in Giorgios's feelings of obligation to provide unexpected visitors somewhere to eat. His desire to assure welcome adheres to the island landscape in which visitors, known or unexpected, have depended upon the delivery of Greek island hospitality for millennia. In ancient Greece, visitors would be warmly received by the officials of city-states, but the current incarnation of Greek hospitality resides primarily in the islands' food and beverage venues and accommodations, which often serve as the first point of greeting and welcoming first-time visitors, returning tourists, seasonal residents, and old friends.

Φιλοξενία may be costly and sometimes burdensome, but it booms like a well-tuned bass drum drowning capitalist logics. The many criticisms of Greece as failing to achieve Northern European models of economy miss what the many entrepreneurs I interviewed have clearly diagnosed—Greek business activity is tuned to a stronger and longer held rhythm of hospitable reception, compromise, and gift-giving.

Vicissitudes of Foreignness

Φιλοξενία also is tied intractably to the Greek "othering" of all foreigners. A social construction of "other" is necessary for producing a "love of foreigners." Yet Greek "othering" is essentially not based in a colonial positionality. In the modern tourist context, φιλοξενία is reinscribed as a subaltern engagement with the imperial gaze (Kaplan 2012), a way in which Greeks are able to receive even discourteous tourists as guests.

The distinction of foreigner—or ξένοι (pl), ξένη (f), or ξένος (m)—continues to be an active part of the vernacular in Greece and in

the Greek diaspora.* For example, ξένοι is applied by first- and second-
generation Greeks living in the US, Australia, and Canada to allude to
non-Greeks or non-Greek social and cultural forms in the country of
immigration. In Lesvos, islanders applied the designation of foreigner
equally, whether they were referring to the upscale tourists from Germany
or England in Molyvos or the young Afghani men working in the fields
of the Eresos valley. The term also is used to classify degrees of localness.
While there is a general Hellenic identity, geographical and cultural
distinctions continue to characterize ethnic Greeks' understanding of
themselves. For example, Greeks traveling from one part of the country
to another are regarded and self-identify as ξένοι.

When I was being introduced to cooperative members in the various
villages, cooperative members who had married into the village were
introduced or introduced themselves as ξένοι, and their village of origin
supplied. In discussing who purchases their pastries, many cooperatives
explained that they sold to both locals and foreigners, confirming that in
speech and practice anyone external to the village was ξένοι. To define a
person as foreign is to recognize that one is not autochthonous—whether
it be a nation, island, village, or family—showcasing a strong bond to
place that is considered characteristic of island societies.

Another occasion that illustrates the profundity of place-based
identities was when a friend, Stacey, from Skala Eresos came with me
for a ride to the village Filia. I had scheduled a meeting with the Filia
cooperative and she asked to join me because her father is originally
from the village. Although the village was an hour's drive away, she had
neither a vehicle nor a driver's license, nor was the village accessible
by bus, and she had not been there for some time. Stacey introduced
herself to the cooperative members and others we met in the square as
ξένη or foreign, born in Eresos, but explained that her father was originally from Filia. The Filia villagers and Stacy clearly held each other
in special regard, with cooperative members querying her so they could
figure out her genealogical ties to the village, but she still was not local.
If she had been, the Filia villagers would not have needed to trace her

---

*ξένοι (pl), ξένη (f), or ξένος (m) (xénos), strange, foreign, unknown, unfamiliar or
alien, stranger, foreigner, guest, irrelevant, unrelated, unconnected, extraneous, not
belonging to, of another, outlandish, having no reference to, having nothing to do
with, not in relation (with), unconcerned.

familial relations or connection to the village, because they likely would have known it.

The deep sense of localness or the embeddedness of geographical identities became apparent when I was discerning if there was a gendered pattern in how both locals and regular visitors referred to the various tavernas and eateries in Skala Eresos. Rather than using a restaurant's official name, local patrons often referred to it by the owner's name, which was sometimes a woman's name and other times a man's. I learned that the designation depended on who in the business was originally from Skala Eresos. For example, a taverna would be referred to as Penelope's or Mixalis's based on whose family was from Eresos. Interestingly, if the business was "foreign-owned," which sometimes included Greeks from another region, it was regularly referred to by the business's official name or as ξένοι.

Ξένοι is a categorization used regardless of one's class, race, ethnicity, or sexual orientation. This is not to suggest that ethnic Greeks may not be classist, racist, gender biased, or homophobic, but that being a stranger is a distinct quality that does not privilege some groups as less foreign than others. Those who are not ethnic Greek or not local may or may not be attributed various statuses and treated or addressed differently, but the first distinction is that they are ξένοι. Even if the qualities of a foreigner or a foreign group may be perceived as favorable, these do not make them any more Greek or less foreign. Within a local community or village, being from it is an asset.

Villages may claim returning tourists, a set of migrants, or a visiting scholar as "foreigners of our own," signifying that they have a special relationship to a place (Cowan 1991). For example, although sometimes imbued with homophobia, owners and local residents of Skala Eresos would refer to the local lesbian community as "τα κορίτσια μας" or "our girls." Some of the women's cooperatives also referred to non-Greek foreigners who annually visited the village as "η ξένοι μας" or "our foreigners."

For a number of Northern tourists and visitors to Greece, the experience of otherness was a challenge, even if they were sufficiently hosted. This was especially the case for many permanent and semipermanent residents in Lesvos, who desired or assumed a local identification. Northern European migrants living in Lesvos commented on what they perceived to be a distant intimacy they held with local Eressians no matter the length of their residence. For many Northern Europeans who are permanent residents or regular visitors to Eresos, the unmistakable experience of not belonging was unsettling. They were dismayed that they could not define or control the meaning of social inclusion. They found the "othering" aspect of φιλοξενία disagreeable.

Daphne, a German dwelling off and on in the Eresos valley for almost twenty years, provides a clear articulation of this sentiment: "I think that everyone who is not Greek, is not the right person in Greece, for the Greeks. It is not easy on an island to be close to the local people. Either if you are from Athens or other countries, because they are also not local." Other long-term Northern European residents believe that Skala Eresos's Greek community has adopted them. For example, Crystal, a white English woman, who has lived in Eresos for more than a decade, addressed the matter: "I am not a typical lesbian here who only sits with the lesbians. And living in the wintertime here I met more Greeks." Throughout my interview with her, Crystal made the case that she was part of the local Greek community, although she could not provide any clear indication of close ties to local Eressians. For example, she did not describe being a regular participant in community or family events or outings, holidays or celebrations, or being invited to a private family meal. I often saw her sitting with the English expatriate community on the village square. Crystal presented examples, such as gifts given to her daughter at Christmas, and assistance when she had a plumbing problem in her house. However, these are likely examples of φιλοξενία rather than any change to her status as foreigner. Meeting with local Greeks publicly in a restaurant or café or being granted κέρασμα is not the same as holding insider status in Greek island communities. Crystal's foreignness is self-evident in her lack of awareness of the code of host-guest relations and her longing to belong to the place as a local and not as a guest.

In another meeting with an English expatriate couple, Gwen and Roger, both in their late fifties, they described their neighbors favorably. They referred to a Greek proverb, "A gift is not a debt to be repaid," shared with them by a neighbor who regularly brings them fruits, vegetables, and jugs of wine. Our conversation turned to traditional Greek home furnishings, a hobby and business for them in Eresos. I asked if they found the type of antique furnishings they merchandized typical of their neighbors' homes. Inadvertently, my question forced the realization that they hadn't visited their neighbors: "We haven't really been to any Greek homes. We haven't even been to Elsa's house, well . . ." Aside from the offerings and exchanges with Greek neighbors the couple's socializing, like Crystal's, remained surrounded by the English expatriate community that has come to reside in the Eresos valley since the mid-1990s.

The Greek business owners who were not originally from Lesvos, including many who have lived and worked in Skala Eresos for more than twenty years, almost always started their tale of entrepreneurship with "I am foreign to here," and then indicated from where in Greece they originate. Although some of these ethnic Greeks had some challenges and duress in establishing themselves, which are explored later in chapter 7, they did not seek inroads into the local Greek community. They did not expect to become locals. Some of these Greek business owners would have preferred greater inclusion while others appreciated or preferred their status as a Greek outsider or as an implanted foreign business owner. Many of the Greeks running enterprises in Skala Eresos that were not local consider themselves part of the alternative or bohemian community that began to develop there in the 1980s, forming their own social circle.

GUESTS WITH AN IMPERIAL GAZE

In Greek cultural and social practices, receiving hospitality is almost as important as providing it. It is a sign of being culturally fluent and more closely connected to the rituals of Greek society. The dialogical nature of φιλοξενία is often absent in stereotypical renditions of Greek hospitality in which Greeks are presented as subservient or fawning over Northern visitors. Greek habits of hospitality are often caricaturized as over-the-top, as is witnessed in the film My Big Fat Greek Wedding (2002). In the movie, a Greek American woman brings her American boyfriend to meet her family, who act as drooling hosts. The play Mama Mia (1999), and the later film adaptation (2008), is another vivid contemporary example of mainstream characterizations of Greek islanders as servile bystanders happily accommodating Northern holiday romances on their isles.

Many of the tourists I spoke with seemed to receive the κέρασμα provided to them by Greeks from a position of privilege or entitlement, rather than from one of reciprocity. They arrived in Greece paradoxically with "western eyes" (Mohanty 1988) or an "imperial gaze," which feminist scholar E. Ann Kaplan (2012, 78–79) defines as "a gaze structure which fails to understand . . . integral cultures and lives that work according to their own, albeit different, logic. . . . The imperial gaze reflects that the white Western subject is central, much as the male gaze assumes the centrality of the male subject. . . . anxiety prevents this gaze from actually seeing the people gazed at." Ironically, Northern Europeans view Greece with an "imperial gaze" despite it serving as the foundation of their Western subjectivity. My exchange with Moira, a Scottish woman who worked as a waiter in Skala Eresos, illuminates this gaze as it plays out in the mixture of locals, tourists, and semipermanent Northern European residents staying in island villages during the summer. In our interview, Moira complained to me that her Greek customers expected her to speak Greek. Clearly offended by this expectation, Moira believed that English should be acceptable for service because Skala Eresos is a tourist destination. Moira failed to consider what would likely occur if the tables were turned, for example, if a Greek restaurateur in a Scottish tourist area did not wait on customers in English. Like many other Northern Europeans living in Lesvos, Moira problematized the marginalization of her "centrality," as her imperial gaze prevented her from considering the dining context from the position of Greek diners in Greece.

The implicit and explicit belittling of Greeks was thematic in my interviews and meetings with tourists, long-term visitors, and privileged migrants from Northern Europe. For example, Northern European interviewees described the generous or hospitable gestures granted by Greeks as being quaint and obliging. Northern Europeans exoticized Lesvos's villages as geographically and culturally exceptional from their own places of origin. Their accounts of locals in Eresos were sometimes favorable but still rather demeaning. For example, an English woman retiree offered that "the Greek villagers, they are gentle, kind, very giving, helpful, nothing is too much trouble. This is carried through their actions both at home and at work." Although the respondent seemed to consider these positive attributes, her characterization of Greeks alludes to the patronizing stereotypes of subservience often used by global Northerners to describe Southern regions.

Another showcase of the imperial gaze was demonstrated by Lizette, a Northern European lesbian, in her description of the relationship between the lesbian community in Eresos and the local Greeks: "It works. I think because the locals are so tolerant. I think it is because in a way in this Greek culture of laissez-faire, of having a major fight, and the next day is good again. This is what I love about Greece, or it is something typical from here. Here things are forgotten soon, and here someone can do extreme things, and next year it is forgiven. It is a very forgiving place." Also a seemingly benevolent account of Greek hospitality, this sentiment neglects to consider the subjective positions of Greek islanders and the reception of guests as determined by φιλοξενία.

Many of the Northern Europeans I interviewed and met with described Eressians as tolerant, a characteristic often cited to explain the village's acceptance of lesbians. For example, a German visitor who had been traveling and living on and off in Lesvos for more than two decades explains, "Very tolerant—they can't be bothered, laziness, and we [lesbians] take it for granted." These evaluations lack an understanding of the extension of φιλοξενία, which includes assisting or facilitating visitors, providing gifts or room to be and act more or less as they wish. Lefebvre and Régulier's (2003, 233) distinction between the "sworn community" of the European north and the Mediterranean's "regime of compromise" applies here. What Northern visitors to Greece overlook is the accommodations they are provided because, unlike contractual arrangements, which oblige citizens as well as visitors to follow rules, the cultural codes of the Greek Mediterranean provide a flexible stance in regard to local rules and norms particularly to strangers and their habits.

For many travelers to Lesvos, the φιλόξενια granted to them was characterized as freedom or lawlessness. A straight-identified Frenchwoman explained: "I didn't really think of Greece as a place. I had no special thought or affinity to it but I like its freedom. The motorbikes can run at night, I can smoke my cigarette when I want, and my child can be free, the children have a freedom." In my interviews, the freedom of children was often given as an example of the distinctiveness of Greek society. In Greek villages, children weave in and out of dining venues and tourist shops to chat with owners, report an incident, cry about a fall, or request a drink and snack. The visibility of children and their claim of village streets is another lens into the conviviality of Greek enterprises.

A lesbian in her late forties, who began visiting Eresos regularly in the last decade, said that she came to live in Greece because of "the freedom, a spirit, a deeper sense of things and to see things from another point of view." Κέφι (kéfi), another rite of Greek hospitality, also informs the "freedom" that Northern European respondents describe experiencing in Greece.* Papataxiarchis (1991) explains that κέφι derives from the Arabic "keyif," or "keyf," signifying pleasure, humor, a healthy state, as well as a state of slight intoxication. It is used to describe a mood of

---

*κέφι (kéfi) n/n. Good humor/temper/disposition, cheerfulness, joviality.

joy and relaxation, when the worries and concerns of the world "are
banished."

For Papataxiarchis (1991), κέφι draws from constructions of Greek
masculinity, to be further elaborated in the next chapter, informing the
social practices that envelop the public space of many island villages
to which tourists and travelers arrive. Many of the Northern European
lesbians and others I spoke with, when expressing what they like about
Greece or what inspires them to return, iterated qualities of κέφι, a few
of them even using the term. Mila, a Dutch lesbian, explained: "What
I like about Greece is the intensity. It's like when you have this night
and you slip into a taverna and suddenly the music starts and an old guy
starts to dance. It's this, you know, for me all this passion, all this, mmm,
freedom, there is a lot of freedom." Many of the Northern European residents compared Greece to their countries of origin. In her mid-thirties,
a young lesbian resident of Skala Eresos compared Greece to Germany,
explaining, "It is not so perfect, the nature is not so cultivated like in
Germany. Here the vegetation and life can be more wild." In comparing
Austria to Greece, Nicole, who had been married to a local Eressian man,
stated: "Everything was too nice, too well organized, every house had the
best materials and built in the right tradition, it was perfect—in Greece
it is totally the contrary. It leaves you space to live because things are
so disorganized and free." The freedom experienced by Northern European is fed by the φιλοξενία or the customary hospitality that structures
Greek host-guest relations in which rules are stretched to accommodate
visitors. As guests, Northern Europeans are extended social and physical
space that they perceive as novel. In addition, the celebratory context of
summertime in Greek villages is a welcoming environment that is based
in Greek economic conviviality. Summer is the time of numerous public
events in the village square, including celebrations of various saints' days
and religious holidays, and family events, such as weddings and baptisms.
Skala Eresos, like many Greek island villages, produces a sort of yearly
homecoming for returning kin, as well as for foreigners, who join in the
splendor of the Aegean summer.

Many Northern European visitors and residents also characterized life
in Lesvos as lawless. At the beginning of my first research visit to Lesvos
in 2008, a seasonal resident of Skala Eresos from Germany who managed a
tourist storefront stated, "Nothing is illegal in Greece." It became a curious
but steady refrain I would hear throughout my fieldwork. For instance, one
long-term Northern European resident of Lesvos states: "I liked the attitude

of Greeks to laws. The relationships in Greece are richer, because there is no state." One German lesbian I spoke with employed a comparison: "Greeks are a bit anarchistic in their ways. They don't like to have laws and try to find a way around it. Everybody has no helmet here, but it is a law to have a helmet. In Germany it would not be possible, the police see you, you get a fine, and then you don't do it next time." A Dutch lesbian, who has lived in Greece for over two decades, also compared her home country with Greece, contending similarities between the nations and attitudes toward the law: "There is a lot of freedom. There is some connection to Holland. Holland is a nation of anarchists and Greece also. You have an idea and you do it, and the law, pleh, is the law."

I brought up the persistence of lawlessness over dinner with a few Greek sociologists, asking them about the claim that "nothing is illegal in Greece." Without hesitation, they addressed the sentiment. A discussion of Greek life ensued where they contrasted autonomy versus regulation, maneuverability around laws, and legal infringements on personal freedoms. One colleague, who had been teaching and living in the UK, explained that he returned to Greece because of what he felt was an overwhelming systemic control over his life. Along with referring to the closed-circuit television or video surveillance of public space in the UK, he critiqued the extensive regulatory code, rules, and social codes that he endured in England. He shared his realization that his day was dictated by a patterned system that controlled both his social and personal life. He explained that he returned to Greece for autonomy and a less formulaic existence.

When I spoke to local Eressians and other Greeks about attitudes toward the law, several used the phrase "All laws have windows (Όλη η νόμει έχουνε παραθηρα)," suggesting that one can wangle their way around a law to achieve their goal. Other Greeks used the analogy of finding the button (τό κουμβί) to work around a law or regulation that was interfering with one's goal.

For example, one restaurant owner, a Greek man originally from the city of Patra in the Peloponnese, who identified with the bohemian set of Skala Eresos, explained: "The laws in Greece are a mess, like entangled spaghetti. In Greece, especially, the law serves the wrong people. There is always a window . . . the law is nothing. Those who make the laws don't follow it, why would anyone else?" Autonomy and the negotiation of the law is a practice that derives to some extent from the sociohistorical and political context of Greece that I described in the previous chapter.

For many islands, including Lesvos, local and autonomous governance dominated the political orientation of remote villages. Immediately following World War II, there was almost an absolute absence of a central government in islands such as Lesvos. The imposition of laws from a distant mainland government, along with a not so distant experience with fascism, makes federal and EU laws suspect to many Greeks, especially when they interfere with autonomy and independent economic pursuits.

However, ethnic Greeks did not conform to the viewpoint that Greece is lawless. In a conversation centered on tourists' perceptions of Greece's legal framework wherein I presented the perspective of lawlessness, an Eressian woman answered rhetorically, "If Greece is lawless, then why do so many foreigners come to spend time on our islands?" She took offense to the characterization of lawlessness because for her it implies an unsafe and freewheeling society, which are quite contrary to Greek cultural norms. Throughout Greece, foreigners and tourists are granted space to act freely and not feel regulated, but this is different from lawlessness.

Northern Europeans' description of Greece as lawless reflects an ethnocentric understanding of φιλοξενία. The sense of freedom frequently referred to by Northern Europeans is due to a long-held rhythm of hospitality. Their "imperial gaze" overlooked the cultural reasons for the liberties they are granted, as they instead characterized Greeks as subservient or lazy. What they perceived as lawlessness, or a lack of constraint, in Lesvos are leniencies afforded to Northern Europeans because guests are not expected to abide by the local social codes.

In my conversation with the Greek academics, they focused on the regulatory environment, rather than the daily conditions of life in Greek villages, which include a remarkable sense of physical safety. In a conversation I overheard in a travel agency in Lesvos, a Northern European lesbian, who had lived and worked in Eresos for at least a decade, was speaking with a customer who was concerned with where to leave her rental car keys upon returning the vehicle to the office after hours. The Dutch travel agent explained, "You haven't been in Greece long enough. You leave your keys in the car, your house open, and your baby in the street." This statement implies the norms she has experienced regarding safety in Greece.

Descriptions of lawlessness were clearly not in reference to concerns about theft, crime, or physical safety. To the contrary, the "freedom" enjoyed by residents and visitors alludes to the strong sense of security experienced in Greece, especially on its islands. As austerity measures grip Greeks, stealing and theft increased but dropped off by 2014 (Tsouvelas et al. 2018). Greek crime rates—including hate crimes—are lower than much of Northern Europe with Greece holding some of Europe's strictest and well developed laws regarding hate speech and crimes. Greece's low crime rate, including one of Europe's lower murder rates (Eurostat 2018), is not the result of extreme policing and regulatory presence. Instead, it is because of a culture of conviviality derived from the historic pulse of a sensitivity and generosity toward strangers and a deep appreciation of preserving place. Roger Cohen (2015) of the *New York Times*, covering the Syrian refugee crises in Lesvos, explains that given its dire economic circumstances, "Greece could serve as a textbook example of a nation with potential for violence against a massive influx of outsiders." As he and many others have documented in Lesvos, Greeks demonstrated generosity and compassion to refugees even at the peak of its economic crisis—although the continued failure of EU response to its immigration crises has recently stressed the reception of immigrants to Lesvos.

As a description of Greece, "lawless" seems to refer to the scarcity of contractual arrangements and enforcement in Greece, rather than criminal concerns or unrestricted hostilities. Contractual arrangements limit the space for negotiations, especially when established laws, regulations, or modes are inhospitable or irrelevant to a particular situation. The triumph of negotiation in Greece explains the flexibility and spontaneity that are conducive to convivial economics that often depend on locally shaped, informal economic exchanges among small and micro businesses that shift with the ebb and flow of the economy and in the interest of community well-being.

The operations of a green grocer in Skala Eresos exemplify this kind of business negotiations at the local level, articulating the particularities of island microeconomies. Fruits and vegetables can only be legally sold in supermarkets or by greengrocers in Greece. Other categories of shops may sell cheese or other general goods, but they are not permitted to sell meats, which are sold by the butcher. As conveyed in chapter 1, in Greece the laws governing what food items can be sold by a type of enterprise are quite specific and are adhered to quite carefully. This may be due to the implicit understanding that this widens opportunities for multiple smaller enterprises, rather than a single large entity.

Figure 4.1. The greengrocer's/courtesy of Tzeli Hadjidimitriou. As the designated sellers of produce, aside from supermarkets, which are minimally present in remote regions, greengrocers are ubiquitous across Greece. There is at least one found in the agora or market area of even the most petite villages on the smallest of islands. This photo is of one of several found in Eresos.

I frequented a certain greengrocer in Skala Eresos to shop and partake in regular chats. On a late summer afternoon when I went to purchase a second round of cherries, I started a conversation with John about the details of his business. John described how he holds a unique relationship with each of the dining venues on the Skala Eresos shoreline. He explained various aspects of these relationships, including whether the produce is delivered prior to or after payment is made, the amount of produce purchased, and whether there was a written document or not. It seemed that monetary exchanges, distribution of product, and levels of formality were individually decided and renegotiated weekly, especially at the start of the tourist season. If his client had some financial duress during a week, John would easily accept a delay of payment, or extend further credit. In addition, if a restaurant had an unexpectedly large number of patrons, John would accommodate evening calls for deliveries of tomatoes, eggplants, or okra. If he needed funds up front, and a business was capable, he could ask for it.

Conviviality or Informality?

Negotiation, rather than obliging one to contract, reflects the generosity that business owners extend to one another, arguably arriving from a society that has operated by the principles of φιλόξενια for millenniums. To demand or force payment is considered crass or a loss of character simply because it is considered to be inhospitable. Negotiated economic ties are reflective of island societies where networks and familiarity often dominate economic exchanges and work (McCall 1994). In Greece's island regions, few are beholden to the Greek national state, which they view as distant and disinterested. Circumventing tax payments is not considered a moral crime, but being stingy to one's own community or guests certainly is because it stands in stark contrast to a cultural rhythm that prioritizes generosity.

Informal economic relations in Greece were regularly blamed in the media for Greece's economic crisis. Rather than EU officials and politicians holding culpable the forces of global capital, the microeconomies of Greek enterprise were censured and faulted. Informal economic activity—for small-scale and autonomous enterprises—is often less about challenging the state and more often a strategy of economic survival (Karides 2007). To suggest that Greece's informal sector is responsible for the nation's economic tailspin neglects that convivial economics existed prior to the corporate-driven financial crisis of 2008 and Greece's relative stability before its entry into the EU. It is often challenging for microenterprises in almost any economic context to survive without some degree of informality, often because laws favor corporate enterprises, rather than supporting the survival of small and micro business. Via an imperial gaze, Northern Europeans are unable to recognize informal economic forms as part of "integral cultures and lives that work according to their own, albeit different, logic" (Kaplan 2012, 78). The informal, the convivial, and the negotiated, rather than contractual enforcement, define the success of ritual forms of association across enterprises in Greece.

The seemingly byzantine system of regulations governing small and micro food businesses in Greece have also been implicated as contributors to the crisis because they disallow the flow of capital. During a visit with a staff member in the mayoral office in Eresos, I was flummoxed by the myriad of exceptions, definitions, and caveats in the governing structure of food enterprises. When I expressed concern to the clerk that my grasp of formal Greek might be insufficient for me to comprehend these policies, she responded kindly by saying, "No, my love, it is just inconsistent, that's how it is." Another business owner explained that when she sought to determine what types of food she could sell at a bar she was opening she was referred to a very large paper volume with a worn binding that was nearly impossible to decipher.

Although appearing arcane, the Greek laws governing small-scale enterprises seem to have sustained and protected them against corporate takeovers. However, the "economic overhaul" commissioned by the bail-out agreements included legislation to disrupt some of the protections of small enterprises (Alderman 2015). For example, pharmacies in Greece are sanctioned by regulations governing hours of operation, profit margins, spatial proximity to one another, and assuring pharmaceutical access throughout Greece including remote locations. While, in some cases, cosseting enterprises may lead to sinecures, the regulations regarding enterprise may protect Greece from the onslaught of corporate capital faced by urban and rural regions across the globe. As of yet, there is no corporate chain of pharmacies in Greece. Instead, pharmacies across Greece continue to be considered a public good.

Lefebvre (1991, 44) asks, "What is an ideology without a space to which it refers?" Φιλοξενία is an ideology or rhythm of Greek island space, providing its residents and visitors with a sense of freedom that is distinctively Greek. Neoliberalism, with its well-oiled ideological machinery, normalizes its logics and reifies them as the correct and proper forms of economic transactions regardless of nation, region, or geography. In effect the informal, the convivial, and the negotiated are considered unacceptable or a farce when one's economic framework is co-opted by neoliberal capitalism. The simultaneous attraction to Greek "lawlessness" and "freedom" and ridicule of Greece's economic and social logic attests to the difficulties people have in making sense of social-economic systems that are inconsistent with their own provincial viewpoint, especially when that viewpoint has been absorbed as a global and prevailing perspective (Chakrabarty 2000). As an orienting principle, φιλοξενία simultaneously enables the acceptance of worldviews different from one's own and protects the local sensibilities and cultural logics of Greek islanders, permitting an organic and attritional economic alterity to coexist and thrive.

During 2015, the global press became fixated on the influx of migrants and refugees that arrived on the island of Lesvos from Turkey. Less attention, however, was given to the grassroots efforts led by Lesvos's islanders who extended φιλοξενία to the thousands of refugees—many of whom were fleeing violence in Pakistan, Syria, and Afghanistan—arriving on the island's eastern coast. Greece's reception of these refugees and migrants was astoundingly distinct from other European nation-states, especially Austria, Slovakia, the Czech Republic, Bulgaria, and Hungary, which either sealed their borders or created increasingly repressive immigration controls (Eddy and Bilefsky 2015). In the case of Hungary, officials fenced in migrants, redirected trains, and created an overall hostile context. On Lesvos, islanders welcomed the migrants and refugees by opening soup kitchens and creating accommodations.

In 2016, at the Fourteenth Island of the World Conference in Lesvos, Thrasyvoulos Kalogridis, head of the Chamber Society for the Development of Greek Islands, shared an anecdote of meeting with EU officials on immigration and imploring them to join him on a vessel in the Aegean. He explained to the conference audience that he wanted these EU policy-setting officials to witness firsthand the numerous rafts holding refugees, and that for him, and Greece, it would be utter cruelty to return the families he saw back to economically ravaged and war-torn places. His reaction exemplifies the approach of Greeks in Lesvos and how it is shaped by φιλοξενία. Despite EU concerns with Turkey's human and civil rights record, the EU's eventual response to the "refugee crisis" was to fund Turkey to implement stricter border controls and hold immigrants and refugees.

The welcoming of refugees during an economic crises highlights φιλοξενία in heroic fashion, but the mundane story of host-guest relations and convivial economics is expressed in the tavernas and kafenions of Greek islands. The small-scale enterprises in Lesvos allow for casual opportunities where people share gifts, drinks, meals, stories, and other novel items. Although they still are engaging in a market exchange, the relationship between guests and hosts on Greek islands is "more than that" (Calhoun 1992, 7–8). Just as the entities that formed the basis of civil society were "institutions of sociability only loosely related to the economy," the convivial economics on Greek islands resist the path of neoliberal-driven economics.

Many practices engaged in by the owners, managers, and workers in the enterprises of Lesvos—whether they were from Lesvos or not—are oriented by the organic rhythms of the island and by Greece generally. These include flexible exchanges rather than contractual obligations, hosting and provisioning guests, and a distinction between local and foreigner that have sustained the island communities of Greece for centuries. In spite of the force by which neoliberalism pressed itself upon the Greek islands, economic practices in Lesvos have yet to be fully co-opted and instead reflect an everyday form of resistance (Scott 1985).

The subaltern geographies of islands lead Greek islanders to construct pathways to greet or receive new visitors based in ancient moral codes. Φιλοξενία informs Greek social life and enterprises, supporting the basis of a convivial economy. Yet φιλοξενία also serves as a form of strategic essentialism. By distinguishing the foreigner and designating her ways and means as distinct, Greek island social codes remain more or less intact. With regular visitations from their diasporic communities and the manifestation of modern tourism, a well-patterned reception of guests continues to dominate the Greek islands. The small and microenterprises that pepper Greek islands play the distinctive role in the provision of hospitality that is at the core of Greek life.

CHAPTER FIVE

The Seasonal Agora

A Gender-Placing Rhythm and a Sexualized Sense of Space

ΠΡΟΒΟΥΛΟΣ ἀλλὰ τί δράσεις;	MAGISTRATE What will you do?
ΛΥΣΙΣΤΡΑΤΗ τοῦτό μ' ἐρωτᾷς;	LYSISTRATA You ask me that?
ἡμεῖς ταμιεύσομεν αὐτό.	We'll control it.
ΠΡΟΒΟΥΛΟΣ ὑμεῖς ταμιεύσετε	MAGISTRATE You mean you're
τἀργύριον;	going to manage all the money?
ΛΥΣΙΣΤΡΑΤΗ τί δεινὸν τοῦτο	LYSISTRATA You consider that so
νομίζεις; οὐ καὶ τἄνδον	strange? Isn't it true we take
χρήματα πάντως ἡμεῖς	care of all the household
ταμιεύομεν ὑμῖν;	money?
ΠΡΟΒΟΥΛΟΣ ἀλλ' οὐ ταὐτόν.	MAGISTRATE That's not the same.
ΛΥΣΙΣΤΡΑΤΗ πῶς οὐ ταὐτόν;	LYSISTRATA. Why not?

—Aristophanes, *Lysistrata*, Johnston's (2017) translation

The sociable sharing of food and drink is found by anthropologists to be a fundamental aspect of personhood in Greece (Cowan 1991), but the public space of Greek villages is coded by gender and dominated by men. The φιλοξενία granted to visitors and tourists and the vibrant sociality of the village agora therefore is shaped by traditions of a public gendered spatiality that is sexualized and heterosexist. When single women—young or middle aged, alone or in the company of one another—have been present in the social venues of the agora, it implied they were sexually available to heterosexual men. With increased tourism since the 1980s, including the rise of independent women tourists and gay and lesbian travelers across Greek islands from Europe, gender and sexualized dynamics of sociality became entwined with traditional and tourist sensibilities of public space, most strikingly in the summer months.

Over the course of three decades, feminist human geographers have established "that space is gendered and gendering has profound consequences for women" (Doan 2010, 1). Engaging in ethnographic and historical methods, feminist geographies describe the processes that contribute to the construction and reconstruction of gendered spaces, including the interactions between local forms and global influences. Feminist human geographers brought to the fore micro- and macro-level analyses of space that helped to articulate the ways gender relations are spatial and inform understandings of nation-states, urban and rural regions, households, the public sphere, and the body (Massey 1994). Initially highlighting the spatial constraints placed upon women that limit their opportunities (McDowell 1999; Massey 1994; Rose 1993), more recent feminist work and queer analyses address how gender and sexuality constitute space such as in the field of lesbian geographies (Browne and Ferreira 2015; Valentine 1993). Gibson-Graham (2006, xxiv), whose work on diverse and community economies I review, summarize: "A feminist spatiality embraces not only a politics of ubiquity (its global manifestation), but a politics of place (its localization in places created, strengthened, defended, augmented, and transformed by women). Feminism is the politics of becoming in a place. In this admittedly stylized rendering, feminism is not about the category 'woman' or identity per se, but about subjects and places. It is a politics of becoming in place."

Feminist and queer geographies have extended analyses to the spatial production of masculinities (Berg and Longhurst 2010), the heteronormative domination of place, and the queering of it (Browne and Ferreira 2015; Talburt and Matus 2014; Doan 2010). As locally defined communities contending with regular tourism, Greek island villages have delivered a convenient prism for researchers attending to the politics of place. The tensions between "Western" modernity and Greek island life have been most visible in the space of the village square and convivial economic entities, where sociosexual and gendered spatial rhythms are transformed.

I begin with an auto-ethnographic account of my own experiences that highlight contemporary Greek island attitudes toward gender and sexuality and women's public socializing. Referring to interviews I conducted in 2008, 2009, and 2012 with "foreign" women and in relation to anthropological literature on gender and space in Greece, I elucidate contemporary arrangements of gender, economy, and public sociality in Lesvos. Next, I review ancient Greek ideals of gendered space and its actual praxis, a contradiction that has hinged on the misrecognition of women's economic contributions in Greece now and in the past. I then turn to modern constructs of Greek masculinity that rely on displays of public sociality in coffee shops and tavernas. I consider how local Greek islanders, especially men on the village square, engaged with the onset of Northern European tourism to reveal the cadence of gender and sexuality in the public sphere and how it shifts seasonally and over time.

In the gendered public landscape of Greek island villages, the lesbian enterprises and the women's cooperatives created their own modes of sociality reworking norms around gender and sexuality in the agora through their economic endeavors. My analytical lens for evaluating convivial economics in Lesvos is also broadened through literature on queer economics (Jacobsen and Zeller 2008) and gay and lesbian tourism, which I take account of to better explain the subalternity of gay and lesbian travel and entrepreneurship in Greece.

Field Stories (Gendered)

As I worked to understand the gendered spatiality based on ethnographic observations, interview data, and my Greek background, I discovered a trove of anthropological literature on the spatiality of gender relations in rural Greece. Edited volumes and ethnographies from anthropological perspectives have investigated constructs of masculinities, gender and kinship, and women's resistance (Loizos and Papataxiarchis 1991; Herzfeld 1985; Loizos 1977). In most of these works, spatiality is identified as central to the constructs of gender in Greece. Papataxiarchis (1991, 157), documenting gender relations in the Aegean in the 1980s, states:

> The most remarkable aspect of social life is the extensive segregation of the sexes: women and men spend most of their time in same-sex contexts and identify strongly with their own sex. The nucleated village seems to be divided into sex-specific territories. The square in the center with the coffee shops and marketplace is dominated by men. The houses that surround the square and constitute neighborhoods are small havens for women and children.

While the anthropological literature identifies some of the social norms organizing Greek villages as tied to rurality, I also draw on an island studies perspective as I consider that these constructs of spatiality might be shaped by their island geography, as well as by broader Greek social norms.

As I routinely drove across the island through and to many of the villages of Lesvos, I noted a limited number of women socializing in public. Invariably, the village squares and agoras of more than twenty villages I passed regularly had groups of men collected together at the kafenions lining the village squares. They met in large groups in the mornings for coffee, again in the late afternoon for more coffee, and sometimes smaller groups would gather in the evenings for ouzo or beer with mezes. On my last research visit to Lesvos in May 2016, even as I am firmly aware of the gendered spatial practice of Greek villages, I confirmed the relative absence of local women socializing together in the kafenions.

While groups of men gather to share drinks in the agora, women might be visible working in a family enterprise, purchasing groceries, or picking up children from school. I experienced the gendered spatiality of socializing, especially on winter mornings when I was the single woman in the kafenion, my only access to the internet. Nearly every morning I went to use the internet and quietly have a cup of coffee, the men who regularly met, many of them agricultural workers, sent me a κέρασμα of coffee.

There were also women-only spaces I frequented in Lesvos. Besides the women's cooperatives, which offered homosocial company, I participated in two gendered communities in Eresos. One was the coffee socials attended by Greek women that were held by the PTA occasionally on winter weekends to benefit the public schools. My participation was as a parent of children who attended the school, but also due to the close connections I made with a well-established teacher in Eresos who sponsored me. The second was lesbian bars in the late evenings. In the summer these were lively scenes with music and dance parties. In wintertime, a small crowd of international foreigners and ethnic Greek women from other regions grouped together for conversation and company.

An instructional personal experience I had regarding the gendering and sexualizing of the time and space in Lesvos's villages were the not-so-indirect comments I received from a taverna owner in Eresos. One early December evening, I joined a Northern European woman

I had interviewed for a casual dinner at a taverna. In a joking manner, the owner questioned how such an affair—two women out on a
winter evening—could be taking place without the company of men
family members. He was trying to grasp the occasion that would lead
us, especially one being married, to publicly dine "alone." The evening
turned out pleasantly, and unexpectedly informative, markedly because
my companion and I had transgressed gender spatial codes. Being out as
two women on our own implied sexual availability. My dining partner
expected goading and teasing from the owner and played along with him,
but it was hazy to me as to whether he was serious about us as being
available due to our nontraditional gender performance (Butler 1990).
Ines delighted in the fact that as a Greek from the US, I was naïve to
the gendered spatiality of Greek islands. She herself had recently divorced
an ethnic Greek man from the island and complained about the isolation
she experienced living in a more traditional village, especially during
winter. She was left with no opportunities to go out on her own and
publicly socialize, as she sometimes could in Eresos and Skala Eresos,
and regularly in her own native France.

Dining alongside us was a family (a heterosexual couple and two
children). I learned that the woman dining with her family was from
Austria and had married into the village at least a decade ago. Unlike
my friend and I, however, I learned the woman dining with her family
adapted to the traditional gender spatial code by only dining publicly
with her family. By following local social codes, one might remain ξένοι
or foreign, but you could be folded into the local society, becoming
less visible than most foreigners, especially single women, who remain
observable outsiders.

Another field story further reveals my sluggishness at coming to
terms with the spatiality of gender and sexuality in Lesvos, despite being
schooled in Greek gender norms as a child of Greek immigrants. By
not growing up in a Greek enclave (by intention of my mother), where
more spaces might have been coded by gender as it is accomplished
in Greece, I had no experiential window into the public sociality of
Greeks. As a child I could freely sit on my father's lap in our suburban
backyard and breathe in exhalations of tobacco, or steal sips of coffee
from my grandmother in the kitchen upstairs. It did not occur to me
that my Greek migrant relatives might have been attempting to reenact
the gender spatial codes of their homeland, as well as parenting codes,
which allow young children of all genders to run freely.

On a gray, cold, wet winter day, a young couple, in their late twenties, a local Eressian man and Dutch woman, generously granted me an extended interview in their cozy home warmed by an active fireplace. I once again transgressed gendered boundaries. Stratos, Gina's husband, had offered that if I wanted more details of the village lore, he would be willing to meet with me again. I suggested we meet at one of the kafenions in the upper village where he worked. Without offense, and with a good deal of amusement, they both explained that meeting him at a café for a further interview would not be possible. In their private interactions the young couple stated that they did not adopt traditional gender norms, but Stratos was a member of a well-known local family in Skala Eresos. The couple explained that if I met with Stratos publicly it would create gossip and require many explanations, especially to Gina's in-laws. Though in my mind this was a professional meeting and I have interviewed single men in multiple contexts, I evidently had not yet acclimated to the perception and sexualization of a meeting at a café between two unrelated persons of different genders.

Although ethnic Greek women from the village were not generally seen publicly socializing unless there was a special event or perhaps on a Sunday after church or as a group on summer evenings, they were regularly visible working in the small enterprises that characterize Greek villages. Though Greek village women "contest the gendered pleasures of everyday sociability" (Cowan 1991, 180), gendered rules of public socializing seem to still apply in many rural island villages. With few exceptions, ethnic Greek women's daily public presence generally is confined to working (in bakeries, tourist shops, bars, or family restaurants), food shopping, major social events, or taking care of errands.

Never Marry a Greek

My interviews with heterosexual-identified women from Northern Europe, including France, Austria, Netherlands, and Sweden, who had married ethnic Greek men further articulated customs of gendered spatiality. The subtitle is a play on a Sandra Cisneros short story, "Never Marry a Mexican," as reference both to the struggles these women faced in their cross-cultural relationships and the borderlands that encompass them (Anzaldúa 1999). I interviewed about ten women, most of them in their forties, who discussed their choice to live in a Greek village and their long-term relationships, marriages, and divorces with ethnic Greek men. They described and confided the challenges they experience with Greek social norms that they felt differed distinctly from their own cultures. Their stories help frame the context of gender, sexuality, and nation in Greek island villages, and the larger social environment in which women's cooperatives and the lesbian businesses developed their enterprises. Suzette, a German in her forties and in the midst of divorcing a Greek man, explained: "Alternative Greeks are the worst. They are pretending to be open, partiers, and hippies but once married they have the traditional expectations." A large part of the diverse community in Eresos include Greek men who reject conventional measures of success, as they are attracted to villages like Skala Eresos because of the social and economic alterity and diverse population. Similar to Lizette, several other Northern European women I interviewed indicated that while earlier parts of their relationships with Greek men were within a counterculture environment, eventually they struggled over Greek traditions of gendered spatiality. This included the expected departure of wives from socializing on the plateia or the village square. When these Northern European women were tourists or casual girlfriends, their presence was accepted as foreigners in the public sphere, but once they married or entered into a more permanent relationship it seems that women's company interfered with the homosocial conviviality of Greek men on the plateia. Several of the women interviewed explained that at first they entertained or romanticized the separation of social spheres, and maintaining a household, but ultimately almost all of them spoke of feeling excluded and trapped at home.

Denise, who lives in the mountain village of Andissa in the same district as Eresos, had visited Lesvos regularly during childhood vacations with her parents from Belgium. She moved to the island as an adult, and explained her difficulties with being married to a Greek man: "In the morning men go to work, they come to eat, wake up, go to work, and then from work they go to the café and then from the café they come home at night, and then they go again to work." The habit of men departing in the mornings and returning only for meals and a midday nap is traditional to Greek society. This routine differs from that of traditional Northern European households that are based in marriages in which men returned home in the evenings where they act as the household head. In Greek domestic order, women generally control the household, and men tend to spend less time in it (Papatraxacharis 1991). Denise, who

I listened to sympathetically, was quite concerned about her marriage, and lamented, "this is no way for family life." Remarkably, Greece holds one of the lowest divorce rates of the EU countries, as well as globally (Eurostat 2017).

Like Denise, many of the Northern European women I spoke with came to loathe Greek cultural norms of gendered space. Greek women's domestic customs, which include keeping the household, raising children, agriculture work, and maintaining cultural traditions, were adopted only by a few of the Northern European women married to Greek men. From the perspective of the women I interviewed, once they married and after having children, the dynamic of the relationship changed as men resumed their public life without them.

Previous research on foreign women married to Greek men and living in Greek villages found that these women felt marginalized, as they were rarely included in village activities coordinated by local Greek village women (Dubisch 1993). For example, they were not invited to the gendered socializing of ethnic Greek women that often occurred in homes, such as morning or afternoon coffee. Nathalie, a French woman in her forties who had moved to Eresos with her young son, explained: "In the beginning it was difficult; they saw me as here to catch a man, no freedom to meet people. All is sexualized, if you drink a whiskey with a man it means you want to fuck him. In Greek society a woman meeting a man for a social drink is perceived as a sexual rendezvous." She offered another example: "When a friend of mine, a local Greek man, came to my house [in the upper village], instead of parking his car in my driveway, he parked away from my home. When I asked him, he said it was to not create any talk or problem in the community. Of course, I said that being secretive is calling attention, but I was sure my friend had no sexual interest." What Nathalie's commentary solidifies is that the persistence of spatial restrictions still dictates when and where people can meet in mixed-gendered company even in present-day Lesvos. She compared the current context in Greece to France, arguing that there is a twenty or thirty year lag in Greece regarding social norms on how men and women socialize. Although younger unmarried Greeks do socialize in mixed-gender company, such as in cafeterias and bars, on weekend evenings, once women are married or move beyond their twenties, they seem generally to not socialize publicly without family members.

Northern European women married to Greek men who were living in Eresos employed various strategies for integrating into village life and public sociality. For example, Marisa—a Northern European woman who

spoke excellent Greek using the local dialect—scrupulously subscribed to local habits of gender and space. She did not publicly socialize at bars, restaurants, or cafés with friends. Yet Marisa was out every summer evening when shops reopened following the afternoon siesta, managing her in-laws' seasonal tourist shop. In between ringing up customers, I often saw her chatting with tourists or European friends at chairs and a table set outside the store. It was because she was engaged in work that Marissa's public presence was consistent with the spatial practice of gender.

Marissa explained that she and her spouse participated in traditional gender norms, as neither saw it as much of a hurdle and it kept them in a comfortable social standing in the village. Yet unlike some of the other European women I spoke with, who had no family business in the agora to manage, Marissa had an opportunity to witness and partake in the liveliness of the seaside village without stigma. The Austrian woman—noted earlier for dining with her family while I was dining with my Frenchwoman acquaintance—also sturdily upheld public gender codes, but she was rarely seen in public except on outings with her family. Whether they resented or adopted them, Northern European women were wittingly aware of the conventions of gender and public socializing in Greece. Once they married into the village or community, foreign women could not easily transgress spatial codes, as a woman tourist might, because it would reflect poorly on their in-laws. However, even when they followed social codes, it is unlikely that these foreign women would be invited to coffee socials by local Greek women, leading at times to loneliness (Dubisch 1993; Cowan 1991).

Women in Ancient Space

The assumed spatial designation of Greek women to the household is an old belief. A number of resources sum up the spatial ideology of women in ancient Greece (White et al. 1995, 8): "Custom dictates that a Greek woman limit her time outside the house to visiting with her nearest female neighbors. Exceptions to this rigid social convention were weddings, funerals, and state religious festivals in which women were expected to play prominent public roles." Significantly, this reflection on the spatial practice of ancient Greece echoes my own observations of social life in contemporary Lesvian villages and the gendered space articulated by anthropologists. Yet throughout villages in Lesvos and Greece, women are also readily visible working in family enterprises, government offices, and carrying out tasks. In her recent ethnography on gender and economic development in rural Crete, Gabriella Lazaridis (2016) argues that women's income-earning activities are regularly overlooked in government record keeping, as it is rarely appreciated as economic activity.

Academically, much examination has been made of the public sphere of Greek society and men's participation in it, but the role of households has received distinctly less attention (Foxhall 1989, 1994). Lazaridis (2016) argues that scholarship on Greece, often blinded by Northern heteropatriarchal norms in which men are retained as head of household, has been unable to address how the gendered public and private spheres have interrelated throughout Greek history. Without appreciating the economic role of Greek women historically, and how women-led households participated in the ancient agora, false assumptions persist into the present-day.

In the 1990s, there seemed to be a heightened interest in gender, sexuality, and laws governing morality in ancient Greece by classicists and historians (see Roy 1997; Foxhall and Lewis 1996; Cohen 1991). Feminist reviews of historical records and artifacts drew attention to the political, social, and economic role of the household in ancient Greece and how women commanded it (Katz 2000; Foxhall 1994). According to archaeologist and historian Lin Foxhall (1994, 136), in Classical Greece of the fourth and fifth century BC women's household duties consisted of "much more than doing housework, since the family's economic enterprises (including factory and farms) were conceptually contained within the household—no notion of independent, corporate, economic institutions existed." The position that women managed household budgets in Classical Greece is echoed in the epigraph to this chapter drawn from Aristophanes's play *Lysistrata*.

Foxhall (1989, 1994) further explains that households were not considered secondary to the public sphere in which men partook in ancient Greece, but were, rather, the foundation by which men engaged in political participation. Men served as representatives of their households, based on the economic resources that were overseen by women. Because of the relative youth of women compared to the men they married, Foxhall (1994) asserts that women in ancient Greece provided cross-generational expertise for the management of household enterprises. The association of the household with entrepreneurial activity in Greece has existed throughout its history and manifests currently in the family businesses on the agora.

Figure 5.1. Woman in the window/courtesy of Tzeli Hadjidimitriou. This photo was taken in one of the rural villages of Lesvos. I include it because it implies the gendering of space in Greece and to tease Virginia Woolf's slighting of Greek women post–Ottoman Empire. Evidence demonstrates that historically Greek women are economically active in household affairs, despite not visibly socializing on the plateia.

In her tour of Greece in the early 1900s Virginia Woolf (1906) made this observation: "I have seen no native women; & indeed you see very few women. The streets are crowded with men drinking & smoking in the open air . . . but the women keep within. You generally see them leading children, or looking from an upper window, where, presumably, they work." Her evaluation, like those of other casual travelers across Greece, is based on cultural codes and biases that assume that the lack of public socializing of ethnic Greek women implies a lack of social and economic engagement. Yet women have been involved in economic activities historically, although public socializing has remained gendered over the eras.

During the ascendance of Christianity in the Byzantine period (or the Eastern Roman Empire), women remained connected to the private sphere of the household, but also played a managerial role in family enterprises, as the Byzantine household was the chief economic unit. A professor of Byzantine art, Ioli Kalavrezou (2003), addresses the scholarly misunderstandings of women's public presence and the contradiction between the ideology and practicality of gendered spatiality in Byzantine Greece. Kalavrezou (2003), who explores women's roles through collected artifacts of the era, explains: "The ideal was that women should stay at home and not leave the house. But for the vast majority of women, this was impractical. Women had to go out, whether to draw water, to work the fields, or engage in other economic activities. Indeed, our sources from the fourth century onwards make it clear that women had a considerable life outside the house. Their participation not only in agricultural labor but in trade has been well attested." Although focused on Byzantine urban centers, Kalavrezou's (2003) summary of how women participated in the agora suggests that the public and private spheres were rather integrated due to women's economic activity. She (2003) elaborates:

> The presence of women in trade and business is unexpectedly strong, considering the powerful stereotype of the housebound woman. . . . In the fourteenth century our sources proliferate. We find women who owned shops in Constantinople and women who managed them. Women invested in business and trade, mostly with family members. Indeed, the shops were small, family-run businesses, and the family network was important in all economic activities. In that sense, women's roles in the economy lay between the public and the private sphere.

Kalavrezou's (2003) assessment provides useful insight for a rhythmanalysis of enterprise and gender in contemporary Greek villages. While women in Greek society are identified with the private sphere of the household, their duties and responsibilities historically included economic control and public engagement.

Women in Greece have been integral in securing the economic welfare of families, including the managing and running of businesses and enterprises. Yet they have been generally absent from the public *socializing*, going out independently, sitting for a cup of coffee or casually having drinks with a group of friends without a special occasion. Greek women's exclusion from public sociality is what materializes the ideology of the housebound Greek woman, but the economic well-being of many Greek families depends on women's activities.

Coffeehouse Masculinity

Evthymios Papataxiarchis, who edited the volume *Contested Identities: Gender and Kinship in Modern Greece* (1991) with sociologist Peter

Figure 5.2. Parea/courtesy of Tzeli Hadjidimitriou. This photo exquisitely portrays the affection and public socializing of men across Greek islands at kafenions. Greek anthropologist Evthymios Papataxiarchis (1991, 21) has described the intimate pairings of men as "friendships of the heart."

Loizos, describes the modern Greek coffeehouse as "a place of refuge for men from women dominated households." In Michael Herzfeld's (1985) study of the social worlds of Cretan shepherds, he also details the accomplishment of masculinity within the coffeehouses. In the kafenion, with tables extending from their inner sanctum to the walkways surrounding it, Greek men have created a world based on "emotional friendship" that sits outside economic and political strategic alliances. The ubiquity of the kafenion in villages throughout Greek islands, the rural mainland, and city centers cannot be overestimated. In these entities the "normative equality among men" that is considered to capture Mediterranean societies is created through public sociability and gathering (Papataxiarchis 1991, 151).

The gendering of the Greek public sphere and its expression of masculinity was intensely investigated by these anthropologists. Panayotis Panopoulos (1999) also considers the political role of the Greek coffeehouse. Referring to the first study of Greek coffeehouse culture by John Photiades (1965), Panopoulos (1999) explains that the men sharing "coffee and spirits" often sort out the political life of the village in their gestures and discussions to deter more volatile political interactions from developing.

According to Papataxiarchis (1991), men's relationships at the coffeehouse are founded on "friendship . . . firmly insulated from the morally suspect practices of economic and political exchange." Unlike research in other nations that often finds friendship (among men) as instrumental in purpose, Papataxiarchis (1991, 158) argues that in the Greek context they are based on "the commensal code of kerasma." In a recent opinion piece in the *New York Times* on the deterioration of US masculinity, Brooks (2017) refers to the virtues of ancient Greek masculinity: "Braying after money was the opposite of manliness. For the [ancient] Greeks, that was just avariciousness, an activity that shrunk you down into a people-pleasing marketer or hollowed you out because you pursued hollow things." The open pursuit of wealth, a lauded trait under neoliberalism, is stunted in some Greek versions of masculinity. Openly seeking gain in sociality and politics for the purpose of advancing oneself was a loathsome trait in ancient Greece and in the anthropological studies of modern Aegean masculinity. Rooted in the social construction of Greek masculinity, the obvious and instrumental pursuit of monetary gain as undignified is a central rhythm permitting conditions for convivial economics to flourish in Greece.

Κέρασμα—described earlier as a gift or a treat given to customers, friends, family, or strangers—also refers to the reciprocity that forms the basis of a deepening friendship between two men (Papataxiarchis 1991). By gifting drinks and exchanging small favors, two men become closer. Eventually the pair is considered to be in company of each other or παρέα (paréa)—a Greek term with wide references, such as a companion at a single event, a temporary companion, or a long-held friendship such as men's coffeehouse pairing.* Papataxiarchis (1991, 21) explains that, "as a married couple in their home," these tightly connected emotional partners occupy the same table in the kafenion with regularity and assume a "friendship of the heart." The food and drink businesses in the agora provide a "home" for the homosocial gatherings of men in Greek villages.

The gathering places throughout Lesvos's villages and much of Greece emphasize egalitarian exchanges, sociality, care, gifting, assistance, and the pleasure of conversation and keeping company as an effectual use of time. These sorts of social rhythms break not only with Northern assumptions of masculinity but also with neoliberalism, where "lived time loses its form and social interest, with the exception that it is of time spent working" (Lefebvre 1991, 95–96). Traditional Mediterranean coffeehouses, founded in the Ottoman Empire, were inseparable from hospitality and socialization just as they were "a preeminently masculinized space" (Quataert 2005, 160). By creating the possibility of the public expression of convivial gathering outside the confines of religion and the household (Karababa and Ger 2010; Panopoulos 2001), the kafenions exploited market forms to produce a social sphere independent of households.

The coffeehouses that spread to Greece from Arab and Ottoman social worlds shaped the food and drink venues in modern Greece (Quataert 2005; Panopoulos 1999). As the first enterprises to serve coffee, spirits, and petite bites in the small villages across Greek islands, the kafenions established a basis for convivial economics prioritizing sociability over economic prowess.

Kamaki: Local Men and Foreign Women

The original proprietors of kafenions financially depended upon catering to the local population of men. They had not imagined the development

---

*παρέα (paréa) n/f. company, companionship party, clique, set comrade, mate.

of a summer tourism that would swell with each season. The organic sociality embedded in Greek islands, a sense of geographic isolation, idyllic scenery, and mythology merged to create a paradisiacal Greek island setting for the European traveler seeking escape and alterity. Neither the coffeeshop owners, the village communities, nor the Greek state could have predicted the new social worlds that rapidly growing tourism would bring to traditional island life.

The freeing social landscape of Greece—the public social life governed by κέφι and κέρασμα—started to attract bohemian tourists and travelers in the 1970s, who had time to spare, and sit at tables with drinks, alongside their Greek hosts, who often expressed φιλοξενία in their interactions with strangers. In essence, the ethno-homosocial dominance of the island village square was interrupted by Northern European travelers, who were generally welcomed rather than considered intruders. The original sociality of the kafenion, which was to supply a location for men to gather outside the confines of women-controlled households, was being undone, at least in the summer months. Northern European women tourists, perhaps, had the largest impact on patterns of gendered public sociality in the Greek islands, particularly foreign women visitors without families, who, traveling on their own or with friends in the summer, gathered at coffeeshops, bars, and tavernas. They established a new dynamism of gender and sexuality on Greek islands beginning in the early 1980s. Most of the foreign women I interviewed who had partnered with ethnic Greek men first arrived as summertime tourists.

As previously stated, the φιλοξενία extended to ξένοι generally entails no obligation for tourists and guests to comply with local cultural norms, including that they are not reprimanded for inattention to the gendered spatial codes of the plateia or village square. Culturally, though, if ethnic Greek women were found socializing outside their households and at coffeehouse or bars, they were stigmatized. "Of the road" or "του δρόμο" has been used to refer to women who did not conform to the spatial traditions of Greek womanhood (Cowan 1991). The negative coding of women's presence in public spaces is a remnant of the honor and shame principles identified by numerous anthropologists as characterizing Mediterranean societies (Lazaridis 2016; Dubisch 1993; Loizos and Papataxiarchis 1991; Cowan 1991; Herzfeld 1985). Women's overt sexuality was considered to reflect negatively on the Greek household. The limited presence of women gathering in dining venues, the warning I received about meeting men for interviews on the public square, and the pestering I received for dining on a winter evening with a woman companion, all affirm the continued existence of the gendered and sexualized spatial countenance in Greek island villages.

As Northern European women tourists started to arrive in Greek island villages in greater numbers, a relational dynamic between Greek men and foreign women arose. This dynamic became widely known as καμάκι (kamaki), which literally translates to a harpoon used for spearfishing.* Καμάκι entered the Greek lexicon as a reference to the homosocial competition of prowess, cunning, and trickery that characterized mostly island men's sexual pursuits of foreign women from the late 1970s through the early 1990s (Zinovieff 1991; Koufopoulou 2010).** Island men would engage in the process of "spearing" a foreign woman over a few days in hopes that it would culminate with one's "prey" partaking in consensual sex (Zinovieff 1991; Koufopoulou 2010). Based on her anthropological research on the phenomenon during the mid-eighties, Sofka Zinovieff (1991, 203), sums καμάκι as

> a system of male competition, whereby men without material and social status establish other grounds for prestige. Second, the act of kamaki highlights the sense of antagonism that many Greeks have toward "Europe" or the West. Kamakia may see themselves as belonging to a poorer, inferior society, and by lying to, tricking, and sexually conquering foreign tourist women from the supposedly superior societies, they have some revenge. The third theme is the desire of many kamakia to change their lives, to escape, or to take material wealth or prestige from the West.

Although καμάκι is often described as a sort of sport or game men would play, Zinovieff (1991) argues that it reveals the larger struggle of nation, gender, sexuality, and identity in which they are engaged. Her analysis affirms the systemized social and economic inequities between Greeks and Northern Europeans, and even more so between Greek islanders

---

*καμάκι (kamáki), n/n. harpoon, fish-spear, gigolo.

**The use of kamáki widened and also implies something like a "hustle." For example, the term can be used in a friendly manner, a customer might use it to question a shopkeeper's prices, or a friend presenting a startling bit of information might be met with the response "Με κάνεις καμάκι?" or "Are you kidding or hustling (spearing) me?" It also can be used as a less amiable challenge when someone feels they are being taken advantage of.

and Northern European tourists, and its recognition by both parties. Zinovieff's use of the phrase "the West" again affirms the separate spheres of which Greece and Europe are conceived and the appropriation of ancient Greece as the basis of Europe and not modern Greece.

Καμάκι became a national issue for Greece in the 1980s. Government officials and Greek newspapers expressed concerns that island cultural norms were deteriorating, as secluded island villages were considered center stage for lascivious pursuits. While Greek island men chased relations with foreign women tourists, Northern European women also traveled to Greek islands seeking affairs with Greek men. Zinovieff (1991, 215) assesses the social power between the island men and foreign women tourists: "It is the woman who leaves the man and returns to her regular life, whereas the kamaki must wait for the next woman to appear, or the last one to invite him to stay. It is the woman who controls the fundamental conditions (arriving, leaving, accepting or refusing the advances of the kamaki), and thus the kamaki ideology of control and male domination can only really be sexual, and is frequently based more on fantasy than reality." For Zinovieff (1991), national and economic status intersect with gender and sexuality, ultimately placing Greek men in a subordinate position, despite their competition to "spear" a foreign tourist. Alongside this, these Northern European women may have been engaging in sex tourism (Taylor 2006), an increasingly global trend by Global North women.

The geographic separation from their continental realities likely imbues tourists with a sense of freedom that many interview participants referred to as experiencing in Lesvos. Islands often present an escape from continental realities because they appear as safe and private, contained environments—a separated physical realm in which privileged tourists feel that they can depart from their social norms. The social and economic privilege of many tourists visiting islands also empowers them to ignore or neglect the mores of local cultures. Armed with an imperial gaze, many Northern tourists are able to discount the rituals of other societies as secondary, and it seems sometimes their own social norms have little bearing on their actions while on vacation.

Island Queer

Islands, provisioning subaltern space, are marginal to continental-centric perspectives. They can offer escape from gender and sexuality constructs not only to privileged women travelers (Kolocotroni and Mitsi 2008) but also to lesbian and gay or queer tourists (Newton 2014). The punitive laws and regulation against non-heterosexual expressions in Northern Europe, particularly through the 1980s, and the hostility toward gays and lesbians in these nations, fueled lesbian and gay tourism to Greek islands and elsewhere in the Mediterranean where reprieve was available. As the lesbian and gay rights movement gained strength in Europe, gay or lesbian tourist zones provided alternative social outlets and enterprises where lesbians and gays could vacation, recouping from activism or eluding the sometimes violent imposition of heteronormativity in their home societies.

Anthropologist and queer theorist Mark Graham (2002) describes how lesbian and gay tourist locations provided an escape from heterosexist social norms. Graham (2002, 19) and others (Boone 2001) argue that gay men historically have traveled to more freely express their sexuality in less repressive and anonymous environments. Anthropologist Esther Newton (2014), who pioneered a lesbian, gay, and queer anthropology, authored a historical ethnography on the development of Cherry Grove, New York a lesbian and gay summer tourist enclave on Fire Island since the 1930s. In her volume, Newton (2014) describes the long distance and ferries required to travel to Fire Island from New York City. She remarks on the freedom Fire Island has offered to the metropolitan New York's lesbian, gay, and queer community, affirming the safety and social escape islands geographies can supply.

Greek islands also supported a liberation from the confines of what had been a repressive homophobic environment in Northern Europe, similar to what Newton (2014) describes Fire Island as delivering to urban New Yorkers. Not only because it is an island but also because, in Greece, homoeroticism is etched into Greeks' sociohistorical memory due to its its ancient past. Combined with the general φιλοξενία granted to strangers, giving visitors the space to engage and act in ways that might not be customary to mainstream Greek society by virtue of their foreignness, Northern European lesbians and gays had found a place of respite.

The homoerotic relationship between ancient Greek philosophers and their pupils also afforded many gay Northern European men to develop an affinity for Greece. Graham (2002) argues that many of these men read the classical texts in the original Latin or Greek, giving them "access to a world of homoeroticism that had often been suppressed in translation." Gay men traveled to the Mediterranean because it offered a gay or alternative space where they could seek sexual liaisons, dodging both stigma and penalization (Waitt and Markwell 2006; Graham 2002). Especially through the last half of the nineteenth century the homoeroticism of classical Greece conferred legitimacy to the sexual expression of gay men.

Renée Vivien, a British poet and openly lesbian, and Natalie Clifford Barney, a US heiress, were similarly inspired to travel to a Greek isle by ancient texts. They are the first two Northern European lesbians documented to voyage to Lesvos in the early 1900s. Vivien was prominent among Paris's artistic and bohemian set during the Belle Epoque, the period in Europe prior to World War I. She wrote the first French translation of Sappho's poetry, which is credited with correcting the heterosexist revisionism that tainted the first translations of Sappho's fragments, which were in English. The association of Lesvos with lesbian travel progressed from literary interests to modes of contemporary tourism over the century. The attraction, as Graham (2002, 37) argues, is at least in part due to the homosexual imaginary of Greek islands: "Homosexual tourism sought an aesthetic whole in the Mediterranean by searching for what was missing from the northern European homelands."

The association of Greece with homosexual expression is not only articulated in ancient texts, but is a formative aspect of Greece's tourist landscape. Gay vacation spaces developed in the Greek islands, becoming a haven where gay and lesbian tourists and semipermanent residents would return annually. Returning almost yearly at the same time of year enabled lesbian and gay tourists to Greece to develop a network of holiday friends that could be "out" together, away from their usual social worlds in which they might remain closeted (Cox 2002). The seasonal rhythm of Mediterranean weather, with days of continuous sunshine, almost guaranteeing a holiday that won't be interfered with by foul weather, facilitates seasonal conviviality for all summer travelers to the Greek islands.

Mykonos, one of the Cycladic islands, preceded the development of gay vacation spots in Europe by decades, and is now recognized for its cosmopolitanism and high-end tourism. Through ethnographic research, Bousiou (2011) follows a group of gay men who re-created livelihoods each summer season in Mykonos for over thirty years. Her documentation of gay men sojourners to Mykonos shows similarities to the lesbians who also have been returning to Skala Eresos for decades. Bousiou (2011) refers to the gay men as "nomads," highlighting their continual return and departures from their collective social lives in Mykonos. What she does not emphasize, which is the heart of this book, is the centrality of businesses that are convivial for gay travelers and often established by gay identified proprietors, which is an essential part of making a gay tourist enclave.

Cox (2002) suggests that gay tourist sites were essential for cultivating lesbian and gay social worlds that could not arise in repressive home environments. In contrast, Graham, in the same volume, *Gay Tourism: Culture, Identity, and Sex* (2002, 21), contends that gay tourism leaves "the homophobia of the home country intact" and that the "subversive potential is blunted" because it is separated from the everyday world so that gay holidaymaking was escapist. These analyses remain a standing debate on gay tourism (Fimiani 2017; Newton 2014). However, little research has been pursued on the communities where gay, lesbian, or queer tourist enclaves may arise. These local and place based residents often play a substantial role in allowing, embracing, or thwarting and suspending gay and lesbian enclaves and enterprises (Hughes, Monterrubio, and Miller 2010; Faiman-Silva 2009).

Theorists have argued that gay tourist sites "chip away at the heteronormative regime" in the places they appear (Cantú 2002; Graham 2002). Graham (2002, 39) argues: "The criss-crossing of place by tourists, homosexual, gay, and queer, who are out to make sense of the world (and have fun in it) knits together previously separate places and trails after signifiers of same-sex eroticism that leave their mark in even the most hetero-normative of sites." Graham's passage gives limited regard to the social and economic privilege of gay and lesbian tourists, to Northern entitlement, or to the local social context. For example, "signifiers of same sex eroticism" were already available in Greece and supported the expansion of gay and lesbian Mediterranean tourism. Postcolonial readings of lesbian, gay, and queer travel have advanced explorations of sexualities in a global landscape and challenged Global North privilege in queer analyses (Browne and Ferreira 2016; Kapur 2010; Boellstorff 2005; Puar 2002). Kapur (2010) uses the term "sexual subaltern" to capture the sexual subjectivities in postcolonial contexts that do not adopt or identify with Global North categories of lesbian and gay. Linking global power relations with a queer perspective supports a queer materialism standpoint (Kapur 2010; Cantú 2002; Spurlin 2001) and is an important nexus for understanding how social marginalization in one national context does not absolve privileges attained in another. Geographers Kath Browne and Eduarda Ferreira (2016) also highlight the privileging of urban over rural, or Global North rather than Global South, as less homophobic and freer when a more thorough analysis is warranted. Almost two decades ago, English professor William Spurlin (2001, 185) called for greater engagement between queer and postcolonial scholarship:

> In its analyses of marginalization and subaltern experience, its emphasis on national identities and borders, and its attention to race, gender, and class, postcolonial studies have seriously neglected the ways in which heterosexism and homophobia have also shaped the world of hegemonic power. A parallel problem is that queer studies . . . have shown little interest in the cross-cultural variations of the expression and representation of same-sex desire; homosexualities in non-Western societies are, at best, imagined or invented through the imperialist gaze of Euroamerican queer identity politics, appropriated through the economies of the West, or, at worst, altogether ignored.

Spurlin (2001) highlights the often white, privileged perspectives of lesbian, gay, and queer identified persons from the Global North and the challenge it presents to recognizing alternative sexual realities and constructs around the globe (Hawley 2001; Spurlin 2001; Cantú 2002; Boellstorff 2005; Browne and Ferreira 2015). Browne and Ferreira (2015) more recently have called for studies of queer spaces to apply an intersectional approach to tease out the simultaneity of privilege and bias. By also addressing how gender and sexuality inform the historical and social context of a place, studies of gay enclave tourism (Fimiani 2014; Waitt 2012; Bousiou 2011) will benefit from paying more attention to why some local settings or geographies may support or deter queer or lesbian and gay tourism more than others.

The regularity of homosociality across Greek island villages provisioned a situation in which lesbian and gay travelers could gather more easily. Groups of men gathering together publicly in Greek villages is common practice. Although Greek women primarily socialize privately, their public appearances occur as part of a homosocial gatherings or with a family. The freedom lesbians and other travelers identified experiencing in Greece is also tied to the carte blanche granted on the plateia. Policing, including strangers' gender or sexual identities, is inconsistent with the expressions of Greek masculinity that embodies the public domain. Constraints or requirements upon strangers would inhibit the verve of φιλοξενία on the village square shaped by a Greek masculinity (Cowan 1991; Papataxiarchis 1991). To patrol the behaviors of visitors in a public setting not only counters Greek reception of visitors but it would also emasculate the public sphere by requiring constraint. The gender coding of space in Greek villages relegates the enforcement of social codes or modification of behaviors to that of the family in the realm of the woman-led household and not to the duties of men. Greek public social forms produced fertile grounds for lesbian and gay tourism to advance in Greek islands.

Moreover, Greek laws regarding gay sexuality were historically more progressive than the laws of many Northern neighbors. In Greece same-sex relations between men were legalized or decriminalized in 1951, nearly two decades before the Northern European nations from which lesbians and gays traveled to summer in the Greek islands. In Germany, homosexual relations for men were decriminalized in 1968 (East) and 1969 (West). Through the 1990s, Germany's conservative party, the Christian Democratic Union, opposed gay rights advocacy. In England, legalization of same-sex relations occurred in 1967, and in Scotland in 1981. In the early decades of the lesbian and gay rights movement, homophobic violence erupted in Northern Europe in ways that did not occur in Greece (European Union Agency for Fundamental Rights 2013; Richardson 2002; Gage 1979). Despite the decriminalization of gay sex by the Sexual Offence Act of 1967 in the UK, the parameters of privacy it set forth increased patrolling of gay sexuality and landed thousands of men in prison. In England a vehement attack on its gay community advanced under Thatcherism and during the AIDS crisis. The year 1988 saw the passage of antigay legislation, and the 1990s brought several high-profile brutal killings of gay men in England. This created an anxious and hostile environment for Britain's gay and lesbian community, which responded with activism (Richardson 2002). The Greek islands served as a refuge for lesbian and gay persons arriving from these more oppressive legal and social environments.

Because lesbian and gay migration has tended to be in the direction of rural to urban regions, lesbian geography (Nash 2015) had focused on the lives and communities of lesbians in cityscapes. The relocation of lesbians to largely rural and remote areas had remained rather under-explored in comparison to the study of urban gay lives (Blidon 2015;

Browne and Ferreira 2015). Yet Browne and Ferreira (2015, 2) note that, for lesbian and gay persons, "rural lives can be havens of safety and where alternative lives can be planned and lived." Lesbians especially sought rural and isolated spaces in which to create separatist communities, such as was formed in Skala Eresos, in rejection of heteropatriarchy and urban consumerism (Gorman-Murray, Pini, and Bryan 2013; Browne 2011; Valentine 2000). This volume contributes to considerations of how island geographies specifically are spaces that provide a counter to the heterosexual grid of continents (King 2016; Lattas 2014; Kantza 2002).

Gender and sexuality research on rural Greek islands captures the generally noncommittal attitude of Greeks toward same-sex relations even when engaged in by local villagers (Lazaridis 2016). Describing interviewees' reaction to two young village women in a relationship, Lazaridis (2016, 179) explains: "Despite the societal taboos related to this, such relationships in rural Greece are left alone, provided that they do not provoke the community." Lazaridis (2016) reports that villagers would explain "this is the way they are, what can we do" and that, in most cases, these relationships go unnoticed. Although Lazaridis (2016, 179) ultimately argues that women in the village involved in same-sex intimacies often marry under pressure, she also explains that their earlier homoerotic ties did not cause them danger and hostility. Lazaridis's (2016) research on sexuality and its cultural constructs in a rural island context indicates a less guarded environment around sexual expression that is consistent with my findings on Lesvos. In my interviews with lesbian tourists, most described experiencing the social context of Skala Eresos with ease. For example, a Swedish woman who identified as lesbian shared: "I can't wait to come back. No violence, peaceful, I can leave my computer and it doesn't get stolen. There is a confirmation of lesbianism. It's a unique lesbian community that is local." A lesbian-identified tourist from Australia shared the following: "I feel very comfortable as a lesbian, but not just that. In the way the Greeks are outside a lot. It is a bit like Perth, Mediterranean climate. People are outside, they eat outside, café dining. I like that it is a mixed community and comfortable." The articulation that lesbian tourism was an integrated part of the social dynamic in Skala was fairly consistent among local lesbian interviewees. In a short interview I conducted with a lesbian couple, one of the pair summed up their attraction to Skala Eresos: "We like that it is not so touristy like other places. That it is OK to be a lesbian here, and that it is not all lesbians." There were some who were more critical in their assessment of Skala's social world. A British lesbian states, "The lesbian community is separate from the Greek world. It's another world, there are no visible connections." Vassoula, a Greek lesbian from the Aegean, drawing from insights as a long-term resident of Lesvos with access to both Greek and lesbian communities, sums up the social situation this way: "Ten percent would like to put us on a big boat and have us go; this used to be 25 percent. Fifty percent tolerate us, they like the tourism because it brings money. Forty percent know us as persons." Although positive assessments by lesbian tourists prevailed, Vassoula's insights as an ethnic Greek accounts for local residents that remain ambiguous or hostile.

Legally, Greece's indefinite path to sexual rights has become increasingly regressive as other European nations improve and establish contractual rights for same-sex marriage. Lesbianism has remained absent in the Greek criminal code, which has not made direct reference to same-sex relationships between women. Across Europe, lesbians have experienced a similar legal invisibility. Several Greek lesbians highlighted this absence as reflecting a society unwilling to see them or unable to conceive of women "who love women." Despite the recognition of men's homosexuality as historically grounded, Sappho's legacy has not influenced Greek civil laws. With the momentum of a legal strategy and lesbian and gay advocacy, there was a recent push to update Greek laws regarding same-sex relationships. The Greek Orthodox Church and Greek conservative parties often have hampered these efforts (COWI 2009). In 2015, Greece legalized same-sex civil unions, providing formal legitimacy to same-sex relationships, although not marriage rights.

Presently, not the laws but the cordial reception of visitors keep Greek islands an attractive gay tourist destination. The Greek orientation toward foreigners as guests with no bearing on the local community extends sexual autonomy. Lesvos and Mykonos, but also other Mediterranean islands, maintain an organic alterity that reflects a negotiated, rather than regimented, approach to social diversity that accommodates the sexual expressions of guests and visitors. Greek islands that host gay and lesbian tourism also accommodated the development of microenterprises by gay and lesbian entrepreneurs. These examples of attritional economic alterity are ventures initiated by lesbians and gays departing mainstream economic lives that often serve their own subaltern communities.

QUEER, SUBALTERN, AND ECONOMIC

In their introduction to *The Queer Economics Reader*, Jacobsen and Zeller (2008, 2) argue for a queer economics "as the examination of and response to the effects of heteronormativity both on economic outcomes and on economics as a discipline." Queer theory's analytic focus has largely been discursive, giving limited attention to a queer material analysis (Cantú, Naples, and Vidal-Ortiz 2009; Klawitter 2008). In calling for a queer sociology, Seidman (1994), Valocchi (2005), Bernstein (2013), and others draw attention to the opportunities the discipline offers for advancing a queer material analysis.

Cantú, Naples, and Vidal-Ortiz's (2009) study of globalization and Mexican men's migration provides a queer material analysis that has implications for the migration of Northern EU lesbians to Lesvos. The authors demonstrate how perceptions of sexual practices are shaped by national context and migration policies and how men redefine and reinvent their sexuality when they emigrate. Economic opportunities interweave with sexual orientation and homophobic bias as they shape individual decisions to migrate permanently or seasonally. Cantú, Naples, and Vidal-Ortiz's (2009) call for a queer political economy that can account for "heteronormative assumptions" in analyses of economic processes.

As noted, though laws across the EU have been put into place to protect gay, lesbian, and queer-identified persons from labor market discrimination, this was not the case in the 1980s when gay and lesbian travel to Greece commenced (D'Emilio 2008). Experiences of marginalization and discrimination, both socially and economically, may incentivize persons to develop their own independent enterprises, even at a loss of earnings, as a strategy to evade bias and discriminatory behavior (Karides 2007). Local and small scale or alternative economic projects are often created by subaltern groups—women, lesbians and gays, indigenous people, immigrants, people of color—as a way to sustain and create community.

Lesbian entrepreneurialism has been given short shrift in the academic literature (Browne and Ferreira 2015; Valentine 1995). Urban sociologist Manuel Castells (1983), relying on gender stereotypes, assumed that business ownership of gay venues was dominated by gay men due to their inherent need for more territorial-based control, a trait he assumed was not held by women and therefore limited lesbian ownership. Lesbian geography responded by showing that lesbian enclaves do exist (Browne and Ferreira 2015; Rothenberg 1995; Valentine 1995) but were based in broader countercultural spaces that included alternative bookstores and cooperatives and were less visible than gay men enterprises. Given the gender difference in wealth and wages, lesbians may not have had the capital to initiate enterprises in Global North urban centers in the same ways as gay men.

Generally, because sexuality regimes shape economic practices (Bedford 2010; Lind 2010; Cantú, Naples, and Vidal-Ortiz 2009), those marginalized by heteronormativity have sought to establish alternative enterprises for sociality and collectivity. Although shifting norms around lesbians and gays have lessened the barriers between gay and straight "leisurescapes" (Browne and Bakshi 2011, 179), gay and lesbian establishments, enclaves, and tourist destinations in previous decades were essential for socializing and community building. Presently, as long as discrimination toward lesbian identities continues, the need for lesbian-specific commercial spaces remains (Courlouer 2013).

John D'Emilio (2008), a leader in gay and lesbian studies, provides a pertinent analysis of the formation of queer communities in relation to capitalist expansion that buttresses my arguments of a convivial economics. Along with others (Katz 2007), D'Emilio claims that gay identities developed with the expansion of capitalism due to the decline of the household in the Global North as the primary economic unit of production where family members were interdependent. As the capitalist mode of mass production eroded the material basis of "family life," it provided an avenue of economic survival that liberated persons with diverse sexual orientations from the confines of the heteronormative family (D'Emilio 2008). Parting from the economic and social constraints of one's biological household often meant a separation from familial intimacies and dependencies but also the initiation of group life for gays and lesbians. D'Emilio (2008, 191) explains: "Already excluded from families as most of us are, we have had to create, for our survival, networks of support that do not depend on the bonds of blood or the license of the state, but that are freely chosen and nurtured. The building of an 'affectionate community' must be as much a part of our political movement as are campaigns for civil rights."

D'Emilio's (2008) analysis is particularly relevant to Global North gay and lesbians and nations with restrictive and aggressive approaches to sexual diversity, and it highlights the necessity of creating places for community to support social activism. Yet the building of "affectionate community" is also economic. His analysis stops short of clarifying where and how communities have been created and sustained themselves and by what economic means. The advent of capitalism may have provided gays and lesbians in the Global North with opportunities to find economic security beyond the borders of the household, but the persistent homophobic bias in formal labor markets, the polity, and social venues throughout Europe and the US fomented the need for alternative establishments where gay and lesbian communities could congregate.

Public community centers generally were increasing in availability for lesbian and gay forums through the 1980s and early 1990s. Nongovernmental or nonprofit organizations, also examples of alternative economics, were enormously important in providing space and support for lesbian and gay identified community members through the AIDS crisis. Yet in many instances it was the development of microenterprises guided by the interest in offering spaces of collective sociality and fun that offered opportunities for affectionate communities of gays and lesbians to develop. It was the private sphere of gay bars, cafés, and nightclubs that offered safe sites, even as they were forced to contend with hazards from law enforcement and local publics regarding lesbian and gay rights. It is no coincidence that the gay liberation movement was sparked by gay and trans protesters of police raids at the Stonewall Inn who were protecting their right to socializing and merrymaking in New York in the 1960s.

Offering escape from the urban frontlines of resistance, gay and lesbian tourist enclaves composed of multiple social venues—hotels, café, restaurants, clubs—developed a network of enterprises that created a safe and convivial web for extended retreat. In Lesvos, the geographical separation and the organic conviviality of the plateia set a context in which lesbians could establish enterprises that more or less merged with the local economic expressions of hospitality. From the homosocial belonging found in Greek coffeeshops and the φιλοξενία in the agora evolved the lesbian enclave in Skala Eresos.

In a contribution to *The Queer Economics: A Reader*, Allen (2008) further articulates sexualized patterns of economy, but spotlights heteronormative patriarchy and offers "lesbian economics" as an alternative. In a starkly lucid description of patriarchal production and economic domination, Allen (2008, 163) explains: "The wheel of patriarchal economics, in which every fulfillment is connected to a loss, continues to turn against women. . . . Work in the patriarchal economy requires so much from us that a lesbian economics often slips by. We may take as inevitable the loss of time, creativity, and female lives in patriarchy—or these may be insistently present, evoking our intense anger at a situation we find impossible to change."

Allen (2008) sums up the inherent losses fixed in an economic regime dependent on heteronormative capitalist patriarchy, which she describes as malevolent for many workers, but particularly women. Allen's (2008) evaluation of mainstream capitalist production echoes Maria Mies's (1986) assessment of patriarchy and accumulation. Mies (1986) argues that, while Northern women are constructed as incessant but unsatisfied consumers, Southern women may be cruelly exploited as workers in the production of the items to be purchased. Allen (2008) articulates a historical practice of aggregating wealth that relies on the subordination and objectification of women and is premised on constraining sexualities.

Allen's (2008) lesbian critique objects to incorporating women into the dominant system regardless of equality policies and attempts of integration—full inclusion will always be the carrot at the end of the stick. The dominant economy depletes women's abilities and opportunities to construct alternative livelihoods, leading to "life exhaustion" and the inability "to develop the tools with which we can, by choice, shape our lives" (Allen 2008, 168). Allen (2008, 168) argues that "if we are to live in an economy in which we can be free, we must disband the heterosexual grid." Allen's (2008, 161) call for a lesbian economics resonates with a range of alternative economic perspectives:

> Material necessity does not require engagement in activity that is repetitive and unfree. Unlike a patriarchal economy, a lesbian economy does not demand that we passively consume it, reproduce it, and leave no trace of ourselves. A lesbian economics is the creation of an economy in which we can claim our individualities, an economy in which we are no longer women. . . . the real possibility of claiming our survival by steadily working out new patterns of economic explanation and effecting economic change.

Allen's (2008) appeal mirrors Illich's (1973) tools of conviviality, but also implies the influence of marginal positionality for the unfolding of an alternative economics. Articulating both the kinds of oppression women experience under dominant economic forms and the challenges women face to withdraw from patriarchal economics, Allen (2008) conceives of a lesbian economics as an alternative but supplies no example of lesbian economics or where it might develop, though Skala Eresos may serve as one.

The queer analytic deconstructs discursive frames that normalize and marginalize expressions of gender and sexualities by hinging them on the correctness of heteronormative patriarchy. The potential of queer materialism is an avenue for bridging economic analyses with sexuality and gender as shifting constructs that accounts for "an integrated concern with place, history, and the social" (Cantú, Naples, and Vidal-Ortiz 2009, 36). Exploring alternative economics with a queer materialist paradigm further elucidates the subaltern involvement in the creation of enterprises that counter both a neoliberal and hetero-patriarchal economics.

Synopsis: Gendered Alternatives and Sexualized Economies

The alternative economics expressed in Lesvos illustrates aspects of Allen's (2008) lesbian economic framework. Those marginalized in the mainstream economy are more likely to create enterprises based on principles of economic conviviality that reject the self-interest at capitalism's core. Greece and its islands offer a subaltern space where neoliberal economics has neither completely zapped the energies of women who work and manage their enterprises nor stumped creative and alternative economic avenues. Instead, Greek islands have attracted those seeking reprieve from bias and oppressive economic demands. This does not mean that poverty and economic insecurity are not experienced on the islands, especially with recent economic crises, but rather that organic economic conviviality distinguishes how this duress is countered in Greece.

The currents of gender and sexuality that run through Greek island villages—the paradox of women and the public sphere, masculinity constructed via public and homosocial displays of generosity and sociality, both shaped and reshaped by tourism—converge as a rhythm of Greek social life. Immediately apparent in the villages throughout Lesvos is the pattern of gender segregation. Daphne Spain (1992), a sociologist who studies the relationship between the built environment and gender, long ago challenged assumptions that gendered segregation is monolithically disempowering to women. For instance, by virtue of having their own places away from the "male" gaze, women might have opportunities for more open engagements with one another. The household has largely provided this space for women in Greek rural villages, one in which outsiders and strangers to the village generally do not have access and which women control.

In Greek island villages, gender segregation persists but the bound-aries—materially and ideologically—have been historically permeable in order for women to complete their gendered work. Village women's access to the public sphere has been through economic and religious concerns, or through family affairs. Greek island men, a marginalized group themselves, largely retain the sphere of public sociality with the first venues established for their conviviality.

The rise of sun and fun tourism in the 1980s to the Greek islands was superimposed on the public social culture of Greek island villages, simultaneously mimicking its patterns of sociality and transforming it. The impact of second wave feminism, which resulted in women's freer expression of sexuality in Northern Europe, merged with the increasing affordability of international travel. Many European women began jour-neying independently of their families and men peers, and the Greek islands yielded a distinctly inexpensive and attractive location for them, fulfilling both the sense of escape and security sought by Northern tourists. The Greeks were both exotic and in close enough proximity. And, for some Northern women, Greek men represented an opportunity for sexual adventures hidden and separate from their mundane lives. The 1980s also gave rise to lesbian and gay social movements in Northern Europe and increased gay and lesbian travel to the Greek islands. For a number of Northern lesbian and gay travelers, life on the Greek islands became a permanent or seasonal oasis where they could establish bars, restaurants, and accommodations, creating the basis of a convivial economy to serve gay and lesbian travelers. The social sphere in Greek village squares that they entered, open and almost completely outdoors, is profoundly shaped by food and drink enterprises and the socializing that occurs in them. They are the places in which convivial economics are grounded. It is in within this sphere that Northern European visitors are hosted munificently in the summertime glory of Lesvos. It is the season that fruits and vegetables ripen in the Eresos valley and Aegean Sea calms for fishers to land their catch.

CHAPTER SIX

Island Food Systems

Lessons for the Continent

There are about 150 million olive trees in the country, either in systematic orchards or scattered across the country. Lower agricultural productivity in Greece, compared to other EU Member States, is correlated to the smaller average-size of holdings. The economies of scale offered by modern farming practices have limited impact on the small plots of land typically used in Greece.

—Export.gov, "Helping US Companies Export" (2018)

The cooking of the Mediterranean shores, endowed with all the natural resources, the colour and flavor of the South, is a blend of tradition and brilliant improvisation. . . . It is honest cooking too; none of the sham Grand Cuisine of the International Palace Hotel.

—Elizabeth David (1958, xv)

Much of the organic and attritional forms of economic conviviality in Lesvos revolve around preparing and provisioning food. Food—the making and eating of it—when conducted communally and combined with stimulants such as coffee and alcohol provides a strong basis for conviviality, as it may help create a place where future possibilities can be mulled over and constructed (Andrews 2020; Harvey

2000).* The significance of the coffeehouses that Habermas (1991) embraced as the primary location in the development of communicative action, critical reflection on life and society, is echoed in the socializing evident in Greek island microeconomies and the lesbian enterprises and women's cooperatives that entered the public sphere.

The cooperatives and the village of Skala Eresos yield space for groups who had been historically marginalized. The lesbian businesses, alongside the traditional Greek tavernas and tourist businesses and restaurants, all abound with conversation and shared discussion over politics, arts, or island history, sites to be seen, and local gossip. The women's cooperatives create an avenue for village women to legitimately participate in the agora by gathering socially, via their enterprises, and engaging in a public social life independent of their families.

These enterprises rely substantially on the local food system of Lesvos, which they also help to expand through the fare that they sell. Though the displacement of subsistence agriculture with commodity crops has occurred across the world, local food systems continue to play a critical role on Greek islands including in relation to tourism. This chapter considers how island agriculture, where food sources have been geographically delimited for centuries, may inform current approaches to local and alternative food systems that has centered on Northern, continental, and urban spaces.

Lesvos maintains a rich agriculture based in its geographical diversity and distinct differences between its eastern and western terrains. The island, with wine that was coveted in ancient times and olive and fig groves that have fed multiple generations, has sustained residents and visitors with a varied and tasteful diet for millenniums. The convivial

---

*Based on his recently completed dissertation, Michael Andrews (2020) argues that the informal associations and creative exchanges that can occur in bars and taverns lead to inventiveness as measured by patents. Focusing on the US prohibition of alcohol (1920–1933), he demonstrates that fewer patents were issued for several years after prohibition went into effect. Women were not granted access to "saloons," so Andrews also compares patents issued by gender in the post-prohibition years. He finds that women and men were granted a similar amount of patents during this period. The current pandemic, with closed or unfrequented bars, provides him a future case study (Vanek and Mayyasi 2020). Andrews manuscript, "Bar Talk: Informal Social Interactions, Alcohol Prohibition, and Invention," is an engaging read on these findings.

economics that has evolved across the Greek islands rests on a rhythm of trading locally sourced foods, agricultural practices based in small land-holdings, and what seems to be a persistent preference by ethnic Greeks for their own cuisine. Even in Athens, there is less international fare than is prevalent in many capital cities in Europe and across the globe.

The generally stubborn attitude of Greeks toward corporate interference together with persistently opaque state policies may negate the spread of foreign multinationals—possibly limiting international foods and keeping fast food conglomerates at bay. Anecdotally, I considered the scope of corporate food incursion in Greece by comparing the availability of McDonald's (the US based and world's largest food chain) in Greece to its European counterparts. Greece is the last original EU nation to host a McDonald's. While most of these nations courted the fast food chain in the 1970s, Greece's first franchise opened in 1991. Of European nations, Greece contains twenty-four McDonald's outlets, which is dwarfed by the one thousand outlets each in France, Germany, and the UK, the five hundred in Italy and Spain, the over one hundred each in Switzerland, Portugal, and Austria, and the eighty-nine in Ireland. Population sizes notwithstanding, the representation of McDonald's in other EU nations overwhelms that of Greece.

A large part of Greek cuisine—including a variety of fruits and vegetables and mainstays such as olive oil, olives, feta cheese, seafood, poultry, lamb, nuts, and wine—are procured from its rural and island regions. This combination of foods that Greek islanders have consumed for centuries has been identified by scientists as healthful, reducing the risk of diabetes, heart attacks, strokes, and cancer, and recently recognized for maintaining brain health (Luciano et al. 2017; Choi 2003). Popularly regarded as the Mediterranean diet, it is based on the eating habits of ethnic Greeks, particularly Cretans, as well as southern Italians and Spaniards, as studied between the 1940s and 1960s. In complete contrast to eating locally, the Mediterranean diet has been exported around the world in recent decades as a nutritional regime.

Contributing to the vibrancy of Greece's local food system are the many Northern visitors who travel to the nation to enjoy its cuisine. Although vacationers have long sought out new tastes and regional foods, culinary tourism has metamorphosed into an independent and thriving travel sector over the last two decades (Yun, Hennessey, and MacDonald 2011; Long 2004). First defined by Long (2004), culinary tourism is "about food; exploring and discovering culture and history through food and food related activities in the creation of memorable experiences." Northern Europeans have traveled to Greece for decades, enjoying fresh and flavorsome meals. Much of this travel is tied to the introduction of Greek and Mediterranean cuisines in their home countries. Celebrated English cooking writer Elizabeth David is credited with doing just this for the British population. Her first volume, *A Book of Mediterranean Cooking*, quoted in the epigraph, was a game-changer for British diets that had been contending with austerity and dietary blandness after World War II.

The rise of food tourism over the last decade is connected to a plethora of tourist development strategies that now target "foodies." The impact of food tourism on local food systems, and island places like Lesvos that still have a taken-for-granted local food economy, is not yet apparent. In this chapter, I turn to recent literature on the impact of food tourism on agriculture communities and the twist of traveling locavores, persons who seek a diet of locally produced foods and now seem to travel for it. Regions across the globe are branding themselves as tourist locations based on local food specialties or creating food items for the purpose of constructing a regional association with them to attract tourists (Sidali, Kastenholz, and Bianchi 2015; Long 2004; Sims 2008). Rather than a ploy for attracting visitors, on Greek islands fresh, scrumptious meals and seaside dining have long been par for the course.

The Greek islands are not food sovereign, especially vastly touristed ones, such as Santorini, Mykonos, or Crete, as they largely depend on imported foods to serve visitors. However, even in these islands, many families maintain traditional food practices, including growing their own vegetables, purchasing bread from the local bakery, and buying fish from the local fishers, who drive around town touting their day's catch on microphones attached to vehicles. Regional foods are also served in the many tavernas and other Greek dining venues visited by holidaymakers and so remain somewhat dependent on traditional systems of agriculture including collective methods of production. The economic crisis impoverished many Greek residents, especially in cities, reducing diets. But the daily consumption of local wine, salads bathed in local olive oil, home-grown vegetables, and island seafoods continued in many island homes and also supported relations in cities.

The following section begins by considering food studies scholarship to locate island food systems and the convivial economics in Lesvos within the field. I also broach perspectives that challenged conventional agriculture as it was first taking root in the postwar era of the 1950s and

1960s. Decades prior to the contemporary interest in alternative food networks, environmentalists, hippies, and food activists were promoting and arguing for healthful food production, fearing the destructive capacities of the Green Revolution. Their advocacy and efforts toward small-scale, locally controlled, and organic agriculture have been fairly overlooked in current food studies literature but deserve further consideration for assessing the potential of alternative food systems.

Local food systems are an important attribute of island societies that has been likewise underexamined in food as well as island studies. Large-scale agriculture, packaging, advances in transportation, and the need to feed tourists may have transformed many islands' foodscapes, but eating locally is entrenched in island communities—numerous fruits, vegetables, and marine life are endemic to islands and provide the basis of an organic economic alterity. Those seeking to depart from mainstream lifestyles often begin by changing their relationship to food—the buying and eating of it.

The chapter concludes with an ethnographic account of how local foods inform the ingredients and preparations in Skala Eresos's dining venues and the women's cooperatives. In my meetings at cooperatives and Skala Eresos's food enterprises, I surveyed owners and workers and cooperative members about their food preparations and where they purchased their items. The food produced, purchased, and traded in the cafés, tavernas, and cafeteria and cooperatives in Lesvos suggests the existence of an island-based food economy. I also informally surveyed tourists about their reasons for traveling to Lesvos and Skala in particular. In my brief interludes, informal conversations, and interviews with the many Northern Europeans who travel to or reside in Lesvos, it was not only the "Sapphic culture" or "bohemian feel" or "the lovely setting" that brought them to Lesvos but also the "food, food, food"—vegetables grown in rich valleys, local cheeses, and Lesvos's famed sardines and ouzo. It may be the privilege of the Aegean islands to hold the climate and geography for a diverse island diet, but future analyses of island food systems should yield lessons for continents as alternative food networks continue to be implemented and attract academic attention.

Cultivating Food Studies

Food studies literature has grown precipitously in current decades with an increasing number of subtopics. Recent attention has been to alternative food systems such as local, organic, and sustainable agriculture, and other efforts such as farmers' markets, guerrilla gardening, or urban gardening (Goodman, DuPuis, and Goodman 2014; Hinrichs 2007). Food activism is another large area of study, including food movements that demand greater access to less chemically produced agricultural products, better treatment of agricultural workers, and address economic and racial inequalities in accessing fresh foods (Karides and Widener 2018; Alkon and Agyeman 2011; Alkon and Norgaard 2009; Slocum 2007). There is also a host of research on food consumption patterns (see Counihan and Van Esterik 2012 and Watson and Caldwell 2005). Food studies researchers are also evaluating public awareness of the toxicity of pesticides and fertilizers used in conventional agriculture and their relationship to soil deterioration and the impact of climate change on regional agriculture (Nestle 2007). Evaluation of government policies toward food safety, the escalating power of chemical companies to dictate or influence government food policy, and how the public might be able to take back the food system are also topics central to food studies (Winne 2008; Lyson 2004; Hassanein 2003).

Early sociological research on food systems was based in a world-systems perspective. The work of sociologists Harriet Friedmann (1987) and Philip McMichael (1994) was revelatory, demonstrating how mass scaled and global agricultural production drove capitalist expansion by providing the sustenance necessary for industrialization and an urbanizing workforce. Their scholarship, along with others, tie the advancement of corporate-controlled food regimes to a decline of healthful and varied diets, the loss of local control over agriculture, and increasing socioeconomic inequalities and environmental harm (Heffernan and Constance 1994).

Much of the early food systems research in sociology applied neo-Marxist approaches to study modes of resistance by laborers, farmers, and peasants (McMichael 2009; Bonanno and Constance 2008; Scott 1985). Agricultural workers demands for better wages, fulfillment of unpaid wages, and safer and less toxic work conditions were not being met while peasants or subsistence farmers began calling for food sovereignty, as they sought to resist the creeping forces of land dispossession (Araghi and Karides 2012; Wittman, Desmarais, and Wiebe 2010). Research in peasant studies overlapped with the sociology of development—both were concerned with the impact of modernization on rural communities and their ability to adapt or resist globalization and the export-driven agriculture that was encroaching on subsistence and sustainable agricultural practices. The budding alternative agriculture strategies—such as food cooperatives, farmers' markets, and small, local, and organic farming—were not on Marxists' radar who did not associate these strategies with the plight of peasant farmers.

Another strain of food research also initiated in the late 1970s and 1980s examined the social dimensions of food consumption. These early studies in the social organization of eating, the relationship of food, health, and well-being, and patterns of food consumption were largely sidelined in the social sciences as insufficiently academic (Bonnano and Constance 2008; Beardsworth and Keil 1997). However, by the early 2000s, the work of sociologist Sharon Zukin demonstrated that consumption matters and the study of consumers and their choices were relevant for understanding global markets and economic processes (Zukin and Smith 2004). The increasing study of consumers and consumption combined with a mounting interest by academics and the public in the availability, health, and safety of food to vitalize a contemporary food studies.

Elaine Power and Mustafa Koc (2008, 2), Canadian sociologists leading the field, defined food studies as research on the "historically specific web of social relations, processes, structures, and institutional arrangements that cover human interactions with nature and with other humans involving production, distribution, preparation, and consumption of food." Many recent contributions in food studies now bridge political-economic analysis with new patterns of food consumption and the growing focus on nonconventional or alternative means of food distribution and production (Goodman, DuPuis, and Goodman 2014; Patel 2012; Johnston 2008; Hinrichs 2007; Guthman 2004).

Many accounts of alternative food production, distribution, and consumption are unpromising. For example, Claire Hinrichs (2003), a rural sociologist and agriculture economist, writes that local food activists may hold an "elitist nativism" that unites them in opposition to outside forces. Local food strategists have been described as parochial or defensive, narrowly concerned with one's immediate social realm, a "privileged escapism" lacking a global perspective on the inequities rendered in food production and distribution (DeLind 2011; Szasz 2007; DuPuis and Goodman 2005; Hinrichs 2003).

Further critiques of alternative food consumption are grounded in the paradox of social change via consumerism or the consumer-citizen approach to healthier fresher food sources (Mares and Alkon 2011). Josée Johnston (2008, 229), another Canadian food sociologist, explains that "ethical consumer discourse is organized around the idea that shopping, and particularly food shopping, is a way to create progressive social change." Johnston (2008) argues that the consumer-citizen models do not necessarily produce a substantive program for health and sustainability. Or, as Hinrichs (2000) explained, although closer social ties develop between food producers and consumers, they continue to be framed by commodity relations.

Researchers such as Johnston (2008), Hinrichs (2000), Guthman (2006), and Allen and Guthman (2006) challenge local and alternative food systems based on arguments that these efforts may be motivated by neoliberal subjectivities. Smart, green, healthy living is not necessarily a matter of food justice, but is often informed by the rhetoric of choice for the economically privileged. The implication is that the movement for food localism, or organic and less chemically produced foods, is advanced by well-off and self-directed populations that neglect the larger challenges in addressing the inequalities of the modern food regime, its corporate enablers, and complicit research programs in public and private sectors.

Academic skepticism of local, small-scale, organic farms and markets as alternatives to conventional agriculture was present in the sixties and seventies when in the Global North the first incarnations of food alternatives—cooperatives, subsistence farming, communes—confronted the dominant logic of mass scale agriculture. However, Warren Belasco's *Appetite for Change: How the Counterculture Took on the Food Industry* (1989) serves as a rare academic analysis that documents how the efforts of hippies and "freaks," or the counterculture of the 1960s and 1970s, in small-scale and organic farming, back-to-the-land movements, and food cooperatives aided the expansion and mainstreaming of health food stores, restaurants, and cafés. Belasco, a professor of American studies, was prescient in appreciating both food as political and the power of economic alterity as a challenge to the status quo. Belasco (1989) illustrates that the organic and local food alternatives initiated at the margins by the counterculture eventually informed mainstream attitudes to conventional food systems. By alerting the public to the potential toxicity of their food, Belasco makes the case that it was hippies who brought healthy, local, and organic foods into the mainstream.

Another rare and early academic publication on food and economic alternatives is Cotterill's (1983) study of the viability of "hippie economics." Cotterill (1983) tests the "small is beautiful" thesis through a study of the expansion of food cooperatives that occurred in the 1970s. The "small is beautiful movement" of the 1960s and 1970s repudiated mass production and the consumerism it engendered. Cotterill (1983) argues that food cooperatives persist because volunteers sustain them by offsetting costs. However, he concludes that the future success of cooperatives depends on their ability to expand in size rather than on continued volunteerism. Guided by neoclassical economic models, his conclusion discards economic alternatives, such as food cooperatives that remain locally rooted and based in community participation, because they do not adopt a growth logic. Like other academics who are oriented by a capitalocentrism (Gibson-Graham 2006), Cotterill (1983) cannot conceive of an alternative economy where, for example, work is traded for reduced grocery costs and community needs are met through collective ownership. Contrary to Cotterill's (1983) prediction of their disappearance, food cooperatives are currently in revival.

There has been a persistent resistance in academia to seriously contend with grassroots alternatives or everyday forms of resistance as engines of social change, even by left-leaning academics (Gibson-Graham 2006). While Marxian analyses succeed in articulating the inequities that global capital creates, models for advancing social and economic justice continue to fall short. Even recent writings, such as Wright's *Envisioning Real Utopias* (2010), yield to traditional left notions that microenterprises, self-employment, and small-scale cooperatives offer little promise for future constellations of alternatives to capitalism. Wright's dismissal (2010, 232) of localized enterprises and collectivities is substantial:

> The hippy [sic] communes of the 1960s may have been inspired by utopian longings and a belief that they were part of the "dawning of the Age of Aquarius," but in practice they functioned more as escapes from the realities of capitalist society than as nodes of radical transformation. Other examples, like organic grocery cooperatives, while not escapes from capitalist society, nevertheless seem constrained to occupy small niches often catering to relatively affluent people who can afford to "indulge" their preferences for a particular kind of "lifestyle." Organic grocery cooperatives may embody some progressive ideals, but they do not pose a threat to the system.

Academic cynicism toward alternative economics casts doubt over the possibilities of dismantling capitalism exclusive of a socialist turn. As formerly addressed, Wright's (2010) critique mirrors early social movement scholars by barring "individual and unobtrusive" activities as concretely resistive. Evaluations like those of Wright (2010) and Johnston (2008) assume that we have submitted to the ideological dominance of neoliberal sensibilities and require macrostructural social change. They overlook localized, small scale, and grassroots forms (Simone 2004; Hau'ofa 1994) that have offered real and immediate options to address the negative health and ecological impacts of conventional agriculture.

Alisa Smith and J. B. MacKinnon's *100 Miles Diet: A Year of Local Eating* (2007), an early prompt of the local food movement, was evaluated unfavorably by academics who identify its proposal as neoliberal and privileged (Guthman 2008; Peck and Tickell 2002). In his rereading of the diet, Harris (2009, 61) challenges these analyses by suggesting that they are limited by frames that "blind us to new political opportunities." Harris (2009, 61) explains that consuming foods grown within a hundred mile range was an attempt to enact "a different negotiation of the ethical dilemmas posed by the food system." He argues for complex or diverse (Gibson-Graham 2006) readings of alternative food systems.

One such approach is the pursuit of redressing the racial and economic inequalities embedded in contemporary food regimes through food justice movements and alternative food networks (Alkon and Agyeman 2011). Neva Hassanein (2003), an environmental studies professor importantly connects food movements with social justice and racial inequalities in the food system. She finds that building a network of alternatives to conventional farming and distribution are incremental steps toward creating access to healthier foods by marginalized communities and for overcoming intensive chemical-dependent corporate agriculture. Hassanein (2003) recognizes that alternative food networks are currently one of the few substitutes available to the conventional food system. McMichael (2009, 141) too, after decades probing food regimes, calls for "a gathering of food sovereignty movements across the world to reverse the modernist narrative of small landholders' obsolescence etched into the development paradigm and current development industry visions of 'feeding the world.'"

There is growing research recognizing that local, organic, and alternative food movements can shift the range of possible options of food production (Hinrichs 2009; Hasanein 2003; Belasco 1989). Recent reviews of alternative food systems suggest moving beyond the early bifurcation between conventional and alternative food production, and to take context and geographies more carefully into account in reimagining food systems (Albrecht et al. 2013; Lehner 2013). At the very least, recent efforts to "remake the food system" showcase that globally groups are taking action to address their concerns with it (Hinrichs 2009). The slow food movement, coordinated by Carlo Petrini, an Italian journalist, who in his opposition to a McDonald's establishment in Rome's Piazza di Spagna in 1986 fomented what is now an international network of organizations and local slow food chapters that are referred to, unsurprisingly, as "convivia." While convivia engage in diverse pursuits such as hosting dinners, conferences, or visits to farmers' markets, they are based in the three central slow food principles of sustainable farming, fair treatment of farm workers, and gastroeconomic pleasure that embraces a slower pace of life (Petrini [2005] 2013).

Efforts to advance alternatives to the conventional food system are actively pursued in marginalized communities and in marginal locations. The limited availability of fresh produce in now well demarcated "food deserts," primarily in low-income black and brown urban communities in which fresh foods are not easily purchasable, has led leaders of these neighborhoods to develop community gardens and local markets. Guided by an interest in food justice and food sovereignty, urban residents are collectively farming empty and abandoned lots and rooftops, and making backyard gardens as a means of securing fresh foods and increasing access to it in their communities that have been left out of white, privileged food movements (Karides and Widener 2018; Alkon and Agyeman 2011; Desjardins 2010).

The spontaneous development of local food systems in marginal communities suggests that these types of efforts are not necessarily driven by a market orientation of consumerism, but are grassroots responses to unjust, unaffordable, and unsafe food practices. In many rural regions, grounded in traditions of small-scale and subsistence agriculture, convivial models of production and exchange continue to dictate the organization of food systems. Whether urban or rural, communities without economic privileges are invested in local, small scale, and organic farms and markets not because they are oriented by neoliberalism but as pursuits for food justice and food sovereignty.

Flocking to many island regions such as Greece, young participants in the counterculture movement in the late 1960s and early 1970s left to initiate small-scale and worker-controlled artisanal and agricultural production units to escape the advancement of mass production. The new social worlds created by these "bohemians," "hippies," "dropouts," "alternatives," or "freaks" on islands may have intruded on local cultures.

However, in many cases the entities they created flowed from the forms and practices they found already existing on islands that organically countered the rigid and chemical organization of industrial food production that was evolving at the time.

Transnational Food and Traveling Locavores

Unlike the bohemian counterculture travelers of the 1960s, who combed islands to live off the land and away from mainstream livelihoods, contemporary food tourists seek consumptive experiences. Privileged Northern travelers who seek to visit places that they perceive as more naturalistic, less stressful, or healthful environments are now also assessing the availability of fresh local food sources when deciding on a travel destination. Although travelers to Greece often remark on the pleasures of dining on fresh local foods, attracting tourism through food has only been approached by the Greek tourist industry in the last few years.

Food tourism is recent and a growing subtopic in the food studies literature (Yun, Hennessey, and MacDonald 2011; Long 2004; Hall and Sharples 2003). Yun, Hennessey, and MacDonald's (2011) study of culinary tourism on Prince Edward Island developed a rubric for categorizing the relationship of food and leisure: "deliberate" food tourists are those who travel to locations with the intention of dining on local cuisine, "opportunistic" food travelers seek out local food and drinks, and "accidental" ones eat local foods because that is what is available. Although it would be difficult to unyoke the essence of the travel experience to Lesvos and other Greek islands from the ubiquity of Greek cookery and beverages, I venture that most of those holidaymaking in Greece are likely opportunistic or accidental food tourists.

In July 2009 and 2012 I conducted a short survey over several afternoons with tourists who had escaped the gleaming sunshine by gathering under the awnings of the cafés and tavernas that run along the shoreline. Of the thirty tourists I surveyed, including married and unmarried lesbian couples, straight married couples with children, young single ethnic Greeks, women and men, and retired couples from the UK, approximately 30 percent mentioned food when I asked, "What brought you to Skala Eresos?" One respondent, a lesbian-identified Irish woman, explains that she vacations yearly in Lesvos with her father because "the food, definitely the food, the lesbians are secondary." Urban Northern

Europeans travel to Greece for the relaxation that rural island life offers, and in the case of Skala Eresos, many travel for the camaraderie available to lesbian travelers and facets of bohemia. Yet they also value the availability of fresh foods and Greek preparations of them.

Food tourism, or tourist development via the branding of regional cuisines, is a recent form of gastronomical commodification. Richards (2002, 3) argues that because gastronomy "has become a significant source of identity formation in postmodern society," it plays a part in the growing interest in cultural tourism. Niched and specialized travel experiences currently drive the tourist industry, the world's largest service sector, as developers around the world attempt to attract visitors to various localities by showcasing exceptional features of a region. In this regard, food—distinct recipes, regional interpretations of them, hard to find ingredients, or their freshness—is now a foremost strategy for tourist development. Local cuisines figuratively feed travelers' desire for an authentic tourist experiences (Sims 2008).

The popularization of Greek cuisine in the Global North, or the exposure to foreign foods generally, is tied to migration, which in turn is shaped by the imperial trajectories of colonizing nations. Greeks largely immigrated to the UK and Germany and further abroad to the US and Australia in the aftermath of World War II and the Greek Civil War. In the UK the earliest group of Greek migrants arrived in the early 1900s after the Greek War of Independence against the Ottoman Empire. While a wealthier set of the Greek diaspora were based in the shipping and export industries, peasant farmers and working class Greeks who migrated abroad often labored in the food or garment sectors (my parents included).

Ethnic enclaves formed by migrant communities are often built around restaurants and small shops that sell cultural items (Portes and Stepick 1993). Many Greek men, often with the help of their families, opened restaurants, particularly diners, to appease the gastronomical desires of fellow immigrants and in the process attracted a diverse clientele (Gabriele 2013). Greeks' dominance of diners has been tied to their ethnic identities and migrant status, which limited their access to other professions (Gabriele 2013). Dan Georgakas, a Greek American and anarchist historian who was quoted in Lewine's (1996) *New York Times* essay, "The Kaffenion Connection: How Greek Diners Evolved," explained: "Most of the immigrants were independent farmers . . . so they knew how to run a small business. And many came from the Ottoman

Empire, where they learned to do business with different kinds of people."
To this I suggest that the Greek diners in the US, and Greek-owned
restaurants globally, attempt to re-create the masculinized sociality of the
Greek plateia for the men who own and work in them.

Just as lesbian and gay establishments provide a place to connect
and feel at home for queer communities, eateries often provide a reprieve
for immigrant communities. They become a meeting place for recent
and seasoned members of a diaspora, an opportunity to connect with
economic opportunities, and a place to assert one's own cultural values
and forms of socializing. Ethnically oriented dining venues in the Global
North, often created in the interest of serving their own populations,
eventually became attractions for Northerners who are seeking new and
unconventional tastes. The early birds in ethnic dining were those first
willing to venture into migrant neighborhoods to try out new foods and
enjoy a novel dining experience.

The contemporary obsession with food and dining, and consuming
new cultures, has reshaped the perceptions of the cuisines of marginalized ethnic groups and migrant neighborhoods. Ethnic restaurants, cafés,
and eateries are now at the forefront of Northern food consumption,
exhibited in the obsessive amount of programming dedicated to eating
and traveling for diverse ethnic cuisines. For Northern European palates,
exposure to Greek cuisine is time-honored—both familiar and foreign
enough to attract Northern diners seeking to "eat culture" (Crowther
2013). The rise of ethnic foods as fine dining, fast casual, or street foods
in the Global North, often catering to a middle class, has been nothing
less than dramatic (Dixon 2014) and belies the humble and localized
roots of many of these cuisines.

Donna Gabaccia (2000), an Italian food scholar at the University of
Toronto, explores the relationship between food and mobility in various
contexts. Gabaccia's (2000) migration-centered approach to food, along
with others (Ho 2018; Rye and Scott 2018; Kershen 2002), is another
growing arena in the field of food studies. It considers how immigrants
influence national cuisines—for example, how couscous from the Maghreb
has been adopted as French—as well as how immigrant groups maintain
their "culinary identity" despite pressures to assimilate. It seems that by
introducing their local cuisines through food enterprises, migrants to
the Global North may have facilitated the expansion of food tourism.
Gastronomes' consumption of foreign cookery in migrant neighborhoods
may have inspired them to travel so they may imbibe these meals in
their region of origin.

When considered in relation to the advancement of alternative food networks, the connection between locavorism, tourism, and the new transnationalism of eating in the Global North is sticky. For instance, the increased importation of foods correlates with a rise of international tourism (Fischer 2010). Migrants and foodies ferment the culinary diversity of Northern cities, making novel food experiences a central part of middle class urban living and postmodern identities. These ethnic dining experiences are commodified as they become constructed as authentic place-based cultural events that cannot be replicated (Sims 2008). The authenticated food experience is further extended when one travels for it. Food tourists may view themselves as progressive locavores, but increased jet setting to indulge in food delights defies much of the ethos of localism and it may interfere with local culture and environment (Bhat 2017). On the other hand, consumptions of local culture has also been linked to sustaining and reviving cultural practices, including foods that had been overshadowed by modernity (Sims 2008; Everett and Aitchison 2008).

A sizable literature, largely found in tourism journals, exists on strategies for creating and marketing food tourism. For example, in pastoral regions, food tourism is posed as an opportunity to "combine the intimacy model and the experience economy as a rural development strategy" (Sidali, Kastenholz, and Bianchi 2015, 1179). Food tourism is also considered an opportunity for advancing sustainable development and supporting local producers. In their recent book, Hall and Gössling (2017, 12), international researchers on sustainability and food tourism, suggest that the planning of a sustainable culinary system "brings to the fore the major role that tourism . . . plays in the food system." By meeting tourists' desires for unique regional experiences through fresh and authentic foods, local food tourism is perceived as a force for resisting multinational corporate tourist development, which is considered less authentic and less sustainable (Sidali, Kastenholz, and Bianchi 2015). As an industry food tourism will require the critical lens that Johnston (2008) and others offer on consumption as a vehicle for progressive change, especially its intrusion on local and community based development.

Despite the impact that freezers, processing, packaging, and transportation have had on local cuisines (Mintz 2006), creating regional identities that are tied to particular foods and preparations is increasingly applied to attract tourism. What makes dining in Greece stand outside the current food tourism models is that the audience is not being catered to with constructions of local dining experience, but they are participating in the everyday practice of al fresco drinking and dining that characterizes Greek life. Even in Plaka, the epicenter of tourism in Athens, most restaurants are locally owned, serving locals and tourists alike ethnic Greek foods in the Greek tradition—authentically authentic.

Eating Locally on Lesvos

The promotion of alternative food networks is a decades-old mobilization (Goodman, Dupuis, and Goodman 2014) and the prominence of food tourism is even more recent. Yet eating locally has endured in small island societies for centuries. The meals served in Skala Eresos, and the pastries, jellies, and breads prepared by the women's cooperatives, suggest that the food and diet of the island population are still guided by geographical scope. Even if the onslaught of corporate tourism and conventional agriculture has made many islands dependent on mainland exports, the ties to local food practices based in small land plots, wild harvesting, and fishing and diving seem to be more intimate on islands than on continents.

Lesvos is one of many Greeks islands that are able to be organized by local food production, offering a model for sustainable local development. Surveying owners on the various products used in the diverse eating venues in Skala Eresos, I learned that many of these items were local. In a majority of venues, olive oil, cheeses, fruits, seafood, and meats came directly from the Eresos valley. In several restaurants, families who owned or managed them often supplied the olive-related products and vegetables from their own harvest. One taverna owner responded to my question on how she sources her vegetables by pointing to the taverna about three shops down and stating "from them." When I asked shopkeepers in Skala about specific items such as seafood, lemons, yogurt, or cheeses, they responded ντόπιο (dopio) or local. I initially interpreted local to mean from the island, but I came to understand that it refers to the immediate region, the Eresos valley. This far narrower conception of local differs distinctly from the broadness with which contemporary food movements in mainland societies apply it. Local and small scale or living off the land and sea is what many island populations have been able to do for generations, and continue to do with no self-conscious effort. A restaurant owner, describing the abundance in the valley, iterated: "Eresos is a place that can live on its own. It could do this very easily, and with its own systems of exchange."

For example, several restaurant owners remarked on the high quality of the products from the local dairy cooperatives as compared to private and foreign dairy producers. All the food businesses in Skala purchased at least some of their dairy products from the local dairy cooperative, as do the women's cooperatives. For many enterprises Lesvos's cooperatives were their single source for cheese. Local shepherds collect goat and sheep's milk and bring it to the cooperative to churn into an assortment of cheeses. Several of the island's noted cheeses, such as kasseri and ladotyri, have won national prizes. To enjoy them, one needs to travel to Lesvos or find them in the shop in Athens that supplies Lesvian products. Lesvos's producers do not export these cheeses beyond Greece.

Farm-to-table in Eresos is routine and enveloped in convivial economics. Local owners use their own olive oil, grow their own herbs or vegetables, and buy seafood from the local fishers, without considering the marketability of local foods dining. Some of Skala Eresos's owners and managers who are not originally from the valley started food businesses precisely because they valued its locally embedded economy and food system. In particular, these attritional alternative economy owners, who left urban regions to reside permanently or seasonally in Skala Eresos, were most interested in furthering the localness and alterity of food production in the region. For example, Pete, who is a successful owner of a bar café in Skala arrived from a city in mainland Greece, advocated for increasing the variety of local cheeses:

> I told the dairy cooperative that they should get a slice machine for kasseri. Toast [a pressed ham and cheese sandwich, ever present on the kafenion menus] could be easily made with kasseri but almost all the shops use Edam, a Dutch cheese that you can purchase sliced. But the cooperative only sells kasseri in a large block. I don't have the time to cut the cheese piece by piece! If they did this, then everyone would buy it. The kasseri could also be used for pizza if they would shred it, but they don't want to change their routine.

Nonlocal business owners, like Pete, appreciate the freshness and quality of local products, and they are considerably interested in deepening the access and efficiency of using local ingredients. These owners, and their native Eressian counterparts, seemed motivated to make the most of local resources and local producers. Not in a single conversation, interview, or observation in Skala Eresos was it suggested that local foods should be exploited to attract tourists nor was the possibility of marketing local delicacies for export discussed. It seems the benefit and delight of eating local foods locally was self-evident.

Lela, an Eressian in her mid-thirties and a member of a family that owns a larger restaurant on Skala's strip, explained that she buys many of their products in Mytilini, adding that while she prefers the village products, she did not want to "clean out" the availability of products sold locally. By concerning herself with the availability of products for smaller venues in the village rather than trying to thwart her competitors, Lela's response is indicative of convivial-minded business practices that take the collective and remote location of the village into account.

The standard among the cooks, servers, and owners of Skala Eresos's dining venues was that local is preferred because the quality is known. This stance may reflect parochialism among islanders, but it likewise reveals a genuine appreciation for fresh local fare and the desire to serve it to customers. Further, while a commitment to serving local food items is evident, it was recognized that not all items served in Skala could be local. A gregarious ethnic Greek owner, who split his time between Athens and Skala Eresos, ran a bar café removed from the village, yielding space for him to remain open until 2 a.m. on busy nights, explains: "We try to buy everything local, but Jack Daniels, it comes from Tennessee." His awareness of the regional location of Jack Daniels may serve as a testament to place-based appreciations of the foods and drinks imbibed in Lesvos.

Caring for Topos

The deep appreciation for local ingredients was also evident in my meetings with the women's food cooperatives. Many of these cooperatives, including Ayiassos, Parakila, Agra, Ayia Paraskevi, and others, revealed the same understanding of "local" as the proprietors of the restaurants in Skala Eresos, using the term to refer to the immediate environment. Cooperative members explained that they drew from their terrain as much as possible. Whether it be in the rich, green region of Ayiassos on the east side of the island or in the villages of Agra and Parakila, cooperatives relied on the agricultural and wild harvesting traditions of their particular villages.

For many of the cooperative members, cooking with locally found ingredients was also about their attachment to place and helping it prosper. As Irini, a former cooperative president from Molyvos, explains: "Everything we use we try to get from the local area, milk, cheese, eggs, and more. If we can get them from our yards, we get them from our yards. Flour, sugar, and chocolate we get from Mytilini." Evangelia, a younger member of the Ayiassos cooperative, elucidates:

> When we started it was not just about making money. For us it was to preserve our land and for ourselves. The economics of the project was not just our priority. We wanted to create a project that was outside our work in the household or in the fields. It is our commitment to our team, to each other, and to the importance of this project for our village, and we think we have been able to preserve our island, despite the setbacks handed to us. If the pursuit of a project is primarily or only focused on money, then it cannot succeed.

Evangelia's statement exudes economic conviviality, as she conveyed an organic understanding that considerations for environment and society must be part of an economic endeavor. Ayiassos is a stunning mountain village that holds a seasonal chestnut and cherry blossom festival, and the women's cooperative is central to it. What seems distinct about island place is that the attachment of islanders is not just to the island, but to a very particular part of it.

Many of cooperatives pointed to how they benefit their village, and how that supersedes their economic goals. Anthi from the Anemotia cooperative explains: "If our goal was money, then we would not last. We are generally interested in what is good for our 'topos' [land] and also for us." For almost all the women's cooperatives, creating an income for themselves was linked to community development. As Lexi, a member from Polichnitos cooperative, states: "We have our own income, we make our own money, and we benefit the entire village. Not only from buying local produce from the [dairy and olive] cooperatives, but also the village gets known from it." One of the cooperative members in Agra shared: "I wanted to do something for my village. My family has a store. I can always work, but I left, to be here."

The cooperative members' positive appraisal of their homes and the bounty of farmed, fished, and wild-harvested items is indicative of

a convivial economy that considers the health of a locality as a significant factor for business operations. Islanders generally seem to hold
a heightened sense of where they are in the world, and this seems to
be associated with an organic stewardship, as reflected in the women's
cooperatives of Lesvos.

The women's cooperative members displayed pride around the
preservation of culture and the rhythms of village life, their gendered
work, and their ability to host and serve their village. The circumstances
of the Parakila cooperative illustrates how food becomes a vehicle for
building attachment to place. Most of the families inhabiting the village
of Parakila arrived as part of the population exchange between Greece
and Turkey after the catastrophe in Smyrna in 1922 described in chapter
3. The cooperative members explained how it was their grandparents that
moved into the homes that were vacated by the Turks who had resided in
the village. The architectural structures in Parakila are visibly influenced
by Ottoman design. A remnant of an old mosque can be seen from the
main road that girds the village. The cooperative members identify with
their "Eastern" roots. The president of the cooperative explained: "We
are Anatolian, our kitchen, the pastries derive from Eastern recipes. Our
cuisine comes from Asia Minor and has its own tastes." The confluence
of Asia Minor cuisine and architecture has a distinct effect on visitors,
and possibly on residents, mostly the children and grandchildren of
refugees. The women's cooperative's fare unites with the structural and
physical spatiality of where their cuisine, less than an hour's ferry ride
over the Aegean, is grounded. The Parakila cooperative prepares foods
that Turks, who originally resided in the village, likely had prepared
before the population exchange.

Cooperatives with a younger membership, such as Parakila, considered themselves more innovative than others. The Parakila cooperative
is the single example among the cooperatives in Lesvos to seek culinary
tourism. As one member of the cooperative shares in a somewhat ageist
observation: "We are constantly thinking of ways to expand our market.
Cooperatives with members in their fifties and sixties make items as they
have. They are not thinking about a new customer base, or understand
the new interest in traditional goods." Several of the cooperatives with
younger membership seemed particularly inspired with ensuring the success of their work. Tessie, another member of the Parakila cooperative
explained: "There is room for expanding the tourism we offer. In Greece
we get the tourist and throw him in the pool, we take him for a walk to

the beach, so he can also have a swim in the ocean, and then bring him to a taverna at night." Tessie was drawing attention to the opportunities for tourist development in Lesvos such as the quiet holidays remote islands can offer urbanites, especially Athenians. Others in the Parakila kitchen added, "We have so much to offer here on the island of Lesvos." The president of the cooperative went on to discuss a recent visit from a Greek cooking show (*Gourmet Alive*), during which they shared their expertise on the televised program. Many members believed that media coverage would draw attention and increase the sales of their products nationally, as one member explained: "The TV people enjoyed being with us. They return regularly just to work with our kitchen. The program now highlights Lesvos generally, so there is a better appreciation of our cuisine in the Greek public." Parakila cooperative members explained that they were strategizing to attract upscale culinary tourists to their village. Julie stated that "we want to make our place known."

Other than Parakila, the women's cooperative in Molyvos, the village known for its upscale tourists and serene medieval architecture, also referred to culinary tourism, although dismissively. The president of the Molyvos cooperative gave her thoughts: "When you are waiting for tourism, others make the plans; you don't make the plans. For now, we are just trying to keep the place open. We are cutting our wages and we are here all day long." Molyvos has drawn Greek artists and actors from Athens since the 1960s, and more recently it has attracted Northern European retirees. It is the only cooperative that has a large foreign clientele, which seems to have jaded Molyvos cooperative members' perspective on culinary tourism. When I asked about their main customers, Thanasia answered, "German, English, Belgium, and Dutch." In 2012 Molyvos was most affected, among villages in Lesvos, by Greece's economic crisis. The protests in Athens and the media's portrayal of Greece discouraged the upscale foreign tourists to which the village catered. When I returned to Molyvos in spring 2016, I was pleased to see that, despite the economic crises, the cooperative had expanded, with a balcony restaurant on the main road leading into the village.

For most of the cooperatives, their economic survival was due to a collective resistance and shared noncompensation. They were able to do this because many of their daily food items, including olive oil, olives, eggs, cheese, chicken, lamb, wine, and vegetables, were from their own small plots of land or that of family members. By deferring the payment of wages, the cooperatives were able to endure the worst of the crisis.

Keeping careful accounts, they planned to pay out what was due to each of them when the economy had stabilized. The cooperatives' survival mattered not only for the cooperative members but also for the villages where they were situated. The endurance of cooperatives and other enterprises signified for many in their communities' resilience in the face of Northern European austerity measures.

Preserving Islandness through Gender and Food

The primary customers of all but one of the cooperatives in Lesvos are the villagers living on the island and further abroad. Parakila's pursuit of the wealthy Athenians drawn to the cosmopolitanism coolness that now characterizes food travel is still rare. The mainstay for most of the women's cooperatives including Parakila in Lesvos are islanders and village kin who have relocated to cities and seek a taste of home. Even the Molyvos cooperative, with its Northern European customers, depends on sales to local families living off island. Ellie, from Agra, elaborates: "The foods we cook are traditional, our mothers and grandmothers taught us—they gave us the traditional skills of women. In this work we promote our culture." Ellie addresses food preparation as a gendered activity and one that is foundational to culture keeping. In the burgeoning food literature, approaches to gender are understated though feminist analyses are being advanced (see Parker et al. 2019). Accounts of alternative food systems, or the food justice movements, give limited attention to the fact that cooking is gendered care work (Szabo 2014; Avakian and Haber 2005). That the preparation of healthful meals requires time and added costs that parents, especially low-income single working parents in the formal sector, do not have is often absent from the writings of the men fronting food movements. Michael Pollan (2009, 137), the US pundit for local foods and home cooking, writes:

> Cooking for yourself is the only sure way to take back control of your diet from the food scientists and food processors, and to guarantee you're eating real food and not edible food like substances. . . . the decline in home-cooking closely parallels the rise in obesity, and research suggests people who cook are more likely to eat a more healthful diet.

Pollan, and his herd of middle-class followers, evidently give little consideration to gender, work, and poverty, and how these relate to food.

He fails to articulate that home cooking became less affordable than fast food due to the expansion of agribusiness and government subsidies of it, increasing obesity among the overworked and underpaid. In addition, as more and more women entered into the formal full-time workforce, men did not pick up additional household duties, including regularly cooking (Hochschild 2012). Though likely not Pollan's intention, unhealthful eating is communicated not as an outcome of neoliberalism and patriarchy, but rather due to lazy home cooks. Even more striking is Pollan's (2009) conspicuous rejection of gender. Pollan (2009) seems to devalue care work and the time household labor requires, which has become increasingly limited. Without making sense of the fact that women historically have been the primary preparers of home cooked meals and continue to be, alternative and health food advocates deny the oppressive forces that Allen (2008) articulates when calling for a lesbian economics. For example, Jane Ellen Brody (2010), a writer who contributes to the *New York Times* on personal health topics, in a review of one of Pollan's books, writes:

> Home cooking need not be arduous or very time-consuming, and you can make up time spent at the stove with time saved not visiting doctors or shopping for new clothes to accommodate an expanding girth. If you eat less, you can afford to pay more for better foods, like plants grown in organically enriched soil and animals that are range-fed.

This passage is steeped in economic privilege and lacks mindfulness of the often grinding work that consumes persons in the Global South and North. Brody (2010) is evidently unaware of the price and time differences between a fast food meal and a home cooked one with fresh ingredients. She also neutralizes food, from a cultural form in which peoples' histories and familial memories intertwine with basic ingredients to produce rich traditions and tasteful meals, to a matter of execution.

Feminist sociologists' scholarly works on women's double duty, the second shift and third shifts as workers and household managers, abound. With few exceptions, much of this classical feminist literature, even as it has come to engage race, ethnicity, nation, and class, needs to further engage food preparation as a site of cultural expression that may sometimes move beyond the carrying out of perfunctory household duties. Contemporary foodies and food writers, such as Pollan (2009), snatched upon this void, critiquing feminism for killing cooking (Williams

2013). Feminism was blamed for reducing cooking to a chore, causing obesity, and "trampling" the culinary arts (Williams 2013).

The current shift toward healthful home cooked meals consumes many middle-class Global North women, who are the most active participants in cooking, canning, gardening, and raising chickens to produce green, ethical, artisanal households. Writer Peggy Orenstein (2010) labels this orientation of educated women as "femivorism." Women with economic means, often dependent on spouse's salaries, are able to devote their labor to farming and cooking from scratch. For some of these women, this culinary do-it-yourself approach may offer a healthier independent household and is perceived as an alternative to formal work or as a cost-saving strategy. For others, "femivorism" often starts with a commitment to healthful living, but without equal participation by partners or spouses, the self-sustaining household becomes a cumbersome chore. Writer and alternative food producer Shannon Hayes (2010) also finds that women's original drive toward self-sufficiency waned when they were not involved in a larger mission with others around food activism, entrepreneurialism, or teaching (Hayes 2010).

These predominantly white, middle class, homesteading women, or femivores, may not have moved to an island, but they reflect the sort of attritional economic alterity demonstrated by many of my interviewees who relocated to Lesvos with similar interests of living independently and away from the formal economy. Conversely, for many women across the Global South, their ability to maintain independent subsistence-driven households was taken from them. Land grabs, in which large tracts of land that had been collectively worked by peasants and indigenous groups for a significant time span are whisked away by corporate entities in allegiance with acquiescent governments, are a hallmark of global capitalism. Vandana Shiva (1988, 2), a foremost environment and food scholar activist, provided a gendered lens on the destructive forces ushered under the guise of economic development:

> The displacement of women from productive activity by the expansion of development was rooted largely in the manner in which development projects appropriated or destroyed the natural resource base for the production of sustenance and survival. It destroyed women's productivity both by removing land, water, and forests from their management and control as well as through ecological destruction of soil, water, and

vegetation systems so that nature's productivity and renew-
ability were impaired.

In many communities across the globe, indigenous and peasant women's
organic economic alterity was debilitated due to the expansion of global
food regimes (McMichael 2009; Friedmann 1987). It is exactly these food
regimes that many well-off Global North women have the privilege to
reject by using their resources to buy or grow less chemically intensive
foods (Hayes 2010; Orenstein 2010).

Food practices—how we grow, cook, and dine—are largely the
work of women, extending well beyond sustenance, as they can embody a
means by which to preserve and transfer one's cultural, ethnic, or island
identities. The neoliberal project razes these kinds of sentiments and
the culture of place if it is not in the interest of economic gain. This is
most evident in the seizure of peoples' lands under neoliberalism in the
Global South (Margulis, McKeon, and Borras 2013; Araghi and Karides
2012), but families in the Global North also suffer from a work/home
crunch that leaves little time for families to gather to cook, eat, and
share in culinary traditions (Counihan 2004; Gerson and Jacobs 2004).

By maintaining small landholdings with vegetable gardens or olive
groves, many Greek islanders have been able to retain their own aesthetic
of food and sociality and survive the negative impact of neoliberalism,
although not without constraint. The loose governance of the Ottoman
Empire that afforded local autonomy to rural communities and the ongoing
absence of central government in island regions (described in chapter 3)
again is a factor facilitating local ownership of plots, economic autonomy, and collective or communal responsibility. Within this context, the
women's cooperatives in Lesvos created a pathway to uphold their island
village culture through the local production and consumption of food.
Creating a collective and convivial social space to prepare local foods,
the women's cooperatives produce items that serve the local population in
their villages, but also for Greek islanders who live and work in Athens.
Foods produced on one's island of origin are sought after by Athenians
in markets or shipped to them by island-dwelling family members.

Hau'ofa (1994, 8) characterizes islanders as historically mobile,
seeking to expand their worlds, yet maintaining deep connections to their
island homes. Speaking of Oceania, Hau'ofa (1994, 12) refers to "the
social centrality of the ancient practice of reciprocity." Whereas economists
interpret remittances as unidirectional, the reciprocity of island residents,

"with goods they themselves produce, and maintain ancestral roots and lands, homes with warmed hearths," is underappreciated. Islanders who migrated for work can return to islands to "re-strengthen their bonds, their souls and their identities." Island identities may sit firm because of the convivial economics practiced by islanders far beyond islands' shores.

In Athens, Peri Lesvou is a shop dedicated to selling products from Lesvos. In 2008, when I visited the store, it was a government entity, but financial strains and corruption resulted in its privatization as a family business. In 2012, when I revisited Peri Lesvou, just about the same products were available: a majority of the food items (including weekly deliveries of fresh yogurt in customary clay pots), such as jams and pastas, were produced by the various women's cooperatives I had visited on Lesvos. The same was true for 2016. The shop also holds a wide selection of ouzo, for which Lesvos is known, and products from the olive and dairy cooperatives. When I met with the managers, it was a matter of fact to them that their customer base was city dwellers with ties to Lesvos.

Some of the women's cooperatives were able to develop national and even global markets that support local development. An important niche for all the cooperatives are weddings and baptisms that occur on Lesvos, but also in Athens and Thessaloniki, and notably as far as Central Africa and Australia. I learned about the cooperatives' export market during a late evening with the Ayia Paraskevi cooperative when I overheard the cooperative president on the phone with a local taxi driver. She was negotiating for more time to finish an order that would be delivered by the taxi driver to the port in Mytilini, so that it could be loaded onto a ferry for arrival in Athens the next morning. I checked with each of the cooperatives, and learned that large social or religious events hosted by islanders in Athens are sometimes catered by a village's women's cooperative. When I asked why, given the range of bakeries in Athens, Ourania, from the Molyvos cooperative, explained: "A private bakery could never provide the quality of product that the women's cooperatives provide and the villagers know that."

Members in the cooperatives' kitchens were preparing orders for weddings, baptisms, holidays, or other family events on a regular basis. Although I did not initially realize the extent to which items were being produced for export, I could see the mass amounts of pastries being prepared for religious festivities. This is because of the notable μπομπονιέρες (boubounieres) or Greek style favors, pervasive in ceremonial celebrations such as weddings and baptisms in Greece and by its diaspora. They usually include sweet almonds wrapped in tulle, sometimes with other crafted items, that cooperatives were responsible for creating as part of their service. Attractive, well-made boubounieres are a status symbol, and having them made in the family's regional locality adds to their charm.

The volume of orders for special occasions was impressive as was the intensity at which the cooperative members worked to meet deadlines. Getting the items to the social event became an almost joint effort among villagers, as the wedding or baptism of kin abroad was talked about in the village. Rather than drawing the line, the women's cooperatives would work late into the evening and meet last-minute requests for additional items, or unexpected changes to the order. The willingness to negotiate or extend deadlines, rather than abide by a contract, is reflective of the hospitality and flexibility embedded in Greek enterprise.

Members from various cooperatives said that they extended themselves because of the economic crisis, as many families could no longer afford to plan a large-scale event at more expensive venues. The successful and timely delivery of a great display of food required the investment of time and energy and coordination that would not be compensated as might occur when one hires a formal caterer. The efforts in preparations were shaped by a sense of community or obligation toward completing the necessary tasks to help create a successful wedding or other event for villagers abroad.

The confidence customers had in the cooperatives meeting the orders was based on the accomplishment of the gendered duties of village women. Greek village women who live on islands are the keepers of traditions that are essential to family and religious celebrations. The cooperatives' members were aware that the needs of village kin living in cities were an important market. Ariadne, from the Agra cooperative, explained, "There is a trend now to have a wedding event in one's own field and garden. This has been to the advantage of cooperatives that are more equipped to do catering, and are better able to organize prepared foods for an event."

In Greece, as elsewhere, there is a preference for gendered local food production, a preference that the women's cooperatives successfully fulfill. Women from Lesvos who live and work in urban contexts, where time and space to make traditional pastries is absent, or perhaps due to a lack of interest in cookery, can rely on the cooperative for the customary gendered production of foods for major events. Or as Meli, from the Petra cooperative, said, "Where is anyone in an Athens apartment going to be able to cook for a large party? It takes a group of women."

Food anthropologist Carole M. Counihan (2004) notes in her book *Around the Tuscan Table: Food, Family, and Gender in Twentieth-Century Florence* that women in urban Italy felt obliged to cook healthful meals for children and pass on family food traditions, but jobs prevented them from meeting this expectation they had for themselves. Despite their new economic power as wage earners, Counihan (2004) argues that women were less secure in their identities because they could not fulfill culinary rituals. To some degree, the system of women's cooperatives in Greece relieves this burden for Greek urban women. The women's cooperatives sustain island identities by serving as a proxy for the gendered culinary arts for urban islanders. The regular purchases of cooperative products by emigrant islanders in Athens or Thesaloniki not only support the retention of distinct cultural fare but economically supports local producers, including the farmers and the various food cooperatives found across Greek islands. Although fulfilling the gendered obligations of preparing traditional foods, the women's cooperatives paradoxically challenge traditional gender norms. Not only do these island village women move from isolation in their household to collective production, but having gained access to the agora, they are publicly visible, sharing coffee in their own cafés or shop fronts.

Diet: The Island Food Phenomenon

Local foods advocates argue that the food—processed, mass produced, with intensive chemicals, sugary, and meat heavy—eaten by sizable continental and urban populations is not only unhealthful but also environmentally unsustainable. Historically, it was the hinterlands of urban zones that would supply agricultural products to the growing number of city dwellers, making locally organized diets dominant less than a century ago. The advancement of conventional agriculture and the establishment of global food regimes removed multitudes from independent farming. The combination of refrigeration, prepackaged and frozen meals, advances in food transport, and genetically modified organisms and chemicals further disconnected populations from the potential of regional agriculture.

The new determination to purchase or grow fresh local produce by means of sustainable agriculture affirms that more and more of us are yearning for connectivity with where and how food arrives at our tables. The contemporary food movements may have been fueled by the success of the counterculture's challenges to modernizing food systems decades ago (Belasco 1989), but guiding current locavorism or femivorism is the mounting evidence of environmental damage and the harm associated with conventional agriculture. Small scale, ecological farming, and food cooperatives are far more mainstreamed presently than they were in the sixties and seventies, though some of the alternative food projects initiated at that time endure.

Assessments of the impact of food movements, in all its forms, are riddled with contradictions. Localist strategies for "taking back our food system" from corporate actors and alternative food networks toward organic and small-scale farming are lauded for improving health and community building, while being critiqued for exclusivity and costliness. Food tourism has gained ground because of increased middle-class interest to travel for freshly prepared foods based in cultural traditions. Yet the culinary tourist industry represents a commodification of experience, as it exploits for economic development the rising interest in food that is local, regionally authentic, ethnic, fresh, exquisite, or traditional. At the same time, food tourism may provide an avenue for rural regions to sustain their long-held agricultural traditions, support local farmers and artisanal food production, and preserve culture.

For the many scholars approaching the ballooning field of food studies in the interest of supporting alternatives, the conundrum remains as to how to advance a food system that does not expose workers or consumers to toxic chemicals without reifying the consumptive and individualistic logics of neoliberalism. It seems that the current discord in recent food scholarship on the transformative power of alternative food systems is tied to the early sociological debates on what counts as resistance or generates social change that was summarized in the opening of this volume. Resistance is identified as "real" when it includes "institutional politics"; in the case of food, it may include changing government policies to limit toxic chemicals, or amending permit laws to allow farmers' markets or farming in neighborhoods. When the focus is on the rights of employees—including farm workers, those in food processing plants, or in the service industry—contemporary food activism is considered "viable class action." Yet alternative food strategies do not fit in either category and are therefore assessed as "token . . . unorganized or individual actions, or behaviors described as opportunistic and self-indulgent, accommodation within the system" (Scott 1985, 287).

Much of James Scott's body of scholarship challenges the academic framing of grassroots and localized independent actions as nontransformative. Gibson-Graham's (2006) arguments on the limited analytical vision of academics to recognize the wide pool of alternative economic exchanges as viable is in the same vein. Urban sociologist and development professional AbdouMaliq Simone (2004, 5–6), who meticulously researched forms of solidarity and convivial economy occurring in African cities that go unnoticed by government officials and development workers, explains:

> Self-responsibility for urban survival has opened up spaces for different ways of organizing activities. Communities have become increasingly involved in one or more aspects of the provision of essential services. . . . Many local associations have been formed to improve sanitation, provide shelter, improve marketing, extend microfinance, and advocate for a broad range of rights. . . . These networks are not constructed in terms of conventional organizations or grassroots associations, but involve large numbers of people who implicitly coordinate their behavior in the pursuit of objectives that have both individual definitions but coherence among participants.

And as cited earlier, Hau'ofa (1994) also communicates the positive results delivered in "the realm of ordinary people, peasants and proletarians . . . that go unnoticed or ignored at the top." These subaltern renderings of social change apply to the many efforts and forms in the food justice and food movements taking hold across the globe. Taking back our food system is not limited to wealthy or middle class consumers, but is reflected in the unobtrusive and attritional undertakings or the interstitial strategies of subaltern populations, even if some of these activities may be co-opted by neoliberal interests.

Island diets have been restricted by geographies far longer than those of continental spaces and are shaped by vast marine resources, varied climate zones, and endemic flora and fauna. Currently in the occupied Kingdom of Hawai'i there is a revival of indigenous food practices that had allowed for a thriving sovereign food system that was able to meet the nutritional needs of at least a million people (Fisher 2015). With only so many roads to travel, islanders often hold intimate knowledge of place—a "shima" that merges culture with natural environment—which is made apparent in island food systems.

Islanders' experience of bounded space sustains a collective identity and is a prelude to the pronounced welcome or hospitality for which islands are known—not a clichéd kind of tourist industry hospitality, but the genuine welcome of visitors and new persons to an island that is hardly expressed toward returning kin or those with ancestral ties to the island. It is well known among Greeks that Athens empties in the summer—beyond the sea of tourists that overtake Plaka, other sites of antiquity, stores, and restaurants, there is a lull in Athens. Many resident Athenians escape to their familial island for a week or two, while some are able to relocate for the entire summer. Regardless of length of stay, many of the returnees that I spoke with were eager for a taste of home, avidly dining at the various tavernas or, depending on what one can afford, sharing drinks and coffee with parea or friends in the plateia. They contribute to a local culinary tourism that supports a Greek island culture. The value placed on local fare becomes a form of cultural and economic resistance with small enterprises retaining substantial control of the Greek island food system.

PART III

HOSPITABLE SHORES

To the Norwegian Nobel Peace Prize Committee

Ordinary residents of Greek islands and other volunteers have been on the front lines of Europe's refugee crisis for months, opening up their hearts and homes to save hundreds of thousands fleeing war and terror. For their compassion and courage, for treating those in danger with humanity, and for setting an example for the rest of the world to follow, we citizens from around the world, nominate these brave women and men for a Nobel Peace Prize.

Since the very beginning of the refugee crisis, **fishermen, housewives, pensioners, teachers—ordinary residents of the Greek islands and other volunteers have opened their homes and hearts** to save refugee children, men and women fleeing war and terror.

They've even risked their own lives to rescue thousands from the freezing sea waters.

With their actions, they drowned fear and racism in a wave of compassion and reminded the whole world that we are one, united humanity, above races, nations and religions. Now we have a massive opportunity to **help them shine their light even brighter, and show governments that people care** and demand urgent action.

AVAAZ.org 2016 petition

CHAPTER SEVEN

Skala Eresos

From Ancient City-State to
Bohemian Seaside Tourist Village

HUGH: Tough folk, your Hellenics. Hard as the crags and boulders that shape the islands and hills of their landscape.

STEPHEN: Tssch. Do you know I wouldn't be surprised if there was a lesson in there somewhere?

HUGH: Certainly there is. I've often thought of putting out a paper on the correlation between landscape and business acumen.

STEPHEN: Great subject, Stu. You could set fire to some arses with a paper like that. The Institute of Executive Salesmen would go ape crazy on all fours for a theory of that sort.

—"Gordon and Stuart Eat Greek," *A Bit of Fry and Laurie* (1987)

The rise of convivial microenterprises in Skala Eresos—local, alternative, and lesbian—is founded on the good life prized by the Eressians, based in men's coffee shop culture with shepherds, farmers, and professionals socializing, and not on contemporary tourism. The symbiotic relationship between agriculture and tourism—and between attritional and organic forms of economic alterity in the Eresos valley—offers a path for island development that is locally defined and considerate of regional culture and the environment. The subaltern space of the Greek islands has made them locations in which many arrive to participate in a convivial logic that persists in social and economic relations conscripted by island geographies. In rewatching the scene of British actors Hugh

171

Fry and Stephen Laurie's sketch comedy quoted in the epigraph, I was doubly amused—as always by their wry humor and also for how it serendipitously drew together multiple elements of this book.

Figure 7.1. The good life/Personal photo of Georgia Rouvalis. I obtained this photo as part of my grandmother's collection in Amaliada, Greece. The photo contains my grandfather (center), my great uncle, and likely another extended family member. The photo was taken on Kourouta Beach in the Peloponnese and captures Greek expressions of masculinity, the κέφι and κέρασμα, of the celebratory atmosphere of Greek summers.

Skala Eresos is built over the ancient city in which Sappho was likely born (Schaus and Spencer 1994). The embankments of Skala Eresos's current port (from which the cover photo was taken) are based in the same seawalls established around the seventh or eighth century BC (Schaus and Spencer 1994). With the exception of some sea level rise, the shoreline of Skala Eresos remains primarily the same since antiquity (Schaus and Spencer 1994). The ancient population of seaside Eresos, like many coastal cities in the Aegean and Mediterranean, relocated to higher elevations in nearby mountains in response to piracy that encompassed the region from around 700 CE, marking the fall of the Roman Empire (De Sousa 2002). The mountains cradling these communities became a refuge and a lookout to observe coming ships, which allowed residents time to prepare for impending attacks. In much of the Mediterranean, piracy again commenced around the mid-1300s. The unceasing conflict between the Ottomans and Western Europe, the lax oversight of the Ottoman Empire, and the distinct geography of the Aegean islands, which includes protected coves and bays and well-etched sea routes, combined to create conditions in which piracy could flourish (Delis 2016).

According to his descendants, it was not until 1901 when Adonis Koukou, a member of Eresos's landed elite, called for the reclamation of the oceanside that reestablished residency along the Aegean. His argument was that "culture arrives by the sea." A residential community soon developed in the ancient port city of Eresos and the construction of the first modern homes was initiated in 1912. The reactivation of the port resulted in the construction of buildings along the coast used to store the products arriving in small boats. These storage units, and other buildings, were eventually rented and refurbished by locals opening general stores, ouzerias, or traditional Greek tavernas to serve villagers and returning kin. Ultimately, bohemian and lesbian restaurants and nightspots also came to dot Sappho's coastline, turning an ancient city-state into a low-key, alternative, tourist seaside village.

Journeying through layered social rhythms of Skala Eresos, this chapter considers the place-making that has transpired since the establishment of modern Skala Eresos. On many Greek islands, lower seaside villages are reached by rocky switchback donkey trails that wind down from the upper or main villages founded on the mountainsides. These walkways, which are referred to as "σκάλα" or "stairs," lead to the lower villages, which are also referred to simply as "skala"—the term, which

Figure 7.2. A mountain view of Skala/courtesy of Tzeli Hadjidimitriou. This photo captures the length of Skala Eresos's shoreline and much of the village at the bottom of Eresos valley. On top of the tall hillside from where this photo was taken are remnants of a medieval castle built on the ruins of the ancient acropolis of Eresos. Both locals and tourists refer to the area as vigla, which is a Greek term that translates to watchtower or perch, as the location served in antiquity. Wild oregano perfumes the surrounding fields during the summer months.

also means harbor or seaport, is used to preface the name of the seaside village. Although the rocky path between Eresos and Skala Eresos makes for a dramatic hike in the valley between the two allied villages, there is now a paved road that links them. As I review the stages of Skala Eresos's transition from a seaside village to a tourist destination over the century, I focus on the sequenced arrival of various social groups that laid the ground for lesbian enterprises to eventually flourish.

Antecedents to Skala

The sociality and κέρασμά guests experience when taking a seat at any of the eateries around Sappho's Square in Skala Eresos are grounded in social and economic forms that are organic to the local population.* Tavernas and kafenions were first established by local entrepreneurs for village residents to enjoy and gather. Only after many decades did their numbers increase as they came to play host to the Northern European visitors that began to trickle into the Greek islands in the 1960s.

Like many seaside island villages in the Greek isles, Skala Eresos witnessed the largest increase in foreign tourism in the 1980s, reflecting a global trend. The extent to which village locals were able to absorb markedly distinct and visible social groups attests to the success of their φιλοξενία and the corresponding interests between organic and attritional economic enterprises. Despite grievances, many Northern European guests were enamored with the routines and rhythms they found in Skala Eresos. As these visitors became residents, they did not seek to change things or introduce large-scale development; instead, they sought to participate as part of a local business community. In setting up enterprises, newcomers to Eresos mingled with locals, as they relied on them to navigate the Greek business environment. Leaving jobs and careers in mainland cities, the small enterprises they built contributed favorably to the convivial economic practices found in Greek island villages. At its core, convivial economics in Skala Eresos include transactions among suppliers, entrepreneurs, property owners, and customers that are oriented by the interest of keeping everyone afloat—indicative of an organic economic alterity that helped many Greek enterprises survive the economic crisis of the 2010s.

Three of the original enterprises in 1950s Skala were traditional Greek coffee shops or kafenions on the village square, the dominion of men. As days warmed and lengthened with summer, the men gathering at the kafenions extended their stay into the evenings when they would dip into the sea bordering the venues, dry off, and return for drinks or a taste of something to eat. The immediacy of dining and swimming on Greek island shores has come to enchant tourists who very easily spend entire days enjoying this routine.

Many elite Eressian families that constructed the original storage units now gain from the rents paid by local and foreign microentrepre-

---

*Sappho's square is officially renamed after the parents of a wealthy shipping magnate who owned a building on the plateia and offered to improve the plateia with cobblestones. This occurred to the chagrin of many of Skala's residents who continue to refer to the square as Sappho's; it still holds a large metallic statue of her at the center of it.

neurs operating businesses in these prized coastal properties. This group of wealthy Eressians inherited tracts of land in the valley from previous generations that had maintained sharecroppers. Many sharecropping families eventually became independent farmers or left for Greece's urban centers or migrated abroad. Others entered into tourism through the development of food enterprises and other small-scale local serving businesses. To have a business in Skala Eresos, one often begins by "buying the air," which refers to purchasing all or most of the equipment, appliances, and tables and chairs, or just the license under which a business operates. "Buying the air" was a phrase used regularly in my interviews with entrepreneurs in Skala Eresos. In one instance, when I asked a more senior proprietor if he had bought the air, he responded, "No, but I sold the air." His parents were one on the families that were early to relocate from the upper village of Eresos to the seaside village of Skala. He and his brother opened one of the first tavernas in Skala by buying and refurbishing a storage house for figs, an agricultural pillar for Eresos until the blight of disease earlier in the century.

The kafenions and ouzerias that advanced in midcentury Skala Eresos were founded on the expression of Greek masculinities based in gendered space and sociality described earlier. In the following decades, a new pattern of gathering in the public sphere began to emerge during the summer. An expansion of ouzerias, tavernas, and kafenions was prompted by the massive return of villagers who had migrated but returned to their island homes for extended summer holiday visits. These eateries began to cater to a seasonal rhythm of summertime hosting.

As described in chapter 4 φιλοξενία, the governing ideology of the Greek public sphere, is essentially hostile to the watchful accounting practices of neoliberalism. The raison d'être of the microenterprises developing in Skala Eresos was to serve its community and support sociality, while also earning an income—a distinctly different logic from the neoliberal goals of accumulation and expansion. Families emigrated and left Lesvos due to fear of political persecution during and after the Greek Civil War (1945–49) and later as a response to the military junta (1967–74), while many others left purely for economic reasons. Because Lesvos was a stronghold of the Greek Communist Party, the outcome of the Civil War placed the island and those associated with the Communist Party in a precarious position. In my interviews, many local respondents referred to parents who had fought for the National

People's Army of Liberation, explaining that Lesvos served as a place of rest and relaxation for leftist soldiers.

During the mid-1960s, the managerial office of the Agricultural Cooperative of Eresos was founded in a new building along the central plateia in Skala. The construction of this office further solidified Skala Eresos as an independent community, one that was separate from the town of Eresos. Though the cooperative relocated to the upper village in the 2000s, my interview participants almost invariably referred to its offices in Skala. The cooperative hosted its own kafenion, apparently with the tradition of Sunday λουκουμάδες (loukoumades), a Greek fried dough specialty saturated with melted honey and sprinkled with ground walnuts. Near the cooperative office off the main plateia was a general store and a government importation office.

Well into the first half of the twentieth century much of the economic exchange in Lesvos was by barter; banks did not arrive in the Eresos valley until the 1990s. Instead, vans would travel to the villages from established banks in Mytilini at regular intervals for those needing to carry out financial transactions through a banking institution. The first ATM appeared in the mid-2000s in Skala. Dealings that rely on barter and cash seem to have been maintained in contemporary Skala Eresos and facilitate convivial economics. For example, I was aware of numerous trades including maintaining grounds in an exchange for housing, providing produce or herbs, or running errands in exchange for regular meals at a shop, artworks traded for housekeeping services, and veterinary assistance swapped for farming plots.

At midcentury, the only formal accommodations available in the valley were in the upper village and included two inns, Sparelos and Babalambros—the last names of the owners—with a few rooms in each. The inns had been established mostly to accommodate professional visitors, such as governmental officials, members of the agriculture cooperative system, or religious visitors who would occasionally tend to the village. During a summer in the late 1950s, Babalambros opened the first few rooms for rent in Skala, marking the first foray in hosting seaside visitors or foreigners.

The first formal hotel on Lesvos was the Delfinia in Molyvos erected in 1961 and the second, a few later, the Delfinia II, in Skala Eresos. The Hellenic Tourism Organization under a conservative government (the National Radical Union under Constantine Karamanlis) was advancing

the establishment of island hotels. These early efforts at tourist development focused on attracting elites or wealthy tourists to the Greek islands
who had largely traveled to Greece to visit antiquities. Until the 1970s,
it was largely Greek islanders who enjoyed the exquisite insular beauty
of the Aegean, Ionian, and Mediterranean Seas.

Governmental efforts toward Greek tourism have occurred in spurts,
and they have been uncannily tied to conservative regimes. The first government tourism body was formed in 1914, just two years after Lesvos was
liberated from the Ottoman Empire. Angelos Vlachos, a Greek historian
who had also worked in the Ministry of Tourism and the Greek National
Tourism Organization, chronicled its early history. According to Vlachos
(2014), Greece began to attract foreign tourists with the first modern
Olympics Games held in Athens in 1896 and after a number of archeological discoveries. The Greek National Tourism Organization was hoping
that in a relatively stable Europe, with a growing leisure class, there would
be an increase in foreign travelers to Greece. European tourism, however,
was paused with the onset of World War I that led to tightened border
controls and limits on visas, curtailing recreational travel around Europe.

The next upturn in tourist development was under the totalitarian
regime of Prime Minister Ioannis Metaxas (1936–41). Under Metaxas,
the Greek state began to craft a national identity based in the classical
period of ancient Greece that would attract Western tourists to ancient
archeological sites (Vlachos 2014). To attract visitors to the islands,
Metaxas sought to further beautify old buildings and structures on islands.
For instance, Metaxas initiated the whitewashing of buildings in the
Cyclades islands, which have become a lasting symbol of Greek island
tourism (Vlachos 2014).

Based on an analysis of newspaper accounts, Vlachos (2014) found
that Northern Europeans who traveled to Greece regularly complained
about the quality of Greek tourist facilities and the lack of regulation.
These complaints resonate with some of the comments Northern
European tourists made regarding contemporary accommodations and
transportation in Lesvos, and those of early English women travelers.
Rather than appreciating that Greece is distinctly less developed than
Northern Europe, tourists continue to frame Greek facilities not by its
own measure, but through an imperial gaze, as perpetually falling short
of "European" standards.

In 1941, Dimitrios Papaefstratiou, known as the father of Greek
tourism, began planning for Greece as a tourist destination with invest-

ments by the National Bank of Greece (Vlachos 2014). It was not until the end of World War II that Greek tourist development began in earnest, again under a conservative regime. Northern European tourists began to arrive in Greece just as Greeks who had fought in the resistance were subject to imprisonment, exile, and violence by Greece's fascist regime. The Regime of Colonels, discussed in chapter 4, led larger scale development efforts in the islands for the purpose of economic growth and employment creation, in hopes of maintaining social control. Many of these projects never came to fruition, and remained partially built. Those that did were not well planned, with many causing detriment to natural island environments (Vlachos 2014).

As is the case with many diaspora populations, development in small town and villages arrives not with the state or capital, but with the generosity of successful immigrants who worked abroad. In Lesvos, remittances contributed to building many of the neoclassical schools found throughout its villages, as well as new homes, improved roads, and tourist businesses. For example, a large number of Eressians who had migrated to the Democratic Republic of the Congo, working in fishing, music recording, and rubber, used earnings to support family members in Eresos. Due to the Congolese movement for independence, many of the Greeks who had immigrated to the Congo returned to Lesvos during the early 1960s and used their earnings from abroad to buy plots of land for agriculture, to build homes, and develop enterprises.*

Tourist Rhythms

One of the more well-known myths among those told of the Greek pantheon is that of Persephone, the god of vegetation and spring's bounty. As a young woman, Persephone is picking flowers in fields in the company of the Oceanids, sent there by her mother to protect her, when Hades, the god of the underworld, abducts her. Upon Demeter's threat that Persephone return to earth or she will continue to scorch it,

---

*The Democratic Republic of Congo was claimed as the Belgian Congo from 1908 to 1960 by its colonial occupants. Although a few of the Eressians I spoke with referred to it as Zaire, as it was named from 1971 to 1997, most Eressians refer to the nation as the Belgian Congo, which reflects the time frame the Eressians arrived and worked there.

Hades feeds Persephone pomegranate seeds, which induces a desire for Hades and to return to the underworld. The solution between Demeter and Hades regarding the plight of Persephone is a negotiated and rhythmical one: she will spend six months in the underworld, and spring and summer on earth with her mother.

Like Persephone, many islanders who live in Greek cities or further abroad return to their island villages annually, around spring, producing a distinct form of tourism. These visitations initiate a season of celebrations that begin with the observation of Greek Orthodox Easter, which can occur between March and May. At this time foreign visitors also filter into Skala Eresos who are either seeking to witness the celebrations of Easter, securing employment for the upcoming tourist season, or watching the vivid display of wildflowers that adorn the valley at springtime.

Prior to the expected arrival of tourists, owners of the various venues make a set of preparations, spurring the transition from the quiet slow rhythm of island winters to the sprightly work pace and social life of summer. Those that closed for winter begin to rebuild decks that were smashed by winter waves, refurbish chairs and tables, perform renovations, and order inventory. In early spring gossip in the agora revolves around the extent of damage incurred by storms and tides and predictions of how many and who will visit (i.e., Germans, English, Athenians, lesbians, young people, Turks) in the upcoming tourist season. Others discuss the planning of new enterprises and the closing of businesses. By 2012, predicting the impact of the economic crises on tourism also became a prominent topic of conversations.

A few enterprises had exchanged hands and some businesses had rebranded themselves between 2008 through 2012, but not a single storefront closed shop, despite the economic crisis. When I returned to Skala in 2016, I learned that a clothing store and a lesbian bar had closed, but several new businesses had opened, including a coffee shop, a pizza place, and a Turkish kebob house. While concerns and discussion of the future impacts of the economic crisis were spirited, several business owners continued to demonstrate confidence in Skala's ability to attract the tourists and visitors who have been returning for decades.

Skala business owners agreed that everyone was spending less—both foreigners and Greeks. Many of them lamented that they could not "host" customers in ways that they preferred because of austerity measures. As one owner complained, "We can't even lower the prices for our customers." The decline in Greek clientele spending was most significant for businesses serving traditional Greek foods. Panayotis, the owner of a taverna that remains open year-round, explained, "If Greeks have money they will go out and spend it on food and drinks. It's just now that they don't have money." But it wasn't just Greeks: foreign visitors who "come to Greece to eat Greek" also reduced their spending. As one regular lesbian tourist from Australia explained, "Last year I ate out a lot, a lot of traditional food: octopus, sardines. I've done less this time to be economical."

Above all months, August is the premier period for tourism. For Greek islanders, it is a prime time for celebrations, which draw extended family to the island. For European vacationers seeking escape from rainy climates and cloudy days in the north, the Greek islands offer a guaranteed sunny holiday and warm weather escape. In the Aegean, August's high daily temperatures cool down considerably by evening and the bright Mediterranean sun tempers into subtle shades of sunset, inescapably witnessed on the balconies that border Skala Eresos. August is the month that the village bustles to its brim with those in the service industry working to the peak of their capacity, as the village's population quadruples. Workers, business and building owners, and households I interviewed both loathed and relished the activity of August.

Attritional Alternatives: Small Is Beautiful

The "small is beautiful" momentum of the late 1960s and 1970s, framed by Schumacher (1973) and referred to throughout this volume, brought together localness, autonomy, and ecological sustainability. For the most part those directly engaged with "small is beautiful" projects—including cooperatives, communes, artisanal businesses, farms, and restaurants with local and organic fare—were privileged young white people who were rejecting consumerism and careerism. Some were politically driven, as they had anticapitalist intentions. Others were less politically motivated, but still selected to "turn on, tune in, and drop out" of mainstream society (Leary 1966). Those involved in such projects were often depicted as noncontributive, lazy, or simply living in a drug-induced haze, but were often quite diligent, as the rejection of mass production, as "femivores" have found, takes work. Hippies' industriousness was evident in their refusal to consume mass-produced goods and foods, or accept automated processes or a trove of appliances. Groups of young individuals were seeking alternative lifestyles that they found possible in more remote and less developed parts of the world, such as the Greek islands, in the 1970s.

One of the earliest academic publications (Howard 1969, 46) that attempted to define hippies includes the following description:

> On the personal level, a rejection of the conventional social system involved dropping out. Given the logic of the hippie ethic, dropping out made sense. The school system prepares a person for an occupational role. The occupational role yields money and allows the person to buy the things which society says are necessary for the "good life." If society's definition of the good life is rejected, then dropping out becomes a sensible action, in that one does not want the money with which to purchase such a life. By dropping out, a person can "do his own thing." And that might entail making beads or sandals, or exploring various levels of consciousness, or working in the soil to raise the food that he eats.

Howard's (1969) summation of a "hippie ethic" is an intriguing angle for activities currently catalogued as alternative economics, and provides an excellent substantiation of attritional economic alterity. By bifurcating convivial economics into organic economic alterity and attritional economic alterity, I recognize the spatial and social inequities that shape each of these practices in the Greek islands. In sum, *organic economic alterity*, or locally embedded convivial economics, has been sustained in regions on the margins of state and capitalist interest and a local refusal to be co-opted by neoliberal notions of enterprise. *Attritional economic alterity* represents a choice often made by privileged groups in the Global North—but also by persons who have been socially restrained by gender, sexuality, or as members of a counterculture—who tire of bias and marginalization, seek an alternative community, and leave mainstream society and contribute to a subaltern cosmpolitanism (Gidwani 2006; Khader 2003).

As presented in the previous chapter, contemporary writings on small-scale and sustainable economies approach localism, or microbusiness and cooperatives, as novel endeavors (see Kassen 2016; Botsman and Rogers 2011; Burlingham 2005) without situating current alternative economic activities as part of a sociohistorical trajectory that includes the efforts of hippies and other practices of attritional economic alterity that deserve further unearthing by the field of alternative economics. Aside for Belasco's (1989) work and a few others, such as Michael Kassen's *Hippie, Inc.: The Misunderstood Subculture That Changed the Way We Live and Generated Billions of Dollars in the Process* (2016), academic research on the counterculture of the late 1960s and early 1970s has focused more attentively on the cultural or political impact of the movement rather than on its economic one. Among many academics and activists and the general public, there tends to be a dismissal and even demonization of hippies or counterculture projects (Kassen 2016). As Belasco (1989) demonstrates in the alternative food movement, hippie undertakings in local, artisanal, small-scale, and collective enterprises precede and inform the current outbreak of activities in alternative food networks.

In the social sciences, a growing influence of Marxism in the 1970s bolstered the imperative of resolving capitalism's contradictions through socialism. Shaped by the political climate of the Cold War period, advances of nationalist or communist movements in the Global South, and the seeming success of the Cuban Revolution, the leftist perspective was dominated by a singular viewpoint on how large-scale social change was to occur. While philosophies of anarchism and economic alterity, such as Schumacher (1973), Illich (1973), and Bookchin (1969), gained popular traction, many political economists dismissed their work as an unviable counter to capitalism because it was not class driven. Marxist concentration on the mobilization of a formal working class deemphasized the theoretical significance or location of everyday strategies of survival or of petty trade and production that explicitly or implicitly rejects mass production.

As I have reviewed, many of the entities that can be catalogued as small, convivial, and alternative are often dismissed as microforms of capitalism, upholding ethics of accumulation and expansion rather than representing a different form of enterprise (Amin 2009; Leyshon and Lee 2003; Ferguson 1999). Yet there is a great deal of difference between an entrepreneur who initiates a business to make it big in hopes of ever increasing income (i.e., the petit bourgeois) that will permit more possessions compared to those who have chosen to create an enterprise, earn a subsistence or modest income, and work in collective or convivial spaces to sustain the natural environment and affectionate communities.

Islands became particularly attractive locations for young privileged travelers who wanted to retreat from mainstream society. This may be due to islands being understood as isolated, rural, or geographically removed from centers of power, and that the lives of islanders and communities that are shaped by island geographies, or shima, attract alternative types. Many island regions across the globe, for example Hawai'i, Indonesia, the eastern Caribbean, and across the Greek islands, continue to host alternative or hippie outposts. Global North travelers leave their home and exploit the low cost of living in poor and peripheral regions. In Greece, they came to islands such as Hydra, Ikaria, Crete, and Lesvos to establish small-scale artisanal enterprises or work alongside Greeks in agricultural production, such as the seasonal gathering of olives.

Lesvos, and Skala Eresos specifically, was a haven for alternative travelers from the 1980s. As one woman I interviewed explained, "Crete was getting too crowded." These early "tourists" to Skala—Scandinavians, Germans, English, Dutch, and French—traveled several days to reach Mediterranean and Aegean islands to spend their summers, or become part of the permanent alternative communities that were developing in the Greek islands, most notably in Crete. Canadian Joni Mitchell, singer-songwriter and counterculture icon, resided for a bit of time in Matala, Crete, the Neolithic caves, at the epicenter of hippie traveler dwellings on Greek islands. Mitchell memorialized the alternative enclaves of Greek islands in her songs "California" and "Carey," both released on her album Blue (1971). She refers to the two songs as "the same music novella" (Myers 2014). In both songs, Mitchell seems to lament leaving the Greek island. In "California," she sings, "I met a redneck on a Grecian isle / who did the goat dance very well / He gave me back my smile / but he kept my camera to sell / oh the rogue, the red, red rogue / he cooked good omelets and stews / And I might have stayed on with him there but . . ." And in "Carey," she sings, "Oh, you know it sure is hard to leave here, Carey / but it's really not my home / My fingernails are filthy / I've got beach tar on my feet / And I miss my clean white linen and my fancy French cologne." Though Mitchell spent less than a year in Crete, she is well associated with it. Her songwriting renders attritional alterity and these songs illuminate it as rhythmical of Greek island place.

Greece offered Northern European alternatives who were at odds with their nations' ideologies and institutions an idyllic place with a cultural and economic context that prizes autonomous work arrangements, local governance, and convivial or familial exchange. Greek islanders generally accepted this growing number of alternative travelers as deserving of φιλοξενία, despite their participation in activities that ran contrary to Greek social codes, such as nude sunbathing. Though tensions rose between the state and the growing groups of hippie travelers, Greek islanders generally recognize them as another set of foreigners visiting their islands.

SKALA ERESOS'S UNCONVENTIONAL DEVELOPMENT

However unexpected and unplanned, a good part of the increase of tourism in Eresos was due to the hippies who began trickling into Skala in the mid-seventies, becoming a sizeable mass by the mid-1980s. A number of the alternatives and lesbians I met in 2008, 2009, 2012, and 2016 had been visiting, living, or working in Skala Eresos for several decades. Studies of Greek tourism generally do not account for the thrifty alternative campers and travelers to its islands. Yet they have played a significant role in the development and social politics of Greek islands, in many instances leading the way for less adventurous tourists by generating travel circuits to Greek islands from Northern cities.

The impact of these bohemian and alternative visitors and new residents to the Greek islands is distinct from that of the mainstream tourism that followed. Less attracted to developed touristed isles, such as Mykonos and Santorini and later Crete, hippies and other alternative types journeyed to less-known Greek islands, where they contributed from slightly to significantly to remote village economies. As young backpackers willing to work in agriculture or setting up self-sustaining enterprises, they often founded synergistic relationships with local Greeks.

Greek residents and owners in Skala date the addition of bohemian enterprises in the village to the mid-1980s. These new set of establishments, often offering both Greek and non-Greek food preparations, such as avocado toast, peanut sauce and noodles, and pizza, brought more choices in venue to the already well-established businesses of Eressians and other Greeks. Local business owners considered this decade the most economically successful in terms of tourism. Zoe, whose family has operated the same tourist shop since the 1980s, remembers the scene fondly:

[The years from] 1988 to 1994 was the biggest [for] tourism. We had four discotheques that were full every night through the summer. The beach was packed, in August you didn't even have a place for an umbrella. There were English tourists

that were coming on their own, Athenians, and Greeks from
other areas. There were charters, [with] preorganized flights
and accommodations, coming from England and Germany.
And also for a few years there were college students from
Austria, a new group arriving weekly throughout the summer.
The places to go were the Blue Sardine, Le Jardine, Glaros,
Sappho Hotel. It was a mess ('εγινε χαμός)!

Other owners I interviewed suggested that "1983–1989 was the biggest
tourist period," or "there was a generation of hippies in 1982–1985, they
crowded the beaches."

The cosmopolitan character of Skala Eresos that makes the village
uniquely attractive is supported by enterprises established by the alternatives or "freakyo," the label for hippies and alternative in Greece, that
arrived from Greek cities and Northern Europe. Many counterculture
visitors passed through Skala Eresos as semipermanent residents, but
others did not want to return to mainstream lives and mainland careers,
and sought a different future. Those that stayed developed small-scale
enterprises that attracted more bohemian travelers. To the traditional
Greek island enterprises "with plastic chairs that hit the Mediterranean
as quickly as the tourists," these bohemian enterprises brought to Skala
a different aesthetic, music, and food and drinks. At least a handful of
these enterprises continue to operate in Skala Eresos presently. Some
of the early proprietors have changed businesses, starting new ones or
relocating old ones to more preferable settings within the village. A few
have retired in the valley and tend to their own gardens. For many, relocating to Eresos meant leaving city life for island life, as one successful
proprietor who started up in the 1980s explains:

> Life is better here. I know it. We don't have many expenses
> here. In Athens it could take you twenty euros to get to work.
> Here, you ride a bicycle. Skala is a place for alternatives. It is
> welcoming here. You can get lost in the valley, live in a tent,
> and live simply. I just got a massage the other day. When I
> asked him when he arrived he said he had been here for five
> years. Five years in this valley and I never knew him! You
> can still make discoveries.

Elke, a woman from Northern Europe who returned in 2012 to settle in
Eresos, had run a popular bar with her ethnic Greek husband for about

two decades. The bar had been referenced and considered a turning point in the character of Skala's tourism. It was a first nexus, where different groups—local, lesbian, and alternative—would come to socialize. Bemused that her enterprise and alternative life could be of such interest to me, and after I answering her questions about my research, she eventually shared some of her story:

> In 1979 I came to Greece and traveled around the islands like everyone. I met my husband. In the 1980s we were in Folegandros and we thought we should do something, we had this idea to look for a place. I remember we came here, someone told us it was a very nice place. We went to Switzerland and worked very hard and saved up money for a year and a half. He wanted Athens, but I did not want that at all. He also went to see a place in Naxos. We then came here. We started with a place in the village, but we didn't like it being right there in the center. We found this place down the road, four cement walls, a mat roof, and a space to make a garden. We asked about it, it was 1984, the owner said we could have it. There was no water or electricity. It was built illegal, but we started from there.

She continues:

> We had a snack bar that started to work as a discotheque without a license for a discotheque in '85–'86. It was a very nice scene and really mixed. It was for everyone, gay-lesbian, people our age, people from Athens, couples from abroad. It was known for having the best music, the Clash, Cure, African music, reggae. I would get in at 8 a.m. and stay open through 9 p.m. And then we would close, go eat in town. One full moon we said let's have a late night party. And then eventually we started doing that regularly.

Elke's story exposes the informality and awareness of licensing in Greek tourist zones. It also outlines a pattern of attritional economic development that is characteristic of alternative economics and the creation of enterprises for the purpose of conviviality. Skala Eresos has sustained a permanent alternative community of approximately a hundred members that presently continues to attract persons of various ages from Greece,

the rest of Europe, and further abroad. Another owner, Basil, who identifies as one of the permanent bohemian residents in the valley, discusses
how he and his wife decided to make a go of Skala Eresos:

> When, we arrived, there were all plastic chairs, traditional
> Greek songs—a sort of decay. I had never come to Eresos. I
> was a DJ in Hydra. I am a barman and my wife a barwoman. I
> was in Athens looking through for sale ads in the newspaper,
> and saw a bar in Eresos for 30,000 euros. We had no money
> at the time, but I said to my wife that we should go look and
> see. We were sure we were leaving it. It was autumn and we
> sat to have a drink and saw the sunset, and then that was
> it for us. Rather than signing a one-year contract, we signed
> for three. And we bought the air. We came with some cash,
> painted it, started serving cocktails in cocktail glasses. We fixed
> the balcony, went to India, and brought back art and wood.
> We've done that twice; it needs to be refurbished again soon.

Skala Eresos's unique character was formed on the synergies of organic
and attritional economic alterity. Local Greek entrepreneurs initiated
and sustained enterprises to host returning families and kin. Similarly,
alternative and lesbian entrepreneurs developed enterprises to host their
own social worlds. While all entrepreneurs were making a livelihood,
their motive was a desire to live a life steeped in economic conviviality
within the subaltern space of Greek islands.

The local ethnic Greek business owners that I spoke with considered
the alternative enterprises developed by newcomers a boon. I did not
anticipate how many would suggest that they added to and improved the
overall quality of enterprises in the village. For example, a local Greek
taverna owner who has been operating for forty years, explains, "They are
good businesses, good service, and they offer something we don't have,
different cuisines." One owner went so far as to distinguish between
the locals in the upper and lower village based on their reception of
alternative tourists and enterprises: "The people in the upper village are
more closed. They don't have interactions with tourists. The people who
live in Skala are more open, in the way we think. Slowly, slowly tourism
opens the mind. . . . The quality of product here has improved—we
have moved past the plastic chairs." The plastic chairs were symbolic of
a past condition of remote Greek islands trying to meet tourist demand.

The alternative enterprises and aesthetic of Skala Eresos settled into an alternative developmentalism, as traditional Greek-made wood chairs replaced plastic ones. Neither local business owners nor landed wealth identified the enterprises that entered Skala Eresos in the 1980s and 1990s as disturbing the status quo of conviviality, only as enhancing it.

According to some of the first alternative business owners there was initial friction. One Greek alternative business owner explains: "The villagers looked at us as a strange thing. We were swimming naked, always. They were not so happy about it, but they did not bother us so much. We never had any problems—somehow they [the locals] go along." Another Greek alternative business owner, Fonda, discussed the hazing he received from Eressian owners, whom he believed called the "tax police." A few others indicated that they were harassed "a little." While most ethnic Greeks accept the distinction of foreign, Fonda problematized it: "They still see me as ξένοι. I started a business here, bought a house here, and have my family here. And they see us as ξένοι. We do have respect from a lot of people." A German woman restaurant owner stated: "I am here sixteen years and I still feel really like a foreigner. Maybe I am more accepted than in the beginning, but still, yeah." The character of φιλοξενία that governs Greek village societies limits local belongingness and designates outside groups as forever foreign. As diagnosed previously, φιλοξενία makes for an effective resistance to the infringement of outside groups on local identities, especially for island societies (McCall 1994). Though social exclusion is not desirable, when it is enacted by less powerful groups as a form of strategic essentialism to protect the integrity of people and place from more powerful groups who have historically subsumed cultures, it can serve as a form of quotidian resistance (Spivak 1993).

An Eressian woman, taking pride in the diversity of tourists and travelers in her village, exclaimed, "Without a doubt there is no xenophobia" when we were taking stock of the groups that visit Skala Eresos. There is a critical degree of difference between ξενοφοβία (xenophobia) and φιλοξενία. Φιλοξενία is characterized by the flexibility to welcome and host outsiders, grant them space and generosity, and give them opportunities to develop enterprises and the freedom to act different from local social codes, but always maintaining them as strangers. In contrast, a 2001 UN Report focused on early signs of full-blown antimigration bias in the EU, citing sociologist Klaude Boehnke, defines xenophobia as "an attitudinal orientation of hostility against non-natives in a given population." As told in Chapter 3, it was frustrating for many Northern Europeans to be in a social arena to which they were marginal even if they were not treated poorly. Some of the hostility this group perceived was less about direct bias, discrimination, or rejection, as was experienced by recent migrants to Northern Europe, and more about the anxiety that occurs for privileged groups that are peripheralized in a place or by a set of circumstances. Alternative ethnic Greeks in Skala may have found their perpetual status as ξένοι vexing, but they were familiar with Greeks' deep ties to place and the geo-cultural forces at play in the region and generally preferred to associate within their own alternative communities.

The establishment of the Osho Afroz Meditation Center in Skala Eresos in 1989 is a keen example of how Greek islanders meet strangers with filoxenia rather than with xenophobia.* The Afroz Meditation Center is linked to a network of meditation centers based on the teaching of Baghwan Rajneeshi or Osho, a controversial guru who became an international figure associated with the New Age movement. Many of those who attended early retreats at the center, which includes group laughing, yelling, and sex-based therapies, and those who led the center became permanent residents of Eresos valley. Even with therapies that are perceived by the local community as offbeat, they are recognized as a part of Skala Eresos's social landscape.

Like most everything else in Skala, the Osho Center is very active during the summer season and comes to a standstill by late fall. In its first years of operation, practitioners would don long maroon robes draped with orange beads, which did not appeal to local residents. Many people who I spoke with about the development of the center said that this fashion faded because the village community's discomfort with it, and the center's sensitivity to these concerns. There was some issue that the attire appeared too similar to those of Greek Orthodox priests. Others

---

*As the story is told in Skala (and found on the Osho Afroz website), Varidhi, the founder of Skala Eresos's Osho Center, was working as a flight attendant on a private plane hired by Baghwan Acharya Rajneeshi. Varidhi became enamored with Osho's teachings and philosophy and became a devotee. Invited to visit Skala Eresos, and attracted to its remoteness and its energy, he bought property on a hill on the southern side of Skala Eresos, establishing the Osho Afroz Meditation Center. The center remains active, offering simple accommodations, and a wide schedule of retreats and workshops, based in teachings around Rajneeshism, attracting international participants and yearlong and seasonal volunteers.

suggested it was also due to the wardrobes' lack of popularity with younger and new visitors to the meditation center.

There was no aggressive response to the establishment of a religious sect that attracted a large alternative community of foreigners, or to the subsequent opening of a restaurant named after Rajneeshi's 1982 book—*Zorba the Buddha*—that was established by urban Greek followers. One evening eating dinner at a taverna in Skala, I asked my dining partner, Litsa, a local Eressian, what she knew of the meditation center. She called out to the owner of the taverna, who was tending to customers on a crowded balcony, "We have a question about the meditation center!," effectively summoning the busy owner to our table, which made me uneasy. Litsa, asked something like "Where did this center come from?" The taverna owner explained in exaggerated hushed tones that it was land sold by a son whose mother had committed suicide. No one in the community wanted the land, and so it was very cheap. He noted that Varidhi, the Greek follower who established the center in Skala Eresos, then bought two more parcels of adjacent properties.

In a muted matter-of-fact voice, my dinner partner stated, "Marina, do you know what they do there? They have orgies. I know it, my cousin heard them," ending her thoughts on the Osho center as she moved on to another subject. Litsa's attitude toward the Osho Center was not hostile, denoting a characteristic trait by which Greek locals tolerate and select to not interfere with foreign persons and their habits. Her insouciant commentary on the Osho Center was fairly regular among local Greek I interviewed and in conversations where I broached the subject. As a foreign entity, the Afroz Osho Center and those associated with it are free to engage in their spiritual activities without too much complaint. Politicians, local business owners, and residents of the small rural village had not once suggested that the center was infringing on the local culture or that it should not exist.

In many parts of the Global North, the opportunities to create communities and enterprises that diverge from the social and cultural forms of a region are often contested in rural areas, and even in large cities (Polat 2018; Bryan 2015; Forest and Dunn 2013). It is a strikingly Greek quality, one inherent to φιλοξενία, to sustain a dubious attitude toward foreign activities and yet permit the freedom and space for their practice. For example, Laki, a man in his late thirties, described the Osho center as such: "It is a center, some of them are my friends, and the younger people, they have their own set of spiritual practices. In the past some thought they were Satanist, did you hear that? It all seemed strange, but they haven't bothered anyone. No one in the village goes there. I have some friends from Mytilini who have gone. I bet they also prefer that we don't go, ha, ha." Pedro, another local Greek, who has operated multiple businesses in Skala, explained:

> Osho, it's a center, many Greeks come to it. Many who are educated, an upper class kind of tourism. What is this thing they come for? I don't know. There was only a problem with the people who lived around them, I don't know the groups were yelling or crying or laughing as their therapy. I don't even know where it is. It's another sector of tourism. In Eresos we have freakyo, lesbians, families, that all arrive here. There is not one character to Skala, we don't have taboos, that is what makes it good.

Locals and foreigners alike herald Skala Eresos as a place that accepts diverse groups. Both visitors and residents are attracted to the "alternative atmosphere" and cosmopolitanism of Skala Eresos. The village has been noted on travel websites as "the coolest most counter-cultural place in the Mediterranean" (see www.lesvos.com). In 2012, a Sunday section in the widely read Greek daily newspaper *TO BYMA* described Skala Eresos as the nation's bohemian capital. While southern Crete continues to be famed for its nonconformist subset of travelers, bohemian or hippie enclaves on numerous Greek islands—Kythira, Ikaria, Donousa, Anafi, Samothraki—are also popular destinations for alternative types.

Alternative Economics and Convivial Place-Making

Producing the kind of sociality for diverse groups to reconvene each year in the same place is grounded in the safety of hospitality—the core of the convivial economics enacted by many of the small and microbusinesses in the Greek island—which was developed by Eressian enterprises for men's public sociality and then for welcoming returning kin. Businesses initiated and managed by foreigners in Skala not only adopted the economic orientation of local Greeks but also created a welcoming social space for "affectionate communities" of marginalized groups (D'Emilio 2008) to flourish. Selections from interviews with various proprietors are shared below to convey the consistency with which convivial economics are practiced in Skala. The approach of the island village agora stands in contrast to "maximizing self-interest" of neoclassical economics. For instance, in a discussion about business expansion, the owner of a popular taverna contemplates: "I don't see how I would do it, if I had one place and another, how could I manage what is going on? I want to see each plate as it goes out, is it cooked well? Or is it a little burnt? Has enough food been served? You can't do that with two places. You can't have something that you love. We give the food with love, it is not fast food—it is slow food. I want it to be personal." Jason, who had married into an Eressian family, intuitively used the phrase "slow food." As I inquired, it became apparent that though Jason articulated the principles of slow food, particularly its commitment to gastronomic pleasure, he was not familiar with the slow food movement (Petrini [2005] 2013).

In addition to the unmistakable commitment to service and quality, the small is beautiful success of Skala Eresos is tied to the collectivity that grounds convivial economics. Autonomy is one of the central features of running a Greek microenterprise, and historically of Greek village life, but the survival of Greece's microeconomies is based in networks of autonomies that exist among enterprises, within enterprises, and even between property owners and enterprises. "Good competition" is how Despina, a self-identified widow, who runs a coffee shop with her sons, describes it: "There is good competition and bad competition. If there is someone who makes something and it makes the plateia prettier or the food better, we are all forced to do it. This is good competition. If on the other hand one is mean spirited and underhanded, this is not good but it also exists. It is not the theme, but it exists." Sophie, a hotel owner, gives her thoughts on local competition: "There is some competition when there is not work. Why did you send someone to this business or that business? But in August no one is complaining." The enterprises in Skala Eresos seem to operate in symphony with one another. When I spoke about the possibility of tensions to one of the three bakeries, I was immediately instructed: "Our relationship with the other bakeries is excellent. People are not trying to put the others out of business. Whereas a foreign tourist might buy a single pastry, your Greek customer will buy a kilo. Especially the locals that return from Athens, they want their traditional foods." A strong collective sense persisted among enterprises despite the economic crisis. Helping to educate me on how businesses succeed in Skala Eresos, an owner of one of the few small food markets offered me the following lesson:

There was the Lesvos supermarket that took up this corner that
now as you see has two shops, a travel agency, a newspaper
shop, and butcher. It opened in the late 1980s and the chain
of these markets failed. In the mid-1990s a local purchased
the supermarket, but it also failed a few years later. It was
too big for the village. Let's say there are five supermarkets
and 1,500 permanent residents. For each shop owner there
are about fifty or so closer relatives. My mother and cousins
will shop at my store and the same for the others. This way
everyone gets some business.

The greatest economic challenge to the small and local markets in Skala
and other village was the establishment of the Lidl market in Mytilini,
a low-cost German corporate chain. Opening in the mid-2000s, the
store is considered to have shifted some household consumption away
from the local markets. Because the store is almost a three-hour drive,
it would not be a regular shopping trip for those living on the west side
of the island. Generally, both business owners and residents in Eresos
seem committed to making their purchases within the village because
of the quality of local production. This was apparent in the approach of
a café-bar owner to my questions around her business purchases. Val, a
Spanish woman in her thirties who has spent about a decade in Lesvos,
told me: "I want the money to go around here [Eresos], mostly here
[points to the ground in her shop] but, if not, the island. You've got to
try to help each other out because this is where you live. It's good for
me if I get items from the local market, then maybe he'll come here and
get crepes, and if you need help." When I asked "What kind of help?,"
she replied, "Well, let's say its 11:00 p.m. and I am running out of beer,
John will come out and bring me over a case." Throughout my research
visit, this sort of give and take and honest support between enterprises to
help them succeed was evident throughout the village, occurring within
and across enterprises by locals, alternatives, and lesbians.

Another display of collective responsibility occurred when I was
doing my own shopping at a greengrocer. A Greek vacationing couple,
not tied to the village, was appraising the vegetables, commenting on
the freshness of the local produce. One of the pair explained that they
had been to the greengrocer down the road and asked for local tomatoes,
but "he told us we should come to you, because his came from Crete.
It's good to know that the truth is the truth." By sharing with custom-

ers where locally grown tomatoes can be found, the greengrocer who referred the Greek couple to the other grocer upholds the practice of hosting. He also selected to send customers to what would be considered his competition in neoliberal framings of economy. Holding a convivial economics proclivity, organic to Greek island place, the owner secured fresh local tomatoes for guests and added another day's transaction to a fellow enterprise.

Seeking to make purchases locally, supportive of other enterprises, and dependent on one another, Skala's microenterprises are committed to a distinct form of local economy. Within enterprises, both employers and employees adjusted wages and hours to ensure the survival of the business, just as the women's cooperatives have done by delaying wages. Stacy, a Greek lesbian owner of a bar-restaurant, disclosed a moment when she was kvetching to her employees about the bills, complaining about how she would not be able to manage the restaurant and about all she had to think about: "One of my workers, also an old friend who has been in Eresos for sixteen years, told me, 'We can work this out.' The employees then got together and told me, 'When there is no business you will pay us less, three euros an hour and if it's a good day we'll take the regular wage of five euros.'" Stacy added, "But these are Greek employees." Though I did not ask her to elaborate, the implication seems to be that ethnic Greek employees were more likely to negotiate compensation as needed to maintain the business.

Most owners in Skala did not see themselves as engaged in a lucrative endeavor. A local woman owner of an eatery explained, "If I wanted to make money I would not be in Eresos." Others who came to Eresos from European cities stated that "only crazy people opens a business here," and that "you don't open a business in Eresos for money." A Greek lesbian from Athens gives her reason for starting a business, "I wanted to make something a little more collective, something different for the world," or, as another owner sums up, "It's not everything about business."

This approach toward community and economy also was evident in the negotiations between real estate owners and the business owners who rented from them. The cost to open a dining venue or to "buy the air" along the seaside promenade in Skala Eresos in 2012 was 25,000 to 35,000 euros, including licenses, legal and accounting fees, and rent for the year. From 2008 through 2012, the yearly rental for an enterprise in Skala was between 8,000 and 12,000 euros. Typically paid in a lump sum at the end of the tourist season for the following year, rents are collected when business owners are considered financially flush.

In 2012, many of the rents were renegotiated to help business owners curtail the costs associated with increased tax rates on businesses and the decreased spending of customers. During the course of Greek government deliberation on how to address the impact of austerity measures, legislation requiring landlords to reduce rents had been considered, but never passed. Instead, it was understood that a reduction in rent would be negotiated independently, rather than contracted, between business owners and their landlords. On this account, an Italian bar-café owner in Skala, whose venue was popular with young English tourists and lesbians, explained: "It was very easy to negotiate. I am going to see if they could come down a bit more, because it's a weird deal this year."

Other microentrepreneurs confirmed that rents were substantially lowered by about 2,500 to 4,000 euros for a few years after the 2010 loan agreement with the troika. Though landowners in Skala were willing to bear some of the costs associated with the economic crisis, it is the microenterprise owners that carry out all levels of maintenance or rebuilding. For the most part the wealthy class in Eresos and their families are landowners and a customer base for many of the enterprises. Many of them are professionals with advanced degrees living in Athens or Mytilini; in my interviews with them they described enjoying the diverse sociality of their seaside village in summer. A long-time lesbian resident working in tourism and real estate offered that because of their elite status, "The old Eressians are a group that cannot be touched." Most of the wealthy Eressians are not financially dependent on tourism, despite the rents they collect from businesses in Skala. They are uninterested in expanding the development of their village paradise or in improving transportation to increase tourism.

It is the small shop owners—the former peasants and new money in the village—as well as the alternative, nonlocal, and lesbian entrepreneurs and business owners that are most concerned with infrastructure development in Skala Eresos. For example, Voula and Dimitri, a couple I met who own various tourist-related businesses in Skala, came from peasant backgrounds, meaning they had no original ownership of land. In a meeting in his café, George explained that the class lines in Eresos remain intact. This was confirmed by Clio, a longtime friend of Dimitri's, who was at the venue and is a member of the landed, wealthy class.

Dimitri, Voula, and Clio laughed together about the entrenched social hierarchy that endures in Eresos, but cherish their friendship, which exists despite it. Along with his kafenion, now managed by his children, Dimitri was one of the first in the village to enter in the Greek island phenomena of "rooms to let," a system of renting rooms to travelers in private homes that preceded AirBnB by decades. Dimitri and Voula also opened a small tourist shop on the strip, filled with mostly beach items such as umbrellas, plastic pails, floaties, snacks, and small gifts. They were able to alter the economic path of their family, shifting from agricultural workers to tourist entrepreneurs, openly hosting and welcoming a bohemian and lesbian crowd.

Old wealth, alternatives, lesbians, and locals coalesced around their preference for small-scale local business rather than large-scale resorts. One local Eressian business owner argued that "Eresos has not changed that much for forty years, a part of the reason for that is that we are remote." Euclid explained that unlike other island tourist destinations, Skala Eresos has only one large tourist hotel resort that Neilson, a UK company that packages high-end activity holidays in Greece and Turkey primarily for British travelers, rents annually. Taking advantage of Eresos's waters, which are ideal for sailing instruction, the company brings yet another group of tourists and summer workers that arrive each summer from various parts of the UK to Skala. For many of the small-business owners experiencing a decline in visitors in the last decades, the lack of development or "undevelopment," as one bar owner called it, is believed to hinder even the small-scale tourism the village usually attracts. Others attribute the decline to the economic crisis, and still others perceive Skala's economic cadence as business as usual.

A business owner from Germany, Hannelora, who had been working and living in the village for eleven years before starting a restaurant with a partner serving Indian inspired cuisine, explains: "I know it is an agricultural village, and no one wants to build skyscrapers—people like it the way it is 'the rough and wild side'—but there should be some support for development." In calling for development, Hannelora was referring to matters such as street lighting and regular public transportation from Mytilini. To make his point about the kind of development he would like to see, Spiros, part of Skala's alternative scene, kidded me by referring to my place of residence during the time of my research, which was South Beach, a highly developed tourist area in Miami Beach, Florida:

"It is not a tourist center; it is agricultural and local. Support goes to that—dairy, agricultural—but we still have tourism. We would like to see development, but we are not really looking for South Beach, right? We don't really have much new tourism." Interest in modest forms of development was consistent among local Eressian, alternative, and lesbian enterprises. Although the village can depend on repeat tourism and the friends and families of the communities that have made Skala Eresos home, most of the business owners were interested in attracting a fresh set of visitors. For instance, many suggested that a summer ferry should arrive at the port of Sigri, a nearby coastal village, as it had in the past. Helene, a young Greek bohemian graduate student, working in one of the few art galleries in Skala and a regular visitor to the island, explains: "Many young people, friends, in Thessaloniki would like to come to Eresos. It is very remote, and it's a good thing. That's why it's not so developed. But then our friends, people have a hard time getting here. A boat from Thessaloniki to Sigri would make it affordable."

Almost half of the business owners I interviewed were concerned with the limited transportation to the village, as it requires either a car rental, a costly taxi, or a public bus that leaves from Mytilini at 6 a.m. Two owners of different eateries, recognizing the kind of low-key tourists that seek out Skala Eresos, proposed a campground to support development. Julia, from another part of Greece, who had lived in Athens, explains: "People who camp want to camp. They are cooped up in a concrete building in Athens, they don't want to come here and be in another concrete building. I know a judge from Athens who comes here to camp. Even your hippies have to buy some water, some bread, and vegetables, and some drinks. The government can set up a campsite with clean toilets." This quote reveals a simultaneous eagerness to attract new tourism to Eresos and a continuation of a low-key and return tourism. Several small hotel owners referred to their bookings, explaining that many visitors come at the same time of year and request to stay in the same room. Skala's business owners seek development not to alter the scale of tourism, but to subdue the effects of a crisis economy by making visiting the village a little more convenient to attract new tourists, as well as retain their regular seasonal visitors.

Many I spoke with pegged a decline of tourism in Skala to the arrival of the euro. One lesbian resident explained, "It was the late 1990s, when the euro arrived, Greek tourism decreased." A longtime Greek shop owner further explained, "The euro killed so many things, the cost of living doubled but salaries remained the same." And another local Greek explained, "The euro added inflation, I felt it in my wallet. It is a shame for this, the loss of drachmas, we could have been booming with tourism."

Alterity and the State

The Greek state was blamed for the negative impact of the euro on local island economies, for agreeing to enter the EU in the first place, and giving up its national currency. In discussing their current economic challenges, business owners in Skala Eresos and the women's cooperatives regarded the Greek government with dismay. Reflective of Greek skepticism of centralized governance, one owner clarified, "In Greece you make your own life. There is no state." When I brought up the role of government in enterprise development, an older Greek man taverna owner responded intensely, "They want to melt us. They do nothing. Success depends on the personal skills of the owner. . . . the system is against microenterprises." Business owners pointed to the labyrinthine laws governing Greek small businesses. Greeks' evaluations were generally antigovernment, as they expressed frustration with the handling of the economic crisis. As one Greek business owner explains: "I don't believe in the law. Nobody does. This confusion over the law is nothing new. This is what has happened all the time. It is intentional so when the state needs money they can harass us." Ares provides a more detailed example:

> The laws are inconsistent. I try to work clean and to work well. But no matter how I operate I can be accused of being illegal. For example, when I first started someone here called the police who came to tell me that I was not giving out tickets for entering. In Greece, the law demands that when entering a club, a ticket stub is provided. However, as a café/ bar with an open balcony it is impossible to hand tickets since it is an open venue. I was fined a million drachmas. I went to the government office and gave them my key [giving up my business], because it was impossible to pay such a fine. I was sent to a high level officer, but I doubted it would change anything. Not only was my fine voided, the higher officer had no idea that a fine had been issued to me.

Ares was complaining about harassment, possibly hazing, when he was first starting out. Owners' concerns centered on the fact that a lack of clarity in laws, or their willy-nilly application, would make them victims to the government squeezing them during times of economic crisis.

Yet to rephrase an earlier argument, the "jungle" of the Greek legal system—as it was referred to me by a Greek attorney, who was assisting me with grant related paperwork, which had become unduly complex—also entangles corporate entities seeking to invade Greek markets, particularly in the food industry. Falling under the "food code" enacted in 1971 (Chaldoupis 2019), these regulations, or Greece's uniquely specific articulation of where and what kinds of foods can be sold by which enterprise, are precisely the laws the troika sought to have ditched during the 2015 loan agreements for the purpose of liberalizing Greece's economy.

For example, bread, its point of sale, weight, and the determination of what type of entity can refer to itself as a bakery was debated at the 2015 EU Summit on Greece's debt (Financial Times 2015) in an attempt to reduce restrictions. The mish-mash of Greek laws that frustrate microentrepreneurs also limit the corporate takeovers of independent microenterprises, such as bakeries and pharmacies. Greece—often repudiated as informal and unregulated—ironically is experienced by its entrepreneurs as a nation with a complicated and monitored business environment, which they must maneuver within.

Several business owners in Skala suggested that upscale tourist locations that maintain numerous and large hotels receive privileged treatment from the state compared to islands with small, local, or what they referred to as "second class tourism." One ethnic Greek hippie and business owner, disgruntled with the state, explains: "Second-class tourism areas in Greece are subject to harassment by tax police and health police that come regularly to survey the practices of business. They come to Lesvos, not to Mykonos [an island celebrated for its high-end tourism]." While local government officials are engaging in conversations at the kafenion like anyone else, the central government, which is responsible for directing tax and health officials to Greek islands to hook and fine businesses for violating regulations, is considered an interloper. Because Greek islanders historically have operated independently, many hold no expectations of their national government. With the onset of the economic crisis, the national government's presence on the islands increased with the imposition of regulatory measures that ran counter to Greek economic traditions.

Many of the new taxation schemes tied to the loan agreements, addressed in chapter 3, ran particularly afoul of islands and microentrepreneurs. Resisting government interference was a collective pursuit among the microenterprises in Skala Eresos. The Greek government has several spheres in which it polices tourist zones, especially, it seems, second-tier tourist zones, which I witnessed in Skala Eresos. For example, unannounced state officials came to Skala checking business permits, verifying that employees are registered with social insurance, or confirming that, as required in Greece, all sales receipts in dining venues are presented to customers (typically placed under a shot glass on the table) upon ordering, rather than at the end of the meal. They also surveyed that menus, now legally required, were presented to customers, rather than guests visiting the kitchen or asking the waiter for a list of freshly made foods as still seems to be the norm across Greece. Employees in restaurants must also be prepared to show health books confirming that their lungs are clear and that they have no communicable disease. In almost every instance of government officials sent to police enterprises in Skala, once they were identified calls went out from one business owner to another and workers were sent from business to business to warn them of the officials' arrivals so if warranted they could save themselves from being fined.

The viewpoint that the government is primarily a tax collector squeezing small and microbusinesses was steady, as was the stealth and humor involved in resisting it. Most owners could not remember the national state providing assistance, or for providing sufficient infrastructure, so they were not beholden to it. When I drew attention to the few government programs for assisting microenterprise development that I knew about, many of the owners I interviewed reacted adversely. Georgia, a middle-aged business owner of a clothing shop, responded: "No, I have not taken a program. I don't want any money from the state. The state and I, we don't get along, but it gets money from me. I sing for the state!" An older business owner who began operations in the 1980s, when the PASOK government was said to have expanded tourist development, said, "No, it's a myth, no one had programs, you had your money and you made a business." Just a few business owners I spoke with had used the Hellenic Organizations of Small and Medium Sized Enterprises and Handicraft (EOMMEX), a government program linked with the EU that withered precipitously under austerity measures. Those who had used these programs seemed to be younger and recent business owners who got involved with enterprises just after 2000, when funding became available with Greece's entry into the EU. One hotel operator explained how she applied for a loan to assist in the renovation of hotel rooms. Another couple interested in expanding a family bakery received a grant. The baker explains: "I used EOMMEX. They covered 50 percent of the cost to modernize and buy material for a business. The return was to be in six months, but they did not get it back to me until after two years. Fortunately, my work went well. I could modernize my oven and update the electrical system." Another program that targeted islands offered assistance with the start-up costs of restaurants if the entity agreed to remain open through winter for at least the first two years. Two lesbian enterprises in Skala used this program. One venue that served Greek food, pizza, and European fare was a hearth for wintertime sociality not only for the permanent lesbian community but for many local residents as well.

The state is decidedly not conceived by most Greeks as an ally to enterprises in their everyday operations. Most owners in Skala saw the state as parasitical, especially as austerity policies squeezed businesses and families. Yet the extent to which the national government was able to ward off a regulatory overhaul proposed by the troika and resist transnational capital from a takeover of Greece's microenterprise sector, it advantaged microenterprises, enabling them to maintain objectives of autonomy and conviviality.

Smallness and Solidarity

Providing nourishment and drink, small, locally owned, and convivial dining enterprises deliver opportunities for impromptu meetings and creativity that could not serendipitously occur at personal dwellings (Andrews 2020). In Greek islands, the cooperatives and cafés, the tavernas, bars, or ouzerias extend the prospect for situations in which conversations flow, alternatives are formed, and subalterns convene. These are spaces of conviviality that counter the overwhelming corporatization of social life toward large, anomic, bland, tasteless, homogenous, and profit-oriented venues.

In Skala Eresos the first kafenions opened to serve men patrons, becoming centers of their social worlds. Later tavernas and bar-cafés were founded to serve returning immigrants and host family celebrations in summer. To this limited array, bohemians, hippies, and those seeking to remove themselves from mainstream society sought remote islands, at first traveling to them for repose, with some joining Skala Eresos's microentrepreneurs. They established smart, attractive restaurants and cafes, drawing a bohemian crowd to Skala and brightening the tourist scene. After varied efforts by government administrations, tourism was established as an important economic sector by the 1980s, as more and more Northern Europeans found the Greek islands a desirable and affordable vacation, contributing to the microeconomies of Greek islands.

What the owners and participants in organic and attritional convivial economic enterprises hold in common is a desire to create intimate social environments, hosting new guests, friends and families, and familiar tourists. They are also intent on maintaining autonomy in the management of their enterprises and in the general operations of the village. The owners I spoke with were skeptical of the state, wanting little interference and desiring nothing more than the caretaking of basic infrastructure and better public transportation to facilitate travel to Eresos. Most pertinent for the appreciation of microenterprises as modes of resistance based in economic logics antagonistic to neoliberalism is how the workers and owners cared for one another. Whether it is a coordinated resistance to the tax police, admiring the success and quality of neighboring enterprises, providing last-minute deliveries, voluntarily reducing wages, making room for new and unconventional entrepreneurs, or a determination to keep purchases local, the relationship across the microenterprises in Skala Eresos firmly counters the competition, the designation of victors and losers, so crucial and valued under neoliberalism.

In 1973, Ivan Illich wholeheartedly believed in the possibility of reversing mass production and the notion that large-scale industry can be replaced by smaller enterprises in which control over the labor process resides with those engaged in it. Placing the enterprises in Skala Eresos within a longer historical frame of their development assists in gauging small, possibly delinked economic microeconomies as a viable strategy to presently overcome the infringements of neoliberalism. If we consider that 10 percent of Europe's businesses are part of the social economy (European Commission 2011), or that less than 50 percent of US production is in the corporate sector (Gibson-Graham 2006), that in Africa 78 percent of the nonagricultural population is employed in the informal sector and in Latin America it's 57 percent (Becker 2004), we have empirical evidence that microenterprises form the basis of a global alternative economy (ILO 2019).*

---

*This claim is consistent with Gibson-Graham's (2006, 2013) model that diverse and community economics are actually more prevalent than capitalist relations, and account for more hours worked or more value produced, or both, than the capitalist sector.

CHAPTER EIGHT

Lesbian Place-Making and the Imperial Gaze

Here it was heaven, you could find Greeks and lesbians.

—Spiridoula Giannopoulos, former business
owner in Skala Eresos (2012)

Liz Lemon: Why did you have to offend the gay community? It is
the most organized of all the communities. They make the Japanese
look like the Greeks.

Tracy Jordan: How is what I said offensive and that's not?

Liz Lemon: Because no one heard me say it.

—30 Rock, season 6, episode 2 (2012)

The advancement of alternative businesses in Skala through the 1980s
synchronized with the village's increasing popularity as a travel
destination for Northern European lesbians. Subaltern enclaves, like the
lesbian community that developed in Skala Eresos and other gay tourist
destinations, have provided opportunities for a collective reprieve from
heterosexism. In the 1980s and 1990s gay and lesbian tourist spaces on
Greek islands offered gay identified persons alternative social opportunities
to what was available in home countries such as Germany and England.
Despite the tensions and confrontations that transpired between "locals"
and "lesbians," Skala delivered many lesbians relief from the homophobia
they experienced in their regular social worlds and rest from the lesbian
and gay activist work that was gaining strength around Europe during
that time.

In part, the tensions between ethnic Greek locals and lesbians were oriented by the negative constructs and stereotypes of these groups that are carried in Europe and around the world. The exchange between characters Liz Lemon and Tracy Jordan in NBC's television series *30 Rock* cited above highlights the subtle maneuvering of conversations around bias toward Greeks and lesbians. The episode, written by Robert Charlock, is in reference to the real life homophobic one-liner at a Nashville comedy show of African-American actor Tracy Morgan, who plays Tracy Jordan, about a year prior to the episode cited above being aired. Tina Fey, who created the series and acts as Liz Lemon, is half Greek. Although Morgan, Fey, and NBC publicly apologized for Morgan's hate speech, the series also addresses the incident across several episodes. This exchange draws attention to negative ethnic stereotypes of Greeks, which were increasingly evident in media during the economic crisis, when this episode was broadcast. It also draws attention to the organizing and activism of the gay community. Also relevant to this chapter is the scene's commentary on how social bias can be subtle and unseen or overt and the prerogative assumed to negatively stereotype groups even by those who face bias and discrimination due to their own social identities.

Although many EU nations have made progressive changes to laws expanding lesbian and gay rights, many lesbians continue to identify Skala Eresos as a respite from their heteronormative worlds. This chapter begins by addressing the period of the 1980s, when an increasing number of lesbians arrived to Skala and developed a large separatist camp on the beach set away from the village. It then turns to the late 1990s and early 2000s, when lesbian enterprises and lesbian place-making moved within the village of Skala, attenuating the strain that had developed between the Greek villagers and Northern European lesbian travelers. The convivial economics engaged in by lesbian entrepreneurs overlap and dub the economic culture (Boellstorff 2005) found in Greek island villages—so do their homosocial forms of engagement.* Interviews

---

*To "dub culture" is a framework conceived by anthropologist Tom Boellstorff (2005). Boellstorff (2005) applies "dubbing" or the translation of film dialogue from one language to another, to describe the ways gay Indonesians may draw from dominant Western frameworks of expressing gay and lesbian identities but create categories distinctly their own. I apply it here to emphasis that while lesbian enterprises and women cooperatives may be engaging in a gendered public sociality, it is not a direct copy of men's public gatherings, in the same way a dubbed film is never a precise interpretation.

with lesbians, alternatives, and locals help explore the struggle and the dynamics of sexuality, gender, and Greek island space. The stories shared by these varied groups addresses the conflict and collaboration among them, demonstrating how subaltern sensibilities eventually fused around convivial economics.

The geographic remoteness and pristine setting of Skala Eresos alone helps travelers depart from their own social world. These spatial qualities help to explain why many lesbian visitors expressed feeling freed from the daily grind of social mores. Unlike privileged traditional vacationers, many of the lesbian travelers to Skala were seeking not only respite but a context that was safe and liberating, or a "place for lesbians." In my interviews, lesbians who visit Skala ritualistically each summer and others who had moved to Eresos permanently describe the village as unique, special, with "different energy" (Kantsa 2002). Sappho's legacy contributed to contemporary Skala becoming a setting in which most lesbian tourists and residents did not feel exceptional or marginal, at a time when homophobia was widespread in Northern Europe.

The account I provide of a transnational lesbian presence in Skala Eresos corroborates in many ways with Kantsa's (2002) descriptions of lesbian sociality and the relational dynamics between lesbians and locals in Skala Eresos. Kantsa (2002) examines Skala Eresos's transition from a "separatist" lesbian encampment to a lesbian tourist destination. Focused on the harassment that lesbians received by local men in particular, Kantsa (2002) suggests that the eventual tolerance of the lesbian community was driven by economic incentives. The next sections attempt to draw a broader and critical reading of the spatial transformation of Skala Eresos that includes a wider array of rhythms shaping Skala's lively lesbian scene, including Greek φιλοξενία and homophobia, the role of alternative enterprises and community, and the bias and entitlement enacted by visiting Northern European lesbians.

Lesbians Land in Skala

Sitting in a cantina with an early afternoon beer, Jeanine describes the first trip she took to Skala Eresos. It was late July and bright sunshine glimmered powerfully on the Aegean just a few feet in front of us. Jeanine pointed to the northern end of the beach, just past the shoreline porches of Skala Eresos. She explained that on the other end of the "limani," using the Greek word for port, is where she and her friend

Nadine found themselves on their first arrival to Skala almost thirty years earlier. They had stopped near some boulders by the port to look through binoculars and assess the situation on the beachfront. Jeanine and Nadine had traveled to Lesvos from their home in Belgium because they had learned through European lesbian networks "that lesbians like themselves were visiting the island." Jeanine added that she had also wanted to give homage to the birthplace of Sappho.

The trip to Lesvos from Belgium in the mid-eighties required a good deal of commitment. Jeanine and Nadine first took a flight from Antwerp to Athens, and then a meandering bus ride from the old Athens airport—the new one was built when Greece hosted the Olympics in 2004—to the port of Piraeus where they boarded one of the many ferries destined for a Greek isle. Greek ferries are the main links to the

Figure 8.1. The summer beach scene/courtesy of Tzeli Hadjidimitriou. Further down from the village shops along Skala Eresos's shoreline, nudist sunbathers have gathered for decades. This includes a group of lesbian tourists, marked by a rainbow flag, and alternatives, foreigners and Greeks, or "freakyo," and travelers to the Osho Center. Local Greeks typically enter the sea nearer to the village.

islands. In the autumn and winter, they carry both supplies and Greek passengers; in the summer months, the ferries are packed with tourists. Presently there is a daily ferry that travels from Piraeus to Mytilini after a stop at a neighboring island. In the early 1980s, however, ferries departed for Lesvos only a few times a week and they stopped at several islands before arriving in Mytilini, considerably lengthening the journey.

It took approximately two days of travel for Jeanine and Nadine to get to Lesvos. Once they arrived at the picturesque port of Mytilini, they had to make their way to Eresos, which is on the opposite side of the island. The limited public transportation that Skala's entrepreneurs had complained about, referred to in the last chapter, has remained in place with a single bus from the capital departing each morning.

A permanent Northern European lesbian resident of Eresos explained, "If people come to this island, they don't come to Eresos; it's the end of the earth." Like many of the lesbians who journey to Eresos, Jeanine and Nadine were looking for more than a package vacation on a Greek island. Jeanine recalls her shock when she peered beyond the port with her binoculars and saw groups of "naked lesbians" lying on the sandy beach. She and Nadine spent the next few hours passing the binoculars back and forth to each other, astounded by the ease and comfort and the number of bare bodies on the beach. When I asked if their next steps were to join the group of women that were sunbathing and socializing, Jeanine replied emphatically, "No, no, we are Belgian, too modest to take our clothes off like that, like the Dutch and Germans." It was after sunset that Jeanine and Nadine eventually joined the lesbian camp. They have continued to travel to Skala Eresos almost every summer since that first visit.

For three consecutive years, from 1983 to 1985, an extensive semi-permanent structure of wood and palms was erected each summer about 200 meters from the shoreline. This camp was the main post for Northern European lesbians' gatherings during the summer season. Informal camping on Greek beaches exploded through the 1970s and 1980s, when Greece was a cheap place to visit, and backpacking had become a phenomenon of young travelers. Although there are only two beaches in Greece where nudity is officially permitted, Skala Eresos continues to be listed as a nudist beach in several contemporary tourist guidebooks and websites. Europeans have been proclaiming and rating the quality of Greek island shores as nudist destinations for decades. Many of these sorts of entries—now found online at travel sites—include patronizing descriptions of Greek toleration of nudity, as they assume entitlement to the nation as a leisure zone.*

By the mid-1980s the estimated number of lesbian campers was in the low hundreds. Locals and lesbians I spoke with provided similar approximations suggesting that up to four hundred individuals were camping there at any given time. Drosula, one of the many Greek lesbians who first came to Skala in the 1980s, described what she felt were the glory days:

> I remember coming with a friend. I said let's go to Lesvos. I had heard that there was a lesbian scene there. We went to the Blu Bar and stayed there for six hours. And I was looking around and couldn't believe what I was seeing. Then a French lesbian stood on the table. Yes, stood on the table, and called out, is anyone here a lesbian? My friend said, "Where are we?" And I said, "We are in paradise." We went back to Athens, where I picked up some of my belongings, put them in my rucksack, and turned around to come to Eresos. I have not missed a summer since.

Skala's beach offered a fun and festive location for lesbians—the majority of whom were from Northern Europe, but the scene in the 1980s included lesbians from Greece, Italy, Spain, and the US. News originally spread of Skala as a vacation destination through lesbian social networks in Northern European cities. Indicative of how knowledge of lesbian enclaves spread (Rothenberg 1995), Skala gained a word-of-mouth reputation as a welcoming lesbian summer retreat at the birthplace of Sappho. Later magazine articles and a few lesbian-centered documentaries, advertisements, or flyers activated a channel for lesbian tourism from Europe to Lesvos. In her claim that Cherry Grove, Fire Island,

---

*For example, one tourist website proclaims: "The ancient Greeks more or less invented nudism—they practised all their games naked, and carved some wonderful nude statues. The modern Greeks, with their marvellous hospitality, continue this tradition, and are generally wonderfully tolerant of being naked, nude or naturist (Cap'n Barefoot)." An observation from the Lonely Planet Guide's website (retrieved April 2012) of the nude beach in Antiparos also suggests Greeks' acceptance of nude sunbathing and camping: "Many people camped there illegally in tents and campervans. The beach was rather secluded, so no accidental passerbys would be offended. I asked some locals about this and they didn't care less. They said, this has always been a hippie beach and people have been sunbathing nude there since the '60s."

was the "the premier lesbian and gay summer colony in the world" Esther Newton (2014) may have overlooked the high times being had by lesbians in Skala Eresos and gay men in Mykonos. Lesbian-identified women I interviewed, who have spent decades of summers in Skala Eresos, echoed Drosula's enthusiasm for the heyday of the 1980s: "You could hardly find a spot on the beach! In the evening they would have volleyball and you would have enough for around four teams. Now you can't even gather enough for one." Several women I spoke with identified themselves as activists in the growing lesbian and gay movements across Europe in the 1980s. They explained that, at the time, Skala was the place that they could more freely express themselves and "take a break from the fighting." Lesbian-identified women recounted the era of the 1980s favorably, but they also provided accounts of harassment by local villagers. In my interviews there was no shortage of reminiscing and gossip about the different women who would arrive and depart from the camp, their love affairs, fashion, the collective preparation of meals, and accounts of nightly campfires with impromptu music and performances.

At the time Skala Eresos provided the only trans-European space for a large number of lesbians to gather socially in public. Privileged European women historically have traveled to the Mediterranean to escape the rigors of gender in their own societies (Kolocotroni and Mitsi 2008). Northern European lesbian-identified women similarly were able to escape constraints and hostility toward their sexual orientation with a stay in Skala. The regular rhythm of seasonal return by lesbian travelers is significant. It supports the development of annual homecoming events, including anniversary celebrations, birthday parties, and festivals just as local families plan family affairs for when relatives return during the summer.

Many of the women who traveled to Eresos, especially in the 1980s, were expressing their identities as lesbians for the first time. Contending with bias and open hostility in their own societies, the birthplace of Sappho provided many lesbians a sense of safety that was difficult for them to achieve in their own nations. Fueled by tides of lesbian and gay activism in the 1980s in their home countries, these early lesbian travelers declared a portion of the seaside as their own, which eventually led to a series of confrontations between local men and lesbians.

As with prior Northern European women travelers (Mahn 2016), many Northern European lesbians arrived to Skala Eresos with an assumption of Greece as an inferior, backward nation, with quaint villages but boorish villagers. These attitudes clearly are not idiosyncratic of lesbian travelers to Eresos, but stem from the biases embedded in Europe's cultural landscape that nurture an imperial gaze (Kaplan 2012). As the lesbian camp continued to expand, the grace of φιλοξενία was lost on many of the lesbians, who felt they had come and conquered, rather than being hosted as foreign guests. For example, the campers depended on the generosity of several business owners who permitted them to use their kitchens for food preparation and cleaning up after the meals they prepared over grills at the camp.

Lesbian travelers and residents I interviewed particularly remarked on the generosity of George, the proprietor of the Blu Bar, a traditional Greek ouzeria that also served cocktails and aperitifs. George gave the women campers unrestricted access to the sinks in his establishment and the use of his bathroom. Many of the women who befriended him described his φιλοξενία as genuine. I was able to make a connection to my meeting of George, when, as a tourist in 1999, I met him on the main plateia. He introduced himself as a sort of self-proclaimed ambassador of the village, assisting travelers disoriented from the lengthy trip to Eresos. I had arrived on a religious holiday, and could not find any affordable accommodations, so I asked George if he knew of any availabilities. He explained that the Sappho Hotel had some space, but it was a woman-only hotel. Though I came to visit the birthplace of Sappho, I had not expected to find a lesbian enclave and women-only accommodations. George helped me find accommodations through his social network. Ever the interviewer, even before I made a career of it, I asked him why he was offering up such hospitality. He explained that he had been a migrant living in New Orleans (coincidentally my home base at the time), and knows "the importance of a warm welcome." Moreover, George explained that φιλοξενία is part of his job in running a bar, a statement I keenly remember and one that likely planted a seed for this study.

One summer evening in 2012, a small group of women were reminiscing about the glory of the 1980s. Jolene, from Amsterdam, shared a telling story of the type of camaraderie that some of the women had with George and other business owners in Skala:

> A friend wanted to use the sink at George's to wash up. There was nothing else for the campers. George teased and asked her, "Why should I let you?" She said, "Because I am a medical student and in a few years I will be a doctor with a large income and won't you be glad to have me as a patron? I could even rent rooms from you." George invites her for a drink later that evening to meet with his friend, a doctor, so

he can be "sure" [laughter]. The village doctor tells George, "This woman wanting to bathe in the washroom of your ouzeria is a medical student!"

The women joked together with unmistakable fondness. I heard many stories about lesbians lining up to wash in the Blu Bar. Other exchanges between the host community and the lesbian campers were not always convivial. The escapades at the public shower, available for rinsing off after a dip in the sea, drew heavy critique, and were considered a major public disturbance by locals. Camping lesbians often took advantage of the public shower, using it not only to rinse off but also to bathe, many times without a bathing suit. Both lesbians and locals I interviewed explained that in the 1980s, women might walk through the plateia topless and also showed physical affection for each other under the shower. This contributed to a period of contentious interactions over the public space of the plateia.

Most of the lesbians who I met referred to the tolerance of the local Eressians and the "over the top behavior" of many of the lesbian tourists in the 1980s. As one English lesbian described the setting: "Some would go into the village and wander around with a dildo, they did a lot of dancing in the square. There was a large degree of exhibitionism. What can I say? We felt free." Some lesbians overtly antagonized local Greeks with provocations around nudity and sexuality. These actions reflected and assumed cultural superiority and a demeaning attitude toward the host society grounded in a general Northern European bias toward Greeks. It also reflects an oppressed status in home countries in which these women found very little opportunity for being out publicly. The cultural inappropriateness of Northern European lesbians in Skala Eresos in the 1980s is not exceptional for Global North tourists at large. For many privileged travelers to Global South nations, vacations are not only for rest and relaxation but also a break from the civility or the social norms by which they are expected to adhere to in their own society. Especially in the case of early lesbian travelers to Skala, the norms Northern European women were escaping were oppressive. Skala Eresos was one of the first places they were able to be out as lesbians without having to explain their sexual preference to family, friends, or coworkers. For some visiting lesbians the taste of liberation combined with their privileged Northern European status provoked extreme incursions on the local norms of sociality. Many of the women I interviewed who have been returning regularly to Skala for decades sympathetically reflected on the actions of their peers who, twenty years younger, may have acted untowardly. Some lesbians were critical of the incursions. Angelina, an ethnic Greek lesbian who has lived in Germany most of her life, offers her understanding of the past: "Some of the German feminists, who were the first to arrive, they were not only playing with the norms of sexuality. They were challenging Greek ethics as well. This consists of throwing one's culture into one's face and that was different for us." By "us" Angelina was referring to Greek lesbians, who served as intermediaries between Greek locals and Northern European lesbians. Another Greek lesbian, Chrissa, also shared that she and other Greek lesbians engaged in double negotiations to sustain discourse between local Greeks and lesbian travelers. As insiders and outsiders in both communities, Greek lesbians were equally empathetic.

Locals cited the most concerning act was the active nudity on the public square and intentional provocations. A former mayor explained: "We know there are nudists all over Greece, Mykonos, Crete, we don't care what you do privately but we have customs in the village, our ethics. Go on the other side of river if you want to do that." Another statement by an elder man, a member of the Eressian community who had sought to facilitate positive exchanges between locals and lesbians, expresses how laws are negotiated to accommodate tourists: "Nudism is forbidden, but just go far away, and the locals [men] won't come to watch you. This way we are all safe from problems and fights from occurring." And yet another member of the Eressian community explains: "Don't go on the square and take off all your clothes where there are people. Do it in your own home." In each of these examples of how Eressians dealt with the past infringement of lesbians, φιλοξενία is evidently guiding them. Their method of addressing nudity on the village square is informed by a hosting mentality working to ignore, tolerate, negotiate, and gradually move nudity off the plateia. Several former mayors I met with prided themselves on their attempts to soothe the anxiety and concerns of the village population who were beginning to feel infringed upon. One mayor describes his conversation with someone he considered to be a "leader" of the lesbian community:

> The lesbian women who came in relation to Sappho felt that this was their natural environment. They thought because of Sappho's school and culture, the place belonged to them. They came here and assumed the place, OK, OK. I don't care

what you do in your bedroom, but could you please not be so provocative when you are on the square. Could you respect our local cultures and customs?

Analytically, the ethos of Greek φιλοξενία—the welcoming of foreigners—is central to Greek public life. As detailed in chapter 4, foreigners that were rude or inconsiderate would not impinge on the social beingness of the local community because foreigners were considered external to the logics and expectations of Greek social norms. As a disposition, φιλοξενία subdues Greeks from responding with hostility to foreigners because aggressive action toward foreigners would encroach upon their own social standing in the community. For ethnic Greek men especially, policing behaviors also runs counter to constructs of Greek masculinity. Although Greek lesbians and alternatives attempted to mediate the tensions and avert clashes, the provocation of some lesbians presented a moral dilemma to Greeks.

The heavy "othering" of Greeks by Northern European lesbians—and their failure to respect not just Greek norms regarding public nudity but those of their home societies—speaks to the assumptions of centrality of the "white western subject" (Kaplan 2012, 78–79). In Skala Eresos, the police were not called to deter or arrest someone for public nudity or to enforce the law. It is worth considering how nudity in town (not beaches) would have been treated by coastal communities in summertime Northern Europe. Postcolonial queer analyses presented in chapter 5 help to explain how white, liberal, and privileged gay and lesbians reduce expressions of sexualities in peripheral regions by forcing them to fit within their own frameworks (Hawley 2001). With an "imperial gaze" structure that prevents seeing people, the historical orientation toward homosexuality and hospitality that many Greek islanders carry were not recognized by some of the early lesbian visitors.

Moreover, there is very little elasticity in the contractual form of association and attending enforcement that characterize Northern Europe society (Lefebvre 2003). As presented in chapter 5, much of England and Germany—nations that dominate Greece's tourist market—were socially oppressive places for lesbian and gay communities in the 1980s. Although the UK and Germany had no overt laws restricting lesbians' sexual expression, many women chose to remain closeted. A survey conducted by a lesbian and gay activist organization in 1993 suggested that two-thirds of gay- or lesbian-identified people in England hid their identities at work.

In Germany, there have been few lesbian-identified women in the public sphere (Blaustein and Newman 2007). For many lesbian-identified women Skala Eresos has been a space of ease and freedom.

The Last Day of Camp

Most of the residents I interviewed between 2008 and 2016, regardless of ethnicity, nationality, or sexual orientation, were aware of the lesbian camp that had existed in the 1980s. All groups I conferred with remembered and alluded to how the lesbian campers restricted men's access to portions of the beach. The encampment hijacked a section of the public beach to serve the interest of a single enclave. The purpose of claiming exclusive territory for the lesbian camp was to protect against and resist harassment by local men and police officers. Interviewees explained that some of the local men were slow to realize that the resistance to their flirtation or kamaki was truly based in disinterest. While a few of the bar owners and return lesbian tourists described these interactions as "good fun," others described the persistent stalking by Greek men as annoying and aggressive.

In hopes of creating protective boundaries, some lesbian campers were aggressive toward local men, including fishers and shepherds, who were not passing to harass them, but traveling by the seaside. The aggressions of the lesbian campers included throwing rocks at men who passed by the camp. In one instance, a single Eressian fisherman was stopped and accosted by a small group of lesbians. Shortly after these interactions escalated, the lesbian camp was set on fire when its occupants were known to be attending an event at the port on the other side of the village. No one was harmed nor was anyone ever caught or charged for the conflagration. Following this attack in 1985, the lesbian camp ceased and was not resurrected the following summer.

Understandably, both local residents in Eresos and Greek and foreign lesbians I spoke with were reticent to talk about the violence perpetrated on the lesbian camp. It seemed to me that both groups felt uneasy to talk about these conflictive moments, despite my gentle prodding and genuine interest. When discussions on the topic transpired, neither lesbian travelers nor local Greeks nor alternative community members took my questions as an opportunity to vent about the hostilities of the past, or to express resentment.

Locals from Eresos seemed particularly discomfited by my questions and investigation into the attacks and fire set at the lesbian camp. For many village residents, the conflagration and violence was an embarrassment that reflects poorly on the island village and far cry from the obligations of φιλοξενία. This was apparent as no one I interviewed or spoke with suggested or alluded that the attacks against the lesbians were explainable or deserved, and there was a sharp expression of shame by some of the older residents. Many of the lesbians I interviewed—who were English, German, Dutch, and Austrian—also seemed uncomfortable, and none seemed to harbor anger toward the local Greek community. Instead, they said the hostile interaction was between "very aggressive lesbians" who were coming to Skala Eresos "at that time" from "very homophobic" places, and believed that a few young village men were culpable for the fire.

Both lesbians and locals seemed interested in making very clear delineations between their past and present relationships. Petros, a long-time local owner of a small café in the village, explained, "At first, there was a problem. They were different kinds of lesbians, getting drunk; we had some problems. Slowly, and from their own perspective, they became closer to the locals." Kantsa (2002) also recognizes a reconciliation between the local and lesbian community in the 1990s, but emphasizes that it was financial interest in tourist development that brought the two groups closer in line. While economic concerns may have played a part, the improving relationship was also informed by a preference for local resolution and φιλοξενία, as well as a local appreciation for lesbianism. Kouli, a small shop owner, shares his understanding of the development of lesbian tourism:

The women tourism here, it wasn't something organized from the village. It was not an industry—a tourist strategy to bring lesbian women here as in Mykonos in which they tried to attract gay men. Here, the lesbians came because of Sappho. For me, it's Sappho. Even the few who may say they don't like it, well, they can't get rid of them. It is the birthplace of Sappho, Skala is their own pilgrimage, their place.

Another Skala Eresos woman, Alexa, who operated a family business, explained: "In the past, maybe there was some shock [over] two women holding hands or kissing each other. Especially when they did not have their own businesses and they did this at the cafés. But now they have their own businesses, so there is no problem—they can do what they want there." Alexa simultaneously shows an openness to same gen-der affectionate expression, and a partiality for it occurring within lesbian enterprises. Ultimately, Alexa does not challenge the advancement of les-bian enterprises in Skala Eresos but seems in favor of their expansion. Her statement affirms both sides of φιλοξενία and the autonomy preferred and granted by ethnic Greeks within the space of one's enterprise. Though ini-tially there were some challenges, the transition of the lesbian community from separatist campers to local entrepreneurs was not deterred by local government or businesses. By claiming space through convivial enterprises, lesbians became entrenched in the seasonal rhythm of Skala's agora.

Lesbian Businesses on the Agora

The convivial economics of Skala—and on Greek islands generally—pro-vide local island communities the ability to absorb tourists, expatriates, and alternative communities without losing their own forms and tradi-tions. The historical legacy of Lesvos or Greece, island place, or shima, an intimacy between geography and people, shapes the achievement of Skala Eresos as a site for diverse communities. Each successive commu-nity is molded by a deep sense of place, as it responds and eventually influences the cultural and environmental context. Islanders, or those living on islands, especially rural or less populated islands but also highly touristed ones, are aware of their surroundings and the ebb and flow of arriving parties including those who decide to remain permanently. By developing enterprises and participating in the convivial economics, new settlers join Greek island microeconomies and are able to embed themselves in the social milieu of the village despite their outsider status.

In Skala Eresos, lesbian enterprises have continued to grow in numbers for over two decades. Between 2008 and 2016 lesbian-identified entrepreneurs continued to open new enterprises, adding to the range of dining options available on the shoreline. The private gatherings and social events of local Eressians, alternatives, and lesbians are quite often segre-gated, but the plateia continues to be a place that allows for the melding of different groups, casual exchanges, and coordinated meetings. Though there may be a concentration of one social group or another depending on the ownership of a venue, in most of the enterprises of contemporary Skala Eresos the diners reflect the diversity of its communities and tourists.

The first few lesbian enterprises to operate in Skala Eresos were met with various amounts of interference by members of the local community. To commence, lesbian enterprises also had to "buy the air" or rent locations. It was Greek lesbians' negotiations with the landed families of Eresos that opened opportunities for lesbian businesses to proceed. The origin stories of the first set of lesbian enterprises are informative about how lesbian spaces were established in the village and the homecoming they provide to returning lesbian travelers. The first lesbian enterprise was a hotel, set away from the agora, established by a Greek-German couple. Lila, a Greek whose family fled from a village in northern Greece for Germany due to their left politics, had been working in a shop in Athens. Lila explains, "I had been looking around for self-employment. I was thinking of a pizza place." She first of heard of the lesbian enclave developing in Skala via word of mouth among lesbians she knew in Germany.

Gillian, her partner, had traveled to Skala Eresos in 1994 and described what she saw in Skala as "a market gap . . . there was no place for just woman," so she got this "hotel idea." Engaging in what seems to be a pattern for starting up an enterprise on Greek islands, Gillian and Lila spent the next few years in wealthier EU countries working to save funds to rent a building in Skala. In 1998, the Antiope Hotel became the first woman-only hotel to open its doors. Lila shared with me her personal photo album of their inaugural year. The hotel had a muted red clay exterior and each room was brushed in different hues that matched the stark landscape surrounding the village. Gillian and Lila adorned the accommodation with the sparse décor of traditional Greek furnishings and wall hangings. The hotel encompassed a well-tended garden from which produce was gathered to serve clients. Lila described the ambience of the hotel as "mellow"; its location, south and uphill, was secluded from the traffic around the central plateias along the coast.

The former owners explained how the Antiope was a fairly successful enterprise from the start, as it was picked up by gay/lesbian "European" travel agencies. Although new visitors arrive each year, return tourism remained the Antiope's clientele for almost a decade. Rather than just managing a hotel, Lila and Gillian were hosting returning acquaintances and tourists who had become good friends. Paralleling the enterprises in Skala, the Antiope Hotel became a place for lesbian friends and family to reunite yearly in welcoming hospitality.

Lila and Gillian sold "the air" of the Antiope to an ethnic Greek lesbian in 2004. Their decision to stop operating the enterprise was rooted in a desire for a hiatus from the work and annual summer hosting, but also due to the challenging familial dynamics of the owners whose property they rented. At first it was agreed that the elderly matriarch of the family who owned the property would continue to live in a room at the hotel. This happened without difficulty, but problems arose with one of her son's occasional tirades around guests. When the mother passed away there was no longer any control over his actions, which had worsened. Lila and Gillian spoke sympathetically about the family and their troubles, and they had sought on their own to find better housing and help for his mental illness, but he refused. They also felt that his behavior and rejection of their assistance was due to homophobia. The compassion Lila and Gillian showed the ill family member is also indic-ative of enterprise development oriented by community membership.

Lila and Gillian were invested in Skala Eresos as a lesbian enclave and were interested in expanding tourism by attracting younger and new lesbian tourists. They left Skala Eresos to operate a kiosk in urban Germany, but returned a few years later, eventually opening an all-year restaurant. Lila and Gillian's goal of operating a business in the interest of developing lesbian community and working within Skala Eresos's community structure embodies the convivial economics reviewed throughout this volume. The Antiope continued to run as a woman-only hotel through 2012. It was then picked up by a young woman seeking to attract young bohemians and artists. The hotel was instrumental in the integration of future lesbian enterprises into Skala Eresos, allowing for extensive social gatherings at the outskirts of the village with lim-ited conflict at its start. The manner of management—which involves personal ties between customers and clients and the hosting of social gatherings—is based in the camaraderie of affectionate communities. The orientation of Antiope's owners defied mainstream business models rooted in expansion; instead, they opted for an economic model based on enterprise as a means for sustaining community.

A year after the Antiope opened, the first lesbian bar, the Tenth Muse, launched on the main square in Skala Eresos. The business owners, a group of Athenian lesbians, had no relationship with the owners of the Antiope. Unlike the Antiope, which was tucked away, the Tenth Muse took center stage on the plateia. As a bar-café, the Tenth Muse was able to operate from morning until late into the evening, serving some form of breakfast, simple meals, and coffee and cocktails.

In conversation with a group of year-round lesbian residents of Skala in a lesbian-owned restaurant on a rainy winter evening, I listened to Penelope, one of the early owners, reminisce on the initiation of the Tenth Muse. With red wine and pizza, we sat at wooden tables behind

καί ποθήω καί μάομαι
κατ' 'εμον στάλαγμον

τάδε νῦν 'εταίραις
ταῖς 'εμαισι τέρπνα κάλως 'αείσω

ΣΑΠΦΩ

CAFE

THE TENTH MUSE

SKALA ERESSOU · LESVOS · GREECE
TEL: (0253) 53287

Figure 8.2. The Tenth Muse. This an image of the leaflet promoting the Tenth Muse in its first years of operation that was given to me by one of the original owners. On the backside is written "The poetess, Sappho, who was born and lived in Eresos . . . was named the 10th muse, by Platon. In that era, society on the island of Lesvos was entirely different from the rest of Greece. There was much greater social and individual freedom . . ." And on the inside, "Sappho's poetry . . . are excellent examples of erotic writing, which can be considered revolutionary, even today, as they express the love of one woman for another. Two thousand and more years later, Eresos still calls women, from all over the world, to cross the Aegean in order to find and enjoy sensual love without boundaries—to actually sense the eroticism which the earth itself exudes."

thick plastic windows protecting us from the rain and only barely from the wet cold. Penelope shared that it was a cool evening toward the end of the season when she was gathered with a few women in just about the same spot we were sitting. At the time it was the Blu Bar, and the women watched the disassembling of the agricultural cooperative's office in preparation for its move to the upper village. The women had been musing on where lesbians could freely hang out in Skala. Penelope had asked her company, "Why don't we open our own place?" Remarking that the agricultural cooperative's location on the plateia would be ideal and visible, Penelope explained that "I wanted to do something where I could provoke." The Tenth Muse was born and became a vital space for lesbian collectivity, shifting the norms around women's public sociality on the plateia.

Through the 1990s, it was the Blu Bar and Marianna's that served as the social gathering place for lesbian travelers and part-time residents. While George, owner of the Blu Bar, was hospitable and offered access to sinks, I asked what made Marianna's attractive as a gathering place for lesbians. Some women I interview responded with "I don't know," or the "food was good." Others, though, offered, "Because it had a woman's name," and that "Marianna" was ultimately a friendly and welcoming proprietor. The owner, who I met with in 2012, explained that she is not named Marianna, but that "it was just a name." She appreciated that her venue had been a central location for lesbians to gather. But she had little to offer as to why: "Maybe the name, maybe the food." When I asked her about what happened when lesbians opened their own enterprises, she stated positively, "good for them, they now they have their own places," and shared no regrets of losing business.

To begin the process of establishing a lesbian bar on the plateia, Penelope approached the owner of the building that had served as offices for so many decades. Tassos, a member of Skala's landed elite, who had made a fortune in the US and was considered a sort of celebrity in the village, was the one to inherit the building among other family members. Each summer he would dock his yacht in the bay, hosting parties that many in Skala's diverse community had attended. Penelope explains that when she met with Tassos regarding her interest in renting the location for a lesbian bar, he was immediately interested and they began negotiating the terms on the yacht. Expecting greater resistance from him and a higher rental fee because she was planning a lesbian bar, Penelope explained that she was surprised when Tassos charged her the standard price for renting a location on the plateia. She and her friends started construction on the Tenth Muse that year.

In the summer of its opening the Tenth Muse contended with harassment from some of the local villagers. The most striking involved a young local woman, an early employee of the bar, who suffered from drug addiction. The owners of the Tenth Muse believed that after they fired her, some members in the village manipulated the young woman to turn against her employers, provoking her to harass customers and workers. This included threatening Penelope with a broken glass. Penelope explained, "The square was full and no one in the village came to help us, even the police took time to arrive." The continuous threats caused Penelope to leave for a year but the other owners continued on with the business.

Despite volatility in its first year, the Tenth Muse eventually became a fixture in Skala Eresos due to the tenacity of its owners and Tassos's decision to continue renting to them. By the early 2000s, the Tenth Muse was a popular place serving a wide customer base that included local Eressians and a range of tourists. Throughout summer days, I witnessed children from the village running in and out of the Tenth Muse for glasses of water. On several occasions, I saw them inside sitting inside at a large table receiving snacks and in lively conversation with one of the owners. When I first came upon the Tenth Muse in 2008, I found a Greek Orthodox bishop, identifiable by his large mitre, having a morning coffee. In the early evening groups of young men, and older women on Sundays, could be seen sharing coffee at the tables set on the plateia. By late evening the inside bar was blaring old disco tunes with a dance floor dominated by lesbians.

Eva, Penelope's partner and co-owner of the business, explained that she employed anyone who could do the job, and keep a positive attitude during the stress of August. For Eva, being a bar-café that caters to lesbians did not mean segregation from the village nor gendered hiring. However, Eva explained that some of the visiting lesbians from Northern Europe requested that only women be employed, to which she acquiesced. Eva explained, "I don't know why this bothered them, it's not how we are here, but they were my friends, so . . . We don't have to be so separate but they did this at the camp, too, but it's not our conditions." Despite the practice of homosocial gathering, employment in village enterprises had not been determined by gender.

Several of the ethnic Greek lesbian business owners in Skala Eresos made similar remarks on the differences between them and Northern

European lesbians, though they were hardly seeking to distinguish themselves. However, in some moments, when asked to reflect on the social
circumstances in Skala, Greek lesbians shared their self-awareness of the
difference in positionality between Greek and Northern European lesbians. Valerie, another early Greek lesbian visitor to Skala and business
owner, tells me: "An English lesbian staying at Skala Eresos said to me
this 'was our place.' I disagreed. There is a misunderstanding by some of
the foreign lesbians. And then taking the beachfront caused unnecessary
problems in the early years." Valerie brought up the lesbian camp to
further her point. She asks me emphatically, "Isn't this illegal?" Though
I was unclear at first, Valerie was referring to denying local men their
ability to walk along the shore or the lesbian policing of the beachfront,
not the illegal camping. The occupation of place by Northern Europeans
runs counter to the permissiveness, or at least the rhythm of negotiation,
provision of space, and free movement found in Greece. The restrictions
that characterized early Northern European tourists' vision of lesbian
place-making ran counter to the ethics of Greek lesbians.

Greek lesbians seemed to shrug at the biased statements and
stereotypical assumptions they noted their foreign lesbian counterparts
made about ethnic Greek culture. Possibly as an extension of φιλοξενία,
Greek lesbians were forgiving of Northern European ignorance about
Greek social life. The Greek lesbians, who chose to reside in a remote
island space, many arriving from cities in Greece and having traveled
in Europe, held wide insights into the social dynamics of Skala Eresos.
Victoria, one the earliest Greek lesbian business owners in Skala, shares
her tale of arrival: "The first time I came was twenty-three years ago or
more [1989]. I came by luck. Some friends in Athens said we should
go. I had some friends from here, from the island. I returned two to
three seasons for vacation. The same friends told me to come work. I
worked for a few years and then I opened my own. Before the Musa
[Tenth Muse] there were gay-friendly places like Marianna's." The discussion then turned to Victoria's business surviving under the imposed
austerity measures. This conversation took place during the summer of
2012 when microenterprises on islands were feeling particularly dragged
down. I quote Victoria's analysis at length:

> I bought the air, yes. When you are young you make crazy
> decisions. When you are a serious business person you don't

do business here. May used to be much busier, July was busy, and then came the currency change. It's a global game, for all the money to go to one pocket. It seemed with the EU like things were going to come out different, but it looks like it will be even worse for Greece. Greece will be chartered by corporate capital, those who are choking the whole world. There is a bigger plan of corporate takeover. Once the corporations are in control you will see the transportation arriving to Eresos. Without transport the small businesses are being choked. We don't even have lights on the square over there, it is the second square of the village and it is not lit! It is all the same. Greece is a great place; it has everything. There is little crime. To tell you the truth, I feel bitterness to live in a beautiful place while you are being choked by the taxes. Everything is being made more difficult. What should we do? We can't all go to America, Australia, or North Europe. I can't do that. I've worked in Germany and in England, just the weather gets on my nerves, and that is the least of it. Greece is one of the most beautiful places in the world, even better than Switzerland. You can ski in Greece with great mountains. Greece has it all. Consider the range from northern Greece all the way to Crete—you can have bananas and the mountains. And this is the main issue. We can grow crops, olives, in all the countries that are Mediterranean. In Germany they only have mushrooms. And I don't think the Mediterranean people are lazy.

Victoria's kaleidoscopic declaration draws together many of the elements captured in this volume: local food systems, neoliberal globalization, conviviality, and the state. Another lesbian enterprise that was early to open, the Sappho Hotel, remembered for its charming balcony, was operated as a women-only hotel from 1998 to 2004. Lesbian-identified women from Northern Europe ran the hotel and they hired workers who were also lesbians. Josie, who identifies as English and as a lesbian, describes how she came to the Sappho Hotel in 2002, and "never moved off the deck." Like many lesbians who found themselves in Skala Eresos in the late 1990s and 2000s, she was not initially aware of the extent of the lesbian community and the atmosphere of freedom:

I arrived here first after deciding to leave another island vacation early. The accommodations were not spacious enough for the group that I was with. I decided to travel to Lesvos because it was the first ferry departing. The woman selling me the ferry ticket told me I needed to go to Skala. When I arrived in the village I had no idea where I was going so I just started walking to the sea and serendipitously checked myself into the Sappho Hotel. I asked for the price of the room and thought I heard sixty euros, which I thought was alright. But the actual price was sixteen! And the room was every dyke's dream.

Josie further relates that she was a women's studies student in the 1980s and had an opportunity to come to Skala as part of a group, but heard bad reports that "the beaches were dirty and the people are unfriendly." She laments, "I could have been here all those years." By the mid-2000s, Skala Eresos had reached a turning point with multiplying lesbian-owned and oriented enterprises. The tensions that the first businesses experienced were gone. The lesbians seeking to maintain community in Eresos did so through enterprise, claiming a place in the agora and participating in the Greek island ritual of summertime hosting and convivial economics.

Sappho's Travel epitomizes the seamless catering to different communities of Skala. It is a typical Greek travel agency, which continue to survive the internet, that offers transportation services, issues ferry tickets, books hotels, and is also the epicenter for coordinating Northern European lesbian tours and travel. The proprietor of the agency was early to recognize the regularity of lesbian tourism to Lesvos, even initiating in 2000 a women's festival that continues to be held annually in Skala Eresos and is now referred to as the International Eresos Women's Festival.

In the first year, the festival drew negative attention because of the sexually explicit advertising a UK tourist agency used to tout the festival. The advertisements attracted the attention of village residents, many of whom wanted the local government to condemn the event. Rather, the international women's festival has since been integrated as a village event, with programming at government buildings, restaurants, and tavernas, and the mayor providing the official welcome. The festival is now recognized as an economic boost for the village's enterprises, as it extends the tourist season into late September. The event has grown in scale to include visual arts and music venues, as well as lectures and workshops and presentations from Greek dance troupes from the neighboring villages. In the last few years some of the women's cooperatives in Lesvos have participated in the festival as caterers. All of Skala's enterprises anticipate the event, and everyone comments on the successes and failures of it each year, with some suggesting that there has been a general decline in participants. The internet promotions I reviewed and the discussions I held describe the festival as a vibrant event, though due to my timing, I was never able to attend.

Collaborations in Alterity

By claiming a piece of the agora, the lesbian enclave, along with other small-scale Greek and alternative entrepreneurs, joined in Skala Eresos as a place for convivial economics. The lesbian enterprises, mostly serving food and drink and providing accommodations, have become an important part of Skala's tourist-traveler-bohemian-scape that still amounts to a traditional Greek island village.

Unlike many lesbian spaces, which are temporary (Nash and Bain 2007; Valentine 1993), the lesbian enclave is a permanent territorially based community (Browne and Ferreira 2016). As mediators, ethnic Greek lesbians facilitated the interactions of lesbian enterprises with other businesses in Skala, enacting a convivial development, as they enabled purchases of local produce from farmers, dairy products from cooperatives, and fish from local fishers, and teamed up with other businesses to resist government patrolling or the tax police. The lesbian enterprises grew from an interest in creating lesbian community that fit with local traditions of small-scale entrepreneurialism and hospitality. Sappho's legacy facilitated the entry of lesbians into the socioeconomic world of Skala Eresos, as it solidified a historical rhythm on the island for lesbian place-making. The earlier presence of bohemian or hippie businesses also smoothed the entry of lesbian enterprises.

The collective spirit governing island economies in Greece of course is not without expressed biases. When I spoke with some local business owners about lesbian tourism and enterprises, they offered a sort of patronizing approval. When I asked one Eressian woman hotel manager about who were her largest group of tourists, she shared: "The women, they are clean, they don't break things, or leave a mess. They are quiet and caring. I hardly had to do anything after they left. I am going to be a lesbian, they read together, cook together, that's very appealing." I had not asked about what kind of tourists "lesbians" might be, and her decision to evaluate them, though positive, rings similar to Northern Europeans patronizing descriptions of ethnic Greeks. Another of the village tavern owners also benevolently assessed: "I love them. They are a large group of tourists and good tourists. What someone does in their bedroom, women sleeping with women, men with men, or whatever, it has no relevance." It seems some ethnic Greek owners were working toward reducing homophobia and attempting to address their implicit bias. Alexo, a long-standing Greek stalwart of locally owned businesses in Skala who beheld the thirty-year transformation of Eresos valley, declares: "They [lesbians] are the best tourists. I had only one issue and it is an example to show you how good they are. One night there was an English woman who was drunk and she threw plates on the ground. I told her please don't do that again. I would have to call a police. The next day seven women came to apologize. They explained that she was drunk and that she had just broken up with her girlfriend. We understood." Alexo was seeking to dilute biases around sexual orientation that he knows exists in the village. Yet intoxicated Northern Europeans on vacation have broken plates in Greece for decades, regardless of sexual orientation. The practice was popularized as a tourist activity in stereotypical accounts of Greece in English-speaking films and TV shows. While plate-smashing was an ancient Greek tradition that has retained currency among Greeks as a form of celebration, it now occurs rarely and mostly in licensed venues.

Members of the Skala Eresos's local Greek community also legitimize the mainstreaming of lesbian enterprises by suggesting that it was lesbians that capitulated to local codes for their own economic interests. A stern elite resident in Skala shares her thoughts: "The lesvias watch their behavior now. They are business owners and they want good relations with the community." Another older proprietor of a small tourist shop shares his take on the collaborative tourist environment: "I did not like the problems with the women that occurred more than fifteen years ago. Now, they are mannered. They cleaned up their act and have businesses."

These homophobic economic explanations showcase the aversion of an older generation to lesbian integration. No one challenged the right of lesbian enterprises, but some of the interview participants implied a preference for segregation—lesbian businesses are for lesbians. These claims are less indicative of current social rhythms found in Skala

Eresos. For the adult Greek children inheriting family businesses, lesbian tourists and neighbors are no longer a segregated community of tourists. Instead, these second- and third-generation owners attempt to counter a global hegemonic homophobia in their awareness and defense of their non-heteronormative village. Most current owners—lesbian, local, or alternative—seem to be compensating for a homophobic past, as they clearly work to distinguish contemporary relations from previous difficulties.

The lesbian enterprises are transforming from an exceptional tourist sector to an integral part of the social, economic, and cultural exchange that can occur in communities governed by locally operating and embedded enterprises. Lesbian entrepreneurs join other alternative and Greek enterprises in their convivial practices of business ownership. At present neither the beachfront nor other properties in the Eresos valley have been commodified for large-scale tourist development. Rather, the various communities in Skala have adopted a "spontaneous development" model (Leontidou 1990) that constructs enterprises in response to the needs of the community. Unlike capital that engages in long-term planning with the intention of developing a region for increasing profits, the enterprises are based in an organic or attritional economic alterity.

Many lesbians who relocated to Eresos expressed satisfaction with their locally oriented livelihoods. The non-heteronormative public sphere of Skala, still steeped in Greek social and economic traditions, provides a center for cosmopolitan subalterness. A Dutch lesbian in her late forties, who has been living and working in Skala for almost two decades, communicating her exuberance for living in the village, makes economic conviviality palpable:

> It is my home, my home, this is my chosen family, my friends, locals and lesbians. I live in the Eresos community. It is where I work and I do my shopping. I go to the local petrol store. I stay local and I am really happy here. There is a community of lesbians that I am really happy can live here all year around. And I am perfectly welcome to stay here. I feel welcomed. I don't feel people have an issue with us being here. I don't reject Greek values, and it's nice to blend in and a fantastic discussion from a Dutch point of view. The Greeks are nice people and the sun is shining. You can get by with a little. I realize I can have a perfectly happy life without much money, with friends, fantastic food, and some

alcohol! It's the essence of this place makes you think about
needing less. I've got nothing, I am happy; you have time to
think of life. I did that—I had a good run at a career, and if
I stayed probably likely not feeling as happy and content as
I am living here. I have time to be philosophical.

An English lesbian, Suzette, explains her decision to come to Eresos
before the age of retirement: "So many people call this their second
home. I had a fantastic job, pension, insurance, but I decided, why
wait another thirty years? Life is to be lived now." These quotes reflect
a distinct pattern where many Northern European professionals opt to
trade their careers and homes to live in Skala Eresos. The movement
toward convivial work arrangements is increasingly a response to the
neoliberal work environment. As Scott (1985, 229) suggested, everyday
forms of resistance adopt long-run campaigns of attrition. The attempts
by lesbians to make it in Skala Eresos—even if they did not all meet the
same success or satisfaction—indicate their desire for a work-life rhythm
through which they can thrive within a lesbian community, in other
words, a lesbian economics. Portia, another lesbian-identified woman
whom I spent time with, explains what she likes about living in Eresos:
"The problem you know is people don't care anymore, you can die in
the street. Life is so hectic you don't have time to care. Not here, here
it is still quiet and traditional. It is a village way of living and thinking.
Only in the summer it is a fun fair, but you look at the houses and you
get glimpses of the past." Given the homosocial nature of Greek social
worlds, the gathering of lesbians in the agora was congruous with the
sociality of summer in island villages that rarely include a heterosexual
dominance unless it involves extended families or a group of teens or
young adults in their early twenties; rather, homosocial company was
distinctly more evident. When I asked where straight couples might go
to socialize without family and children, I was directed to a bar in the
upper village that afforded such a scene, but only on Saturday nights.

    Skala Eresos has been a place in which lesbians can exist and
interact where they are unlikely to encounter homophobia or marginalization, which was especially crucial before Northern European nations
enacted progressive lesbian and gay legislation. The expression one
lesbian described feeling in Skala is the "normality of day-to-dayness."
The term "ghetto" was raised several times to distinguish Skala Eresos
from other gay tourist destinations. Daniella explains: "This is not a

lesbian ghetto, but very mixed, travelers come here alone, to be alone and not to be alone. There is the Osho Center and other alternatives and singles. Then in August it gets conservative with Greek families. Then September is the women's festival. The energy of the place, it is a magical place."

Skala Eresos's Heterotopia

Skala Eresos has become a small heterotopia that supports a socially diverse milieu of small enterprises and a cosmopolitan crowd. The village squares reflect a transformed, though Greek, sociality. Greek men continue in homosocial gatherings at kafenions, yet the existence of a permanent lesbian and alternative community has resignified the social space of Skala Eresos. While groups may primarily gather at places with hosts of similar identities, there is a cross-fertilization with groups visiting other venues for the taste of various cuisines and to be cosmopolitan. In Skala this occurs not only in summer months, when many Greek islands refigure themselves to host European tourists, but throughout the year. Greek *organic economic alterity* imbues most, if not all, of the enterprises in Skala Eresos because of the strength of community that convivial economics wields, but also because those attracted to it developed an *attritional economic alterity* that purposely sought spaces and places outside of dominant neoliberal economic forms of work and expectations of enterprise. Further, the clear parameters of φιλοξενία free outsiders from being chastised for not adhering to local social codes. The uncustomary actions of tourists and guests, such as public drunkenness or nudity, are condoned so long as they don't directly impede local sociality or the cadence of the public square.

The harmony of the communities in Eresos valley is grounded in the seasonal rhythm of Greek island life—quiet and isolated through the winters, permitting communities to regroup and rekindle a local sense of being and return to the mundane, in contrast to the intensive and socially interactive tourist season. The kefi or celebratory atmosphere of Greek island summers is locally grounded as new groups and residents adopt and create their own forms of summertime merrymaking.

The persistence of convivial economic practices in Greece and the preference for autonomous livelihoods in its islands defy neoliberalism as a matter of course, attracting those ready and able to abandon the scale and materialism in Northern European cities. For Northern European lesbians, and subaltern groups, who simultaneously face oppression and seek social worlds based on their own rhythms, Greek islands offered space. Island studies confront stereotypes of islands as isolated and insular, instead making a strong case that many islands groups are cosmopolitan, having been at the center of global interactions and transnational exchange, while still maintaining a local culture. As Marissa, a senior who enjoys the diversity of her village, explains: "In Eresos we are not a melting pot. We maintain our society and move with changes in cultures. We don't stay closed. We are elastic, open but not too open."

CHAPTER NINE

The Women's Cooperatives of Lesvos

The dichotomy between domination and resistance, as we currently conceive it, bears all the marks of the dominant discourse,
in its insistence that resistance itself should necessarily take the
virile form of a deliberate and violent onslaught. . . . We should
look for resistances of a different kind: dispersed in fields we don't
conventionally associate with the political; residing sometimes in
the evasion of norms or the failure to respect ruling standards of
conscience and responsibility. . . . From this perspective, even with-
drawal from or simple indifference to the legitimating structures of
the political, with their demand for recognition of the values and
meanings which they incessantly manufacture, can be construed
as a form of resistance.

—Rosalind O'Hanlon (2000, 110)

In the early nineteenth century, cooperatives were a socioeconomic
response to the inequities and harm caused by capitalist expansion
(Wright 2010; Moulaert and Ailenei 2005). Small producers interested
in maintaining their livelihoods formed agricultural and consumption
cooperatives to resist the rise of industrialized agriculture that was
threatening their autonomy and economic survival. Rejecting cooperatives, Marxists were unyielding in the position that "conquering political
power" was "the great duty of the working classes" as Marx stated at the
First International, a global meeting of workers, in 1864. Cooperatives
were regarded as interfering with revolutionary progress by diverting
ardent political challenges and making no significant impact. Another
substantial critique waged was that cooperatives cannot truly engender

233

economic change. Marx dismissed cooperatives or associations in the *Communist Manifesto* as "little experiments." In the *Eighteenth Brumaire of Louis Bonaparte* he described cooperatives as a "movement which, having given up the struggle to overthrow the old world despite all the means at its disposal, prefers to seek its own salvation behind society's back, privately, inside the narrow framework of its existence, and which will thus necessarily come to grief" (cited in Buber 1996, 80).

Contemporary authors (Wright 2010; Gibson-Graham 2006) grapple with Marxist critiques of cooperative movements that consider them as apolitical, economically ineffective, or likely to be incorporated into capitalist logic (Gasper 2014). Gibson-Graham (2006), for example, were concerned with the hybridization of cooperatives and the exploitation of labor as they expand in size. Wright (2010, 166), also uncertain of their effect, argues that "with a few notable exceptions, they are mostly relatively small, local operations. When they are successful, they often tend to evolve in the direction of more conventional capitalist firms, hiring non-member employees as a way of expanding production rather than enlarging the full membership of the producer coop itself." Concerns over whether cooperatives or microenterprise or interstitial strategies and autonomous and unobtrusive acts are sufficiently revolutionary or resistant to capitalism is an intransigent motif in the assessment of alternative economics, and one that seems unproductive. Rather, more attention to the workings, intentions, and geographies of these entities that have persisted and have provided safe haven to many groups deserve evaluations for what they contribute as a counterspace and how they integrate and exist in the locations where they are found.

The success of many convivial entities—such as the village women's cooperatives on Lesvos—is not determined by their ability to network, expand, or formalize. Nor is it tied to unionization and working class activism that are both rather hearty in Greece. For the women's cooperative on the island, their ability to remain independent, small-scale, and sustainable is their own measure of success (Koutsou, Iakovidou, and Gotsinas 2003). This chapter adds to the discussion on women's cooperatives in chapter 5, focusing on the beginnings of the cooperatives and the day-to-day practices of running a cooperative in a Greek island village, including a fuller discussion of prickly interactions with the state. The following sections offer a thematic analysis that centers on the voices of cooperative members.

Cooperative Days

"Rain, Coffee, and a Fireplace"

Walking through the empty village streets in the utter quietness of winter months, I experienced the solitude that island residents live in for much of the year. The initiative for a women's cooperative was driven by the isolation many women felt in their households and a yearning to not be idle after the summer tourist and fall harvest seasons were over. In most of Lesvos women indicated that the development of their cooperative came from their own volition and financing, while others were prompted by government gender equity programs for rural development. As Phoebe, one member of the Ayia Paraskevi cooperative, explained, "We did it by ourselves, we did it with supporting each other." The women's cooperatives all found a location in their village and invested their own resources, such as household pots and pans, when they began to produce as a cooperative. Thereafter assistance often came from local sources, including community members and families. Resources also arrived from regional nonprofits and the Greek government. One of the younger members from the Agra cooperative summarily talks about the origin of the cooperative: "How did we get started? It was the rain, the fireplace, and the coffee. We started as friends, and then we began to talk. First three of us came together; we spoke with others and engaged them. We wanted to give life to our village and to get out of our house. Then we learned that government would provide us with some help once we got started." In its first steps, the Agra cooperative acted autonomously. Similarly, members of the Filia cooperative describe their beginnings: "We started in a small location in the village that was empty. We found it ourselves. It was more like a kitchen in our house. We were on top of each other trying to produce, so we decided to find another place and we set it up, painted it ourselves, and used our money to do this. At the start some of us actually did our cooking for the cooperative in our house." Elina, a member from the Ayia Paraskevi cooperative, portrays their start-up process:

> In our first location we didn't have to pay rent, one person let us use their house. Then two of the local shopkeepers, a general store, and the butcher let us put some of our products

in their stores. Now we have a place and pay rent. It was a storage unit that we fixed and we did it all and paid for it ourselves. We paid rent upfront for the year. We then applied for government funds, less than 5,000 euros, to buy the big appliances, refrigerators, and a machine to make filo.

These grassroots efforts by the cooperatives show a form of resourcefulness often found in geographically constricted locations, such as islands. The Parakila's cooperative start-up story echoes the others: "It was a difficult economy. We figured we had to come up with 10,000 euros. We believed in ourselves and we became friends. Before we got started there was nothing here, no evidence of a women's cooperative. We gave ourselves one year to see how it would work. The most important thing was that we would get along with each other. There were some who couldn't get on; they didn't want to do what most of the others wanted." The Parakila cooperative has been quite successful, opening a warmly decorated storefront. Other cooperatives also indicated that their success was dependent on getting along and achieving harmony. For example, a Filia member declared: "At the start there were forty women and finding agreement was a challenge but now we are fine. We had a lot to learn, we asked for assistance or mediation to work out our organizational problems. Those that didn't break, learned." All of the cooperatives experienced reduction in membership. The year of initiation often had bloated numbers because many of the women who initially signed were less serious or unable to make a long-term commitment. Over the course of my research, the cooperatives I had visited showed little change in membership from my first meeting in 2008 through 2016. Some of the cooperatives with older members, such as Ayiassos and Asomotos, lamented that they had not attracted new and younger women.

The most widely used source of government assistance for cooperatives in the early 2000s was the Ministry of Agriculture. This was tied to the establishment of the EU and its investments to address gender equity and rural development in Europe by supporting women agricultural workers and agrotourism development (Lassithotaki and Roubakou 2014). Once some of the cooperatives felt established, they sought forms of government funds, as the Ayia Paraskevi cooperative did. Cooperatives could receive between 2,500 and 5,000 euros to help purchase industrial kitchen items, such as a stove, refrigerator, or filo dough maker. In several cases, these items already had been purchased by the cooperative, so they used the funds to assist with rent. In addition, the Ministry of Agriculture would offer trainings in food preparation by professional bakers in which attendance was required to receive government support. The cooperatives' response to these seminars was mixed; a few valued the training, but most indicated that that they had their own recipes and own routines for producing baked goods that they had learned from their mothers and grandmothers.

The cooperatives that did have a relationship with the Ministry of Agriculture—including Molyvos, Ayia Paraskevi, Anemotia, and Agra—all emphasized that it was one women, Kyria or Mrs. Kofou, who served as their greatest source of support. Referred to only by her last name, it took a few visits to cooperatives for me to realize that she was not an independent supporter, but rather a representative of the state. They all hailed her as a key resource for questions regarding things like trade regulations, health and safety codes, and access to governmental funds. They also expressed appreciation for the inspiration or encouragement given by Kyria Kofou when they were struggling to sort out procedures, gain a foothold in sales, or overcome gender bias.

I was lucky to meet with Kyria Kofou at the Ayia Paraskevi cooperative in 2009. She humbly described her office and a career stretching over three decades. Kofou explained that the PASOK or the socialist government was the first to establish a set of programs for agrotourism in the islands during the 1980s. This included rooms for rent, restaurants, and activities such as horseback riding and sea sports. In the early 2000s, the second round of rural island development was initiated by the European Union's interest in regional agricultural growth. Kofou explained that in some instances the development of women's cooperatives, such as the one in Anemotia, was to assist older women to engage in productive activity. For the most part, the funding for cooperatives was an attempt to incorporate the productive capacities of women agricultural workers.

By 2012, Kofou retired and many cooperative members lamented her departure, especially in the context of the economic crisis and other state failures in relation to Lesvos's cooperatives. A member of the Molyvos cooperative explained, "There is no one in the office to assist us now. If we have a question, there will be no one to answer, and Kyria Kofou will not be replaced because there is no money."

Other cooperatives, such as Filia and Skalachori, did not garner initial funds from the government and suggested that it might be due to their political leanings. In the case of Filia, they received support from the local government, not the Ministry of Agriculture, to launch the cooperative. The cooperative members in Filia explained, "The mayor agreed to forgive two years of rent and lent us funds for refrigeration and ovens to help us start the cooperative."

One of the members at Filia added that she served as a counselor in the local government and was able to bring up cooperatives' issues in meetings of the municipality. Some of the cooperatives were disappointed with the limited support they received from spouses and their communities during their start-up. Another Filia cooperative member explains: "We really had no support here, but we help the community. We were told you are not going to make it. They [the local villagers] don't understand that our food is fresh and it is different than what is made by the machine. The villagers are still not sure if it is worth paying a little more. They didn't believe us because we were women." In Ayiassos, Kikki explained: "At first our husbands did not like it. It was a big problem, especially early on when the wife wasn't home. Our men have the attitude from the East." Another instance in which gender traditions were brought up: "The village didn't take us seriously. They didn't believe that us women together would get along; we showed the opposite and captured a market. . . . It hasn't changed much at home. My God, if that changed, they would be up in arms." And Alexia from the cooperative in Polichnitos explained: "In this village, the spouses were not supportive. They did not see the economic value in the project, but now they support it. Our spouses saw it as a hobby, ha, we were working nine hours a day for a hobby!"

Women throughout villages of Lesvos resisted gender stereotypes and worked together on a venture that would provide them new opportunities, satisfaction, and remain under their control. In their planning they identified methods for constructing an enterprise that began by drawing on their collective resources. These women shifted the long-held rhythms of isolation and exclusion from the agora, continuing local food traditions but in the form of a collective enterprise.

"THE HOUSE ISN'T ENOUGH, IT CHOKES US"

In my meetings with the various women's cooperatives, members expressed that engaging in collective work outside the home was a central reason for making the financial investment to enter into a cooperative. Gianoula, a member of the Ayia Paraskevi cooperative, directly stated, "The

cooperatives presented a path for village women to develop not only
an economic enterprise but also a method by which to overcome their
isolation." As a member of Anemotia explained, "Yes, we are doing it
for income, but it was to get out of the house."

Anastacia from the Molyvos cooperative explained: "I wanted
to help create a place for women to go. You couldn't go out." And as
another member explained, "The women in the cooperative are more
free. You have more good in your life."

In most cases, the cooperatives are housed in buildings around the
village square, meaning that they receive daily traffic from shoppers and
seasonal tourists. Almost all of the cooperatives combined production
facilities with a shop front and a small café. The cooperatives gave local
women the opportunity to capture a portion of the village center where
they can convene. Just as the local men often meet to have coffee or a
drink together, women's cooperative members do the same, though it is
in conjunction with earning a living. As a senior member of the Molyvos
cooperative explained: "For us, for the girls, we can't stay at home; we
have learned to work. I can't stay at home and watch the TV all day.
We take great interest in our work, and the development of the cooperatives. It exhausts us, but we love it." The mental health benefits of the
camaraderie of the cooperatives were not lost on members. A woman
at the Agra cooperative explained, "Work is good company, women go
crazy in the house, they had many psychological problems." It is the
opportunity to be "out" that contributes to the women's cooperatives'
endeavors. A member in Molyvos explained her reason for participation:
"I joined the cooperative to get out. It helped a lot." Describing the
general benefit of the cooperative for island women, a member from
Mesotopos explained: "We are more full, we have things to do; we are
not stuck here. Now we work with people, we have more self-esteem."

The Agra cooperative sits on the Kalloni-Eresos road, which is the
only thoroughfare on the southwestern side of the island that hugs the
coast as it makes its way down from the mountain town. The cooperative members explained that if they were going to continue living in
their villages they needed to do something. They shared how the public
middle school had already closed, and there are concerns over the clo-
sures of the local elementary school, due to the departure of villagers
for Athens. The decline in village populations is a condition found not
only on Greek islands experiencing monumental economic and social
insecurities, but is a general concern for island societies in the context
of globalization (King 2009).

Figure 9.1. Cooperative members at work/courtesy of Tzeli Hadjidimitriou. Women's cooperative members work in concert with each other and never alone. Village family members living in Athens or further abroad often place large orders for pastries and food items to serve a taste of home at major events such as weddings and baptisms. This photo renders palpable the camaraderie among women's cooperative members and the joyful elements of cooperative labor and ownership.

Women's cooperative members recognized the necessity of changing the traditional spatial gender norms and the development of projects that extended their work of household manager. The cooperative members said their work did not replace their traditional gender duties, as they instead managed them along with participating in the marketplace. The benefits of being publicly engaged in work were tied to the caring and intimate relationships that women's cooperative members held with each other, especially as they negotiated and maintained the collectivity of their enterprise. As Georgia, one cooperative member in Agra, explained: "We have a big love for each other. When one of us is missing, we ask where could she be? Then we check on her and keep track of each other." Several of the cooperatives (Parakila, Skalachori, and Mesotopos) referred to the ways in which the children of the cooperative members grew up as extended family, as they often played together in the patio of their facilities. Merging home and work, cooperative members maintained gendered duties, but they also blur the lines of the public and private spheres—a long-established trait of Greek enterprises, and women's participation in them, that preserves a work-life rhythm that is livable.

Another cooperative member from Ayiassos humorously conveyed the priority that the cooperative takes in their lives. Alicia explained, as other members chuckled: "First we do work here, *then* we do work at home. I would not leave this company for anything. We talk about everything here." The friendship and company found in collective work mattered greatly to the women's cooperative members, as their associations differed from social or family events found in village life. The operation of an enterprise requires a specific form of engagement, especially a collectively owned or a laterally functioning enterprise that offers the opportunities for deeper relationships based on ties of collaboration.

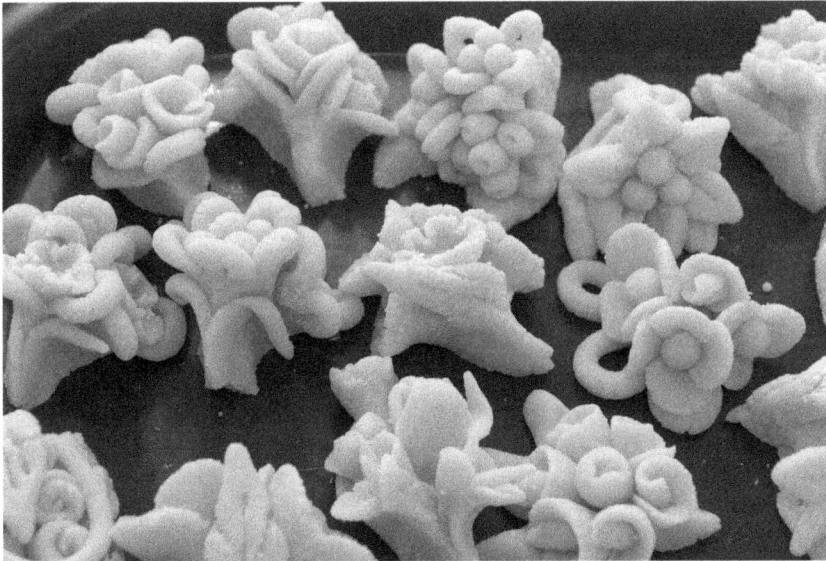

Figure 9.2. Greek pastries, cooperative style/courtesy of Tzeli Hadjidimitriou. The high style and artisanal work of women's cooperative members are showcased in this preparation of αμυγδαλωτά λουλούδια Μικρασίας or Asia Minor almond flour flower cookies, which are prepared for special occasions. Members of a few of the women's cooperatives are from families that fled violence against ethnic Greeks in what is now eastern Turkey about one hundred years ago.

In addition to camaraderie, friendship, and public engagement, many of the cooperative members highlighted the pleasure of being involved with others in a creative activity or an artistic project. As a member of the Asomotos cooperative explained: "We have artistry, we want to see beautiful things. We have dreams for our future and we love what we do. This isn't something that we are made to do. We love our life with the cooperative." Artistry is apparent in the production of cooperative products, as well as in the packaging and displays. The rhythm of making handmade pasta, such as orzo, requires repetition and a trained hand, as does the shaping of roses out of carefully mixed almond paste. Rather than flaunting their individual skills, the cooperatives highlight the pleasure of collective culinary arts.

Success and Survival in the Cooperative Model

The survival and success of these women-led enterprises was often attributed to the cooperative model. There was a consistency among the cooperatives in the way that they described the decision-making process, the negotiation of wages, and the setting of work hours. After my first few interviews, where I asked about why they formed a collective or cooperatively owned enterprise, I soon realized the question made no sense in a Greek village context. While many cooperative members were generous and explained the obvious, the question did not fit in the same way if I had queried a private business owner (especially in the US) about why they had not started as a cooperative. The responses I received reveal cooperatives as an entrenched form of economic organization in Greek village life.

In raising this question at the Ayia Paraskevi cooperative, members began with the ABCs of what it means to be a cooperative, to illuminate for me why they operate as one. The advantage of a cooperative model over independent ownership was self-evident to cooperative members: collective rather than individual distribution of work, company with others or parea, and a greater ability to withstand financial crunches. The cooperative members never considered that the structure of cooperatives were examples of alternative economics or subversive. Among Lesvos's enterprises the purpose of the continued process of negotiation among consumers and suppliers was to arrive at the best terms to sustain all concerned. Despite the demands of austerity programs, the cooperatives continued to operate by principles of convivial economics that, without intention, defied the plan of the European Union, the European Central Bank, and the International Monetary Fund to modernize Greek business practices through austerity measures. The logic of engagement among Greek businesses is to as much as possible float an entity in greatest need, even a competitor, rather than driving its dissolution.

The Mesotopos cooperative offers a case of how convivial economics—or self-organized and small-scale collectives—that are embedded in place succeed. The Mesotopos cooperative is made up of thirty-four members with fifteen working on a daily basis and others casually throughout the week. It is the largest cooperative in Lesvos, and it is often recognized as the most productive women's cooperative on the island.

After years in operation, in 2012 the Mesotopos cooperative moved into a large new building. They bought land directly on the main road using cooperative savings to construct a building in which they could work and host a shop. The first level of the structure houses a spacious room, tiled throughout, with lovely showcases. Traditional Greek pastries such as kouroubedes, blaziztes, theeples, flouxeria, baklava, koulourakia, and cookies in various shapes basted with butter, sometimes rolled in sesame seeds or drizzled with chocolate, are decoratively placed. Set on top of counters are carefully made pyramids of jars filled with colorful sweet preserves made from quinces, olives, watermelon, cherries, oranges, lemons, apricots, and more. There is also a large stacked display of "gliko tou koutaliou" or "dessert of the spoon," dazzlingly sweet desserts served in a small spoon with coffee. Upon entering the shop one is met with shelves of multicolored homemade pastas in various shapes that are decorously placed; each product is labeled with a production and expiration date written by hand.

The Mesotopos cooperative was recognized for their achievement with an award by the National Women's Agriculture Association. When I asked the Mesotopos cooperative about their success, one member explained: "We are a cooperative. We all make decisions together and we have achieved our success because we have maintained the cooperative model. We all come together and make our decisions and agreements. We decided together to purchase the land and agreed on the plans for the building. We took out a loan. We began the efforts for the new building three to four years ago." Another member added, "We have synergy and we love what we do. We really like our work." Emphasis on the success of the cooperative model was widely evident.

For example, the Anemotia cooperative noted: "A cooperative is unique. We can work within ourselves. To owe, to borrow, we can fight, and you can start your battle. We see the unemployment out there. We make our plans, we begin our projects together." A member from the Molyvos cooperative explained: "The cooperatives can survive because collectively we can agree to reduce our wages. A small businessperson who hires someone is still responsible for paying their wages." And a member of the Polichnitos cooperative had a strikingly similar statement: "The cooperative has more strengths. We can agree to make cuts to our salaries and work longer hours. When you have someone working for you have to pay them. Here we decide together to make cuts. We fight besides each other and together to maintain it."

Unfortunately, the reduction of wages and an increase of work hours were significant examples of the collective decision-making process that cooperatives underwent between 2009 and 2012 to address the effects of the crisis. In many cases the cooperatives cut wages by half. In a few instances, rather than pay wages they kept an account of the monies owed to each cooperative member for future payment. The delay and reduction in wages may demonstrate the type of self-exploitation waged by those critical of alternative economics. However, most cooperatives kept track of their losses, for future reimbursement, agreeing together that it was worth the good the cooperative provides them and their village.

For many, the social space provided by the cooperative was more important than individual wages. In the Anemotia cooperative, wages were reduced as low as one euro per hour. One of the members explained, "This is OK for us, but a younger woman could never make it on this." The cooperative members had the option to reduce wages because they are not singularly dependent on a cash economy. Many had some savings, but most held small plots of land that they gardened and olive groves sufficient for personal use; by living on remote and rural islands one evades the incessant consumerism of cities and continents.

The cooperative model employed by Lesvos's women's cooperatives, which include localized control, equal distribution of income or hourly wages, and a collective decision-making process, manifest what Illich (1973) meant by self-defined work. Collective decision-making incorporated how many orders they were willing to accept and the organization of production. In some cooperatives, the member who excelled at a particular task stayed with it. For example, in Parakila: "Our work is organized in two shifts per day. Everybody must work one and if we are very busy two. We

don't really change jobs around, each has their job and they hold it."
Others, like Agra, altered work and shifts: "We work and we talk but we
don't want to form cliques so we vary schedules and change the groupings
and jobs. In the summer, we have one person assigned to the storefront
to deal with customers. But we are also flexible so that someone can do
what they are best at." This type of negotiated flexibility is a defining
feature of Greek businesses, which avoid hard-and-fast rules that defy the
constant figuring required for survival at the margins.

In terms of the governing structure, the cooperatives held regular
elections for president, vice president, secretary, and treasurer every
two to four years, depending on the cooperative. In various ways the
cooperatives indicated that, although they have an official administrative hierarchy, the collective made the decisions. For example, Alicia,
an Ayiassos cooperative member, stated: "We have regular elections,
but we do not have a dictator. We have a collective decision-making
process. We debate, argue, and disagree with how to proceed, but we
do not have permanent fights. Up until now we are fine, but we don't
know if we will last." Alicia's concern with being able to last reflects the
constant need to reduce wages due to the pressure of the economic crisis
and the state's neglect in the survival of the cooperatives. Similarly, in
Parakila and Molyvos, those in office took a leadership role, but members
indicated that important decisions were made collectively. A member
of the Skalachori cooperative explained: "We hold elections every four
years and we have a president, vice president, and secretary, but when
there is a very big decision we have to all agree." Consensus building
seemed to be a strategy for many of the cooperatives. Another member
of Agra cooperative explained: "In terms of decision-making, everyone
gives their position. We go around from one to fifteen [the number of
members in the cooperative] and we give our opinion." The cooperatives
prized a flexible organizational form that considered the various needs
of the cooperative and its members. The cooperatives were intent that
the voices of each members were considered as the organization made
decisions and addressed various challenges.

Cooperatives in Crisis

Several of the women's cooperative members suggested that their ability
to continue to operate through the economic crisis was tied to a growing

interest in purchasing Greek or local products. Rather than the growth of the local food movement found elsewhere, buying local in Greece was a matter of course, due to the preference for Greek cookery, but during the crisis it was considered a response to the harshness of the loan agreements involving the EU. Nikki from Ayiassos specified that the resolve to purchase Greek products was driven by a desire to support the local economy. A member at the Filia cooperative made this assessment: "I think now many people are reading labels and trying to figure out if the product came from Greece. This is a new consciousness. We [Greece] have been importing without developing our exports. But Greece has a great deal that it can grow and produce and we have to organize and exploit it; there would be less need and less debt."

More than a decade ago, as a strategy of island development, the prefecture of Lesvos and Limnos, which governed the island, subsidized the Lesvos Shop. The Lesvos Shop was a central topic that cooperative members wanted to discuss, especially in 2008 and 2012, and it provides an avenue for considering organic economic alterity and its relationship to the Greek state. Essentially, the Lesvos Shop was a state-run entity in the port of Mytilini (and Athens) that showcased the goods produced by the women's cooperatives of Lesvos as well as island products such as ouzo, olive oil, cheese, honey, and crafts. The cooperatives that brought items to the Lesvos Shop kept a record of what was due to them based on the pricing of products. Products were not being sold on commission, but purchased via invoice and then sold by the Lesvos Shop. For some of the cooperatives, especially those in smaller villages with an elderly membership, the Lesvos Shop was a major source of earnings. Other cooperatives used the Lesvos Shop only as a source of added income.

Unfortunately, the greatest challenge for many of the cooperatives' financial success was that the Lesvos Shop did not make payment on many of the invoices for the goods provided by the cooperatives. Discussions about the Lesvos Shop, its mismanagement, and lack of payment was an ongoing point of contention in all my meetings with the cooperatives. The Lesvos Shop drew the ire of the public and the potential of corruption was covered in the island's newspaper. The payment owed to the cooperatives by the prefecture in 2008 was hefty, ranging from about 10,000 euros to over 40,000 euros per cooperative. The issue had come to a head, and the prefect was threatening the closure of the Lesvos Shop, which was not what the cooperatives wanted. In fall 2008 the Lesvos Shop and the women's cooperatives was addressed at the prefecture's meeting that occurred during my first research visit.

In a coffee shop garden, with vined banisters and a raised wooden platform on a rainy November evening, just prior to the prefecture meeting set to consider the Lesvos Shop, members from various cooperatives met to coordinate their efforts. Seventeen members from the islands' cooperatives, including Molyvos, Ayiassos, Ayia Paraskevi, and Polichnitos, and Kyria Kofou from the Ministry of Agriculture participated. They were troubled by the amounts owed to them, but more so with the mismanagement of the Lesvos Shop by someone all agreed was ill-equipped for the job. Senior cooperative members explained to newer ones that at its inception, the Lesvos Shop was managed effectively by the cooperatives and that they would prefer that it fell under their management again, but they did not want it closed under any account. All agreed in their preparation for the prefect meeting that the goal was to keep the Lesvos Shop open rather than focusing on still owed debts. The cooperatives were seeking to manage or at least improve the management of the Lesvos Shop so they could maintain it as a place to sell their products at the island's main port.

Those participating in the premeeting also recognized the lifeline the shop provided some of the smaller cooperatives. They shared designs to improve the shop, such as collaboratively running it with representatives from different cooperatives. This hour and a half meeting was the very first time members of the islands' women's cooperatives had met together and planned across cooperatives. Most of the cooperatives I spoke with had little interest in a formal association among Lesvos's cooperatives. Although they did not identify other cooperatives as competitors, they preferred to operate autonomously (despite advice from academics and development practitioners that they should unify). The women attending this meeting engaged in friendly conversation and in serious discussion, but there was also plenty of humorous commentary about state officials. Cooperatives members with more political experience, or those who were more comfortable with public speaking, offered warnings to expect loud and bombastic rhetoric by members of the council but to not be intimidated.

The prefect meeting, open to the public, was held in a large and packed auditorium in the port of Mytilini. I estimated that at least three hundred people were in attendance with standing room only. The forty-feet-high ceiling in an oval shaped ballroom was ideal for political grandstanding. There was arena seating on one side and the president and secretary of the prefecture were on a raised platform down at the center with councilors sitting around an overly large but beautifully constructed wood table. Photocopied "No Smoking" signs were hanging around the auditorium, but burning tobacco could be smelled throughout the space. Along with the attractive lighting, warm and muted rather than florescent, watching Greek politics at work up close and off-screen was a striking experience.

Another item on the agenda, the establishment of an army shooting range near Agra, attracted numerous citizens who had been protesting outside the auditorium. Earlier in the week the protesters blocked the single highway through the eastern part of the island, which I experienced firsthand, having to turn around and take the only other route to get across the island. When discussion of the Lesvos Shop started it was about 10:00 p.m., not considered too late for the Greek political sphere.

The deliberations over the Lesvos Shop were heated, more than I expected, even after hearing the warnings at the cooperative premeeting. While most of the council members listened to various arguments, several politicians loudly lambasted the Lesvos Shop as a wasteful entity and accused the cooperatives of inefficiency. Other politicians argued stridently in favor of the cooperatives. Seasoned politicians used the matter of the Lesvos Shop for posturing, but for many cooperative members it was their first time speaking in such a forum. In this large-scale public setting, members individually made a case for the prefect to reorganize the Lesvos Shop, explaining that it was profitable when run by them and could be again when managed appropriately. The members who spoke were openly critical of the government employee that mismanaged the shop, accusing him of selling items that were not from the island and that he "ate the money" due to the cooperatives. They voiced their identity with their land and implored the prefect to consider that the cooperatives kept their communities alive. The loudest politicians were those trying to drown members' testimonies on the failure of the shop to be economically responsible. One council member cautioned another to calm down and to stop taking a hard line with the women agricultural workers. A cooperative member from Mesotopos explained to those governing the prefecture: "The Lesvos Shop owes us money, twenty thousand euros, but I am not here for the money. We want our products in the store. The customer is waiting for us at the Lesvos Shop; the goods are being sold." The council member on the board representing the village's region added that the Mesotopos cooperatives had payment owed to them put off first for five months, then for seven months, and now for nine months.

Meri, a cooperative member of Ayiassos, moved to the table and sat in front of the microphone, looking up at the president and then taking in a panorama of the audience as she spoke: "The economics is one thing, but it is getting out of the house, getting to be free. I was able to throw away the pharmaceuticals I took for my mental health. It is not just economic—to work with each other is for our health, to maintain tradition and the community. Don't give us a hard time again, let us do our work, the cooperatives are everywhere." Another cooperative member from Filia asked, "We have learned the routine of work. What are we supposed to do now, return to our houses?"

The Lesvos Shop was not shuttered after the tumultuous meeting that ended well after midnight. The decision to sell, privatize, and or give the shop to cooperatives to manage was tabled, with the claim that more information was necessary for the case to be decided. However, by March 2011 all locations of the Lesvos Shop were closed; the decision was tied to the restructuring of Greek government administration in connection with the austerity measures. In 2010, the Kalikratis Reform reduced the number of prefectures in Greece from fifty-seven to thirteen regional authorities, and the 1,034 municipalities were slashed to 325.

After consisting of thirteen municipalities, the Aegean region was headquartered in Piraeus, the port of Athens, and was reduced to one municipality. The stated goal of the Kalikratis Reform was to increase subnational participation in government and decentralize domestic policy (Chardas 2012). Instead, the experience of the cooperatives reflects that of many in Greece: reduced access to policymakers and weaker local governments. The centralization that occurred with the Kalikratis Reform counters the localized political control that historically has characterized Greek islands. One cooperative member from Ayia Paraskevi captured islanders' perspective, "What does Pireaus have to do with us? Now they will really forget us."

By 2012, the Lesvos Shop owed 550,000 euros to suppliers and 160,000 euros to the cooperatives, compounding the strain of the economic crisis felt throughout Greece. The president of the Filia cooperative spoke animatedly about the Lesvos Shop. As she prepared the industrial mixer for a batch of dough, bringing out news clippings she had kept regarding the issue, she explained that if the debt owed to them by the state was fulfilled, "we wouldn't have a problem, we would have had ourselves paid and instead of owing money to ourselves, we would be very advanced. Even if the state had provided us with a partial payment, 10,000 euros, that would have assisted us." The indebtedness of the Lesvos Shop to the cooperatives started somewhere between 2003 and 2006, according to the cooperatives I surveyed. Although cooperatives kept records and paid taxes on the products given to the Lesvos Shop, the state claimed it held no public record of the products it had purchased from them. A member of the Ayiassos cooperative states: "The Lesvos shop has not paid us. We chased them. We would ask them for money from their cash register. They would say we can't pay you and we would ask again. Now we do business with Peri-Lesvos [in Athens]. The work is very good—she takes them and she pays immediately, hand with hand." The Parakila cooperative president, who also addressed the prefect at the public meeting, explained the following to me a few days later:

> The Lesvos Shop owes us 26,000 euros. We spent about a year pursuing a payment, hiring lawyers, and filing in court. We were initially led to believe that we would receive payment. While we were pursuing a legal case, the Lesvos Shop closed. And the governing structure of Lesvos changed. This increased the challenges and difficulties of attaining payment. The 26,000 euros are considered paid, but they haven't paid. We paid the 3.5 percent taxes on these earnings, all the cooperatives have paid their taxes, even when they didn't receive payment, or they couldn't operate.

When the Parakila cooperative complained to the tax office regarding payment on earnings yet to be received by the government, the response she received was that the tax office would need to take a closer look at their books. She explained, "If they do that, no matter how accurate our accounting, they will surely find something." Her sentiment is similar to the concerns shared by the small shop owners in Skala. Most microenterprises avoided interactions with governing bodies to avoid interference with their survival and autonomy, preferring a loss over state entanglement.

According to cooperatives that were seeking repayment, the change in governmental structure failed to provide fair governance. Government officials seemed to use the Kalikratis Reform to avoid responsibility for the debt owed by the Lesvos Shop under the prefecture. They explained that all legal cases would be tabled for three years during which there would be a "cleaning of accounts" to determine what funds were available to pay the debts owed by the Lesvos Shop. Once this is determined, then the cooperatives can pursue their funds legally. Resigned, the Parakila president stated, "Everyone knows that the state is bankrupt and there will be no funds left over and that the state is buying time in order to delay addressing the matter." They were also told that they would be required to go to court. Frustratingly, the president continued: "We have made many efforts, but have won nothing. The change of the Kalikratis has unraveled the legal system and no one is sure which office attends to which matter or exactly what the law is." As has been demonstrated throughout this volume, Greek islanders hold a dubious relationship with its mainland government. As more than one islander explained to me, "the further away from Athens, the less you matter." With the new government structure, it seems that Lesvos residents are expecting to be further taxed and ostracized by the central government.

Another change in government policy discussed by the cooperatives was the official recognition of the social economy by the Greek government in 2012. Cooperatives worried about the adoption of requirements for a minimum number of members and less favorable tax policies. For larger men-dominated agricultural or industrial cooperatives, minimum membership is not a problem. However, for women's agricultural cooperatives, especially those located in island villages with small populations, it was a major concern. Some members worried that new regulations would interfere with earnings or that they would be further taxed. Across cooperatives, most members identified the new laws as another hurdle they must address to conduct their business—none saw it as an advantage.

The new legislation also requires additional paperwork, including bookkeeping, meeting minutes, and the recording of votes. One member in Ayiassos fretted: "We are having a difficult time, a challenging economic time. They want us to keep track of everything, but this costs money. Everything is rising, our taxes, our overhead, and now we have to cover this?" Several of the cooperatives were resolute on ignoring the government, which they only saw as meddling with their livelihoods. Evident in my conversations with cooperative members was the perspective that the institutionalization of the social economy would lead to more challenges for the economic survival of their cooperative. Nasioulas (2012, 159) traced changes in the legal structure of social economic development in Greece: "Law 4019/2011 on Social Economy and Social Entrepreneurship now provides for the institutional recognition of Social Economy in Greece for the first time. By introducing new forms of social entrepreneurship, such as the Social Cooperative Enterprise, it enriches the available organizational forms for economic self-expression." According to Nasioulas (2012, 159), while a step forward, the new law governing social enterprises and the social economy is limited "because the Greek administrative system is yet able to address long standing issues regarding the structuration of social economy in Greece, through a detailed, operational and inclusive recognition." Nasioulas's (2012) position is based in the social economy perspective (Wright 2010; Moulaert and Ailenei 2005; Laville, Levesque, and Mendell 2006) that argues for the institutionalization of alternative economics within the state as the best way forward for challenging capitalist economics. Cooperative members across Lesvos felt differently. Autonomy, local control, and decentralization have long been considered the hallmark to the success of cooperatives. The implementation of state-level policies is viewed as a hindrance, as they could interfere with the local coordination of convivial economic practices.

Greece's economic crisis took center stage in my meetings and interviews with the cooperatives in the summer of 2012. One cooperative member in Parakila, who I had met in prior meetings, captured the attitude toward the current crisis with an adage, "When you are soaking wet, it doesn't matter how much more it rains, you are already wet." Other members of the cooperative nodded. The comments made by cooperative members around the Greek economic crisis indicated that they had been through this before. Many members were also defiant in response to the Memorandum of May 2010, which introduced the first set of austerity measures. When I asked how they thought the economic crisis might impact them, I received staunch responses such as "we are not for closings."

The women's cooperatives members are committed to working and working hard, taking pay cuts or withholding pay in order to secure the survival of their collective enterprise. Many of the cooperatives had used this strategy during other moments of financial distress, such as the failure of the Lesvos Shop. They were resolute that the current crisis was just another bridge to be crossed. In my visits with the cooperatives in 2008, 2010, 2012, and 2016, members were constantly engaged in production, with continuous orders to fill, and phones ringing with new ones. As economic units, cooperatives in Greece and globally demonstrate resilience and fared better than other enterprises in similar industries during the economic crisis (CICOPA 2013, 5).

Finale: Women's Cooperatives as a Liberatory Project

Across Lesvos, the women's cooperative members were conscious of their island place and what it took to make a living there, how to secure personal well-being, and how to support their community and their land. Unlike many other island villagers, these women and their immediate families chose not to leave the island for Athens. While challenging long-held norms around space and place that circumscribe gender and sexuality in the remote villages of Greek islands, the women's cooperatives simultaneously upheld deeply rooted traditions around food and collective and local production. Sasa, from the Skalachori cooperative, provided a particularly acute depiction of islandness and gender:

> An island is a wonderful place to come and to relax, but living here it can also strangle you. If you live on a mainland, the thought to leave your circumstance, or to escape, is there even if it may not be a real possibility. On an island you are a captive of the ocean. So you have to birth wings to get past it. For us, the cooperatives are those wings.

The women's cooperatives of Lesvos are economic entities that affirm the effectiveness of the cooperative organization of production, especially within a challenging economic context. Earnings and the financial success of the cooperatives were driven or motivated by a desire to engage in work, collectively and for sociality in the company of other women. The deep regard these women have for the betterment of their community through their engagement in local production and for their own survival was plain. They were aware of the rhythms that grounded their Aegean villages in cooperative traditions and their villages' communal orientations toward autonomous governance and convivial economy. Their local identities did not lapse into provincialism, as they hold a coastal awareness and generational experiences of varied interactions—colonization, expulsion, migration, tourism, transnational commerce—with the world.

Coda

Its ruling classes were destroying each other at a great rate while its
land system (the basis of its economic structure) was coming loose,
with considerable reorganization moving in the direction of a far
more egalitarian distribution than had been the norm. Furthermore,
small peasant farmers were demonstrating great efficiency as producers. The political structures were in general getting weaker and
their preoccupation with the internecine struggles of the politically
powerful meant that little time was left for repressing the growing
strength of the mass of the population. . . . *Things were indeed falling apart.* Had Europe continued on the path along which it was
going it is difficult to believe that the patterns of medieval feudal
Europe with its highly structured system of orders could have been
re-consolidated. *Far more probable is that the European feudal social
structure would have evolved towards a system of relatively equal small-scale
producers,* further flattening out the aristocracies and decentralizing
the political structures.

> —Immanuel Wallerstein, *Historical Capitalism with
> Capitalist Civilization* (1983, 41–42) (italics mine)

Spring is the most startling season in Eresos valley: the campo, drenched
in wildflowers, after a cold wet winter, is a vivid first reminder that
the stern and quiet weather that blankets the Aegean islands is ending.
During this time of year, the dining venues in Skala Eresos engage in a
seasonal awakening that arrives with Persephone's annual arrival from
the underworld. Likewise, spring spurs the women's cooperatives to
prepare for festivities such as those attached to Greek Orthodox Easter
that require ample servings of island-prepared savories.

Figure C.1. The Eresos valley/courtesy of Tzeli Hadjidimitriou. This last photo from Tzeli Hadjidimitriou, cinematographer and photographer based in Lesvos and Athens, depicts the splendor of the Eressian valley in spring. Her photographs throughout this book have lent a vivid visualization to stories I've attempted to articulate.

The rhythm of return and departure in Greek islands profoundly shapes the lives of Greek islanders. It is not only natural rhythms, such as the sun's regular return—large and overwhelming in the warmth it provides, dissipating the rain and dark clouds—but the social ones that are connected to them. The arrival of family members and tourists to the Greek islands each spring and their exodus by autumn is like clockwork. The economic and political crises of Greece also stand out as rhythmical. Though not quite as regular, Greece bears the mark of a crypto-colonized nation (Herzfeld 2002)—impertinently regarded by its Northern neighbors, appropriating Greek society and culture as European and discounting or scapegoating them when expedient for political or economic benefit.

This study of Lesvos's convivial economics—the lesbian enclave, the women's cooperatives, the island microeconomy, and the organic and attritional alternative economics they reflect—contributes to a growing body of scholarship that looks into the shadows to identify the scope and possibilities of economic alternatives outside capitalism as a viable route to lasting social change. The social and solidarity economy, localism, and community or diverse economies as articulations of alternative economics espouse various approaches for advancing a counter to neoliberalism. This includes embeddedness in the state (social economy), collective ownership (solidarity economy), local ownership (localism), and changing the discourse (diverse economies). The last decade has witnessed a substantial increase in the output of writings on alternative economics that modify, nuance, or add to the four dominant perspectives outlined in this volume. To these perspectives *Sappho's Legacy* contributes an appreciation that alternative economics reside in the subaltern.

Convivial economics are a Mediterranean- and island-centered approach toward resisting tenets of capitalism and opposing neoliberalism's emphasis on competition as the way forward. The spontaneous alternative culture that shapes Greece's economic system, the easy coexistence of modernity, informality, and the ancient, has evidently been a formidable opponent to neoliberalism. On Greek islands alliances among and within enterprises for the collective interests of economic subsistence and autonomy or self-defined work is characteristic and preferred over large-scaled enterprises, centralized capital, and government interventionism.

The organic economic alterity of place is an essential reading of alternative economics. David Harvey (1996, 310) argues: "Places acquire much of their permanence as well as much of their distinctive character from the collective activities of people who dwell there, who shape the land through their activities and who build institutions and social relationships within a bounded domain." Harvey (1996) affirms that places are defined by the actions of people living in them, and not necessarily by the rampage of global capitalism. This connection between place and the people who dwell there is especially pertinent to islands. Encompassed by the concept of shima (Suwa 2007), the intimacies between people and with their environment are experienced more acutely in these geographies with many of its denizens holding an "island worldview" (Fisher 2015, 8).

In remote geographies, peripheral to centers of capitalism, the profit-seeking, expansionary goals, and material accumulation of our dominant economic model is more easily repelled. While islands may facilitate relationships that prioritize the well-being of others, urban neighborhoods, isolated mountain villages, and small towns are also

spaces in which convivial transactions can prevail. Local ownership and
political control are key features of convivial economics that are also
highlighted by localism. The state can support microbusinesses and the
development of cooperatives, by keeping large-scale capital at bay. All
too common is the story of the large corporate conglomerate that enters
and crushes numerous small and microbusiness, even as members of the
local community fought to resist it. This not only ruins livelihoods but
breaks down community ties. Taxation policies as well should favor
small businesses and microbusiness, not debilitate them or force them
to operate underground. Governments worldwide need to come to terms
with the sizable portion of their population that is engaged in alternative
economics. By generously provisioning the education, health, and social
services that people require, rather than the parsimony by which they are
currently granted under neoliberalism, microenterprises and cooperatives
could flourish, operating independently but in concert with one another,
and organized by local rather than centralized political control. Because
of their marginalization from the mainstream economy or preference
to work outside of it, subalterns have created spaces of production and
consumption that are based in conviviality and in support of community.

Among the women's cooperatives in Lesvos and the microenterprises
of Skala Eresos, mutual aid and cooperation are cornerstones. For the
most part the cooperatives and microenterprises operate autonomously
and are unlikely to organize laterally to make demands. Only when a
proposed government policy or state action intervenes or impacts their
ventures negatively, such as the closing of the Lesvos Shop or when
the "tax police" arrive in Skala Eresos, do all respond in concert. They
employ Gramscian ideals of the creativity and adaptiveness of subordinate cultures that build impromptu social formations in the context of
a metastable environment.

The adoption of neoliberalism as the rightful economic practice
relies on demonizing other forms of exchange as weak or detrimental
(Steger 2010; Gibson-Graham 2006). Neoliberal proponents' constant
coaxing have depended on "cultural and ideological appeals" that were
"seeking to make a persuasive case for a new global order based on
their values" (Steger 2010, 177–178). Despite the adherence of some
Greek politicians and wealthy elites to the marketization extremes of
neoliberalism, ultimately the Greek population has not succumbed to it.

The utter stinginess of neoliberalism is probably the most striking
contrast to the economic culture of Greece. Austerity and thrift are
often considered, by those who value them, designations of a moral

superiority, despite the clear excesses of an economic system organized around these principles. The result of the referendum in the summer of 2015, when the majority of the Greek population was willing to leave the EU rather than adopt stringent austerity measures and lose autonomy, was an unmistakable show of resistance to neoliberalism as the premium economic practice, as were the regular protests in Athens.

Yet the persistence of small and local enterprises and cooperatives in Greece, where the economy continues to be embedded in social relations, is a vibrant daily demonstration of how Greek society resists neoliberal logic. By broadening conceptions of resistance, Scott (1985, 2012) widened interpretations of how social transformation occurs. In numerous historical moments and presently, subaltern groups, and those in subaltern locations, have sought to construct small, independent, and autonomous solutions. The artisanal producers in medieval Europe gradually built a postfeudal model of conviviality and solidarity through their guilds and lateral associations. Rejecting mass production and mass consumption, hippies' small autonomous enterprises, including cooperatives, communes, restaurants, cafés, and farms, have succeeded as convivial enterprises and underpin some of the current activities in alternative economics around food. And research on the growth of the informal sector in Global South cities and peasant farmers demonstrates that discriminated and poor populations endeavor in local solutions and social collaborations to provide sustenance and basic needs.

Further deliberation is needed by scholars with feminist, queer, Marxist, world-systems, geographical, historical, and intersectional perspectives on the extent to which autonomous subaltern paths of economy serve as transformative motors of history. AbdouMaliq Simone's (2004, 9) documentation of such efforts in urban Africa, which recognizes that "the economies and activities themselves might act as a platform for the creation of a very different kind of sustainable . . . configuration than we have yet generally to know," is an admirable case for how communities figure their own paths of development. The four perspectives of alternative economics reviewed in this volume collectively recognize the possibilities in alternative economics. What convivial economics highlights is how those on the margins tend to engage in economic activities that provide independence and are defined by the social success and survival of community.

Negative stereotyping of ethnicities and races is a fixed explanation for the tragedies of capitalism and the corporate takeover of lives by blaming the culture of economies in postcolonial and crypto-colonial spaces (Césaire 2001). Rather than acting as an ally in a union, North-ern Europe, deflecting their responsibility by discrediting Greece as the nation struggled with an economic and migration crisis, persisted in a historical continuity of belittlement. EU rhetoric rationalized Greece's financial troubles as a matter of Greek society and social norms, labeling them as slack, informal, and deceitful. In 2015, when Volkswagen was found employing "German ingenuity" to veil the emissions level of its diesel vehicles, this ruse was hardly used to define German economic habits. The ethnic bias toward Greece by privileged EU populations that I have chronicled tells how global stories of wealth and poverty are deeply ingrained in narratives of race and ethnicity.

Dismissing small, local, or collective economic entities as an economically viable development strategy alludes to a cultural narrow-ness. By maligning "a system of relatively equal small-scale producers" (Wallerstein 1983, 42), modernization and Marxist researchers ideolog-ically and materially deflated the range of development alternatives for newly independent nations. Leaders of these nations sought alternatives to capitalism and socialism independently and collectively, such as at the Bandung Conference held in 1955 in Indonesia, with the purpose of cooperatively sketching out varied development frameworks.

Instead of a swath of small-scale enterprises, large-scale production facilities, envisioned as modernizing entities, were imposed through debt and development agencies in the Global South even on small islands, such as in the Caribbean. Unable to recognize the abilities and potential of small and local enterprising activities to employ persons and sustain livelihoods across these regions, scholars and policy-makers holding a continental perspective and imperial gaze "overlook or misinterpret grassroots activities because these do not fit in with prevailing views about the nature of society and its development" (Hau'ofa 1994, 2). Yet when it was becoming clear that the modernization project was failing to achieve all it promised in terms of employment, development, and well-being, microenterprise development entered as an IMF solution, with no regard as to its grassroots origin (Karides 2005).

Greece's circumstances around gender, work, and spatiality differ from Northern European household models because households and enterprises often combine and are a centrifugal force on the Greek economy. Maxine Berg, Pat Hudson, and Michael Sonenscher (1983, 10), historians of Europe's economic transition, describe the diminishment of household-centered economics that occurred with the rise of industrial production: "The time discipline of housewives is conditioned by children's demands for feeding, clothing, sleeping and the maintenance of health and learning. This time discipline of family life has very important implications for the time discipline of the pre-industrial artisan. The rhythms of life of the artisan intersected with the rhythms of domestic life because home was in most cases the place of work."

In its organization of its economy, Greece seems to operate by the time discipline of family life that has continued from ancient times and likely molded by "the islands and hills" of its geographies. Greek women in small villages generally are household managers tending to the home and the operations of family enterprises. Greek village life and gender codes were jolted by tourism. In Lesvos the seasonal shift of gender spatial codes and sexuality arrived with the summertime tourists in the early 1980s. It was the presence of independent Northern European women tourists and the village men's kamaki pursuits that altered the cadence of island villages' public social pleasures. For many ethnic Greek island women, access to the sphere of sociality on the plateia is captured through their involvement in enterprise.

Lesvos is anchored in the alternative economic rhythm of Greece, where shops either shut down or slow down during midafternoon, and are generally closed Wednesday and Saturday afternoons and all day Sundays, even in summer when it seems everyone is serving guests. The recent expansion of alternative economics globally reflects an unspoken goal of patterning daily life in rhythms that provide more moments for the repose that is sorely lacking under neoliberalism, and more time for communing with loved ones and strangers.

The lesbians who arrived to Lesvos were seeking an environment that provided a sense of home and a place of return but also opportunities for economic sustenance. Skala Eresos provisioned a space for affectionate community to develop that has been fostered by the continued development of lesbian enterprises. For decades many of the Northern European lesbians traveling to the island could only be "out" in Skala Eresos. Northern European lesbians, who are marginal in the dominant economic system by virtue of their gender and sexuality, searched for alternatives to "disband the heterosexual grid," which neoliberalism relies on (Allen 2008, 168).

Sappho's legacy, the network of counterculture enterprises, an expanding tourism greeted with φιλοξενία, and the homosocial non-competitive expression of the sociality of Greek men in kafenions are rhythms that facilitated the growth of lesbian enterprises in Skala Eresos. The apparent concern for the overall success of the diverse and multiple enterprises by all those that participate in Lesvos's island microeconomies quashes the revered principle of competition of neoliberalism. It attests to Greece's "own ways of opposing capitalism and confronting poverty and exploitation" (Leontidou 1990, 2).

Greece after the Crisis?

Because Greece returned on August 20, 2018 to borrowing on the private market and no longer in arrangements with the IMF, EU, and European Central Bank, it has officially recovered by neoliberal terms. Tourism is burgeoning with the number of tourists to Greece in 2017 doubling since 2012 (Wilder 2018). Greece is also recognized as undergoing a cultural resurgence, with many of the spontaneous and creative alternative economic entities forming in Athens over the decade of the crisis, paving the way for an organic resuscitation. This includes a range of new restaurants that are not only serving Greek cuisine. A *New York Times* travel reviewer (Wilder 2018) declares, "In so many ways, Athens feels more alive, more culturally prolific, than ever, and it's hard to understand how this could have happened in the midst of the worst economic catastrophe in the history of the European Union." In December 2020, as I ready this volume to go to press, it is unclear what the recent spike of Covid-19 cases in Europe portends for Greece, but Greece's ability to avoid the most severe outcomes so far suggests its orientation of care, familiarity, and conviviality may provide a stable avenue for economic revival.

To an extent, the thickness of government policies and their clever implementation by an array of Greek officials outwitted Europe's fiercest efforts to liberalize Greece. A slew of corporative takeovers that Victoria, a lesbian Greek entrepreneur, worriedly predicted as an outcome of the measures demanded of Greece by the European Union, the European Central Bank, and the International Monetary Fund, has yet to materialize. Yet the underbelly of neoliberalism looms as Greece's conservative party, New Democracy, takes charge of the national government with the promise to stop Greece from being Europe's "problem child."

A main concern for Greece is the extreme levels of tourism. Nikos Chrysogelos, a Greek member of the European Parliament representing the Ecological Greens, explained in an interview: "We can't have small islands, with small communities, hosting 1 million tourists over a few months. There's a danger of the infrastructure not being prepared, of it all becoming a huge boomerang if we only focus on numbers and don't look at developing a more sustainable model of tourism" (Smith 2018). The mayor of a popularly touristed island, Santorini, selected to limit the number of cruise ships seeking to dock in the summer of 2018. The exponential rise in tourism is drawing attention to social and environmental concerns and its disruption of the shima of small island societies. It seems that privileged global travelers are seeking spaces of conviviality and environmental beauty that are shrinking in numbers as neoliberalism continues to damage our planet.

Recent advocacy for food tourism and the interest in local products have caused many Greek urbanites to return to island villages to appreciate local, Greek, artisanal foods, which are also an attractive purchase for European tourists and the growing numbers of Asian tourists. Indeed, the first Lesvos Foodfest was held over a long weekend in Molyvos during July 2017. New enterprises and farms focused on local and organic production are mushrooming in Greece. Their future success remains in the ability of Greek islanders to continue to protect their autonomy, retain the health of island ecologies, and develop their enterprises without interference or the consequences of a global economy that continues to place profits over people and environment. A January 2019 article in the *Wall Street Journal* referring to Greece as the European California describes multimillion dollar investments in a growing cannabis industry, which may also influence Greece's financial, social, and agricultural landscape in the future. Most prominently will be how Greece navigates a postpandemic future.

Greece's unemployment in the autumn of 2020 was the highest in Europe and remains strikingly high at 15.8 percent and almost double that for young persons. Wages and pensions have been drastically reduced and Greece's debt is at 180 percent of its GDP. Although Greece has been granted a buffer period in that loans to be repaid have an extended maturity for about fifteen years, the expected growth rate of Greece seems likely out of reach to meet the repayment plan even prior to the stark economic conditions ushered in with the pandemic. Yannis Varoufakis, continuing to engage politically after serving SYRIZA, founded the political party MeRA 25, which is part of a coordinated political venture of EU leftists. Varoufakis recently described Greece as a debtors' prison likely to last for two more generations. He also acknowledges that Greece "is a great place to revive your human spirit. . . . Because if people can have such fun in miserable circumstances, then there is hope for all of us" (Quest and Pisa 2018). On a positive note, some of Greece's previous debt will be rolled over with loosening EU policies on the permissible rate of national debt. Whether the Berlin Consensus relents under the economic pressures caused by the pandemic remains to be seen; regardless, Greece's peripheral and border geography in the EU will likely continue to present challenges.

Although not battered by the racist and colonial expropriation and exploitation experienced by nations of the Global South, Greece historically has been subjugated by Europe. Indebted and dominated as a front against the Ottoman Empire (1821–32), Greek soldiers shot under command of UK's prime minister Winston Churchill after resisting Nazi expansion (1941–44), and its population sacrificed and divided by the first US proxy war in the Cold War period (1946–49) are a few episodes of suppression. Greece was also left by Europe to assail its modern fascist regime (1967–74), and more recently abandoned in addressing the plight of immigrants and refugees arriving to its shores while being issued merciless austerity measures.

Like populations in Global South nations, many Greeks have created their own means of subsistence and rely on local community structures to meet social and economic responsibilities. Opportunities exist in Greek islands such that, without the investment of large amounts of capital, the Greek and lesbian enterprises in Skala Eresos and the women's cooperatives across the island are able to provide some income and support for community, sociality, and survival. They constructed a situation for personal and political growth that arrives with deep relationships among themselves and their communities and not through the dictates of bureaucratic hierarchies. The cooperatives and lesbian enterprises, and the microeconomies of Greek island villages, might fit into David Harvey's (2000, 264) own vision of utopia: "centers of intense sociality and cultural experimentation, places where the art of after-dinner conversation, of musical performances and poetry readings, of 'spirit talk' and storytelling, [that] are so tenderly cultivated as to make them sites of continuous social engagement. . . . They are places where people who want to be different can express that want with the greatest *freedom*."

Both in the forms of organic economic alterity and attritional economic alterity, those on the fringe or not benefiting directly from the dominant economic system continue to enact and figure out on a day-to-day basis how to sustain livelihoods that are founded in social systems and cultural rhythms of their own making rather than ones imposed upon them. In *Provincializing Europe* (2000) subaltern historian Dipesh Chakrabarty notes that the dominant ideologies of Europe that have been exported globally stem from localities and histories of their own. In his critique of the Eurocentrism of global knowledge, Chakrabarty (2000) explains that theorizing is shaped by particular places. He is explicitly critical of the spatial or contextual neutrality attributed to Western thought. Making it more complex is that what is considered Western economic thought has no grounding. If it is to be connected to Greece's total (ancient and modern) history, then its result is a convivial economics, that differs from the capitalist economies of continental Europe that have trampled the world.

By studying little corners of the globe, the everyday lives of people in them, and their approaches to production and consumption in the spaces in which they live, the makings of the world-system can be found and understood along with the possibilities of its transformation (Naples 2003). Scholarship on alternative economics, utopian prospects, and subaltern strategies deserves further grounding in everyday examples of how and where they exist for deeper practical insight and theoretical purpose.

Works Cited

30 Rock. 2012. "Idiots Are People Two!" Season 6, episode 2. National Broadcasting Company, January 19.

Acosta-Belen, Edna, and Christine E. Bose. 1995. "Colonialism, Structural Subordination, and Empowerment: Women in the Development Process in Latin America and the Caribbean." In *Women in the Latin American Development Process*, edited by C. Bose and E. Acosta-Belen, 15–36. Philadelphia: Temple University Press.

Adorno, Theodor. 1966. *Negative Dialectics*. London: Routledge and Kegan Paul.

Albrecht, Cayla, Rylea Johnson, Steffi Hamann, Lisa Ohberg, and Michael CoDyre. 2013. "Toward Alternative Food Systems Development: Exploring Limitations and Research Opportunities." *Journal of Agriculture, Food Systems, and Community Development* 3 (4): 151–159.

Alderman, Liz. 2015. "Greeks Worry about Bailout's Push for an Economic Overhaul." *New York Times*, July 19. Retrieved July 19, 2015. https://www.nytimes.com/2015/07/20/business/international/greeks-worry-about-bailouts-push-for-an-economic-overhaul.html.

Alkon, Alison H., and Julian Agyeman. 2011. "Introduction: The Food Movement as Polyculture." In *Cultivating Food Justice: Race, Class, and Sustainability*, edited by A. H. Alkon and J. Agyeman, 1–20. Cambridge, MA: MIT Press.

Alkon, Alison H., and K. M. Norgaard. 2009. "Breaking the Food Chains: An Investigation of Food Justice Activism." *Sociological Inquiry* 79: 289–305.

Allard, Jenna, Carl Davidson, and Julie Matthaei. 2008. "Introduction." In *Solidarity Economy: Building Alternatives for People and Planet*, edited by J. Allard and J. Matthaei, 1–19. Chicago: Changemakers.

Allen, Jeffner. 2008. "Lesbian Economics." In *Queer Economics: A Reader*, edited by J. Jacobsen and A. Zeller, 160–175. New York: Routledge.

Allen, Patricia, and Julie Guthman. 2006. "From 'Old School' to 'Farm-to-School': Neoliberalization from the Ground Up." *Agriculture and Human Values* 23: 401–415.

Althusser, Louis. 2014. *On the Reproduction of Capitalism: Ideology and Ideological State Apparatuses*. New York: Verso.

Amin, Ash. 2009. "Locating the Social Economy." In *The Social Economy: International Perspectives on Economic Solidarity*, edited by A. Amin, 3–21. London: Zed Books; New York: Room 400.

Andrews, Michael. 2020. "Bar Talk: Informal Social Interactions, Alcohol Prohibition, and Invention" Working paper, October 11. Retrieved October 28, 2020. https://drive.google.com/file/d/1LyQ4KdENPHNYYiolfY9p7XIvnvDHwk79/ view.

Anzaldúa, Gloria. 1999. *Borderlands/La Frontera: The New Mestiza*. San Francisco: Aunt Lute Books.

Applebaum, Herbert. 1992. *The Concept of Work: Ancient, Medieval, and Modern*. Albany: State University of New York Press.

Araghi, Farshad, and Marina Karides. 2012. "Land Dispossession and the Global Crisis." *Journal of World Systems Research* 18 (1): 1–5.

Arnold, David. 2000. "Gramsci and Peasant Subalternity in India." In *Mapping Subaltern Studies and the Postcolonial*, edited by V. Chaturvedi, 24–49. London: Verso and New Left Review.

AVAAZ.org. 2016. "Nobel Peace Prize for Greek Islanders." Retrieved December 2, 2016. https://secure.avaaz.org/en/nobel_to_greek_islanders_fb_en/.

Avakian, Arlene, and Barbara Haber. 2005. "Feminist Food Studies: A Brief History." In *From Betty Crocker to Feminist Food Studies: Critical Perspectives on Woman and Food*, 1–28. Amherst: University of Massachusetts Press.

Bachelard, Gaston. 1991. *Dialectic of Duration*. Manchester, UK: Clinamen Press.

Badgett, M. V. Lee, and Rhonda M. Williams. 2008. "The Economics of Sexual Orientation: Establishing a Research Agenda." In *Queer Economics: A Reader*, edited by J. Jacobsen and A. Zeller, 11–18. New York: Routledge.

Baldacchino, Godfrey. 2005. "The Contribution of 'Social Capital' to Economic Growth: Lessons from Island Jurisdictions." *Round Table* 94 (1): 31–46.

Baldacchino, Godfrey. 2006. "Islands, Island Studies, Island Studies Journal." *Island Studies Journal* 1 (1): 3–18.

Barnard, Mary. 1958. *Sappho: A New Translation*. Berkeley: University of California Press.

BBC News. 2008. "Lesbos Locals Lose Lesbian Appeal." July 22. Retrieved July 30, 2008. http://news.bbc.co.uk/2/hi/europe/7520343.stm.

Beardsworth, Alan, and Teresa Alan Keil. 1997. "Sociological Perspectives on Food and Eating." In *Sociology on the Menu: An Invitation to the Study of Food and Society*, edited by A. Beardsworth and T. A. Keil, 47–70. New York: Routledge.

Becker, Kristina F. 2004. "The Informal Economy." SIDA Department for Infrastructure and Economic Co-operation. Retrieved June 15, 2010. https:// www.rrojasdatabank.info/sida.pdf.

Bedford, Kate. 2009. *Developing Partnerships: Gender, Sexuality, and the Reformed World Bank*. Minneapolis: University of Minnesota Press.

Bedford, Kate. 2010. "Markets and Sexualities: Introduction." *Feminist Legal Studies* 18 (1): 25–28.

Belasco, Warren. 1989. *Appetite for Change: How the Counterculture Took on the Food Industry*. New York: Pantheon Books.

Bell, David, and Gill Valentine. 1995. "Queer Country: Rural Lesbian and Gay Lives." *Journal of Rural Studies* 11 (2): 113–122.

Berg, Lawrence D., and Robyn Longhurst. 2010. "Placing Masculinities and Geography." *Gender, Place and Culture: A Journal of Feminist Geography* 10 (4): 351–360.

Berg, Maxine, Pat Hudson, and Michael Sonenscher, eds. 1983. *Manufacture in Town and Country before the Factory*. Cambridge: Cambridge University Press.

Bernal, Martin. 1987. *Black Athena: The Afroasiatic Roots of Classical Civilization*. New Brunswick, NJ: Rutgers University Press.

Bernstein, Mary. 2013. "The Sociology of Sexualities: Taking Stock of the Field." *Contemporary Sociology* 42: 22–31.

Bernstein, Paul. 1982. "Necessary Elements for Effective Worker Participation in Decision-Making." In *Workplace Democracy and Social Change*, edited by J. Rothschild-Whitt and F. Lindenfeld, 51–81. Boston: Porter Sargent Press.

Besancenot, Oliver, and Pierre François Grond. 2010. "The Greek People Are the Victims of an Extortion Racket." *Le Monde*, May 14, 2010. Retrieved May 24, 2013. http://www.spectrezine.org/greek-people-are-victims-extortion-racket.html.

Billington, Michael. 2020. "Triumph from Tragedy: How Greece's Theatre Roared out of National Crisis." *Guardian*, March 2, 2020. Retrieved November 10, 2020. https://www.theguardian.com/stage/2020/mar/02/triumph-from-tragedy-how-greeces-theatre-roared-out-of-a-national-crisis.

Binnie, Jon. 2004. *The Globalization of Sexuality*. London: Sage.

A Bit of Fry and Laurie. 1989. "Gordon and Stuart Eat Greek." Series 1, episode 3. British Broadcasting Corporation, January 27, 1989.

Bhat, Rajeev. 2017. *Sustainability Challenges in the AgroFood Sector*. Hoboken, NJ: Wiley-Blackwell.

Black, Antony. 1984. *Guilds and Civil Society in European Political Thought from the Twelfth Century to the Present, Part 2*. Ithaca, NY: Cornell University Press.

Blidon, Marianne. 2015. "Putting Lesbians Geographies on the Geographical Map: A Commentary." In *Lesbian Geographies: Gender, Place, and Power*, edited by K. Browne and E. Ferreira, 243–248. New York: Routledge.

Boehnke, Klaude. 2001. *NGO Working Group on Migration and Xenophobia for the World Conference (in International Migration, Racism, Discrimination and Xenophobia, 2001)*. Jointly produced by International Labor Organization, International Organization for Migration, Office of the High

Commission for Human Rights Commissioner, in consultation with the United Nations High Commissioner for Refugees. Retrieved November 3, 2018. http://www.unesco.org/new/en/social-and-human-sciences/themes/international-migration/glossary/xenophobia/.

Boellstorff, Tom. 2005. *The Gay Archipelago: Sexuality and Nation in Indonesia.* Princeton, NJ: Princeton University Press.

Bonanno, Alessandro, and Douglas Constance. 2008. "Agency and Resistance in the Sociology and Agriculture of Food." In *The Fight over Food: Producers, Consumers, and Activists Challenge the Global Food System,* edited by W. Wright and G. Middendorf, 29–44. University Park: Pennsylvania State University Press.

Bookchin, Murray. 1969. "Anarchy and Organization: A Letter to the Left." *New Left Notes,* January 15. Retrieved June 12, 2012. https://theanarchistlibrary.org/library/murray-bookchin-anarchy-and-organization-a-letter-to-the-left.

Boone, Joseph. 2001. "Vacation Cruises: or, The Homoerotics of Orientalism." In *Post-colonial, Queer: Theoretical Intersections,* edited by J. C. Hawley, 3–78. Albany: State University of New York Press.

Botsman, Rachel, and Roo Rogers. 2011. *What's Mine Is Yours: How Collaborative Consumption Is Changing the Way We Live.* New York: HarperCollins.

Bourdieu, Pierre. 1977. *Outline of a Theory of Practice.* Cambridge: Cambridge University Press.

Bousiou, Pola. 2011. *The Nomads of Mykonos: Performing Liminalities in a 'Queer' Space.* New York: Berghahn Books.

Brabant, Malcolm. 2008. "Lesbos Islanders Dispute Gay Name." *BBC News,* May 1. Retrieved January 3, 2010, http://news.bbc.co.uk/2/hi/7376919.stm.

Braiziel, Jana Evans, and Anita Mannur. 2003. *Theorizing Diaspora: A Reader.* Hoboken, NJ: Wiley-Blackwell.

Brecher, Jeremy, Tim Costello, and Brendan Smith. 2000. *Globalization from Below: The Power of Solidarity.* Boston: South End Press.

Briguglio, Lino. 2000. "Small Island Developing States and Their Economic Vulnerabilities." Retrieved June 7, 2011. http://www.gdrc.org/oceans/lino.html.

Brinklow, Laurie. 2011. "The Proliferation of Island Studies." *Griffin Review.* Retrieved November 3, 2020. https://www.griffithreview.com/articles/the-proliferation-of-island-studies/.

Brody, Jane E. 2010. "Rules Worth Following for Everyone's Sake." *New York Times,* February 1. Retrieved March 2, 2016. https://www.nytimes.com/2010/02/02/health/02brod.html.

Brooks, David. 2017. "Before Manliness Lost Its Virtue." *New York Times,* August 1. Retrieved October 3, 2018. https://www.nytimes.com/2017/08/01/opinion/scaramucci-mccain-masculinity-white-house.html.

Browne, Kath. 2011. "Beyond Rural Idylls: Imperfect Lesbian Utopias at Michigan Womyn's Music Festival." *Journal of Rural Studies* 27 (1): 13–23.

Browne, Kath, and Leela Bakshi. 2011. "We Are Here to Party? Lesbian, Gay, Bisexual and Trans Leisurescapes beyond Commercial Gay Scenes." *Leisure Studies* 30: 179–196.

Browne, Kath, and Eduarda Ferreira. 2015. "Introduction to Lesbian Geographies." In *Lesbian Geographies: Gender, Place, and Power*, edited by K. Browne and E. Fereira, 1–28. New York: Routledge.

Bryan, Miles. 2015. "Rural Wyoming Town's First Mosque Sparks Anti-Muslim Rhetoric" *National Public Radio*. December 25, 2015. Retrieved January 10, 2021 https://www.npr.org/2015/12/25/461046585/rural-wyoming-towns-first-mosque-sparks-anti-muslim-rhetoric.

Buber, Martin. 1996. *Paths in Utopia*. Syracuse, NY: Syracuse University Press.

Buettner, Dan. 2015. *The Blue Zones Solutions: Eating and Living Like the World's Healthiest People*. Washington, DC: National Geographic Society.

Burawoy, Michael. 2000. *Global Ethnography: Forces, Connections, and Imaginations in a Postmodern World*. Berkeley: University of California Press.

Burlingham, Bo. 2005. *Small Giants: Companies That Choose to Be Great Instead of Big*. New York: Portfolio.

Butler, Judith. 1990. Gender Trouble: Feminism and the Subversion of Identity. New York: Routledge.

Butlin, R. A. 1986. "Industrialization in Europe: Concepts and Problems." *Geographical Journal* 52 (1): 1–8.

Calame, Claude. 1996. "Sappho's Group: An Initiation into Womanhood." In *Reading Sappho: Contemporary Approaches*, edited by E. Greene, 113–124. Berkeley: University of California Press.

Calhoun, Craig. 1992. "Introduction: Habermas and the Public Sphere." In *Habermas and the Public Sphere*, edited by C. Calhoun, 1–48. Boston: MIT Press.

Calhoun, Craig, and Georgi Derlugian. 2011. "Introduction." In *Business as Usual: The Roots of the Global Financial Meltdown*, edited by C. Calhoun and G. Derlugian, 43–52. New York: New York University Press.

Campbell, Horace. 1987. *Rasta and Resistance: From Marcus Garvey to Walter Rodney*. Trenton, NJ: Africa World Press.

Cantú, Lionel. 2002. "De Ambiente: Queer Tourism and Shifting Boundaries of Mexican Male Sexualities" *GLQ: A Journal of Lesbian and Gay Studies* 8 (1–2). 139–166.

Cantú, Lionel, Nancy A. Naples, and Salvador Vidal-Ortiz. 2009. *The Sexuality of Migration: Border Crossings and Mexican Immigrant Men*. New York: Routledge.

Cap'n Barefoot Naturist Guide to the Greek Islands. "Lesbos." Retrieved July 13, 2009. http://www.capnbarefoot.info/neaegean:lesbos.

Carson, Anne. 2003. *If Not, Winter: Fragments of Sappho*. New York: Vintage Books.

Carson, Rachel. 1962. *Silent Spring*. New York: Houghton Mifflin.

Castells, Manuel. 1983. *The City and the Grassroots: A Cross Cultural Theory of Urban Social Movements*. Berkeley: University of California Press.

Césaire, Aimé. 2001. *Discourse on Colonialism*. New York: Monthly Review Press.

Chakrabarty, Dipesh. 2000. *Provincializing Europe*. Princeton, NJ: Princeton University Press.

Chaldoupis, Charis A. 2019. "How Is the Regulatory Framework for Food and Beverage Constructed in Greece?" *Greek Law Digest: The Official Guide to Greek Law*. May 3. Retrieved December 21, 2019. http://www.greeklawdigest. gr/component/k2/item/108-food-beverage.

Chandra, Uday. 2015. "Rethinking Subaltern Resistance." *Journal of Contemporary Asia* 45: 563–573.

Chardas, Anastassios. 2012. "Multi-Level Governance and the Application of the Partnership Principle in Times of Economic Crisis in Greece." *Hellenic Observatory Papers on Greece and Southeast Europe* 56. Retrieved December 18, 2018. https://ideas.repec.org/p/hel/greese/56.html.

Chase-Dunn, Christopher, and Thomas Hall. 1997. *The Rise and Demise: Comparing World Systems*. Boulder, CO: Westview Press.

Chaturvedi, Vinayak. 2000. "Introduction." In *Mapping Subaltern Studies and the Postcolonial*, edited by V. Chaturvedi, vii–xvii. New York: Verso.

Chirico, Jennifer, and Gregory Farley. 2015. *Thinking Like an Island: Navigating a Sustainable Future in Hawai'i*. Honolulu: University of Hawai'i Press.

Chirot, Daniel. 1985. "The Rise of the West." *American Sociological Review* 50: 181–195.

Choi, Stephen. 2003. "Benefits of Mediterranean Diet Affirmed, Again." *Canadian Medical Association Journal* 169 (4): 316.

Choo, Hae Yeon, and Myra Marx Ferree. 2010. "Practicing Intersectionality in Sociological Research: A Critical Analysis of Inclusions, Interactions, and Institutions in the Study of Inequalities." *Sociological Theory* 28 (2): 130–149.

CICOPA. 2013. "Promoting Cooperatives and the Social Economy in Greece." Final Report to the International Labor Organization. Retrieved January 11, 2017. https://www.cicopa.coop/fr/publications/promoting-cooperatives-and-the-social-economy-in-greece-2013/.

Cisneros, Sandra. 1991. "Never Marry a Mexican." In *Women Hollering Creek and Other Short Stories*. New York: Random House.

Clayton, Daniel. 2010. "Subaltern Space." In *The Sage Handbook of Geographical Knowledge*, edited by J. A. Agnew and D. N. Livingstone, 246–260. London: Sage Publications.

Coggin, Ross. 1976. "The Development Set." Owen.org blog. Retrieved November 8, 2018. https://www.owen.org/blog/116.

Cohen, David J. 1991. *Law, Society and Sexuality: The Enforcement of Morals in Classical Athens*. Cambridge: Cambridge University Press.

Cohen, Roger. 2015. "Battered Greece and Its Refugee Lesson." *New York Times*, September 21. https://www.nytimes.com/2015/09/22/opinion/roger-cohen-more-efficiency-less-humanity.html.

Collins, R. 1986. *Weberian Sociological Theory*. Cambridge: Cambridge University Press.

Comaroff, Jean. 1985. *Body of Power, Spirit of Resistance: The Culture and History of a South African People*. Chicago: University of Chicago Press.

Corlouer, M. 2013. "Quelles places pour les lesbiennes?" In *Géographie des homophobies*, edited by A. Alessandrin and Y. Raibaud, 1954–1955. Paris: Editions Armand Colin.

Cotterill, Ronald. 1983. "Retail Food Cooperatives: Testing the 'Small Is Beautiful' Hypothesis." *American Journal of Agricultural Economics* 65 (1): 125–130.

Counihan, Carole. 2004. *Around the Tuscan Table: Food, Family, Gender in Twentieth-Century Florence*. London: Routledge.

Counihan, Carole, and Penny Van Esterik. 2012. *Food and Culture: A Reader*. New York: Routledge.

Cowan, Brian. 2001. "What Was Masculine about the Public Sphere? Gender and the Coffeehouse Milieu in Post-Restoration England." *History Workshop Journal* 51: 127–157.

Cowan, Jane. 1991. "Going Out for Coffee? Contesting the Grounds of Gendered Pleasures in Everyday Sociability." In *Contested Identities: Gender and Kinship in Modern Greece*, edited by P. Loizos and E. Papataxiarchis, 180–202. Princeton, NJ: Princeton University Press.

COWI—Danish Institute for Human Rights. 2009. "The Social Situation concerning Homophobia and Discrimination on Grounds of Sexual Orientation in Greece." Retrieved August 25, 2018. https://fra.europa.eu/sites/default/files/fra_uploads/376-FRA-hdgso-part2-NR_EL.pdf.

Cox, Martin. 2002. "The Long-Haul out of the Closet: The Journey from Smalltown to Boystown." In *Gay Tourism: Culture, Identity, and Sex*, edited by S. Clift, M. Luango, and C. Callister, 151–173. London: Continuum.

Creevy, Lucy. 1996. *Changing Women's Lives and Work: A Study of Eight Microenterprise Programs*. London: International Technology Development Group.

Crowther, Gillian. 2013. *Eating Culture: An Anthropological Guide to Food*. Toronto: University of Toronto Press.

David, Elizabeth. 1958. *A Book of Mediterranean Food*. New York: New York Review of Books.

Debord, Guy. 1967. *The Society of Spectacle*. Kalamazoo, MI: Black and Red Publishing.

de Certeau, Michel. 1984. *The Practice of Everyday Life*. Berkeley: University of California Press.

D'Emilio, John. 2008. "Capitalism and Gay Identity." In *Queer Economics: A Reader*, edited by J. Jacobsen and A. Zeller, 181–193. London: Routledge.

DeLind, Laura B. 2011. "Are Local Food and the Local Food Movement Taking Us Where We Need to Go? Or Are We Hitching Our Wagon to the Wrong Stars?" *Agriculture and Human Values* 28 (2): 273–283.

Delis, Apostolos. 2016. "A Hub of Piracy in the Aegean: Syros during the Greek War of Independence." In *Corsairs and Pirates in the Eastern Mediterranean, Fifteenth to Nineteenth Centuries*, edited by G. Harlaftis, D. Dimitropoulos, and D. J. Starkey, 41–54. Athens: Sylvia Ioannou Foundation.

Desjardins, Ellen. 2010. "The Urban Food Desert: Spatial Inequality or Opportunity for Change?" In *Imagining Sustainable Food Systems*, edited by A. Blay-Palmer, 87–114. London: Routledge.

de Soto, Hernando. 1989. *The Other Path: The Invisible Revolution in the Third World*. New York: Harper and Row.

De Sousa, Philip. 2002. *Piracy in the Graeco-Roman World*. Cambridge: Cambridge University Press.

Dixon, Alex. 2014. "Ethnic Cuisine Takes Root." *QSR Magazine*, June 19. Retrieved October 3, 2017. https://www.qsrmagazine.com/exclusives/ethnic-cuisines-take-root.

Doan, Petra L. 2010. "The Tyranny of Gendered Space—Reflections from beyond the Gender Dichotomy." *Gender, Place, and Culture: A Journal of Feminist Geography* 17 (5): 635–654.

dos Santos, Lucio Alberto Pinheiro. 1931. "La rhythmanalyse, Rio de Janeiro: Société de Psychologie et de Philosophie." Unpublished manuscript.

Dubisch, Jill. 1993. " 'Foreign Chickens' and Other Outsiders: Gender and Community in Greece." *American Ethnologist* 20 (2): 272–287.

DuPuis, Melanie E., and David Goodman. 2005. "Should We Go 'Home' to Eat? Toward a Reflexive Politics of Localism." *Journal of Rural Studies* 21 (3): 359–371.

Eddy, Melissa, and Dan Bilefsky. 2015. "Austria, Slovakia, and the Netherlands Introduce Border Controls." *New York Times*, September 14. Retrieved September 14, 2015. https://www.nytimes.com/2015/09/15/world/europe/europe-migrants-germany.html.

Empros Newspaper. 2007. "Lesvos English Guide." Retrieved April 13, 2018. https://issuu.com/empros/docs/agglikos_odigos.

Escobar, Arturo. 1995. *Encountering Development: The Making and Unmaking of the Third World*. Princeton, NJ: Princeton University Press.

Etter, Daniel. 2016. "Ode to Lesvos: The Villagers Who Helped Refugees—in Pictures." *Guardian*, October 5. Retrieved December, 16, 2016. https://www.theguardian.com/world/gallery/2016/oct/05/ode-to-lesvos-the-villagers-who-helped-refugees-in-pictures.

European Commission. 2011. *Small and Medium Enterprises: The Situation in EU Member States*. Retrieved July 2012. https://ec.europa.eu/growth/content/small-and-medium-sized-enterprises-situation-eu-member-states-2010_en.

European Commission. 2020. "Cooperatives." *Internal Markets, Industry, Entrepreneurship, and SMEs*. Retrieved October 2020. https://ec.europa.eu/growth/sectors/social-economy/cooperatives_en.

European Union Agency for Fundamental Rights. 2013. *EU LGBT Surveyeurostat European Union Lesbian, Gay, Bisexual and Transgender Survey.* Luxembourg: Publications Office of the European Union. Retrieved September 21, 2018. https://fra.europa.eu/en/publication/2013/eu-lgbt-survey-european-union-lesbian-gay-bisexual-and-transgender-survey-results.

Eurostat. 2017. "Marriage and Divorce Statistics." Retrieved August 23, 2018. https://ec.europa.eu/eurostat/statistics-explained/index.php/Marriage_and_divorce_statistics.

Everett, Sally, and Cara Aitchison. 2008. "The Role of Food Tourism in Sustaining Regional Identity: A Case Study of Cornwall, Southwest England." *Journal of Sustainable Food Studies* 16 (2) 150–167.

Export.gov. 2018. "Greece Agricultural Sector." Retrieved December 2, 2018. https://www.export.gov/apex/article2?id=Greece-Agricultural-Sector.

Faderman, Lilian. 1992. *Odd Girls and Twilight Lovers: A History of Lesbian Life in Twentieth-Century America.* New York: Penguin.

Faiman-Silva, Sandra. 2009. "Provincetown Queer: Paradox of 'Identity, Space, and Place.'" *Journal of Tourism and Cultural Change* 7 (3): 203–220.

Ferguson, James. 1999. *Expectations of Modernity: Myths and Meanings of Urban-Life on the Zambian Copperbelt.* Berkeley: University of California Press.

Fernandez, Sofia M. 2011. "Tina Fey, NBC Apologize for Tracy Morgan Anti-Gay Comments." Retrieved October 20, 2020. https://www.hollywoodreporter.com/news/tina-fey-nbc-apologize-tracy-196917.

Fimiani, Roberta. 2014. "The Role of Gay Space for Gay Destinations." Master's thesis, Department of Human Geography, Högskalan, Dalarna.

Financial Times. 2015. "Greek Bakers Rise to Reform Challenge." July 13. Retrieved September 2016. https://www.ft.com/content/832f1e24-2af9-11e5-8613-e7aedbb7bdb7.

Finlay, M. I. 2002. *The World of Odysseus.* New York: New York Review of Books.

Fischer, Christian. 2010. "The Influence of Immigration and International Tourism on the Demand for Imported Food Products." *Acta Agriculturae Scandinavica, Section C—Food Economics* 1 (1): 21–33.

Fisher, Scott. 2015. "Hawaiian Culture and Its Foundation in Sustainability." In *Thinking Like an Island: Navigating a Sustainable Future in Hawai'i,* edited by J. Chirico and G. Farley, 7–27. Honolulu: University of Hawai'i Press.

Flint, Peter B. 1994. "Melina Mercouri, Actress and Politician, Is Dead." *New York Times,* March 7. Retrieved October 28, 2018. https://www.nytimes.com/1994/03/07/obituaries/melina-mercouri-actress-and-politician-is-dead.html.

Flynn, Daniel. 2008. "Court Rules That Lesbians Are Not Just from Lesbos." *Reuters,* July 22. Retrieved July 29, 2008. http://www.reuters.com/article/2008/07/22/us-lesbians-idUSN2231197820080722.

Fonte, Maria, and Ivan Cucco. 2017."Copperatives and Alternatives Food Networks in Italy: The Long Road to a Social Economy in Agriculture." *Journal of Rural Studies* 53: 291–302.

Forrest, James, and Kevin Dunn. 2013. "Cultural Diversity, Racialization, and the Experience of Racism in Rural Australia." *Journal of Rural Studies* 30: 1–9.

Forster, Edward S. 1958. *A Short History of Modern Greece, 1821–1956.* Westport, CT: Greenwood Press.

Foxhall, Lin. 1989. "Household, Gender, and Property in Classical Athens." *Classical Quarterly* 39: 22–44.

Foxhall, Lin. 1994. "Pandora Unbound: A Feminist Critique of Foucault's *History of Sexuality*." In *Dislocating Masculinity*, edited by A. Cornwall and N. Lindisfarne, 133–146. London: Routledge.

Foxhall, Lin, and A. D. E. Lewis. 1996. *Greek Law in Its Political Setting: Justification Not Justice.* New York: Oxford University Press.

Frank, André Gunder. 1996. *The World System: Five Hundred Years or Five Thousand Years.* London: Routledge.

Friedmann, Harriet. 1987. "International Regimes of Food and Agriculture since 1870." In *Peasants and Peasant Societies*, edited by T. Shanin, 258–76. Oxford: Basil Blackwell.

Frydman, Carola, and Mark Koyoma. 2018. "Summaries of Doctoral Dissertations." Retrieved October 28, 2020. https://www.cambridge.org/core/services/aop-cambridge-core/content/view/DD78EAE43AB1EB27E18465E3E05DA032/S0022050719000123a.pdf/summaries_of_doctoral_dissertations.pdf.

Fukuyama, Francis. 1992. *The End of History and the Last Man.* New York: Free Press.

Gabaccia, Donna. 2000. *We Are What We Eat: Ethnic Food and the Making of Americans.* Cambridge, MA: Harvard University Press.

Gabriele, Michael. 2013. *The History of Diners in New Jersey.* Charleston, SC: American Palate, The History Press.

Gage, Nicholas. 1979. "Greeks' Crime Rate Is Lowest in Europe." *New York Times*, August 19. Retrieved January 22, 2021 https://www.nytimes.com/1979/08/19/archives/greeks-crime-rate-is-lowest-in-europe-absence-of-violence-is.html.

Gandhi, Leela. 1998. *Postcolonial Theory: A Critical Introduction.* New York: Columbia University Press.

Garlofis, Manthos. Untitled webpage detailing various Greek rhythms for hand percussion. Retrieved December 5, 2013. http://www.khafif.com/rhy/garlofis/garlofis.htm.

Garrigós, Alfons. 2002. "Hospitality Cannot Be a Challenge." In *The Challenges of Ivan Illich*, edited by L. Hoinacki and C. Mitcham, 113–126. Albany: State University Press of New York.

Gasper, Philip. 2014. "Are Workers' Cooperatives the Alternative to Capitalism?" *International Socialist Review* 93. Retrieved August 8, 2015. http://isreview.org/issue/93/are-workers-cooperatives-alternative-capitalism.

Geertz, Clifford. 1963. *Peddlers and Princes: Social Development and Economic Change in Two Indonesian Towns*. Chicago: University of Chicago Press.

Gerson, Kathleen, and Jerry Jacobs. 2004. "The Work-Home Crunch." *Contexts* 3 (4): 29–37.

Gibson-Graham, J. K. 1996. *The End of Capitalism (as We Knew It): A Feminist Critique of Political Economy*. Oxford: Blackwell.

Gibson-Graham, J. K. 2002. "Beyond Global vs. Local: Economic Politics outside the Binary Frame." In *Geographies of Power: Placing Scale*, edited by A. Herod and M. Wright, 25–60. Oxford: Blackwell.

Gibson-Graham, J. K. 2006. *A Postcapitalist Politics*. Minneapolis: University of Minnesota Press.

Gibson-Graham, J. K. 2009. "Diverse Economies: Performative Practices for Other Worlds." *Progress in Human Geography* 32: 613–632.

Gibson-Graham, J. K., Jenny Cameron, and Stephen Healy. 2013. *Take Back the Economy: An Ethical Guide for Transforming Our Communities*. Minneapolis: University of Minnesota Press.

Gidwani, Vinay K. 2006. "Subaltern Cosmopolitanism as Politics: A Radical Journal of Geography." *Antipode* 38: 7–21.

Gille, Zsuzsa, and Seán Ó Riain. 2002. "Global Ethnography." *Annual Review of Sociology* 28: 271–295.

Goodman, David, Melanie E. Dupuis, and Michael K. Goodman, eds. 2014. *Alternative Food Networks: Knowledge, Practice, and Politics*. London: Routledge.

Gorman-Murray, Andrew, Barbara Pini, and Lia Bryant. 2013. "Introduction: Geographies of Ruralities and Sexualities." In *Sexuality, Rurality, and Geography*, edited by A. Gorman-Murray, B. Pini, and L. Bryant, 1–20. Plymouth, UK: Lexington Books.

Graham, Mark. 2002. "Challenges from the Margins: Gay Tourism as Cultural Critique." In *Gay Tourism: Culture, Identity, and Sex*, edited by S. Clift, M. Luango, and C. Callister, 17–41. London: Continuum.

Gramsci, Antonio. 2003. *Selections from* The Prison Notebooks. New York: International Publishers.

Greene, Ellen. 1996. "Introduction." In *Reading Sappho: Contemporary Approaches*, edited by E. Greene, 1–11. Berkeley: University of California Press.

Grimes, Kimberly, and Lynne Milgram, eds. 2000. *Artisans and Cooperatives: Developing Alternative Trade for the Global Economy*. Tucson: University of Arizona Press.

GSEVEE, ESEE, KEEE, TFGR, SETE. 2014. *The Development of SMEs in Greece: Policy Document*. Athens: Voulgaridis. Retrieved February 21, 2018. https://www.gsevee.gr/press/mme_eng.pdf.

Gueye, Mohamed. 2015. "Lessons Not Learned." *Development and Cooperation*, July 29. Retrieved July 17, 2016. https://www.dandc.eu/en/article/greeces-crisis-reminds-african-observers-failed-structural-adjustment-programmes.

Giugliano, Fernando. 2020. "Greece Shows How to Handle the Crisis." *Bloomberg Opinion*, April 9. Retrieved September 21, 2020. https://www.bloomberg.com/opinion/articles/2020-04-10/greece-handled-coronavirus-crisis-better-than-italy-and-spain.

Guillen, Mauro. 2001. "Civilizing, Destructive, or Feeble? A Critique of Five Key Debates in the Social Science Literature." *American Review of Sociology* 27: 235–260.

Guthman, Julia. 2004. *Agrarian Dreams: The Paradox of Organic Farming in California*. Berkeley: University of California Press.

Guthman, Julia. 2006. "From 'Old School' to 'Farm-to-School': Neoliberalization from the Ground Up." *Agriculture and Human Values* 23 (4): 401–415.

Guthman, Julia. 2008. "Neoliberalism and the Making of Food Politics in California." *Geoforum* 31: 1173–1183.

Habermas, Jurgen. 1991. *The Structural Transformation of the Public Sphere*. Boston: MIT Press.

Hacker, Sally. 1989. *Pleasure, Power and Technology: Some Tales of Gender, Engineering and the Co-operative Workplace*. Perspectives on Gender. London: Routledge.

Hadjidimitriou, Tzeli. 2012. *A Girl's Guide to Lesvos*. Mytilini, Greece: Tzeli Hadjidimitriou.

Hall, C. Michael, and Stefan Gössling. 2017. "Sustainable Culinary Systems: An Introduction." In *Sustainable Culinary Systems: Local Foods, Innovation, Tourism, and Hospitality*, edited by C. M. Hall and S. Gössling, 3–44. New York: Routledge.

Hall, C. Michael, and Liz Sharples. 2003. "The Consumption of Experiences or the Experience of Consumption? An Introduction to the Tourism of Taste." In *Food Tourism around the World: Development, Management, and Market*, edited by C. M. Hall, L. Sharples, R. Mitchell, N. Macionis, and B. Cambourne, 1–24. Oxford: Butterworth-Heineman.

Hall, Stuart. 2003. "Cultural Identity and Diaspora." In *Colonial Discourse and Post-colonial Theory: A Reader*, edited by P. Williams and L. Chrisman, 392–401. London: Harvester Wheatsheaf.

Harris, Edmund. 2009. "Neoliberal Subjectivities or a Politics of the Possible? Reading for Difference in Alternative Food Networks." *Area* 41: 55–63.

Harris, William. 1996. "Sappho and the World of Lesbian Poetry." Retrieved June 23, 2011. http://wayback.archive-it.org/6670/20161201174348/http://community.middlebury.edu/~harris/Translations/Sappho.html.

Hart, Keith, Jean-Louis Laville, and Antonio Dave Cattani. 2010. *The Human Economy*. Cambridge: Polity.

Hartocolis, Anemotia. 2015. "Greek Merchants Fear a Way of Life Is Disappearing." *New York Times*, July 13. Retrieved July 13, 2015. https://www.nytimes.com/2015/07/14/world/europe/greeks-welcome-debt-deal-but-reservations-linger.html.

Harvey, David. 1996. *Justice, Nature, and the Geography of Difference*. Hoboken, NJ: Blackwell.

Harvey, David. 2000. *Spaces of Hope*. Berkeley: University of California Press.

Harvey, David. 2005. *A Brief History of Neoliberalism*. Oxford: Oxford University Press.

Hassanein, Neva. 2003. "Practicing Food Democracy: A Pragmatic Politics of Transformation." *Journal of Rural Studies* 19: 77–86.

Hau'ofa, Epilu. 1994. "Our Sea of Islands." In *In a New Oceania: Rediscovering Our Sea of Islands*, edited by E. Hau'ofa, V. Naidu, and E. Waddell, 2–16. Suva, Fiji: University of the South Pacific, in Association with Beake House.

Hawley, John C. 2001. "Introduction." In *Post-colonial, Queer: Theoretical Intersections*, edited by J. Hawley, 1–18. Albany: State University of New York Press.

Hay, Peter. 2006. "A Phenomenology of Islands." *Island Studies Journal* 1 (1): 19–42. Retrieved April 13, 2009. https://www.researchgate.net/profile/Pete_Hay/publication/26486348_A_Phenomenology_of_Islands/links/550bbc900cf290bdc1120284.pdf.

Hayes, Shannon. 2010. *Radical Homemakers: Reclaiming Domesticity from Consumer Culture*. Richmondville, NY: Left to Write Press.

Heffernan, William D., and Douglas Constance. 1994. "Transnational Corporations and the Globalization of the Food System." In *From Columbus to ConAgra: The Globalization of Agriculture and Food*, edited by A. Bonanno, L. Busch, W. H. Friedland, L. Gouveia, and E. Mingione, 29–51. Lawrence: University Press of Kansas.

Herzfeld, Michael. 1985. *The Poetics of Manhood: Contest and Identity in a Cretan Mountain Village*. Princeton, NJ: Princeton University Press.

Herzfeld, Michael. 1987. "As in Your House: Hospitality, Ethnography, and the Stereotype of Mediterranean Society." In *Honor and Shame and the Unity of the Mediterranean*, edited by D. Gilmore, 141–143. Arlington, VA: American Anthropological Association.

Herzfeld, Michael. 2002. "The Absent Presence: Discourses of Crypto-Colonialism." *South Atlantic Quarterly* 101 (4): 899–926.

Hess, David. 2009. *Localist Movements in a Global Economy: Sustainability, Justice, and Urban Development in the United States*. Cambridge, MA: MIT Press.

Higgins, Andrew, and James Kanter. 2015. "Greece Given until Sunday to Settle Debt Crisis or Face Disaster." *New York Times*, July 7. Retrieved July 7, 2015. http://www.nytimes.com/2015/07/08/business/international/greece-debt-eurozone-meeting.html.

Hill-Collins, Patricia. 1990. *Black Feminist Thought: Knowledge, Consciousness, and the Politics of Empowerment*. Boston: Unwin Hyman.

Hinrichs, Clare. 2000. "Embeddedness and Local Food Systems: Notes on Two Types of Direct Agricultural Markets." *Journal of Rural Studies* 16 (3): 295–303.

Hinrichs, Clare. 2003. "The Practice and Politics of Food System Localization." *Journal of Rural Studies* 19: 33–45.

Hinrichs, Clare. 2007. "Practice and Place in Remaking the Food System." In *Remaking the North American Food System: Strategies for Sustainability*, edited by C. C. Hinrichs and T. A. Lyson, 1–15. Lincoln: University of Nebraska Press.

Hinrichs, Clare. 2009. "Sustainable Food Systems: Challenges of Social Justice and a Call to Sociologists." *Sociological Viewpoints* 26 (2): 7–18.

Ho, Elaine Lynn-Ee. 2018. "African Student Migrants in China: Negotiating the Global Geographies of Power through Gastronomic Practices and Culture." *Food, Culture, and Society: An International Journal of Multidisciplinary Research* 21: 9–24.

Hochschild, Arlie. 2002. *The Second Shift: Working Families and the Revolution at Home*. New York: Penguin Books.

Hoinacki, Lee. 2002. "Reading Ivan Illich." In *The Challenges of Ivan Illich*, edited by L. Hoinacki and C. Mitcham, 1–8. Albany: State University Press of New York.

Homer. 2013. *The Odyssey*. Translated by Stephen Mitchell. New York: Atria Books.

hooks, bell. 1984. *Feminist Theory: From Margins to Center*. Boston: South End Press.

ho'omanawanui, ku'ualoha. 2014. *Voices of Fire: Reweaving the Literary Lei of Pele and Hi'iaka*. Minneapolis: University of Minnesota Press.

Howard, John R. 1969. "The Flowering of the Hippie Movement." *Annals of the American Academy of Political and Social Science* 382: 43–55.

Hughes, Howard, Juan Carlos Monterrubio, and Amanda Miller. 2010. "Gay Tourists and Host Community Attitudes." *International Journal of Tourism Research* 12 (6): 774–786.

Illich, Ivan. 1973. *Tools of Conviviality*. Berkeley, CA: Heyday Books.

Inman, Philips. 2015. "A Decade of Overspending: How Greece Plunged into Economic Crisis." *Guardian*, July 3. Retrieved July 3, 2015. http://www.theguardian.com/world/2015/jul/03/greece-overspending-defence-wages-taxation-economic-crisis.

International Labor Organization. 2002. "Promotion of Cooperatives Recommendation (No. 193)." Retrieved August 21, 2017. https://www.ilo.org/dyn/normlex/en/f?p=NORMLEXPUB:12100:0::NO::P12100_ILO_CODE:R193.

International Labor Organization News. 2019. "Small businesses and self-employed provide most jobs worldwide, new ILO report says" October 10, Retrieved January 26. https://www.ilo.org/global/about-the-ilo/newsroom/news/WCMS_723409/lang--en/index.htm.

Itano, Nicole. 2009. "Showcased at Greece's New Acropolis Museum: Missing Artifacts." *Christian Science Monitor*, June 21. Retrieved July 13, 2016. https://www.csmonitor.com/World/Europe/2009/0621/p06s16-woeu.html.

Jacobs, Jane. 1961. *The Death and Life of Great American Cities*. New York: Vintage Books.

Jacobsen, Joyce, and Adam Zeller. 2008. "Introduction." In *Queer Economics: A Reader*, edited by J. Jacobsen and A. Zeller, 1–4. London: Routledge.

Jazeel, Tariq, and Legg, Stephen. 2019. *Subaltern Geographies*. Athens: University of Georgia Press.

Jessop, Bob. 2001. "Institutional Re(turns) and the Strategic-Relational Approach." *Environmental Planning* A 33 (7): 1213–1235.

Johnston, Ian, trans. 2017. *Aristophanes' Lysistrata: A Dual Language Edition*. Oxford, OH: Faenum Publishing.

Johnston, Josée. 2008. "The Citizen-Consumer Hybrid: Ideological Tensions and the Case of Whole Foods Market." *Theory and Society* 37: 229–270.

Jones, Owen. 2011. "The EU Treaty Is a Disaster for the Left." *New Statesman*, December 9. Retrieved January 3, 2012. http://www.newstatesman.com/blogs/the-staggers/2011/12/european-treaty-cameron-stop.

Josling, Tim. 1998. "Trade Policy in Small Island Economies." Paper presented to IICA/NCFAP Workshop on Small Economies in the Global Economy, Grenada, August 1998. Retrieved November 9, 2009. http://ctrc.sice.oas.org/geograph/caribbean/Jossling.pdf.

Jurik, Nancy. 2005. *Bootstrap Dreams: US Microenterprise Development in an Era of Welfare Reform*. Ithaca, NY: ILR Press.

Kalavrezou, Ioli. 2003. *Byzantine Women and Their World*. Cambridge, MA: Harvard University Art Museum.

Kantsa, Venetia. 2002. "'Certain Places Have Different Energy': Spatial Transformation in Eresos, Lesvos." *GLQ: A Journal of Lesbian and Gay Studies* 8: 35–55.

Kaplan, E. Ann. 2012. *Looking for the Other: Feminism, Film and the Imperial Gaze*. New York: Routledge.

Kapur, Ratna. 2010. "Regulating Perversion: The Role of Tolerance in De-radicalising the Rights Claims of Sexual Subalterns." In *Queer Theory: Law, Culture, and Empire*, edited by K. Brooks and R. Leckey, 37–52. London: Routledge.

Karababa, Eminegül, and Güliz Ger. 2010. "Early Modern Ottoman Coffeehouse Culture and the Formation of the Consumer Subject." *Journal of Consumer Research* 37 (5): 737–760.

Karides, Marina. 2005. "Whose Solution Is It? Development Ideology and the Work of Micro-entrepreneurs in Caribbean Context." *International Sociology and Social Policy* 25: 30–62.

Karides, Marina. 2007. "Working Off the Books: Women and the Informal Economy in New Orleans." In *Socio-Economic Development and Social Cohesion*, 129–156. In Greek. Athens: Papazisis.

Karides, Marina. 2010. "Theorizing the Rise of Microenterprise Development in Caribbean Context." *Journal of World-Systems Research* 17 (2): 192–216.

Karides, Marina. 2012. "Local Utopia as Unobtrusive Resistance: The Greek Village Micro-Economy." *Journal of World Systems Research* 18 (2): 151–156.

Karides, Marina. 2017. "Why Island Feminism?" *Shima: The International Journal of Research into Island Cultures* 11 (1): 30–39.

Karides, Marina, and Patricia Widener. 2018. "Race, Class, Privilege, and Bias in South Florida Food Movements." In *Food and Poverty: Food Insecurity and Food Sovereignty among America's Poor*, edited by L. Hossfeld, B. Kelly, and J. Waity, 191–203. Nashville, TN: Vanderbilt University Press.

Kassen, Michael. 2016. *Hippie, Inc.: The Misunderstood Subculture That Changed the Way We Live and Generated Billions of Dollars in the Process*. Boston: SixOneSeven Books.

Katz, Jonathan Ned. 2007. *The Invention of Heterosexuality*. Chicago: University of Chicago Press.

Katz, Marilyn A. 2000. "Sappho and Her Sisters: Women in Ancient Greece." *Signs* 25 (2): 505–531.

Kellner, Douglas. 2002. "Theorizing Globalization." *Sociological Theory* 20: 285–305.

Kelly, Marjorie. 2010. *Owning Our Future: The Emerging Ownership Revolution*. Oakland, CA: Berrett-Koehler Publishers.

Ken, Ivy. 2011. *Digesting Race, Class, and Gender: Sugar as a Metaphor*. New York: Palgrave Macmillan.

Ken, Ivy, and Benjamín Elizalde. 2016. "'We Began to See That We Were Valuable': Rural Chilean Women's Transformation from Depressed Wives to Organic Farmers." In *Yearbook of Women's History 36, Special Issue: Gendered Food Practices from Seed to Waste*, edited by B. Bock and J. Duncan, 61–77. Amsterdam: Verloren.

Kershen, Anne J. 2002. *Food and the Migrant Experience*. Aldershot, UK: Ashgate Publishing.

Khader, Jamil. 2003. "Subaltern Cosmopolitanism: Community and Transnational Mobility in Caribbean Postcolonial Feminist Writings." *Feminist Studies* 29 (1): 63–81.

King, Rosamond. 2016. *Island Bodies: Transgressive Sexualities in the Caribbean Imagination*. Gainesville: University Press of Florida.

King, Russell. 2009. "Geography, Islands, Migration in an Era of Globalization." *Island Studies Journal* 4 (1): 53–84.

Kitidi, Katerina, and Aris Chatzistefanou. 2011. *Debtocracy*. Film produced by Kostas Efimeros.

Klak, Thomas, and Dennis Conway. 1998. "From Neoliberalism to Sustainable Development." In *Globalization and Neoliberalism: The Caribbean Context*, edited by T. Klak, 257–277. Lanham, MD: Rowman and Littlefield.

Klawitter, Marieka M. 2008. "Why Aren't More Economists Doing Research on Sexual Orientation?" In *Queer Economics: A Reader*, edited by J. Jacobsen and A. Zeller, 45–50. London: Routledge.

Koktzoglou, Savvas, and Robert Shenk. 2020. *The Greek Genocide in American Naval War Diaries: Naval Commanders Report and Protest Death Marches and Massacres in Turkey's Pontus Region*. New Orleans: University of New Orleans Press.

Kolocotroni, Vassiliki, and Efterpi Mitsi. 2008. "Introduction." In *Women Writing Greece: Essays on Hellenism, Orientalism and Travel*, edited by V. Kolocotroni and E. Mitsi, 5–18. Amsterdam: Rodopi.

Konstatopoulou, Zoe. 2015. "Speech Delivered to Greek Parliament." July 11. Retrieved July 15, 2015. http://www.cadtm.org/Zoe-Konstantopoulou-NO-to.

Koufopoulou, Maria. 2010. *The Collossi of Love*. Documentary film international coproduction: XYZ Productions, ARTE, ERT.

Koutsou, Stavriani, Olga Iakovidou, and Nicolas Gotsinas. 2003. "Women's Cooperatives in Greece: An On-going Story of Battles, Successes, and Problems." *Journal of Rural Cooperation* 3 (1): 47–57.

Kraidy, Marwan. 2005. *Hybridity, or Cultural Logic of Globalization*. Philadelphia: Temple University Press.

Kulish, Nicholas, and Jack Ewing. 2012. "Greek Voting Past, Europe Returns to Fiscal Rescue." *New York Times*, June 18. Retrieved June 19, 2012. https://www.nytimes.com/2012/06/19/world/europe/greek-vote-past-europe-returns-to-fiscal-rescue.html.

Lassithotaki, Aikaterini, and Argiro Roubakou. 2014. "Rural Women Cooperatives at Greece: A Retrospective Study." *Open Journal of Business and Management* 2: 127–137. Retrieved July 20, 2015. http://dx.doi.org/10.4236/ojbm.2014.22016.

Lattas, J. 2014. "Queer Sovereignty: The Gay and Lesbian Kingdom of the Coral Sea Islands." *Shima: The International Journal of Research into Island Cultures* 8 (1): 59–71.

Laville, Jean-Louis, Benoit Leveseque, and Marguerite Mendell. 2006. *The Social Economy: Diverse Approaches and Practices in Europe and Canada*. Cahier de l'ARUC=ES, Cahier No C-11-2006. Montreal: University of Quebec.

Lazaridis, Gabriella. 2016. *Women's Work and Lives in Rural Greece: Appearances and Realties*. New York: Routledge.

Leary, Timothy. 1966. *Turn On, Tune In, Drop Out*. Reissued on CD. 2009 ESP Disk.

Lefebvre, Henri. 1984. *Everyday Life in the Modern World*. New Brunswick, NJ: Transaction Publishers.

Lefebvre, Henri. 1991. *The Production of Space*. Hoboken, NJ: Wiley-Blackwell.

Lefebvre, Henri, and Catherine Régulier. 2000. "Rhythmanalysis of Mediterranean Cities." Pp. 228–240 in *Writings on Cities* translated and edited by Eleonore Kofman and Elizabeth Lebas. Oxford: Blackwell.

Lefebvre, Henri. 2003. *Rhythmanalysis: Space, Time, and Everyday Life*. London: Continuum.

Lehner, Mathias. 2013. "Alternative Food Systems and the Citizen-Consumer." *Journal of Agriculture, Food Systems, and Community Development* 3 (4): 49–53.

Leon, Dawn. 2018. *What is Rhythmanalysis?* London: Bloomsbury Academic.

Leontidou, Lila. 1990. *The Mediterranean City in Transition.* Oxford: Oxford University Press.

Leontidou, Lila. 2014. "The Crisis and Its Discourses: Quasi-Orientalist Attacks on Mediterranean Urban Spontaneity, Informality and Joie de Vivre." *City: Analysis of Urban Trends, Policy, Culture, Theory, Action* 18 (4–5): 551–562.

Leroi, Armand Marie. 2015. "The Gift of Eternal Greece." *New York Times,* July 3. Retrieved July 3, 2015. https://www.nytimes.com/2015/07/04/opinion/the-gifts-of-eternal-greece.html.

Lewine, Edward. 1996. "The Kaffenion Connection: How Greek Diners Evolved." *New York Times,* April 14. Retrieved August 18, 2018. https://www.nytimes.com/1996/04/14/nyregion/the-kaffenion-connection-how-the-greek-diner-evolved.html.

Leyshon, Andrew, and Roger Lee. 2003. "Introduction." In *Alternative Economic Spaces,* edited by A. Leyshon, R. Lee, and C. C. Williams, 1–26. London: Sage Publications.

Lind, Amy. 2010. *Development, Sexual Rights, and Global Governance.* New York: Routledge.

Lipinski, Jed. 2010. "A Commune Grows in Brooklyn." *New York Times,* September 10. Retrieved September 10, 2010. https://www.nytimes.com/2010/09/19/fashion/19Bushwick.html.

Lobao, Linda M., Gregory Hooks, and Ann R. Tycamyer. 2007. *The Sociology of Spatiality.* Albany: State University Press of New York.

Logan, R. John, and Harvey L. Molotch. 1987. *Urban Fortunes: The Political Economy of Place.* Berkeley: University of California Press.

Loizos, Peter. 1977. *The Greek Gift: Politics in a Cypriot Village.* New York: St. Martin's Press.

Loizos, Peter. 1994. "A Broken Mirror: Masculine Sexuality in Greek Ethnography." In *Dislocating Masculinity: Comparative Ethnography,* edited by A. Cornwall and N. Lindisfaire, 66–81. New York: Routledge.

Loizos, Peter, and Evythymios Papataxiarchis. 1991. "Gender, Sexuality, and the Person in Greek Culture." In *Contested Identities: Gender and Kinship in Modern Greece,* edited by P. Loizos and E. Papataxiarchis, 221–234. Princeton, NJ: Princeton University Press.

Lonely Planet. *Nude Beaches of Greece.* Retrieved April 14, 2012. https://www.lonelyplanet.com/thorntree/forums/europe-western-europe/greece/nude-beaches-61ac7f39-e70a-453d-b878-fb07882c1135.

Long, Lucy. 2004. "Culinary Tourism: A Folklorist Perspective on Eating and Otherness." In *Culinary Tourism,* edited by L. Long, 20–50. Lexington: University Press of Kentucky.

Lorde, Audrey. 1984. *Sister Outsider: Essay and Speeches*. Berkeley, CA: Crossing Press.

Lovelock, James. 1979. *Gaia: A New Look at Life on Earth*. London: Oxford University Press.

Luciano, Michelle, Alexander David Dickie, Sherif Karama, Geraldine M. McNeill, Mark E. Bastin, Joanna M. Wardlaw, and Ian J. Deary. 2017. "Mediterranean-Type Diet and Brain Structural Change from 73 to 76 Years in a Scottish Cohort." *Neurology* 88 (5): 449–455.

Lynch, Caitrin. 2007. *Juki Girls, Good Girls: Gender and Cultural Politics in Sri Lanka's Global Garment Industry*. New York: Cornell University Press.

Lyson, Thomas A. 2004. *Civic Agriculture: Reconnecting Farm, Food, and Community*. Medford, MA: Tufts University Press.

MacCannell, Dean. 2013. *The Tourist: A New Theory of the Leisure Class*. Berkeley: University of California Press.

MacLean, John. 2000. "Philosophical Roots of Globalization and Philosophical Routes to Globalization." In *Globalization and Its Critics*, edited by R. D. Germain, 3–66. New York: St. Martin's Press.

Mahn, Churnjeet. 2016. *British Women's Travel to Greece, 1840–1914: Travels in the Palimpsest*. London: Routledge.

Malamidis, Haris. 2020. *Social Movement and Solidarity Structures in Crisis Ridden Greece*. Amsterdam: Amsterdam University Press.

Malkoutzis, Nick. 2011. "Hey Merkel, Leave the Greeks Alone." *Inside Greece, News and Opinion*, May 19. Retrieved November 13, 2012. http://inside-greece.wordpress.com/2011/05/19/hey-merkel-leave-the-greeks-alone/.

Malkoutzis, Nick. 2012. *Greece's Painful Political Transition: Analysis of the Upcoming National Elections*. Friedrich-Ebert Stiftung, International Policy Analysis. Retrieved November 13, 2012. http://library.fes.de/pdf-files/id/09061.pdf.

Mandesson, A. 1995. *Modern Greek–English Dictionary*. Athens: I.B.D. Limited.

Mares, Teresa, and Alison Hope Alkon. 2011. "Mapping the Food Movement: Addressing Inequality and Neoliberalism." *Environment and Society: Advances in Research* 2 (1): 68–86.

Margaras, Vasilis. 2010. "Do Not Shoot the Greeks!" March 5. Retrieved March 6, 2010. http://blogs.euobserver.com/margaras/2010/03/05/do-not-shoot-the-greeks/.

Margulis, Matias E., Nora McKeon, and Santornino Borras. 2013. "Land Grabbing and Global Governance: Critical Perspectives." *Globalizations* 10 (1) 1–23.

Marx, Karl. 1864. "Inaugural Address and Provisional Rules of the International Working Men's Association." Marx and Engels Internet Archive (marxists.org). Retrieved July 5, 2014. https://www.marxists.org/archive/marx/works/1864/10/27.htm.

Mason, Paul. 2016. *PostCapitalism: A Guide to Our Future*. New York: Farrar, Straus and Giroux.

Massey, Doreen. 1994. *Space, Place, and Gender*. Minneapolis: University of Minnesota Press.

Matthaei, Julie. 1998. "Some Comments on the Role of Lesbianism in Feminist Economic Transformation." *Feminist Economics* 4 (2): 83–88.

Mazower, Mark. 2000. *After the War Was Over: Reconstructing the Family, Nation, and State in Greece, 1943–1960*. Princeton, NJ: Princeton University Press.

McCall, Grant. 1994. "Nissology: The Study of Islands." *Journal of the Pacific Society* 17 (2–3): 1–14.

McClelland, David C. 1967. *The Achieving Society*. New York: Free Press.

McDowell, Linda. 1999. *Gender, Identity, and Place: Understanding Feminist Geographies*. Minneapolis: University of Minnesota.

McMichael, Philip. 1994. "GATT, Global Regulation and the Construction of a New Hegemonic Order." In *Critical Perspectives on Rural Change, Vol. 5: Agricultural Regulation*, edited by P. Lowe, T. Marsden, and S. Whatmore, 163–90. London: David Fulton Publishers.

McMichael, Philip. 2008. *Development and Social Change: A Global Perspective*. Thousand Oaks, CA: Sage/Pine Forge Press.

McMichael, Philip. 2009. "A Food Regime Genealogy." *Journal of Peasant Studies* 36 (1): 139–169.

Mendelsohn, Daniel. 2015. "Girl Interrupted: Who Was Sappho?" *New Yorker*, March 16. Retrieved February 2, 2017. https://www.newyorker.com/ magazine/2015/03/16/girl-interrupted.

Mercouri, Melina. 1971. *I Was Born Greek*. Garden City, NY: Doubleday and Company.

Mies, Maria. 1986. *Patriarchy and Accumulation on a World Scale: Women in the International Division of Labor*. London: Zed Books.

Mignolo, Walter. 2005. *The Idea of Latin America*. Hoboken, NJ: Wiley-Blackwell.

Mignolo, Walter. 2011. "Geopolitics of Sensing and Knowing: On (De)Coloniality, Border Thinking, and Epistemic Disobedience." Retrieved March 28, 2017. http://eipcp.net/transversal/0112/mignolo/en/print.

Mignolo, Walter, and Madina V. Tlostanova. 2006. "Theorizing from the Border: Shifting to Geo and Body-Politics of Knowledge." *European Journal of Social Theory* 9 (2): 155–169.

Miller, Ethan. 2006. "Other Economies Are Possible! Building a Solidarity Economy." *Grassroots Economic Organizing*, January 29. Retrieved June 8, 2010. http://www.geo.coop/node/35.

Miller, Joe. 2015. "How Do Greeks in Germany Feel amidst the Debt Crisis?" *BBC News*, July 9. Retrieved July 10, 2015. https://www.bbc.com/news/ business-33446985.

Milton, Giles. 2008. *Paradise Lost, Smyrna 1922*. New York: Basic Books.

Mintz, Sidney. 2006. "Food, History, and Globalization." *Journal of Chinese Dietary Culture* 2 (1): 1–22.

Mitchell, Joni. 1971. "California." From the album *Blue*, A&M Records. Copyright Joni Mitchell. Retrieved April 8, 2014. http://jonimitchell.com/ music/song.cfm?id=86.

Mitchell, Stephen, trans. 2011. *The Iliad by Homer*. New York: Free Books.

Mitchell, Stephen. 2018. "Stephen Mitchell on Translation and Beowulf." *Yale University Press Blog*, February 4. Retrieved January 2019. http://blog.yalebooks.com/2018/02/04/stephen-mitchell-on-translation-and-beowulf/.

Mohanty, Chandra. 1988. "Under Western Eyes: Feminist Scholarship and Colonial Discourses." *Feminist Review* 30: 61–88.

Moore, Barrington. 1978. *Injustice: The Social Basis of Obedience and Revolt*. London: Palgrave Macmillan.

Morton, Donald E. 2001. "Global (Sexual) Politics, Class Struggle, and the Queer Left." In *Post-colonial, Queer: Theoretical Intersections*, edited by J. Hawley, 207–238. Albany: State University of New York Press.

Moulaert, Frank, and Oana Ailenei. 2005. "The Social Economy: Third Sector and Solidarity Relations, a Conceptual Synthesis from History to Present." *Urban Studies* 42 (11): 2037–2053.

Myers, Marc. "Joni Mitchell on the Muse behind 'Carey.'" *Wall Street Journal*, November 11, 2014. https://www.wsj.com/articles/the-muse-behind-joni-mitchells-carey-1415721658.

Naples, Nancy. 2003. *Feminism and Method: Ethnography, Discourse Analysis, and Activist Research*. London: Routledge.

Naples, Nancy, and Manisha Desai. 2002. "Women's Local and Translocal Responses." In *Women's Community Activism and Globalization: Linking the Local and Global for Social Change*, edited by N. Naples and M. Desai, 33–43. New York: Routledge Press.

Nash, Catherine. 2015. "A Commentary." In *Lesbian Geographies: Gender, Place, and Power*, edited by K. Browne and E. Ferreira, 249–260. New York: Routledge.

Nash, Catherine, and Allison Bain. 2007. "'Reclaiming Raunch': Spatializing Queer Identities at Toronto Women's Bathhouse Events." *Social and Cultural Geography* 8 (1): 16–42.

Nasioulas, Ioannis. 2012. "Social Cooperatives in Greece: Introducing New Forms of Social Economy and Entrepreneurship." *International Review of Social Research* 2 (2): 141–161.

Naughtie, James. 2015. "Interview with Louis de Berniéres." BBC *Bookclub* podcast. Retrieved August 10, 2015. https://www.bbc.co.uk/programmes/p00fpsmg.

Nestle, Marion. 2007. *Food Politics: How the Food Industry Influences Nutrition and Health*. Berkeley: University of California Press.

Newton, Esther. 2014. *Cherry Grove, Fire Island: America's First Gay and Lesbian Town*. Durham, NC: Duke University Press.

Nicholas, Nick. 2016. "How Do You Say Welcome in Greek?" *Quora.com*. Retrieved March 28, 2017. https://www.quora.com/How-do-you-say-welcome-in-Greek.

O'Hanlon, Rosalind. 2000. "Recovering the Subject: Subaltern Studies and Histories of Resistance in Colonial South Asia." In *Mapping Subaltern Studies and the Postcolonial*, edited by V. Chaturvedi, 72–115. New York: Verso.

Orenstein, Peggy. 2010. "The Femivore's Dilemma." *New York Times Magazine*, March 11. Retrieved September 18, 2018. https://www.nytimes.com/2010/03/14/magazine/14fob-wwln-t.html.

Osho Afroz Meditation Center. "About Osho Afroz." Retrieved November 13, 2018. http://www.oshoafroz.com/site/content/9/osho-afroz.

Osirim, Mary. 2009. *Enterprising Women: Gender, Microbusiness, and Globalization in Urban Zimbabwe*. Bloomington: Indiana University Press.

Otero, Maria, and Elisabeth Rhyne. 1994. *The New World of Microenterprise Finance: Building Healthy Financial Institutions for the Poor*. Sterling, VA: Kumarian Press.

Panopoulos, Panoyotis. 1999. "Drinking to Identities: Coffee and Alcohol in Greek Ethnography." Paper presented at the Fifth Early Fall School in Semiotics: Semiotic Space and Cultural Time, South-eastern European Semiotic Centre and New Bulgarian University, Plovdiv, Bulgaria, September 14–18, 1999.

Pantazi, Florian. 2015. "Why the Berlin Consensus Is Toxic for the EU." *Blog Activ.eu*, August 31. Retrieved January 17, 2016. https://blogactiv.eu/blog/2015/08/31/why-the-berlin-consensus-is-toxic-for-the-eu-2/.

Papataxiarchis, Evthmios. 1991. "Friends of the Heart: Male Commensal Solidarity, Gender, and Kinship in Aegean Greece." In *Contested Identities: Gender and Kinship in Modern Greece*, edited by P. Loizos and E. Papataxiarchis, 156–180. Princeton, NJ: Princeton University Press.

Parker, Barbara, Jennifer Brady, Elaine Power, and Susan Belyea. 2019. *Feminist Food Studies: Intersectional Perspectives*. Toronto, Ontario: Women's Press.

Patel, Raj. 2012. *Stuffed and Starved: The Hidden Battle for the World Food System*. Brooklyn, NY: Melville House.

Peck, Jamie. 2013. "Disembedding Polanyi: Exploring Polanyian Economic Geographies." *Environment and Planning A: Economy and Space* 45 (7): 536–544.

Peck, Jamie, and Adam Tickell. 2002. "Neoliberalizing Space." *Antipode* 34 (3): 380–404.

Pepper, David. 1984. *The Roots Of Modern Environmentalism*. London: Routledge.

Petrini, Carlo. (2005) 2013. *Slow Food Nation: Why Our Food Should Be Good, Clean and Fair*. Translated by C. Furlan and J. Hunt. New York: Rizzoli Ex Libris.

Petropoulo, Christina. 1993. "Some Historical Notes on the Greek Cooperative Movement." *Diálogos, Propuestas, Historias para una Ciudadania Mundial*, August. Retrieved January 19, 2015. http://base.d-p-h.info/es/fiches/premier dph/fiche-premierdph-744.html.

Photiades, John. 1965. "The Position of the Coffeehouse in the Social Structure of the Greek Village." *Sociologia Ruralis* 5: 45–53.

Piven, Frances Fox, and Richard A. Cloward. 1977. *Poor People's Movements: Why They Succeed, How They Fail*. New York: Vintage Books.

Polanyi, Karl. 1944. *The Great Transformation*. Boston: Beacon Press.

Polat, Kdioglu Defne. 2018. "'Now the German comes': The Ethnic Effect of Gentrification in Berlin." *Ethnicities* 20 (1): 155–176.

Pollan, Michael. 2009. *In Defense of Food: An Eaters' Manifesto*. New York: Penguin Books.

Portes, Alejandro. 1983. "The Informal Sector: Definition, Controversy, and Relation to National Development." *Fernand Braudel Center Review* 7 (1): 151–174.

Portes, Alejandro, and Alex Stepick. 1993. *City on the Edge: The Transformation of Miami*. Berkeley: University of California Press.

Power, Elaine, and Mustafa Koc. 2008. "A Double-Double and Maple Glazed Doughnut." *Food, Culture, and Society* 11 (3): 263–267.

Puar, Jasbir. 2002. "Introduction: Queer Tourism: Geographies of Globalization." *GLQ: Gay and Lesbian Quarterly* 8 (1–2): 1–6.

Pyle, J., and K. B. Ward. 2003. "Recasting Our Understanding of Gender and Work during Global Restructuring." *International Sociology* 18 (3): 461–489.

Quataert, Donald. 2005. *The Ottoman Empire, 1700–1922*. Cambridge: Cambridge University Press.

Quest, Richard, and Katie Pisa. 2018. "In Athens, Having Fun Is the Only Way to Survive." *CNN Travel*. Retrieved January 2, 2019. https://www.cnn.com/travel/article/athens-crisis-fun/index.html.

Rakowski, Cathy A. 1994. *Contrapunto: The Informal Sector Debate in Latin America*. Albany: State University of New York Press.

Rayor, Diane. 1991. *Sappho's Lyre: Archaic Lyric and Women Poets of Ancient Greece*. Berkeley: University of California Press.

Redfield, Robert. 1962. *Human Nature and the Study of Society: The Papers of Robert Redfield, Vol. 1*. Chicago: University of Chicago Press.

Reid-Musson, Emily. 2017. "Intersectional Rhythmanalysis: Power, Rhythm, and Everyday Life." *Progress in Human Geography* 42 (6): 881–897.

Restakis, John. 2010. *Humanizing the Economy: Cooperatives in the Age of Capital*. Gabriola Island, BC, Canada: New Society Publishers.

Reynolds, Margaret. 2000. *The Sappho Companion*. New York: Palgrave.

Richards, Greg. 2002. "Gastronomy: An Essential Ingredient in Tourism Production and Consumption." In *Tourism and Gastronomy*, edited by A. M. Hjalager and G. Richards, 3–20. London: Routledge.

Richardson, Colin, 2002. "The Worst of Times." *Guardian*, August 14. Retrieved April 20, 2017. https://www.theguardian.com/world/2002/aug/14/gayrights.comment.

Rodríguez, Ileana. 2001. "Reading Subalterns across Texts, Disciplines, and Theories: From Representation to Recognition." In *The Latin American Subaltern Reader*, edited by I. Rodríguez, 1–34. Durham, NC: Duke University Press.

Rose, Gillian. 1993. *Feminism and Geography: The Limits of Geographical Knowledge*. Minneapolis: University of Minnesota Press.

Rothenberg, Tamar Y. 1995. "'And She Told Two Friends': Lesbians Creating Urban Social Space." In *Mapping Desire: Geographies of Sexualities*, edited by D. J. Bell and G. Valentine, 165–81. London: Routledge.

Roy, J. 1997. "An Alternative Sexual Morality for Classical Athenians." *Greece and Rome* 44 (1): 11–22.

Rye, Johan F., and Sam Scott. 2018. "International Labour Migration and Food Production in Rural Europe: A Review of the Evidence." *Sociologia Ruralis* 58 (4): 928–952.

Said, Edward W. 1994. *Culture and Imperialism*. London: Vintage.

Schaus, Gerald, and Nigel Spencer. 1994. "Notes on the Topography of Eresos." *American Journal of Archaeology* 98 (3): 411–430.

Schumacher, E. F. 1973. *Small Is Beautiful: Economics as if People Mattered*. London: Blond and Briggs.

Scott, James C. 1979. *The Moral Economy of the Peasant: Rebellion and Subsistence in Southeast Asia*. New Haven: Yale University Press.

Scott, James C. 1985. *Weapons of the Weak: Everyday Forms of Peasant Resistance*. New Haven, CT: Yale University Press.

Scott, James C. 2012. *Two Cheers for Anarchism: Six Pieces on Autonomy, Dignity, Meaningful Work, and Play*. Princeton, NJ: Princeton University Press.

Scott, James C. 2017. *Against the Grain: A Deep History of the Early States*. New Haven, CT: Yale University Press.

Seidman, Steven. 1994. "Queering Sociology, Sociologizing Queer Theory." *Sociological Theory* 12 (2): 166–177.

Servon, Lisa J. 1999. *Bootstrap Capitalism: Microenterprise and the American Poor*. Washington, DC: Brookings Institute Press.

Sheller, Mimi. 2003. *Consuming the Caribbean: From Arawaks to Zombies*. New York: Routledge.

Shiva, Vandana. 1988. *Staying Alive: Women, Ecology, and Development*. London: Zed Books.

Shofield, John, and Jennifer J. George. 1997. "Why Study Islands." In *Island Studies: Fifty Years of the Lundy Field Society*, edited by J. Shofield, J. J. George, and C. J. Webster, 5–14. Bideford, UK: Lundy Field Society.

Shuman, Michael. 2000. *Going Local: Creating Self-Reliant Communities in a Global Age*. New York: Routledge.

Shuman, Michael. 2007. *The Small-Mart Revolution: How Local Businesses Are Beating the Global Competition*. San Francisco: Berrett-Koehler Publishers.

Shuman, Michael. 2012. *Local Dollars, Local Sense: How to Shift Your Money from Wall Street to Main Street and Achieve Real Prosperity*. Hatford, VT: Chelsea Green Publishing.

Sidali, Katia L., Elisabeth Kastenholz, and Rossella Bianchi. 2015. "Food Tourism, Niche Markets, Products in Rural Tourism, Combining the Intimacy Model and the Experience Economy as a Rural Development Strategy." *Journal of Sustainable Tourism* 8–9: 1179–1197.

Silva, Noenoe K. 2004. *Aloha Betrayed*. Durham, NC: Duke University Press.

Simone, AbdouMaliq. 2004. *For the City Yet to Come*. Durham, NC: Duke University Press.

Sims, Rebecca. 2008. "Food, Place, and Authenticity: Local Food and the Sustainable Tourism Experience." *Journal of Sustainable Tourism* 17 (3): 321–336.

Slatkin, Wendy. 2000. *Women Artists in History*. London: Pearson.

Slocum, Rachel. 2007. "Whiteness, Space, and Alternative Food Practices." *Geoforum* 38: 520–533.

Smith, Alisa, and J. B. MacKinnon. 2007. *The 100-Mile Diet: A Year of Local Eating*. Toronto: Random House.

Smith, Helena. 2018. "Greece Tourism at Record High amid Alarm over Environmental Cost." *Guardian*, June 3. Retrieved September 8, 2020. https://www.theguardian.com/world/2018/jun/03/greece-tourism-at-record-high-amid-alarm-over-environmental-cost.

Smith, Jackie, Marina Karides, Marc Becker, Christopher Chase-Dunn, Dorval Brunelle, Donnatella Della Porta, Rosalba Icaza, Jeffrey Juris, Lorenzo Mosca, Ellen Reese, Jay Smith, and Rolando Vasquez. 2008. *The World Social Forums and the Challenges for Global Democracy*. Boulder, CO: Paradigm Publishers.

Smith, Stacy Vanek, and Alex Mayyasi. 2020. "What's the Impact of Bars Shutting Down on Innovations and New Ideas?" Retrieved October 18, 2020. https://www.npr.org/2020/10/16/924648133/whats-the-impact-of-bars-shutting-down-on-innovations-and-new-ideas.

Smith, Valene L. 1989. "Introduction." In *Hosts and Guests: The Anthropology of Tourism*, edited by V. L. Smith, 1–18. Philadelphia: University of Pennsylvania Press.

Snyder, Jane McIntosh. 1994. *Sappho*. New York: Chelsea House Publishers.

Snyder, Jane McIntosh. 1997. *Lesbian Desire in the Lyrics of Sappho*. New York: Columbia University Press.

Spain, Daphne. 1992. *Gendered Spaces*. Chapel Hill: University of North Carolina Press.

Spiegel, Peter. 2014. "Inside Europe's Plan Z." *Financial Times*, September 14. Retrieved October 10, 2018. https://www.ft.com/content/0ac1306e-d508-11e3-9187-00144feabdc0.

Spivak, Gayatri. 1993. "Can the Subaltern Speak?" In *Marxism and the Interpretation of Culture*, edited by C. Nelson and L. Grossberg, 271–313. Urbana: University of Illinois Press.

Spurlin, William J. 2001. "Broadening Postcolonial Studies/Decolonizing Queer Studies: Emerging 'Queer' Identities and Cultures in Southern Africa." In *Post-colonial, Queer: Theoretical Intersections*, edited by J. Hawley, 181–206. Albany: State University of New York Press.

Stamouli, Nektaria. 2019. "Joint Ventures: Greece Cultivates Business Opportunities in Cannabis." *Wall Street Journal*, January 9. Retrieved January 13, 2019. https://www.wsj.com/articles/joint-ventures-greece-cultivates-business-opportunities-in-cannabis-11546957800.

Stanhope, Lady Hester. 1846. *Travels of Lady Hester Stanhope: Forming the Completion of Her Memoirs Narrated by Her Physician*. London: Henry Colburn.

Starr, Amory. 2000. *Naming the Enemy: Anti-Corporate Social Movements Confront Globalization*. London: Zed Books.

Steger, Manfred B. 2010. "From Market Globalism to Imperial Globalism: Ideology and American Power after 9/11." In *Globalization: The Greatest Hits*, edited by M. Steger, 31–46. Boulder, CO: Paradigm Publishers.

Stenning, Alison, Adrian Smith, Alena Rochovská, and Dariusz Świątek. 2010. *Domesticating Neo-Liberalism: Spaces of Economic Practice and Social Reproduction in Post-Socialist Cities*. Hoboken, NJ: Wiley-Blackwell.

Stratford, Elaine, Godfrey Baldacchino, Elizabeth McMahon, Carol Farbotko, and Andrew Harwood. 2011. "Envisioning the Archipelago." *Island Studies Journal* 6 (2): 113–130.

Suwa, Jun'ichiro. 2007. "The Space of Shima." *Shima: The International Journal of Research into Island Cultures* 1 (1): 6–14.

Szabo, Michelle. 2014. "Men Nurturing through Food: Challenging Gender Dichotomies around Domestic Cooking." *Journal of Gender Studies* 23 (1): 18–31.

Szasz, Andrew. 2007. *Shopping Our Way to Safety: How We Changed from Protecting the Environment to Protecting Ourselves*. Minneapolis: University of Minnesota Press.

Talburt, Susan, and Claudia Matus. 2014. "Confusing the Grid: Spatiotemporalities, Queer Imaginaries, and Movement." *Gender, Place, and Culture: A Journal of Feminist Geography* 21 (6): 785–801.

Taylor, Jacqueline Sanchez. 2006. "Researching Female Sex Tourism: A Contradiction in Terms?" *Feminist Review* 83: 42–59.

Tax, Sol. 1956. *Penny Capitalism: A Guatemalan Indian Economy*. Washington, DC: Smithsonian Institution for Cultural Anthropology.

Terrell, John Edward. 2004. "Islands in the River of Time." Paper presented at Islands of the World VIII International Conference, "Changing Islands— Changing Worlds." www.giee.ntnu.edu.tw/island.

Thompson, E. P. 1978. *The Poverty of Theory and Other Essays*. New York: Monthly Review Press.

Trichopoulo, Antonia, Tina Costackou, Christina Bamia, and Dimitrios Trichopoulos. 2003. "Adherence to a Mediterranean Diet and Survival in a Greek Population." *New England Journal of Medicine* 348 (26): 2599–2608.

Tsai, Lily. 2007. "Solidary Groups, Informal Accountability, and Local Public Goods Provision in Rural China." *American Political Science Review* 101 (2): 355–372.

Tsouvelas, Giorgos, Georgios Konstantakapoulos, Antonios Vakirtzis, Orestis Giotakos, T. H. Papaslanis, and V. P. Kontaxakis. 2018. "Criminality in Greece during the Years of Financial Crisis: 2008–2014." *Psychiatriki* 29 (1): 19–24.

Valentine, Gill. 1993. "Desperately Seeking Susan: A Geography of Lesbian Friendships." *Area* 25: 109–116.

Valentine, Gill. 1995. "Out and About: A Geography of Lesbian Communities." *International Journal of Urban and Regional Research* 19: 96–111.

Valentine, Gill. 2000. "Introduction: From Nowhere to Everywhere: Lesbian Geographies." In *From Nowhere to Everywhere: Lesbian Geographies*, edited by G. Valentine, 1–11. New York: Routledge.

Valocchi, Stephen 2005. "Not Yet Queer Enough: The Lessons of Queer Theory for the Sociology of Gender and Sexuality." *Gender and Society* 19 (6): 750–770.

Varoufakis, Yannis. 2017. *Adults in the Room: My Battle with the American and European Deep Establishment*. New York: Farrar, Straus and Giroux.

Vinthagen, Stellan, and Anna Johansson. 2013. "'Everyday Resistance': Exploration of a Concept and Its Theories." *Resistance Studies Magazine* 1: 1–46.

Vlachos, Angelos. 2014. "Tourism Development and Public Policy in Modern Greece (1914–1950)." PhD thesis, Department of Archeology and History, University of Athens.

Vulliamy, Ed, and Helena Smith. 2014. "Athens 1944: Britain's Dirty Secret." *Guardian*, November 30. Retrieved May 30, 2015. https://www.theguardian.com/world/2014/nov/30/athens-1944-britains-dirty-secret.

Waitt, Gordon. 2012. "Queer Perspectives on Tourism Geographies." In *The Routledge Handbook of Tourism Geographies*, edited by Julie Wilson, 82–89. Abingdon, UK: Routledge.

Waitt, Gordon, and Kevin Markwell. 2006. *Gay Tourism: Culture and Context*. London: Routledge.

Wallerstein, Immanuel. 1974. *The Modern World-System I: Capitalist Agriculture and the Origins of the European World-Economy in the Sixteenth Century*. New York: Academic Press.

Wallerstein, Immanuel. 1983. *Historical Capitalism with Capitalist Civilization*. London: Verso Books.

Watson, J. L., and M. Caldwell. 2005. *The Cultural Politics of Food and Eating: A Reader*. Hoboken, NJ: Wiley-Blackwell.

Watson, Sarah Burges. 2013. "Muses of Lesbos or (Aeschylean) Muses of Pieria? Orpheus' Head on a Fifth-Century Hydria." *Greek, Roman, and Byzantine Studies* 53: 441–460.

Way, Arthur. 1920. *Sappho and the Vigil of Venus*. London: Macmillan and Co.

Weber, Max. 1978. *Economy and Society*. Berkeley: University of California Press.

Weeks, Kathi. 2011. *The Problem with Work: Feminism, Marxism, Anti-work Politics, and Post-work Imaginaries*. Durham, NC: Duke University Press.

White, Donald, Keith Devris, David Gilman, Irene Romano, and Yelena Stolyarik. 1995. *The Ancient Greek World: The Rodney S. Young Gallery*. Philadelphia: University of Pennsylvania Press, 1995.

Wilder, Charly. 2018. "Athens, Rising." *New York Times*, June 18. Retrieved June 18, 2018. https://www.nytimes.com/2018/06/18/travel/athens-after-the-economic-crisis.html.

Williams, Mary E. 2013. "Feminism Didn't Kill Cooking." *Salon*, October 21. Retrieved September 1, 2018. https://www.salon.com/2013/10/21/feminism_ didnt_kill_cooking/.

Williamson, Margaret. 1995. *Sappho's Immortal Daughters*. Cambridge, MA: Harvard University Press.

Wilson, Emily, trans. 2017. *The Odyssey*. New York: W. W. Norton and Company.

Wilson, Lyn H. 1996. *Sappho's Bittersweet Songs*. London: Routledge.

Winne, Mark. 2008. *Closing the Food Gap: Resetting the Table in the Land of Plenty*. Boston, MA: Beacon Press.

Wittman, Hannah, Annette Desmarais, and Nettie Wiebe. 2010. *Food Sovereignty: Reconnecting Food, Nature, and Community*. Halifax, CA: Fernwood Publishing.

Wright, Andy. 2008. "Hey! We Were Lesbians First!" *SF Weekly*, June 11. Retrieved July 11, 2011. http://blogs.sfweekly.com/thesnitch/2008/06/hey_we_were_ lesbians_first.php.

Wright, Erik Olin. 2010. *Envisioning Real Utopias*. New York: Verso Books.

Wolf, Eric. (1982) 2010. *Europe and the People without History*. Berkeley: University of California Press.

Woolf, Virginia. (1906) 1992. *Passionate Apprentice: The Early Journals, 1897–1909*. San Diego, CA: Mariner Books.

World Bank. 2016. "International Tourism, Number of Arrivals." Retrieved October 4, 2017. https://data.worldbank.org/indicator/ST.INT.ARVL.

Yi, Ilcheong, Samuel Brülisauer, Gabriel Salathé-Beaulieu, and Martina Piras. 2019. *Conference Summary of "Implementing the Sustainable Development Goals: What Role for Social and Solidarity Economy?"* UN Inter-Agency Task Force on Social and Solidarity Economy. Geneva: TFSSE. Retrieved June 17, 2019. http://unsse.org/wp-content/uploads/2019/10/Conference-summary-UNTFSSE-Conference-16.10.2019-Final.pdf.

Yun, Dongkoo, Sean M. Hennessey, and Roberta MacDonald. 2011. "Understanding Culinary Tourists: Segmentations Based on Past Culinary Experiences and Attitudes toward Food-Related Behaviour." International CHRIE Conference-Refereed Track 15. Retrieved August 17, 2017. https://scholar works.umass.edu/refereed/ICHRIE_2011/Friday/15.

Zarkadakis, George. 2011. "Modern Greece's Real Problem? Ancient Greece." *Washington Post*, November 4. Retrieved April 9, 2019. https://www. washingtonpost.com/opinions/modern-greeces-real-problem-ancient-greece/ 2011/11/01/gIQACSq9mM_story.html.

Zinovieff, Sofia. 1991. "Hunters and Hunted: Kamaki and the Ambiguities of Predation in a Greek Town." In *Contested Identities: Gender and Kinship in Modern Greece*, edited by P. Loizos and E. Papataxiarchis, 203–220. Princeton, NJ: Princeton University Press.

Zsolanai, Laszlo. 1993. "A Framework of Alternative Economics." *International Journal of Social Economics* 20 (2): 65–75.

Zukin, Susan, and Jennifer M. Smith. 2004. "Consumers and Consumption." *Annual Review of Sociology* 30: 173–197.

Index

www.ingramcontent.com/pod-product-compliance
Lightning Source LLC
Chambersburg PA
CBHW031357270326
41929CB00010BA/1221